D0599262

WAS
HUCK
BLACK?

Mark Twain and
African-American
Voices

SHELLEY FISHER FISHKIN

WAS HUCK BLACK?

Mark Twain and African-American Voices

New York   Oxford
OXFORD UNIVERSITY PRESS
1993

Oxford University Press

Oxford   New York   Toronto
Delhi   Bombay   Calcutta   Madras   Karachi
Kuala Lumpur   Singapore   Hong Kong   Tokyo
Nairobi   Dar es Salaam   Cape Town
Melbourne   Auckland   Madrid

and associated companies in
Berlin   Ibadan

Published by Oxford University Press, Inc.,
200 Madison Avenue, New York, New York 10016

Oxford is a registered trademark of Oxford University Press

Library of Congress Cataloging-in-Publication Data
Fishkin, Shelley Fisher
Was Huck Black? : Mark Twain and African-American voices / Shelley
Fisher Fishkin
p.   cm.   Includes bibliographical references and index.
ISBN 0-19-508214-1
1. Twain, Mark, 1835–1910. Adventures of Huckleberry Finn. 2. Twain,
Mark, 1835–1910—Characters—Afro-Americans. 3. Twain, Mark,
1835–1910—Friends and associates. 4. Authors, American—
19th century—Biography. 5. Afro-Americans in literature.
6. Afro-Americans—Biography.
I. Title.   PS1305.F57   1993
813'.4—dc20   92-31228

1 3 5 7 9 8 6 4 2

Printed in the United States of America
on acid-free paper

In memory of my mother,
Renée B. Fisher,
writer and musicologist,
who taught me to listen to
the music and the words
and the music *of* the words

Acknowledgments

The following people read this book in its entirety in manuscript form and offered invaluable criticism: William Andrews, David Barrow, David Bradley, Louis J. Budd, Emily Budick, Evan Carton, Sherwood Cummings, Vic Doyno, Ralph Ellison, Victor Fischer, Milton Fisher, Henry Louis Gates, Jr., Susan Harris, Elaine Hedges, T. Walter Herbert, Hal Holbrook, Karla F. C. Holloway, William Howarth, Justin Kaplan, Paul Lauter, James A. Miller, Toni Morrison, Carla Peterson, Arnold Rampersad, Lillian Robinson, Jeffrey Rubin-Dorsky, David E. E. Sloane, David L. Smith, Bill Stott, Eric Sundquist, and Richard Yarborough.

Milton Fisher, my father, believed in this project all along. His advice, support, and excitement from the beginning helped nurture it to fruition.

David Bradley started all the trouble when he gave a talk on *Huckleberry Finn* at the Mark Twain Memorial in Hartford in 1985 titled "The First 'Nigger' Novel." His provocative questions and important insights have shaped this book from start to finish.

Carla Peterson, Jeffrey Rubin-Dorsky, Richard Yarborough, and Lillian Robinson each played a key role in helping me structure this project in its earliest stages. Their patience and generosity reached levels worthy of the *Guinness Book of World Records*. Toni Morrison, whose work has helped spark much of my thinking on these issues, provided crucial encouragement during this early period, as well. Arnold Rampersad strongly supported my preliminary forays into this material, helped give me the confidence to push ahead, and continued to offer sage advice as the book neared completion.

I am enormously grateful to Ralph Ellison for having agreed so graciously to an extended interview; his ideas inform virtually every aspect of this project, and his enthusiasm for the manuscript meant the world to me.

Skip Gates's generous encouragement and support of my work has always been and continues to be very important to me; his groundbreaking work in African-American literature and theory has been central to the development of my argument in this book.

I am indebted to Bill Howarth for his interest and encouragement; to Vic Doyno for his meticulous reading and prolific comments; to Louis J. Budd, Victor Fischer, Justin Kaplan, David E. E. Sloane, Susan Harris, Sherwood Cummings, and David Barrow for having shared their comprehensive knowledge of Twain scholarship as generously as they did; to Jim Miller for innumerable conversations about potential links between Mark Twain and African-American writers; and to Karla Holloway for having shared her understanding of linguistic issues. T. Walter Herbert helped reshape dimensions of my central thesis. Bill Andrews, Eric Sundquist, Emily Budick, Elaine Hedges, Paul Lauter, Evan Carton, and David Smith asked hard questions and made useful comments. Bill Stott deconstructed and reconstructed my prose. Lillian Robinson brought her good sense and poet's sensibility to bear on both the first and final drafts of the manuscript, calling out the "metaphor police" early and often. Hal Holbrook listened to the voices in his head, and read the voices on my pages, and told me I was right; his interest from the start helped spur me on.

I would like to thank Robert H. Hirst, General Editor of the Mark Twain Papers at Berkeley, for having created an atmosphere in which scholars like myself can feel welcome and be productive. Bob Hirst and Mark Twain Papers Editors Robert Pack Browning, Richard Bucci, Michael B. Frank, and Kenneth Sanderson were cheerful co-conspirators on my scholarly prospecting ventures, gamely answering endless questions and searching out dusty scrapbooks and nearly forgotten files. Staff members Sunny Gottberg and Carol Kramer helped make mining the rich resources of the Mark Twain Papers a source of pleasure as well as profit.

R. W. B. Lewis's support for my work on Mark Twain and race was central to the completion of this project. I am grateful for the encouragement of Lawrence Berkove, Everett Emerson, Gary Saul Morson, Werner Sollors, and Tillie Olsen, all of whom read parts of the manuscript. People whose conversation and correspondence during the last few years helped shape my thinking about the general issues involved in this book include Kate Adams, Gloria Anzaldúa, Joanne Braxton, James M. Cox, Robert Crunden, Thadious Davis, Margo Feeley, William Ferris, Fritz Fleischmann, Neil Foley, Flora Gibson, Susan Gillman, William Goetzmann, Alan Gribben, Doris Harris, Hamlin Hill, Gordon Hutner, Calvin Johnson, Maria Johnson, William Jones, Peter Kardon, Charles Kupfer, Jane Marcus, Michael North, Barry O'Connell, Forrest Robinson, Russell Rosenberg, William Sisler, Sterling Stuckey, Thomas Tenney, Robert Farris

Thompson, Lindsey Traub, Don Walden, and the graduate students in my seminar, at the University of Texas at Austin, on race, class, gender, and ethnicity at the turn of the century.

I would like to thank the Mark Twain Memorial in Hartford, Connecticut, for having invited me to participate in two conferences on new research on Mark Twain, which helped stimulate my thinking on a range of subjects that developed into the work at hand. Executive Director John Boyer and Curator Marianne Curling were particularly helpful, as were Diana Royce and Earl French of the Stowe-Day Foundation. I would also like to thank the participants in the four Mark Twain Summer Teachers' Institutes in Hartford in which I taught, for having helped clarify my thinking about Twain in the classroom.

I am grateful to Robert King, Dean of the College of Liberal Arts, and to Robert Abzug, Director of American Studies, for having helped create an atmosphere at the University of Texas at Austin in which scholarship is encouraged and rewarded. The staffs of the Perry-Castaneda Library and the Harry Ransom Humanities Research Center extended every courtesy. Janice Bradley and Julie Pulliam, administrators of the American Studies Program, stopped me from dropping the ball, even when the pulls of writing, teaching, parenting, and being Graduate Advisor threatened to throw even the tamest juggling act into total disarray.

I would also like to thank the staff of the Schomburg Center for Research in Black Culture, a branch of The New York Public Library, for their generous assistance.

I am indebted to Anthony and Belle Low, John Garrod, and the Fellows and staff of Clare Hall, Cambridge University, for having provided the stimulating and pleasant environment in which I was able to complete this book.

I greatly appreciate Helen K. Copley's having granted me permission to publish portions of Mark Twain's unpublished "Family Sketch," which is now in the Mark Twain Collection of the James S. Copley Library, La Jolla, California. I am indebted to Robert Hirst and the Mark Twain Foundation for permission to print previously unpublished portions of Twain's letters, manuscripts, and journals (material noted throughout the book by an asterisk [*]); to the Pierpont Morgan Library, New York, for permission to quote from Mark Twain's Autograph Manuscript of *Pudd'nhead Wilson,* MA 241–42; and to Michael Plunkett for permission to reproduce part of the manuscript of "A True Story," which is in the Mark Twain Collection (#6314) of the Clifton Waller Barrett Library, Manuscripts Division,

Special Collections Department, University of Virginia. I would also like to thank Ethel L. Robert for permission to publish a copy of her photograph of Charles Ethan Porter; Tom Otwell of the University of Maryland at College Park for permission to publish the photograph of Mary Ann Cord; the Huntington Library for permission to use the photograph of Frederick Douglass; Ann Allen Shockley of the Fisk University Library's Special Collections, for the photograph of the Fisk Jubilee Singers; and Arthur Murphy of the *Baltimore Afro-American* for the photograph of Warner McGuinn.

Oxford Senior Editor Elizabeth Maguire has been a delight to work with: her fine judgment, combined with her warmth, energy, and enthusiasm, has led me to value her not only as an editor, but as a friend. T. Susan Chang has been extremely helpful and conscientious. The entire staff at Oxford has made publishing this book a remarkably painless process.

Mark Caffey and Stephanie Shaw were exemplary research assistants, tracking down obscure articles and illustrations with painstaking care and creativity. Helen Chron helped free me to spend those umpteen happy hours mucking about in all those great primary sources Stephanie and Mark helped me unearth.

I am grateful to Carol Fisher, Fannie Fishkin, and David Fishkin for their warm encouragement. They helped make writing this book both possible and enjoyable.

My son Joey was often the first to hear or read the latest bulletin from the front, his bedroom being situated next door to my study; an astute and sensitive critic, his intuitions proved right more often than not. My son Bobby—who was, as I wrote this book, nearly the same age "Jimmy" was when Twain met him—served as a constant reminder to me of how truly engaging and delightful a loquacious ten-year-old child can be.

My husband Jim—who knows firsthand about intense scholarly activity—put up with my intermittent extended trances at my laptop with saintly patience and indulgence. I could not have written this book without his unselfish support and understanding.

Clare Hall   S. F. F.
Cambridge, England
November 1992

Contents

PART FOUR
BREAK DANCING IN THE DRAWING ROOM
109

Illustrations

WAS HUCK BLACK?

Mark Twain and
African-American
Voices

Introduction

The Negro looks at the white man and finds it difficult to believe that the "grays"—a Negro term for white people—can be so absurdly self-deluded over the true interrelatedness of blackness and whiteness.

RALPH ELLISON[1]

The range of models critics cite when they probe the sources of Mark Twain's *Adventures of Huckleberry Finn* is wide. It includes the picaresque novel, the Southwestern humorists, the Northeastern literary comedians, the newspapers Twain contributed to and read, and the tradition of the "boy book" in American popular culture.[2] Twain himself weighed in with a clear statement about the roots of his main character, claiming that Huck Finn was based on Tom Blankenship, a poor-white outcast child Twain remembered from Hannibal, and on Tom's older brother Bence, who once helped a runaway slave.[3] These sources may seem quite different. On one level, however, they are the same: they all give Twain's book a genealogy that is unequivocally white.

Although commentators differ on the question of which models and sources proved most significant, they tend to concur on the question of how *Huckleberry Finn* transformed American literature. Twain's innovation of having a vernacular-speaking child tell his own story *in his own words* was the first stroke of brilliance; Twain's awareness of the power of satire in the service of social criticism was the second. Huck's voice combined with Twain's satiric genius changed the shape of fiction in America.

In this book I will suggest that Twain himself and the critics have ignored or obscured the African-American roots of his art. Critics, for the most part, have confined their studies of the relationship between Twain's work and African-American traditions to examinations of his depiction of African-American folk beliefs or to analyses of the dialects spoken by his black characters.[4] But by limiting their field of inquiry to the periphery, they have missed the ways in which African-American voices shaped Twain's creative imagination at its core.

Compelling evidence indicates that the model for Huck Finn's voice was a black child instead of a white one and that this child's speech sparked in Twain a sense of the possibilities of a vernacular narrator. The record suggests that it may have been yet another black speaker who awakened Twain to the power of satire as a tool of social criticism. This may help us understand why Richard Wright found Twain's work "strangely familiar," and why Langston Hughes, Ralph Ellison, and David Bradley all found Twain so empowering in their own efforts to convert African-American experience into art.[5]

As Ralph Ellison put it in 1970, "*the black man [was] a co-creator of the language that Mark Twain raised to the level of literary eloquence.*"[6] But his comment sank like a stone, leaving barely a ripple on the placid surface of American literary criticism. Neither critics from the center nor critics from the margins challenged the reigning assumption that mainstream literary culture in America is certifiably "white."

This book suggests that we need to revise our understanding of the nature of the mainstream American literary tradition. The voice we have come to accept as the vernacular voice in American literature—the voice with which Twain captured our national imagination in *Huckleberry Finn*, and that empowered Hemingway, Faulkner, and countless other writers in the twentieth century—is in large measure a voice that is "black."

Mark Twain was unusually attuned to the nuances of cadence, rhythm, syntax, and diction that distinguish one language or dialect from another, and he had a genius for transferring the oral into print.[7] Twain, whose preferred playmates had been black, was what J. L. Dillard might have called "bidialectal"; as an engaging black child he encountered in the early 1870s helped reconnect Twain to the cadences and rhythms of black speakers from Twain's own childhood, he inspired him to liberate a language that lay buried within Twain's own linguistic repertoire and to apprehend its stunning creative potential. Twain, in turn, would help make that language available as a literary option to both white and black writers who came after him. As Ellison put it in 1991, "he made it possible for many of us to find our own voices."[8]

Mark Twain helped open American literature to the multicultural polyphony that is its birthright and special strength. He appreciated the creative vitality of African-American voices and exploited their potential in his art. In the process, he helped teach his countrymen new lessons about the lyrical and exuberant energy of vernacular speech, as well as about the potential of satire and irony in the service of truth. Both of these lessons would ultimately make the culture more responsive to the voices of African-American writers in the twentieth century. They would also change its definitions of what "art" ought to look and sound like to be freshly, wholly "American."

Am I suggesting that the sources and influences that scholars have documented over the last hundred years are not important to our understanding of Twain's career as a whole? No. Southwestern humor, for example, clearly played a key role in shaping Twain's art, particularly in such early works as *Innocents Abroad* and *Roughing It*. But there is something about *Huckleberry Finn* that sets it off from Twain's earlier work and makes it seem less a continuation of the art he had been developing and more of a quantum leap forward; its unrivalled place in both the Twain canon and in the American literary canon reflects this special status.[9] In *Huckleberry Finn* something new happened that would have an enormous impact on the future of American literature. That "something new" has never been adequately accounted for. My suggestion is this: here, more than in any other work, Twain allowed African-American voices to play a major role in the creation of his art. This fact may go a long way toward clarifying what makes this novel so fresh and so distinctive.[10]

Twain's responsiveness to African-American speaking voices should come as no surprise to us, for the intense and visceral nature of his response to African-American *singing* voices has been widely documented. After entertaining the Fisk Jubilee Singers in his home in Lucerne, Switzerland, in 1897, Twain wrote,

> Away back in the beginning—to my mind—their music made all other vocal music cheap; and that early notion is emphasized now. It is utterly beautiful, to me; and it moves me infinitely more than any other music can. I think that in the Jubilees and their songs America has produced the perfectest flower of the ages; and I wish it were a foreign product so that she would worship it and lavish money on it and go properly crazy over it.[11]

Twain acknowledged his admiration for the beauty and power of these songs and their singers in the publicity blurb he wrote for the Fisk Jubilee Singers on their European tour: "I do not know when anything has so moved me as did the plaintive melodies of the Jubilee

The Fisk Jubilee Singers whose talents Twain lauded in the publicity blurb he wrote for their European tour in 1873. (Courtesy, Special Collections, Fisk University Library)

Singers." Calling their music "eloquent" (underlining the close connection in his mind between speech and song), Twain wrote, "I heard them sing once, and I would walk seven miles to hear them sing again. You will recognize that this is strong language for me to use, when you remember that I never was fond of pedestrianism."[12]

Katy Leary, a servant of the Clemens family, reports that one evening as a group of guests were sitting in the music room looking out at the moonlight at the home of Charles Dudley Warner, a neighbor in Hartford, Twain "suddenly got right up without any warning" and began to sing "negro Spirituals." He sang "low and sweet," Leary recalled, and "became kind of lost in it." When he came to the end of the song, "to the Glory Halleluiah, he gave a great shout—just like the negroes do—he shouted out the Glory, Glory, Halleluiah!" Those who were there said that "none of them would forget it as long as they lived."[13]

As his voice projected in song black voices from his childhood, Twain's bearing would become strangely transformed. Drawing on accounts by guests who were present, Justin Kaplan describes an evening at Twain's Hartford home in 1874:

> After dinner, with a log fire blazing in the red-curtained drawing room, he sang "Swing Low, Sweet Chariot," "Golden Slippers," "Go Down,

Moses". . . . He swayed gently as he stood; his voice was low and soft, a
whisper of wind in the trees; his eyes were closed, and he smiled strangely.
Through the sadness and exultation of these songs which he had known
through boyhood, he transported himself far from the circle of polite letters and from the New England snowscape, and he found it difficult to go
back. . . .[14]

Twain could often be found singing his favorite African-American
spirituals when he was farthest from home—in Liverpool in 1873, as
well as in Florence in 1904, the night his wife, Livy, died.[15] William
Dean Howells recalled the "fervor" and "passion" with which
Twain's "quavering tenor" sang these songs during his last visit to
Twain's home in Redding, Connecticut, shortly before Twain's
death.[16] Twain identified with these songs in ways that went to the
core of his being; they spoke uniquely to a part of himself that no
other art could touch.

African-American speaking voices played much the same role, on
a subliminal level, in Twain's consciousness.[17] Twain never expressed
his admiration for the power of African-American speaking voices as
publicly as he expressed his admiration for the Fisk Jubilee Singers,
but many such voices, in addition to the two that I will focus on in
this book, made deep impressions on him during the years preceding
Huckleberry Finn. During his childhood, Twain had stood in awe of
the storytelling powers of a slave named Uncle Dan'l, whom he
remembered from summers spent on his uncle's farm in Florida, Missouri. In his autobiography, when Twain described "the white and
black children grouped on the hearth" listening to Uncle Dan'l's folk
tales, he recalled "the creepy joy which quivered through me when
the time for the ghost story of the 'Golden Arm' was reached—and
the sense of regret, too, which came over me for it was always the
last story of the evening."[18]

In the late 1860s and 1870s, Twain was impressed by the narrative skills of black speakers like Frederick Douglass and Mary Ann
Cord (a servant at the Clemenses' summer home in Elmira, New
York). In 1869, the "simple language" in which Douglass told a story
in the course of social conversation struck Twain as so remarkably
"effective" that he described it in detail in a letter to his future wife:

Had a talk with Fred Douglas, [*sic*] to-day, who seemed exceedingly glad
to see me—& I certainly was glad to see *him,* for I do so admire his
"spunk." He told the history of his child's expulsion from Miss Tracy's
school, & his simple language was very effective. Miss Tracy said the
pupils did not want a colored child among them—which he did not
believe, & challenged the proof. She put it at once to a vote of the school,
and asked "How many of you are willing to have this colored child be
with you?" And they *all* held up their hands! Douglas added: "The children's

*Frederick Douglass, whose elo-
quence in the course of social
conversation impressed Twain in
1869.* (Reproduced by permission of the
Huntington Library, San Marino, California)

*Mary Ann Cord, former slave,
and servant at Quarry Farm, the
Clemenses' summer home in
Elmira, New York, whose storytelling inspired Twain's first
contribution to the* Atlantic
Monthly, *"A True Story" (1874).*
(Courtesy, University of Maryland, College Park)

hearts were right." There was pathos in the way he said it. I would like to
hear him make a speech. . . .[19]

And in 1874, the "vigorous eloquence" with which former slave
Mary Ann Cord told the story of her reunion with her son after the
Civil War inspired Twain's first contribution to the esteemed *Atlantic
Monthly*; a quarter-century later, Twain would still recall her stun-
ning "gift of strong & simple speech."[20]* Twain wrote that he found
the story she told a "curiously strong piece of *literary work* to come

---

*Mark Twain's previously unpublished words quoted here and throughout the
book are copyright © 1993 by Edward J. Willi and Manufacturers Hanover Trust
Company as Trustees of the Mark Twain Foundation, which reserves all reproduction or dramatization rights in every medium. Quotation is made with the permission
of the University of California Press and Robert H. Hirst, General Editor of the Mark
Twain Papers. Each quotation is identified by an asterisk (*).

unpremeditated from lips untrained in the literary art," showing his awareness of the close relationship between speaking voices and "literature." "The untrained tongue is usually wandering, wordy & vague," Twain wrote; "but this is clear, compact & coherent—yes, & vivid also, & perfectly simple & unconscious."[21]* Throughout his career as a lecturer and as a writer, Twain aspired to have the effect upon his listeners and readers that speakers like Frederick Douglass and Mary Ann Cord had upon *him*.[22]

Ernest Hemingway declared that "All modern American literature comes from one book by Mark Twain called *Huckleberry Finn*."[23] William Faulkner called Twain "the father of American literature."[24] The African-American roots of Twain's art, however, have never been fully recognized or explored. In 1987 Toni Morrison issued a call for critics to examine "literature for the impact Afro-American presence has had on the structure of the work, the linguistic practice, and fictional enterprise in which it is engaged."[25] This book is a response. My goal is to foreground the role previously neglected African-American voices played in shaping Mark Twain's art in *Huckleberry Finn*. Given that book's centrality in our culture, the points I make implicitly illuminate, as well, how African-American voices have shaped our sense of what is distinctively "American" about American literature.[26]

Part
<u>One</u>

JIMMY

1

Been a listening all the night long,
Been a listening all the night long[1]

Twentieth-century American criticism abounds in pronouncements about how Twain's choice of a vernacular narrator in *Huckleberry Finn* transformed modern American literature. Lionel Trilling, for example, felt that

> The prose of *Huckleberry Finn* established for written prose the virtues of American colloquial speech. . . . It has something to do with ease and freedom in the use of language. Most of all it has to do with the structure of the sentence, which is simple, direct, and fluent, maintaining the rhythm of the word-groups of speech and the intonations of the speaking voice. . . . [Twain] is the master of the style that escapes the fixity of the printed page, that sounds in our ears with the immediacy of the heard voice. . . .[2]

"As for the style of the book," Trilling concluded, "it is not less than definitive in American literature."[3] As Louis Budd noted in 1985, "today it is standard academic wisdom that Twain's central, precedent-setting achievement is Huck's language."[4]

Before Twain wrote *Huckleberry Finn*, no American author had entrusted his narrative to the voice of a simple, untutored vernacular speaker—or, for that matter, to a child. Albert Stone has noted that "the vernacular language . . . in *Huckleberry Finn* strikes the ear with the freshness of a real boy talking out loud."[5] Could the voice of an *actual* "real boy talking out loud" have helped Twain recognize the potential of such a voice to hold an audience's attention and to win its trust?

Twain himself noted in his autobiography that he based Huck Finn on Tom Blankenship, the poor-white son of the local drunkard whose pariah status (and exemption from school, church, etc.) made him the envy of every "respectable" boy in Hannibal.[6] Twain wrote,

> In *Huckleberry Finn* I have drawn Tom Blankenship exactly as he was. He was ignorant, unwashed, insufficiently fed; but he had as good a heart as any boy had. His liberties were totally unrestricted. He was the only really independent person—boy or man—in the community, and by consequence he was tranquilly and continuously happy, and was envied by all the rest of us. We liked him, we enjoyed his society. And as his society was forbidden us by our parents, the prohibition trebled and quadrupled its value, and therefore we sought and got more of his society than of any other boy's.[7]

What demands our notice is that although Tom Blankenship may have been the model for Huck's place in society, Twain never suggested that there was anything memorable about the nature of his "talk." Huck's talk, on the other hand, as many critics have noted, is the most memorable thing about him.[8] I suggest that there was another "real boy talking out loud" whose role in the genesis of *Huckleberry Finn* has never been acknowledged.

On 29 November 1874, two years before he published *Tom Sawyer* or began *Adventures of Huckleberry Finn*, Mark Twain published an article called "Sociable Jimmy" in the *New York Times*.[9] *"Sociable Jimmy" takes the place of honor as the first piece Twain published that is dominated by the voice of a child.* This fact alone would seem to mark it as deserving of scholars' attention. Strangely enough, however, it has been almost totally ignored.[10]

In this article, Twain says he originally sent the sketch of "Jimmy" home in a letter in the days when he was a public lecturer. Although this initial letter has disappeared, subsequent letters Twain wrote home to his wife allow us to determine that the encounter he relates happened in December 1871 or January 1872, in a small town in the Midwest, probably Paris, Illinois, and that the child in question definitely existed.[11] Twain reports that he had supper in his room, as was his habit, and that a "bright, simple, guileless little darkey boy . . . ten years old—a wide-eyed, observant little chap" was sent to wait on him. The intensity of Twain's response to the child is striking. He notes that he wrote down what the child said, and sent the record home because he

> . . . wished to preserve the memory of *the most artless, sociable, and exhaustless talker I ever came across*. He did not tell me a single remarkable thing, or one that was worth remembering; and yet he was

himself so interested in his small marvels, and they flowed so naturally and comfortably from his lips, that his talk got the upper hand of my interest, too, and *I listened as one who receives a revelation.* I took down what he had to say, just as he said it—without altering a word or adding one.[12]

Twain's "revelation" involved his recognition of the potential of a "bright, simple, guileless . . . wide-eyed, observant" child as narrator. I suggest that the voice of Jimmy, the "most artless, sociable, and exhaustless talker" Twain had ever come across, became a model for the voice with which Twain would change the shape of American literature.

It was a voice that Twain contained within himself, a language and set of cadences and rhythms he could generate fluently on his own, having been exposed to many such voices in his youth. Jimmy triggered his recollection of those voices, and sparked his apprehension of the creative possibilities they entailed. We can view the remarkable impression Jimmy made upon Twain, then, as connected to Twain's awareness of the ease with which he could speak in that voice himself. As he put it in a letter to Livy written shortly after he met Jimmy, "*I think I could swing my legs over the arms of a chair & that boy's spirit would descend upon me & enter into me.*"[13]* It was a crucial step on the road to creating Huck.

"Sociable Jimmy" consists mainly of what Twain presents as a transcription of Jimmy's engaging conversation (see Appendix). Twain had been intrigued for several years by the possibilities of a child as narrator, but this was the first time that he developed this perspective at any length in print.[14] Along with "A True Story," which ran in the *Atlantic Monthly* the same month "Sociable Jimmy" ran in the *Times,* it also represented one of Twain's first extended efforts to translate African-American speech into print. Indeed, to the extent that critics took notice of the piece at all, it was as an experiment in African-American dialect. Jimmy's defining characteristic for critics seemed to be the fact that he was black. For Twain, however, Jimmy was mainly a charming and delightful *child* who captured his heart and captivated his imagination.

In the "Explanatory" with which *Huckleberry Finn* begins,[15] Twain enumerates seven dialects used in the book, one of which is "Missouri negro dialect." Critics have debated whether Twain did, in fact, use seven dialects, or more, or fewer; but they have generally assumed that the only "negro dialect" in the book is that spoken by African-American characters. On a phonological level, that assumption is correct: only African-American characters, for example, say "dat," as opposed to "that." But phonology alone does not describe a *voice*, as the voluminous criticism about what makes Huck's voice distinctive clearly shows. Voice involves syntax and diction, the cadences and rhythms of a speaker's sentences, the flow of the prose, the structures of the mental processes, the rapport with the audience, the characteristic stance as regards the material related.

The cadences and rhythms of Jimmy's speech, his syntax and diction, his topics of conversation, attitudes, limitations, and his ability to hold our interest and our trust bear a striking resemblance to those qualities of speech and character that we have come to identify indelibly with Huck. Both boys are naive and open, engaging and bright. They are unpretentious, uninhibited, easily impressed, and unusually loquacious. They free-associate with remarkable energy and verve. And they are supremely self-confident: neither doubts for a minute that Twain (in Jimmy's case) or the reader (in Huck's) is completely absorbed by everything he has to say. I am not suggesting that Twain was being intentionally misleading either in his "Explanatory" or in his comments about the roots of Huck in Tom Blankenship: rather, I put forth the far from controversial notion that artists are notoriously unreliable critics of their own work. As I point out later on, Twain's blending of black voices with white to create the voice we know as Huck's may well have been unconscious.

On a linguistic level, my discussion of what Huck and Jimmy have in common is indebted to the work of three critics whose sophisticated analyses of Huck's characteristic speech patterns provide invaluable points of departure: Richard Bridgman, Janet Holmgren McKay, and David Carkeet.

One of the key elements Richard Bridgman identifies as emblematic of Huck's speech patterns and of Twain's organizing structure in the novel is *repetition*. Bridgman comments that repetition reaches a particularly "conscious structural function in extended passages where phrases are repeated." Huck:

> We got a LICKING every time one of our snakes come in her way, and she allowed these LICKINGS warn't NOTHING to what she would do if we ever loaded up the place again with them. I DIDN'T MIND THE LICKINGS because they didn't amount to NOTHING; but I MINDED the trouble we had to LAY IN another lot. But we got them LAID IN.[16]

The same subtle repetition of key words and phrases characterizes Jimmy's speech in "Sociable Jimmy," as the following examples show:

> 1. But de res' o' de people, *DEY* HAD A GOOD TIME—mos' all uv 'em HAD A GOOD TIME. DEY ALL GOT DRUNK. DEY ALL GITS DRUNK heah, every Christmas, and carries on and has AWFUL GOOD

TIMES. . . . Pa used to GIT DRUNK, but dat was befo' I was big—but he's done quit. He don' GIT DRUNK no mo' now.

2. Dat's an AWFUL BIG church—AWFUL HIGH STEEPLE. An' it's all solid stone, excep' jes' de top part—de STEEPLE. . . . It's gwine to kill some body yit, dat STEEPLE is. A man—BIG man, he was—BIGGER'n what Bill is—he tuck it up dare and fixed it again—an' he didn't look no BIGGER'n a boy, he was so HIGH up. Dat STEEPLE's AWFUL HIGH.[17]

In a passage Bridgman does not cite but that makes the point about repetition as well as the one he does cite, Huck says,

I set down again, a shaking all over, and got out my pipe for a smoke; for the house was all STILL as death, now, and so the widow wouldn't know. Well, after a long time I HEARD the clock away off in the town go BOOM—BOOM—BOOM—twelve licks—and all STILL again—STILLER than ever. Pretty soon I HEARD a twig snap, down in the dark amongst the trees—something was a stirring. I set STILL and LISTENED.[18]

In a similarly repetitive passage in "Sociable Jimmy," Jimmy characterizes the sound made by a clock in town with the identical onomatopoetic construction.

It mus' be awful to stan' in dat steeple when de CLOCK is STRIKIN'—dey say it is. BOOMS and jars so's you think the world's a comin' to an end. *I* wouldn't like to be up dare when de CLOCK'S A STRIKIN'. Dat CLOCK ain't just a *STRIKER*, like dese common CLOCKS. It's a BELL—jist a reglar *BELL*—and it's a buster. You kin hear dat BELL all over dis city. You ought to hear it BOOM, BOOM, BOOM . . .[19]

Another dimension of Huck's vernacular speech that Bridgman identifies as particularly significant is Twain's willingness to "invest words with new meaning."

The surface of his prose is littered with queer ore quarried from Huck's mine. A melodeum is "pretty *skreeky*," . . . Huck "*smouches*" a spoon, he has "*clayey*" clothes . . . he speaks of an undertaker's "soft *soothering* ways,". . . the king inquired what he was "*alassing* about" . . . he guts a catfish by "*haggling*" it open with a saw; and finally he says that a certain surprise would make "most anybody *sqush*." . . .[20]

"The effect of these words," Bridgman writes,

—dialect, nonce, slang—is that of poetry. Carrying expository meaning, they flash out with a light unique for prose. They are employed less to build an effect cumulatively, more to make an effect immediately. And they contribute to the gradually accumulating feeling in American literature for the importance of the single word. . . .[21]

Jimmy's lexicon is, in its own way, equally creative. When his employer's daughters catch a cat in the house, "dey jis' *scoops* him."

The clock Jimmy admires "ain't just a striker, like dese common clocks . . . it's a *buster*." The brother named Bob "don't git drunk much—jes' *sloshes*, roun' de s'loons some, an' takes a dram sometimes."[22]

Bridgman also notes "the frequent use of present participles in Huck's prose."

> Huck uses participial constructions especially when there is a violent or otherwise memorable action. . . ."They swarmed up the street towards Sherburn's house, A-WHOOPING and YELLING and RAGING like Injuns. . . . Lots of women and girls was CRYING and TAKING ON, scared most to death."[23]

Jimmy, too, favors participial constructions to describe memorable actions: "You don't never see Kit A-RAIRIN an' A-CHARGIN' aroun' an' KICKIN' up her heels like de res' o' de gals in dis fam'ly does gen'ally."[24] Linguist Janet Holmgren McKay observes, as well, that "frequently, Twain adds the colloquial 'a-' prefix to Huck's present participles, and he couples these forms with two-syllable adverbials for even greater rhythm." Jimmy does the same.[25]

Finally, Bridgman notes that "the participle and the reiterated conjunction of a long list 'and . . . and . . . and . . . and . . . and . . .'— are two of the least evident yet most pervasive forms of repetition to be found in Huck's version of the vernacular."[26] "Huck's remembering mind," Bridgman writes, "lays in these details one after the other without any urge toward subordination."[27] McKay also comments on Twain's propensity to make Huck's sentences "seem simple by a lack of overt indications of subordination between clauses and phrases. For example, Huck characteristically uses the conjunction *and* to link any number of subordinate and coordinate ideas, a practice that suggests a lack of linguistic sophistication."[28]

"And" is a common conjunction in Jimmy's speech as well: "He tuck de bottle AND shuck it, AND shuck it—he seed it was blue, AND he didn't know but it was blue mass . . . AND so he sot de bottle down, AND drat if it wa'n't blue vittles. . . ." Or, as he says elsewhere, "Dey all gits drunk heah, every Christmas, AND carries on AND has awful good times." The particularly long list of names Jimmy rattles off, also connected by "and"—"Bill, an' Griz, an' Duke, an' Bob, an' Nan, an' Tab, an' Kit, an' Sol, an' Si, an' Phil, an' Puss, an' Jake, an' Sal," and so on—so impresses Twain that he quickly scribbles it all down on "the flyleaf of Longfellow's *New-England Tragedies*," presumably the closest thing handy on which to write.

McKay enumerates several other dimensions of Huck's voice, virtually all of which characterize Jimmy's voice, as well. "The kinds of errors that Huck makes are by no means haphazard," McKay writes. "Twain carefully placed them to suggest Huck's basic illiteracy but not to overwhelm the reader." McKay notes that "nonstandard verb forms constitute Huck's most typical mistakes. He often uses the present form or past participle for the simple past tense . . . and he often shifts tense within the same sequence."[29] She identifies "the frequent occurrence of double negatives" as the second most prominent nonstandard feature in Huck's speech other than the verb forms.[30] McKay underlines "a redundancy of subjects" as characteristic of Huck's speech patterns. Each of these nonstandard features characterizes Jimmy's speech as well.[31]

Yet another dimension of Huck's style that McKay emphasizes is his "skillful use of . . . verbal imagery of all sorts, particularly hyperbole, metaphor and onomatopoeia." McKay cites such similes as "like the whole world was asleep," and such onomatopoeia as thunder "rumbling, grumbling, tumbling down the sky."[32] Jimmy, too, is no stranger to simile (the drowned cat is "all swelled up like a pudd'n") or to onomatopoeia (the clock "booms and jars so's you think the world's comin' to an end," and "Bob . . . jes' sloshes roun' de s'loons").

McKay notes Huck's preference for using adjectives in place of adverbs.[33] Interestingly, two of the specific adjectives Huck uses most frequently in this way—"powerful" and "considerable"—are also in Jimmy's lexicon.[34] Jimmy says, "He's powerful sickly." Huck says, "I was most powerful sick"; "he got powerful thirsty"; "I was powerful lazy and comfortable"; "[they] had such a powerful lot to say about faith"; and "I was powerful glad to get away from the feuds." Jimmy says, "Some folks say dis town would be considerable bigger . . ." Huck says, "I read considerable to Jim about kings, dukes and earls and such"; "This shook me up considerable"; "I beat it and hacked it considerable"; "He hopped around the cabin considerable"; and "We've heard considerable about these goings on."[35]

Jimmy and Huck both use "snake" rather unconventionally as a verb. Jimmy says, "Dey snake him into de cistern," and Huck asks, "What do we want of a moat, when we're going to snake him out from under the cabin?"[36] The words "particular" (as in "choosy" or "discriminating") and "reckon" (as in "think") are standard elements in both boys' speech patterns, and both boys end sentences for negative emphasis with their dialect variant of the word "scarcely": Jimmy

SOCIABLE JIMMY.

BY MARK TWAIN.

[I sent the following home in a private letter, some time ago, from a certain little village. It was in the days when I was a public lecturer. I did it because I wished to preserve the memory of the most artless, sociable, and exhaustless talker I ever came across. He did not tell me a single remarkable thing, or one that was worth remembering; and yet he was himself so interested in his small marvels, and they flowed so naturally and comfortably from his lips that his talk got the upper hand of my interest, too, and I listened as one who receives a revelation. I took down what he had to say, just as he said it—without altering a word or adding one.]

I had my supper in my room this evening, (as usual,) and they sent up a bright, simple, guileless little darkey boy to wait on me—ten years old—a wide-eyed, observant little chap. I said:

"What is your name, my boy?"

"Dey calls me Jimmy. Sah, but my right name's James. Sah."

I said, "Sit down there, Jimmy—I'll not want you just yet."

He sat down in a big arm chair, hung both his legs over one of the arms, and looked comfortable and conversational. I said:

"Did you have a pleasant Christmas, Jimmy?"

"No, sa.—not zackly. I was kind o' sick den. But de res' o' de people dey had a good time. Dey all got drunk. Dey all gits drunk heah, every Christmas, and carries on and has awful good times."

"So you were very sick, and lost it all. But unless you were very sick I should think that if you had asked the doctor he might have let you get—get—a little drunk—and—"

"Oh, no, Sah—I don' never git drunk—it's de white folks—dem's de ones I means. Pa used to git drunk, but dat was befo' I was big—but he's done quit. He don' git drunk no mo' now. Jis' takes one nip in de mawnin', now, cuz his stomach rules up, he sleeps so soun'. Jis' one nip—over to de s'loon—every mawnin'. He's powerful sickly—powerful—sometimes he can't hardly git aroun', he cayn't. He goes to de doctor every week—over to Ragtown. An' one time he tuck some stuff, you know, an' it mighty near fetched him. Ain't it dish-yer blue-vittles dat's pison?—ain't dat it?—truck what you pisons cats wid?"

"Yes blue vittles [vitriol] is a very convincing article with a cat."

"Well, den, dat was it. De ole man, he tuck de bottle and shuck it, and shuck it—he seed it was blue, and he didn't know but it was blue mass, which he tuck moe' always—blue mass pills—but den he 'spected maybe dish-yer truck might be some other kin' o' blue stuff, and so he sot de bottle down, and drat if it wa'n't blue vittles, sho' nuff, when de doctor come. An' de doctor he say if he'd a tuck dat blue vittles it would a highated him, sho'. People can't be too particular 'bout sich things. Yes, indeedy!

"We ain't got no cats heah, 'bout dis hotel. Bill he don't like 'em. He can't stan' a cat no way. Ef he was to ketch one he'd slam it outen de winder in a minute. Yes he would. Bill's down on cats. So is de gals—waiter gals. When dey ketches a cat bummin' aroun' heah, dey jis' scoops him—'deed dey do. Dey snake him into de cistern—dey's been cats drownded in det water dat's in in yo' pitcher. I seed a cat in dare yistiddy—all swelled up like a pudd'n. I bet you dem gals done dat. Ma says if doy was to drownd a cat for her, de fust one of 'em she ketched she'd jam her into de cistern 'long wid de cat. Ma wouldn't do dat, I don't reckon, but 'deed an' double, she said she would. I can't kill a chicken—well, I kin wring its neck off, cuz dat don't make 'em no sufferin scacely; but I can't take and chop dey heads off, like some people kin. It makes me feel so—so—well, I kin see dat chicken nights so's I can't sleep. Mr. Dunlap, he's de richest man in dis town. Some people says dey's fo' thousan' people in dis town—dis city. But Bill he says dey aint but 'bout thirty-three hun-I'd. And Bill he knows, cuz he's lived heah all his life, do' dey do say he won't never set de river on fire. I don't know how dey fin' out—I wouldn't like to count all dem people. Some folks says dis town would be considerable bigger if it wa'n't on accounts of so much lan' all roun' it dat ain't got no houses on it." [This in perfect seriousness—dense simplicity—no idea of a joke.] "I reckon you seed dat church as you come along up street. Dat's an awful big church—awful high steeple. It's all solid stone, excep' jes' de top part—de steeple, I means—dat's wood. It falls off when de win' blows pooty hard, an' one time it stuck in a cow's back and busted de cow all to de mischief. It's gwine to kill some body yit, dat steeple is. A man—big man, he was—bigger'n what Bill is—he tuck it up dare and fixed it again—an' he didn't look no bigger'n a boy, he was so high up. Dat steeple's awful high. If you look out de winder you kin see it." [I looked out, and was speechless with awe and admiration—which gratified Jimmy beyond expression. The wonderful steeple was some sixty or seventy feet high, and had a clock-face on it.] "You see dat arrer on top o' dat steeple? Well, Sah, dat arrer is pooty nigh as big as dis do' [door.] I seed it when dey pulled it outen de cow. I mos' be awful to stan' in dat steeple when de clock is strikin'—dey say it is. Booms and jars so's you think de worl's a comin' to an end. I wouldn't like to be up dare when de clock's a strikin'. Dat clock ain't jest a striker, like dese common clocks. It's a bell—jist a reglar bell—and it's a buster. You kin hear dat bell all over dis city. You ought to hear it boom, boom, boom, when dey's a fire. My sakes! Dey ain't got no bell like dat in Ragtown. I ben to Ragtown, an' I ben moe' halfway to Dockery [thirty miles.] De bell in Ragtown ain't got so ole now she don't make no soun', scasely."

[Enter the landlord—a kindly man, verg ng toward fifty. My small friend, without changing position, says:]

"Bill, didn't you say dat dey was only thirty-three hurd'd people in dis city?"

"Yes, about thirty-three hundred is the population now."

"Well, some folks says dey's fo' thousan'."

"Yes, I know they do; but it isn't correct."

"Bill, I don't think dis gen'leman kin eat a whole prairie-chicken, but dey tole me to fetch it all up."

"Yes, that's all right—he ordered it."

[Exit "Bill," leaving me comfortable; for I had been perishing to know who "Bill" was.]

"Bill he's de oldest. And he's de bos', too. Dey's fo'teen in dis fam'ly—all boys an' gals. Bill he suppo'ts 'em all—an' he don' never complain—he's real good, Bill is. All dem brothers an' sisters o' his'n ain't no 'count—all ceptin' dat little teeny one dat fetched in dat milk. Dat's Kit, Sah. She ain't only nine year ole. But she's de mos' lady-like one in de whole b'ilin'. You don't never see Kit a-rairin' an' a-chargin' aroun' an' kickin' up her heels like de res' o' de gals in dis fam'ly does gen'ally. Dat was Fan dat you hearn a-cuttin' dem shines on de pi-anah while ago. An' sometimes ef she don't rastle dat pi-anah when she gits started! Tab can't hole a candle to her, but Tab kin sing like de very nation. She's de only one in dis family dat kin sing. You don't never hear a yelp outen Nan. Nan can't sing for shucks. I'd jes' lloves hear a tom-cat dat's got scalded. Doy's fo'-teen in dis fam'ly 'sides de ole man an' de ole 'ooman—all brothers an' sisters. But some of 'em don't live heah—do' Bill he suppo'ts 'em—lends 'em money, an' pays dey debts an' he'ps 'em along. I tell you Bill he's real good. Dey all gits drunk—all 'cep Bill. De ole man he gits drunk, too, same as de res' uv 'em. Bob, he don't git drunk much—jes' sloshes roun' de s'loons some, an' takes a draw sometimes. Bob he's next to Bill—'bout forty year old. Dey's all married—all de fam'ly's married—cep' some of de gals. Dare's fo'teen. It's de biggest family in dese parts, dey say. Dare's Bill—Bill Nubbles—Nubbles is de name; Bill an' Griz, an' Duke, an' Bob, an' Nan, an' Tab, an' Kit, an' Sol, an' Si, an' Phil, an' Puss, an' Jake, an' Sal—Sal she's married an' got chil'en as big as I is—an' Hoss Nubbles, he's de las'. Hoss is what dey mos' always calls him, but he's got another name dat I somehow dis-remember, it's so kind o' hard to git de hang of it." [Then observing that I had been taking down this extraordinary list of nicknames for adults, he said:] "But in de mawnin' I can ask Bill what's Hoss's other name, an' den I'll come up an' tell you when I fetches yo' breakfast. An' may be I done got some o' dem names mixed up, but Bill, ho kin tell me. Dey's fo'teen."

By this time he was starting off with the waiter, (and a pecuniary consideration for his sociability,) and, as he went out, he paused a moment and said:

"Dad-fetch it, somehow dat other name don't come. But, anyways, you jes' read dem names over an' see if dey's fo'teen." [I read the list from the fly-leaf of Longfellow's *New-England Tragedies*.] "Dat's right, Sah. Dey's all down, I'll fetch up Hoss's other name in de mawnin', Sah. Don't you be oneasy.'

[Exit, whistling "Listen to the Mocking-bird."]

"Sociable Jimmy." Facsimile page from the New York Times, 29 November 1874.

says, "she don't make no soun', scasely," while Huck says, "there warn't no room in bed for him, skasely."[37] Both boys use the word "disremember" for "forget" in contexts that are virtually identical in the two texts. Jimmy says, "he's got another name dat I somehow disremember . . . ," while Huck says, "I disremember her name."[38]

Huck's style, McKay writes, "is so colloquial and seemingly unaffected and unrehearsed that we frequently feel as if he is carrying on a conversation with us"—a quality that is less surprising if we accept the basic point I'm making here: that it was real conversation that inspired Huck's voice in the first place. This sense, McKay continues, "is heightened by [Huck's] liberal use of direct addresses to 'you,' the reader."[39] Jimmy, too, in Twain's rendition of his conversation, frequently uses the direct address, "you," to his listener—although Twain's responses in the conversation are largely superfluous: all that was needed to spark Jimmy's monologue was Twain's presence. Both boys' use of the word "you" helps establish the conversational intimacy that McKay rightly finds so memorable in Huck's case.

Victor Doyno has observed that Huck's "self-interrupting style" creates the illusion that we are watching and listening to him "thinking aloud."[40] Jimmy's talk, in Twain's rendition of it, is characterized by this same "self-interrupting" quality, often established through sentences that spurt fitfully across the page in a breathless blur of dashes. "Because he interrupts himself for clarification or for qualification," Doyno notes, Huck "seems open-minded, as if he is not enshrining his own statements. Because we hear the thought process, not the final product of the thought-to-language development, we tend to trust the thinking as honest. Yet we should realize that in his rush of statements we find little subordination, and that he verifies his remarks mostly by repetition."[41] This description applies equally well to Jimmy.

Clearly, Twain is experimenting with African-American dialect in "Sociable Jimmy," just as he was in "A True Story, Repeated Word for Word as I Heard It," which appeared in the *Atlantic Monthly* the same month that "Sociable Jimmy" appeared in the *New York Times*. But although on the phonological level Jimmy's dialect bears some obvious resemblances to the speech of black characters in the novel, particularly Jim's, in a number of other ways his speech is closer to that of Huck.[42] It is not just linguistically, however, that Jimmy and Huck have much in common.[43] Even more striking than the similarities between Jimmy and Huck on the level of cadence, syntax, and diction, are the similarities between the two boys' character traits and topics of conversation.

The adult world remains rather confusing and cryptic to both

Jimmy and Huck, who are blissfully oblivious to the gaps in their understanding. Part of the humor in both "Sociable Jimmy" and *Huckleberry Finn* stems from the reader's awareness that sometimes neither Jimmy nor Huck understands that a joke is being perpetrated. Twain finds Jimmy's "dense simplicity" so engaging that he devotes a bracketed aside in the piece to explicating it:

> "Some folks say dis town would be considerable bigger if it wa'n't on accounts of so much lan' all roun' it dat ain't got no houses on it." [This in perfect seriousness—dense simplicity—no idea of a joke.]

Huck, too, sometimes fails to "get" a joke. At the circus, for example, the "drunk" who had argued with the ringmaster until he gave him a chance to ride jumps on a charging horse, pulls off his outer clothes, and turns out to be one of the regular circus performers in disguise. Huck says,

> . . . then the ring-master he see how he had been fooled, and he *was* the sickest ring-master you ever see, I reckon. Why, it was one of his own men! He had got up that joke all out of his own head, and never let on to nobody. Well, I felt sheepish enough, to be took in so, but I wouldn't a been in that ring-master's place, not for a thousand dollars.[44]

Huck has been taken in even more than he realizes, of course, since he is oblivious to the fact that the ringmaster's "embarrassment" is part of the circus routine as well. His typical stance is dead earnestness, particularly in the face of circumstances that would strike most readers as funny. As Walter Blair put it, "since he was almost completely humorless, he was bound to be incongruously naive and somber on many laugh-provoking occasions."[45] (It is interesting that in "Sociable Jimmy," written early in his career, Twain felt the need to flag the gaps in the child's understanding for the reader; by *Huckleberry Finn*, he would allow that character trait to emerge without authorial comment.) A year or so before Twain met Jimmy, in "Disgraceful Persecution of a Boy" (1870), Twain had experimented with creating a narrator too bigoted to understand the full import of what he related. In "Sociable Jimmy," Twain gave his reader an early glimpse of a narrator too *innocent* to understand the meaning of all he said. By the time he wrote *Huckleberry Finn*, of course, Twain had figured out how to use a narrator's naive responses to the world around him to unmask the hypocrisy and pretensions of that world, a strategy with which he had begun to experiment in 1870 and 1871 in "Goldsmith's Friend Abroad Again." Although Jimmy's naiveté, as conveyed by Twain, serves no satirical purpose, it *is* completely convincing. That totally believable, authentic innocence would be a crucial component of what readers would find compelling about Huck.[46]

Both Jimmy and Huck casually pepper their conversation with accidents that are simultaneously bizarre, grisly, and preposterous. In Jimmy's case, it is the cow that got skewered by the church steeple:

> I reckon you seed dat church as you come along up street. . . . [I]t's all solid stone, excep' jes de top part—de steeple, I means—dat's wood. It falls off when de win' blows pooty hard, an' one time it stuck in a cow's back and busted de cow all to de mischief. . . . You see dat arrer on top o' dat steeple? Well, Sah, dat arrer is pooty nigh as big as dis do' [door]. I seed it when dey pulled it outen de cow.

For Huck, it is the flattening of Hank Bunker:

> . . . I've always reckoned that looking at the new moon over your left shoulder is one of the carelessest and foolishest things a body can do. Old Hank Bunker done it once, and bragged about it; and in less than two years he got drunk and fell off of the shot tower and spread himself out so that he was just a kind of a layer, as you may say; and they slid him edgeways between two barn doors for a coffin, and buried him so, so they say, but I didn't see it. Pap told me. But anyway, it all come of looking at the moon that way, like a fool.[47]

As David Sloane notes, "Effortlessly blended into Huck's comments on omens of bad luck, this anecdote disappears in the run of his talk."[48] Jimmy's anecdote slips unobtrusively into his talk, as well. Both boys apparently wish to be scrupulously accurate about whether their reports are first- or secondhand, reinforcing, in the process, the reader's trust in the candor of their narratives.

Another element Jimmy and Huck have in common is an aversion to violence and cruelty. Both boys have bad dreams about cruel and violent acts they've witnessed, and have difficulty talking about the subject. Jimmy tells us,

> I can't kill a chicken—well, I kin wring its neck off, cuz dat don't make 'em no sufferin scacely; but I can't take and chop dey heads off, like some people kin. It makes me feel so—so—well, I kin see dat chicken nights so's I can't sleep.

After the mindless killings during the feud, Huck comments:

> It made me so sick I most fell out of the tree. I ain't agoing to tell *all* that happened—it would make me sick again if I was to do that. I wish I hadn't ever come ashore that night, to see such things. I ain't ever going to get shut of them—lots of times I dream about them.[49]

While Jimmy's comments involve chickens and Huck's involve human beings, the visceral rejection of violence and cruelty in each case is similar, as is each child's reluctance to talk about it, and the expression of personal anguish with the barely understood sleep disturbance of a child.

When either Jimmy or Huck is truly determined to fascinate his listener he launches into a long, name-filled family narrative. In neither case is the family his own. Jimmy talks about the family that runs the inn in which he works, and Huck about an invented family designed to make convincing whatever identity he has chosen (for pragmatic reasons) at that moment. "Dey's fo'teen in dis fam'ly," Jimmy notes,

> —all boys an' gals. Bill he suppo'ts 'em all—an he don' never complain—he's *real* good, Bill is. . . . Dat was Nan dat you hearn a cuttin' dem shines on de pi-anah while ago. . . . *Tab* can't hole a candle to *her*, but Tab kin *sing* like de very nation. She's de only one in dis family dat kin sing. You don't never hear a yelp outen Nan. Nan can't sing for shucks. I'd jes lieves hear a tom-cat dat's got scalded. Dey's fo'teen in dis fam'ly 'sides de ole man and de ole 'ooman—all brothers an' sisters . . . Dey all gits drunk—all 'cep Bill. . . . Dey's all married—all de fam'ly's married—cep' some of de gals. Dare's fo'teen. It's de biggest family in dese parts, dey say. Dare's Bill—Bill Nubbles—Nubbles is de name; Bill, an' Griz, an' Duke, an' Bob, an' Nan, an' Tab, an' Kit, an' Sol, an' Si, an' Phil, an' Puss, an' Jake, an' Sal—Sal she's married an' got chil'en as big as I is'—an' Hoss Nubbles, he's de las'. Hoss is what dey mos' always calls him, but he's got another name dat I somehow disremember, it's so kind o' hard to git the hang of it.

Jimmy is convinced that all of these details will intrigue his listener—and, as it turns out, they do. Twain interjects,

> [Then, observing that I had been taking down the extraordinary list of nicknames for adults, he said]: "But in de mawnin' I can ask Bill what's Hoss's other name, an' den I'll come up an' tell you when I fetches yo' breakfast. An' may be I done got some o' dem names mixed up, but Bill, he kin tell me. Dey's fo'teen." . . . By this time he was starting off with the waiter, (and a pecuniary consideration for his sociability), and, as he went out he paused a moment and said: "Dad-fetch it, somehow dat other name don't come. But, anyways, you jes' read dem names over an' see if dey's fo'teen." [I read the list from the flyleaf of Longfellow's *New-England Tragedies*.] "Dat's right, sah. Dey's all down. I'll fetch up Hoss's other name in de mawnin', sah. Don't you be oneasy."
> [Exit, whistling "Listen to the Mocking Bird."]

Jimmy's concern that Twain might lose sleep over the fact that Jimmy hadn't been able to recall all the names reveals a blithe self-assurance that Twain found utterly charming and delightful.

Similarly, when the Grangerfords quiz Huck on who he is, he

tells them a tale about "pap and me . . . and Mary Ann . . . and Bill . . . and Tom and Mort." Huck offers the fugitive-slave-hunters a family narrative about "pap, and mam, and sis, and Miss Hooker," and regales the king and the duke with a tale about "Pa and my brother Ike . . . [and] uncle Ben [and] our nigger, Jim." The language Huck uses in one such tale echoes Jimmy's precise phrasing. Huck says, "All of us was saved but Bill Whipple—and oh, he *was* the best cretur!"[50] As Jimmy had put it years earlier, "Bill, he's de oldest. An he's de bes', too."

The only "real" family that each boy has is "Pa" or "Pap" and in both cases the father has a history of alcohol problems that both children describe with unembarrassed frankness. In both cases (despite Jimmy's assertion that Pa's drinking days are over), the problem is ongoing.[51]

Jimmy and Huck also share some matters of taste: each boy is especially awed by a particular clock, and both set themselves up as judges of refinement.[52] Jimmy and Huck are both easily impressed by other things as well—Jimmy by the size of the church steeple and the weather vane at its top, Huck by the Grangerfords' fake plaster fruits and Emmeline's dreadful poetry.[53]

Finally, Jimmy and Huck are both at home with dead animals—dead cats, dead fish. These are simply a part of their world and they wouldn't dream of omitting them from their chatty conversation. They bring them in casually and comfortably, unaware that details about the dead animal might disrupt their listener's equilibrium or digestion. Jimmy entertains Twain at dinner, apropos of nothing in particular, with an anecdote about the dead cat in the well that supplied Twain's drinking water:

> Bill's down on cats. So is de gals—waiter gals. When dey ketches a cat bummin' aroun' heah, dey jis' *scoops* him—'deed dey do. Dey snake him into de cistern—dey's been cats drownded in dat water dat's in yo' pitcher. I seed a cat in dare yistiddy—all swelled up like a pudd'n. I bet you dem gals done dat.

With similarly jarring candor, Huck fails to edit out of his lyrical description of dawn on the river a decidedly pungent dead fish:

> then the nice breeze springs up, and comes fanning you from over there, so cool and fresh, and sweet to smell, on account of the woods and the flowers; but sometimes not that way, because they've left dead fish laying around, gars, and such, and they do get pretty rank . . .[54]

Perhaps Jimmy's sociable chatter about the dead cats remained in Twain's subconscious, when, a few years after his encounter with

Jimmy, he introduced Huck Finn to the world in *Tom Sawyer* carrying a dead cat.

> Tom hailed the romantic outcast:
> "Hello, Huckleberry!"
> "Hello yourself, and see how you like it."
> "What's that you got?"
> "Dead Cat."[55]

Dead cats enter the scene in *Huckleberry Finn* as well, this time *en masse*, when the Bricksville crowd is gunning for the king and the duke at their third performance of "The Royal Nonesuch." Huck says,

> If I know the signs of a dead cat being around, and I bet I do, there was sixty-four of them went in.[56]

Both Jimmy and Huck are proud that they "know the signs of a dead cat being around" and are only too glad to share their knowledge.

Twain had long admired the artful presentation of many of those qualities Jimmy so fully embodied. For example, referring to a story James Whitcomb Riley told, Twain commented,

> The simplicity and innocence and unconsciousness of the old farmer are perfectly simulated, and the result is a performance which is thoroughly charming and delicious. This is art—and fine and beautiful.[57]

If "simplicity and innocence and unconsciousness" are to be desired, who better to embody these traits than a child?

"Sociable Jimmy" was Twain's first published work in which the voice of a child took center stage.[58] In the years that immediately followed its publication, Twain became increasingly aware of the distinctive possibilities of the choice of a child narrator. As he once put it, "Experience has taught me long ago that if ever *I* tell a boy's story . . . it is never worth printing. . . . To be successful and worth printing, the imagined boy would have to tell the story *himself* and let me act merely as his amanuensis."[59] That was, of course, precisely the role in which Twain placed himself as he copied down Jimmy's speech that evening. It is the same role Twain assumed in his imagination when he began writing *Huckleberry Finn*. In the recently discovered manuscript of the beginning of the novel, Huck's opening lines, "You don't know about me . . ." are preceded by the words,

> Huck _{leberry} Finn
> reported by Mark Twain[60]

Asked to explain his writing process, Twain said to an interviewer in 1907,

I never deliberately sat down and "created" a character in my life. I begin to write incidents out of real life. *One of the persons I write about begins to talk this way and another,* and pretty soon I find that these creatures of the imagination have developed into characters, and have for me a distinct personality. These are not "made," they just grow naturally out of the subject. *That was the way Tom Sawyer, Huck Finn and other characters came to exist.*[61]

Twain's comment that his characters develop from their "talk" adds credence to the idea that the "revelation" that Twain experienced listening to Jimmy speak was a vital part of the process by which Huck Finn came into being. Whenever we encounter a sentence we like, Twain wrote, "we unconsciously store it away in our model-chamber; and it goes with the myriad of its fellows to the building, brick by brick, of the edifice which we call our style. . . ."[62] Reading over his transcription of the encounter with Jimmy, Twain may have stored away in his "model-chamber" some of the texture from the child's speech.

It would not have been unusual for Twain to have taken some of Jimmy's topics of conversation, habits of expression, and turns of phrase (as recorded in his own rendition of them) and unknowingly recycled them as Huck's. For Twain had a habit, as he recognized himself, of unconsciously borrowing ideas and phrases from others. Walter Blair notes,

In 1869, as [Twain] put it, he had "stolen" the dedication of a book by Oliver Wendell Holmes "almost word for word" quite unconsciously, and on apologizing had been reassured by Holmes of the "truth" that we all unconsciously work over ideas gathered in reading and hearing, imagining they were original with ourselves. Midway in *Tom Sawyer* he again caught himself committing "unconscious plagiarism." In a letter of 1876, the year *Tom Sawyer* appeared, he indicated that he often unknowingly transplanted ideas from stories by others into stories of his own.[63]

Later in life Twain would express the doubt that "there was much of anything in human utterance *except* plagiarism!"

The kernel, the soul—let us go further and say the substance, the bulk, the actual and valuable material of *all* human utterances—is plagiarism. For substantially all ideas are second-hand, consciously and unconsciously drawn from a million outside sources, and daily used by the garnerer with a pride and satisfaction born of the superstition that he originated them.[64]

If Twain found himself "garnering" some of Jimmy's ideas and expressions for Huck's world, his comments here suggest he felt that such a process was central to the production of his art.[65]

What enabled Twain to transform the voice of a black child into the voice of a white one so effortlessly, confidently, and, possibly, unconsciously? A good deal of the puzzle may be explained by the element of class. As contemporary accounts testify, there were many similarities between the speech of Southern whites and blacks at the lower reaches of the economic spectrum in the nineteenth century. A traveller in the South shortly after the Civil War observed, for example, that "the language of the lower class of the whites is so much like that of the negroes that it is difficult to say where the English ends and the African begins."[66] Although we know nothing whatsoever about Tom Blankenship's patterns of speech, his rock-bottom economic status as the offspring of "paupers and drunkards"[67] suggests that the dividing line between his speech and the speech of blacks in his community may have been quite faint. Twain could thus have plausibly borrowed habits of speech from Jimmy and put them in the mouth of Tom Blankenship or Huck without any sense of incongruity, without violating his own "pains-taking" efforts to have his characters speak in accurate (as well as accurately rendered) dialect. Although Twain distinguishes between the speech of white and black characters in the novel on a phonological level, on the level of syntax and diction, Jimmy's and Huck's speech is similar, as we have shown.

There may be another reason, however, for the ease with which Twain was able to blend elements of black and white experience in Huck: Tom Blankenship, the boy on whom Twain says he modeled Huck, had a black sidekick. On 22 August 1917, an old playmate of Twain's, John W. Ayres (who is mentioned in the *Autobiography*), wrote a letter to the *Palmyra Spectator* that was published under the headline, "Recollections of Hannibal." A clipping of it appears in a scrapbook owned by the Mark Twain Museum in Hannibal.[68] Here one "Black John" makes the following, rather startling appearance—startling because this is the only reference to him that we have. Ayres writes, "I spent part of my early childhood with my grandmother and many a day have chased rabbits over 'The Broadax'" [an open tract of land occupied by "squatters"]

> with "Black John," a half grown negro belonging to my grandmother, and Tom Blankenship. My grandmother told us that Tom Blankenship was a bad boy and we were forbidden to play with him, but when we went on a rabbit chase he joined us. Tom Blankenship was in fact "some kid." He was not subject to laws of conventionality and did not have to go to school and "behave himself" as the rest of us boys did, and therefore was much envied. Black John and Tom Blankenship were naturally leading spirits and they led us younger "weaker" ones

through all our sports. Both were "talented," bold, kind, and just and
we all "liked" them both and were easily led by them. . . .

Ayres adds that he saw Clemens frequently in those days.

We know tantalizingly little about this slave named Black John,
a "'talented,' bold, kind, and just" young man with natural leadership qualities who was at Tom Blankenship's side in "all our sports,"
and to whom Ayres refers in the same breath when Blankenship's
name comes up.[69] But it is tempting to think that a fleeting memory
of this high-spirited black companion of Tom Blankenship's, this
"black Huck Finn," may have encouraged Twain to forge ahead
with his daring project of blending, in Huck Finn, the voice of
a black child (Jimmy) with the status and actions of a white child
(Tom Blankenship).[70]

Can we assume that Twain's meeting with "Sociable Jimmy"
actually happened and that Jimmy really existed—that neither was an
invention on Twain's part? I believe we can. The most compelling evidence for Jimmy's existence is a letter Twain wrote to his wife on
10–11 January 1872, while on the lecture circuit. The letter reads, in
part, as follows:

> . . . If I had been at Mrs. Stowe's reading & they wanted any help, I
> would have read about "Fat-Cholly Aithens" & the rest of my little
> darkey's gossip. I think I could swing my legs over the arms of a chair
> & that boy's spirit would descend upon me & enter into me. I'm glad
> Warner likes the sketch. I must keep it for my volume of "Lecturing
> Experiences"—but I'm afraid I'll have to keep it a good while, for I
> *can't* do without those unapproachable names of the Aithens family—
> nor "Tarry Hote,"—nor any of those things—& if I were to print the
> sketch *now* I should have the whole "fo'teen" after me.[71]*

Twain evidently changed the family name from "Aithens" to
"Nubbles" when he published the sketch in the *Times* two years later,
and Jimmy's name may have been changed, as well. He also masked
some details about the scene's locale (no reference to "Tarry Hote"
survives in the published sketch). But Twain's references to the "boy"
and the "fo'teen" members of the family for whom he worked (and
Twain's fear of the "fo'teen" coming after him if he published the
sketch) clearly establish that Jimmy was a real child whom Twain
met in late December 1871 or early January 1872.

Even without this documentary proof of Jimmy's existence, textual and contextual evidence lend support to the idea that Jimmy was
real. The manner in which Twain framed his transcription of Jimmy's
speech echoes his transcription/re-creation during this period of the
speech of two notable vernacular speakers, in "The Jumping Frog"

(1865) and "A True Story" (1874). In both of these latter cases, the specific individuals who served as models for the speakers in the story have been identified.

Twain introduces Simon Wheeler, the narrator in "Jumping Frog," as follows:

> . . . I found Simon Wheeler dozing comfortably by the bar-room stove of the dilapidated tavern in the decayed mining camp of the Angel's, and I noticed that he was fat and bald-headed, and had an expression of winning gentleness and simplicity upon his tranquil countenance. . . . He never smiled, he never frowned, he never changed his voice from the gentle-flowing key to which he tuned his initial sentence, he never betrayed the slightest suspicion of enthusiasm; but all through the interminable narrative there ran a vein of impressive earnestness and sincerity, which showed me plainly that, so far from his imagining that there was anything ridiculous or funny about his story, he regarded it as a really important matter, and admired its two heroes as men of transcendent genius in *finesse*. I let him go on in his own way, and never interrupted him once.[72]

Simon Wheeler was based on an Illinois river pilot named Ben Coon,[73] whom Twain had met at Angel's Camp, Calaveras County, California, in the company of his friend Jim Gillis in December 1864 or January 1865. As Albert Bigelow Paine described it, "one dreary afternoon, in his slow, monotonous fashion, [Coon] told them about a frog—a frog that had belonged to a man named Coleman, who trained it to jump, but that failed to win a wager because the owner of a rival frog had surreptitiously loaded the trained jumper with shot."[74] Twain entered a brief reminder of Coon's story in his notebook.[75] His own version of the story, "Jim Smiley and His Jumping Frog" (as it was originally called), appeared in the *Saturday Press* on 18 November 1865, and brought him immediate national fame.

Twain's introduction of Aunt Rachel resembles his initial presentations of both Ben Coon and Jimmy. He presented Aunt Rachel, the narrator in "A True Story, Repeated Word for Word as I Heard It," in this manner:

> It was summer-time, and twilight. We were sitting on the porch of the farmhouse, on the summit of the hill, and "Aunt Rachel" was sitting respectfully below our level, on the steps—for she was our servant, and colored. She was of mighty frame and stature; she was sixty years old, but her eye was undimmed and her strength unabated. She was a cheerful, hearty soul, and it was no more trouble for her to laugh than it is for a bird to sing. That is to say, she was being chaffed without mercy, and was enjoying it. She would let off peal after peal of laughter, and then sit with her face in her hands and shake with the throes of enjoyment which she could no longer get breath enough to express. At such

a moment as this a thought occurred to me, and I said:

"Aunt Rachel, how is it that you've lived sixty years and never had any trouble?"[76]

From that point on, Twain allows Aunt Rachel to tell her moving story in her own words.[77] The result was Twain's first contribution to the *Atlantic Monthly*, whose editor, William Dean Howells, credited Twain with having successfully put "the best and reallest kind of black talk in it."[78] Twain was paid at the highest rate the magazine had ever offered.

The model for Aunt Rachel, as Twain and others readily acknowledged, was Mary Ann Cord, an ex-slave who worked as a servant at Quarry Farm, the Clemenses' summer home in Elmira, New York. Several sources corroborate the accuracy of Twain's description of Mary Ann Cord, in terms of both her character and her physical presence.[79] As Twain himself put it in 1906,

> she was cheerful, inexhaustibly cheerful, her heart was in her laugh & her laugh could shake the hills. Under emotion she had the best gift of strong & simple speech that I have known in any woman except my mother. She told me a striking tale out of her personal experience, once, & I will copy it here—& not in my words but her own. I wrote them down before they were cold. (Insert "A True Story.")[80]*

On 18 November 1875, Twain presented a copy of the first edition of *Sketches New and Old* to Mary Ann Cord with the following inscription,

> The author of this book offers it to Aunty Cord with his kindest regards, and refers her to page 202 for a well-meant but libelous portrait of herself & also the bit of personal history which she recounted to him once at "Quarry Farm."[81]

Mary Ann Cord is buried in the same Elmira cemetery as Mark Twain.[82] In 1986, her great grandson, Leon W. Condol, of Silver Springs, Maryland, presented Twain's inscribed volume to the University of Maryland.[83]

Both of Twain's national successes through 1874 involving vernacular speech were thus based on real and identifiable people. His introduction of these speakers in these pieces resembles his introduction of Jimmy, supporting the belief that Jimmy was, indeed, a real child. In "A True Story," Twain was proud of having told the tale "not in my words" but in those of Mary Ann Cord. It is quite possible that some three years earlier he did just what he said he did and wrote down Jimmy's words, too, "before they were cold."

A fair amount has been written on Ben Coon and Mary Ann

Cord, but no scholar has persisted enough to track down Jimmy, presumably because until now his significance has not been recognized.[84] There is no record of any letters or response to "Sociable Jimmy," Twain never reprinted it, and he never referred to it elsewhere. All the evidence indicates that he was probably unaware of the role this material could play in his career. He was initially blind to the significance of "A True Story," as well, minimizing its importance as he casually slipped it in the envelope when he mailed another manuscript to William Dean Howells.[85]

"Sociable Jimmy" seemed so obscure and trivial to George Hiram Brownell, editor of the *Twainian*, that in 1937 when Irving S. Underhill sent him a "photostat copy of ['Sociable Jimmy'] as it appears in printed form on the page of a magazine, name, date and place of publication unknown," Brownell casually filed it away for six years before printing it. When in February 1943 he finally reprinted the piece in the *Twainian*, he noted that when he was given "Sociable Jimmy,"

> In an accompanying letter, Mr. Underhill explains that the magazine page was pasted, without any identification data whatever, in a scrapbook purchased by him from a printer who had worked in Chicago during the period 1870–1875; and other clippings on the same page of the scrap-book were taken from newspapers and magazines published during the year 1874.[86]

He urged readers to come forth with any information about where the article had initially appeared. In April, Brownell announced that no readers had written the *Twainian* with any leads.[87]

By the time Paul Fatout reprinted "Sociable Jimmy" in *Mark Twain Speaks for Himself* in 1978, he was able to identify it as having run in the *New York Times*. Neither after its first republication in 1943, nor after its second in 1978, did the piece elicit any additional critical comment. In the brief note that Fatout appended to the piece, he wrote that Twain "may have been attuning his ear to the variations of Negro dialect and attempting to get it down credibly on paper." Fatout suggests that "perhaps Mark Twain wrote 'Sociable Jimmy' partly as an exercise in vernacular language."[88] The challenge of rendering speech in print had long intrigued Twain, and it is indeed quite possible that he used his encounter with Jimmy as an occasion for linguistic experimentation. It is, of course, impossible to determine precisely which phrases and sentences Twain heard and which he created in this as in other pieces rooted in real encounters. In "A True Story," for example, when Twain changed " 'I ain't no hound dog mash to be trod on by common trash' "* in the manuscript to " 'I wa'nt bawn in de mash to be fool' by trash' " in the printed version, was he improving on Mary Ann Cord's original story, or merely revising his record of it to read more accurately?[89]

Jimmy's speech may have reminded Twain of voices from his childhood. Twain himself was candid about his preference for black playmates throughout his youth. He recalled, "I was playmate to all the niggers, preferring their society to that of the elect. . . ."[90] As Twain noted in his *Autobiography*, "All the negroes were friends of ours, and with those of our own age we were in effect comrades."[91] Bernard DeVoto observed of the atmosphere in which Twain was raised,

> Black and white children grew up together, without distinction except that when wills crossed blacks must yield. . . . They investigated all things together, exploring life.[92]

Some reminiscences of summers on the Quarles farm by Twain's favorite cousin, Tabitha Quarles Greening, that were published around 1917 mentioned, for example, "the slave girl, Mary, little Sam's playmate" as an important companion of Twain's (see photo).[93] Throughout the article Greening emphasized the central role Twain's "darky playmates" played in his childhood and her own and in their memories.[94]

The unquestioned, important presence of black children in Hannibal as well as at the Quarles farm in Florida, Missouri, is captured by Twain in the pump scene in *Tom Sawyer*. When Tom Sawyer is forced to whitewash the fence on a sunny Saturday morning, he tries to switch chores with one of the servants who has been sent to fetch water:

> Bringing water from the town pump had always been hateful work in Tom's eyes, before, but now it did not strike him so. He remembered that there was company at the pump. White, mulatto and negro boys and girls were always there waiting their turns, resting, trading playthings, quarreling, fighting, skylarking.[95]

Whether Jimmy's voice belonged solely to the ten-year-old black child Twain met in 1871 or 1872, or whether it also drew on voices from Twain's past, it was rooted, as are all of Twain's most memorable creations, in real events and real people: "I confine myself to life with which I am familiar, when pretending to portray life . . ." he wrote in 1890. "[T]he most valuable capital, or culture, or education usable in the building of novels, is personal experience."[96] In his journal in late 1887, Twain wrote,

> If you attempt to create & build a wholly imaginary incident, adventure or situation you will go astray, & the artificiality of the thing will be detectable. But if you found on a *fact* in your personal experience, it is

When she was a young girl and Sam Clemens was a child, Mary Quarles, a slave (pictured here in 1907), was Sam's constant companion on his uncle's Missouri farm during summers, responsible for looking after him. (Photo by Albert Bigelow Paine, 1907. Courtesy, the Mark Twain Papers, The Bancroft Library)

an acorn, a root, & every created adornment that grows up out of it & spreads its foliage & blossoms to the sun will seem realities, not inventions. You will not be likely to go astray; your compass of fact is there to keep you on the right course. . . .[97]

Further, as he told an interviewer in 1895,

I don't believe an author, good, bad or indifferent, ever lived, who created a character. It was always drawn from his recollection of someone he had known. Sometimes, like a composite photograph, an author's presentation of a character may possibly be from the blending of . . . two or more real characters in his recollection. But, even when he is making no attempt to draw his character from life, . . . he is yet unconsciously drawing from memory.[98]

Did Twain's meeting with Jimmy take place as he described it? A number of contextual clues suggest that it did. The scene Twain recreated in "Sociable Jimmy" matches other scenes during his lecture tours, as described by his daughter and others. We know, for example, that after several years of being irritated with the lack of privacy when he stayed in people's homes while on the lecture circuit, Twain preferred to stay in obscure inns, where he often took meals in his room in an atmosphere resembling the one he describes in "Sociable Jimmy."[99]

We also have outside corroboration of the fact that Twain did, indeed, take a copy of Longfellow's *New England Tragedies* on his lecture tour that year. "To relieve the tedium of long train rides he always carried with him literary classics that had come to his attention, books by prominent literary contemporaries, and such things as Livy wanted him to read."[100] One book Livy urged on him was Longfellow's *New England Tragedies*, which came out in 1868. On 9 January 1872, Twain wrote Livy from Steubenville, Ohio, that he had "read & sent home" that particular volume.[101] The book was listed in the MTLAcc entry #2055, as a volume donated from Twain's library to the Mark Twain Library in Redding in 1910 by his daughter Clara Clemens Gabrilowitsch. Clara and her father donated 1,751 documented volumes to the Redding Library, but by 1977, when Alan Gribben prepared *Mark Twain's Library: A Reconstruction*, only 240 books that could be identified as having been donated by Twain or his daughter remained. The other books had been lost through circulation or "unwittingly sold to provide more shelf space for newer books."[102] Unfortunately, Twain's copy of Longfellow's *New England Tragedies* was evidently one of the volumes that had disappeared, for when Mark Twain's library was transferred to the Stowe-Day Library of the Mark Twain Memorial and later to the Watkinson Library of Trinity College, Hartford, this volume was missing. The book may turn up yet, in some Connecticut garage or estate sale, with Twain's list of names on the flyleaf.

It is also entirely plausible that Twain would have taken "down the extraordinary list of nicknames for adults" on the flyleaf of the nearest book he had at hand. Twain had the habit, throughout his life, of scribbling miscellaneous notes to himself on the flyleaves of books he owned when they were the most convenient things on which to write.[103]

If we assume that Twain met Jimmy while on tour some time shortly before 9 January 1872, when Longfellow's book still would have been in his room, we can narrow down somewhat where Jimmy may have lived. After a twenty-month absence from the platform, Twain had begun that season's lecture tour on 16 October in Bethlehem, Pennsylvania.[104] His tour took him to Washington, D.C., Wilmington, Delaware, and numerous cities and towns in Pennsylvania, Massachusetts, Connecticut, New York, New Hampshire, Vermont, Maine, New Jersey, Michigan, Indiana, Illinois, and Ohio.[105] From mid-December through early January, Twain's lecture dates were concentrated in the Midwest. The encounter, as we have noted, probably took place in Paris, Illinois.[106] Jimmy's boast that he had been as far as halfway to the town that was about 60 miles away (probably Decatur)[107] suggests that he had probably lived all of his life in the same small Midwestern town in which he was born. This assumption is consistent with his dialect, as Twain transcribed it, and helps explain why his speech is quite different from that of other black speakers whose voices Twain recreated in his fiction, most of whom hailed from Missouri or points farther south.

When he met Jimmy, some time between October 1871 and January 1872, Twain, who had just finished *Roughing It*, was in a good frame of mind to appreciate the child's innocence and exuberance. Jeffrey Steinbrink writes of Twain's persona on the lecture circuit that season: "Twain had ceased for the most part to be an innocent himself and had become instead a commentator on innocence, frequently the innocence of his earlier life."[108] Twain may have had only the vaguest notion, at this point, of where that role would take him. But a note he wrote his wife while he was on the lecture circuit suggests that he knew he was on the verge of something "big." "When I come to write the Mississippi book," he wrote Livy, "*then* look out!"[109]

What happened between Twain's first encounter with Jimmy in 1871 or 1872 and his decision to let a voice much like Jimmy's be the narrator of a novel some four years later, when he began *Huckleberry Finn*? For one thing, Mary Ann Cord told her story. That evening in 1874 when Mary Ann Cord captivated Twain and Livy on the porch of Quarry Farm may have been almost as important a step on the road to *Huckleberry Finn* as Twain's encounter with Jimmy two years earlier. For, while Jimmy's vernacular speech intrigued Twain, Mary Ann Cord showed Twain the possibilities of combining vernacular speech with accomplished narrative skill. She told her story so artfully that Twain felt he had to do little to its structure other than

Mark Twain at his writing desk in his octagonal study at Quarry Farm in 1874, the year he published "Sociable Jimmy" and "A True Story."
(Courtesy, the Mark Twain Papers, The Bancroft Library)

start it at the beginning rather than in the middle. Her story impressed Twain as a "curiously strong piece of literary work to come unpremeditated from lips untrained in literary art."[110]* Quite possibly, the "curiously strong" nature of Cord's "literary work" may have been as much of a "revelation" to Twain in 1874 as the vitality of Jimmy's vernacular speech had been two years earlier.[111] It may be no accident that several months after hearing Cord tell her story, and after recording it on paper himself, Twain decided to return to the story his "little darkey" had told him two years earlier, change the names and places, and put it into print. Perhaps Cord's example, and Howells's unexpected enthusiasm for Twain's rendition of it, helped Twain recognize the great potential that lay in vernacular storytelling. Cord's narrative power in that vein, combined with Jimmy's cadences, rhythms, innocence, good-heartedness, and ebullient loquaciousness, may have moved Twain gradually closer to *Huckleberry Finn*.

Critics have long insisted that Huck Finn was a direct literary descendant of such earlier vernacular figures as Johnson J. Hooper's "Simon Suggs," Augustus Baldwin Longstreet's "Clown," George W. Harris's "Sut Lovingood," David Ross Locke's "Petroleum V. Nasby," and Charles Farrar Browne's "Artemus Ward."[112] Fine scholars including Kenneth Lynn, Walter Blair, Pascal Covici, Jr., and David Sloane developed the idea that Twain knew and admired the work of these popular newspaper humorists who preceded him, that these authors played a role in shaping his own career as a writer, and that they left their mark on Twain's writing in *Huckleberry Finn*. There are major differences, however, between Huck and these early comic "precursors" that scholars have never fully explained.

Twain's earliest sketches are clearly indebted to the work of many of the Southwestern humorists and Northeastern literary comedians. Browne left his mark on *Innocents Abroad* and *Roughing It*,[113] and Longstreet left his on *Tom Sawyer*.[114] These newspaper humorists played a role in the creation of *Huckleberry Finn*, as well. For example, Twain drew on Johnson J. Hooper's "Simon Suggs Attends a Camp-Meeting" when he created the character of the dauphin,[115] and "Aunt Polly" bore such a close resemblance to B. P. Shillaber's "Mrs. Partington" that "Mrs. Partington's" picture was actually used to represent her in *Tom Sawyer*.[116]

One can easily see political satirist David Ross Locke's "Petroleum V. Nasby" as a forerunner to "Pap":

> . . . Deekin Pogram sed he'd bore with them niggers til his patience wuz gin out. He endoored it till last Sunday. After service he felt pensive, ruther, and walked out towards Garrettstown, meditatin, as he went, on the sermon he hed listened to that mornin on the necessity uv the spread of the Gospil. Mournin in sperit over the condition of the heathen, he didn't notis where he wuz till he found hisself in the nigger settlement, and in front uv one uv their houses. There he saw a site wich paralyzed him. There wuz a nigger, wich wuz wunst his nigger,—which Linkin deprived him uv,—settin under his porch, and a profanin the Holy Bible by teachin his child to read it! "Kin this be endoored?" the Deekin asked.[117]

Twain knew and liked Locke, and it is quite possible that he took some tips from him on how to let his most blatantly racist character shoot himself in the foot. Locke's (Nasby's) "Ethnology at Confedrit x Roads: 'Possibly the Seat uv the Intelleck Is in the Heel,'" published in 1867, bears a strong resemblance to Pap's "Call this a govment!" speech in *Huckleberry Finn*.[118]

But what of Huck himself? Kenneth Lynn considers Harris's "Sut Lovingood" a major precursor. But Huck neither sounds, acts, nor feels like Sut Lovingood does. Listen, for a moment, to Sut Lovingood's speech:

> I seed a well appearin man onst, ax one ove em [the proprietors of taverns, evidently carpetbaggers] what lived ahine a las' year's crap ove red hot brass wire whisters run tu seed, an' shingled wif har like onto mildew'd flax, wet wif saffron warter, an' laid smoof wif a hot flat-iron, ef he cud spar him a scrimpshun ove soap? The "perpryiter" anser'd in soun's es sof an' sweet es a poplar dulcimore, tchuned by a good nater'd she angel in butterfly wings an' cobweb shiff, that he never were jis' so sorry in all his born'd days tu say no, but the fac' were the soljers hed stole hit. . . . When the devil takes a likin tu a feller, an' wants tu make a sure thing ove gittin him he jis' puts hit intu his hed to open a cat-fish tavern, with a gran' rat attachmint, gong 'cumpanimint, bull's neck variashun, cockroach corus an' bed-bug refrain, an' dam ef he don't git him es sure es he rattils the fust gong. . . .[119]

Sut's cadences, lexicon, and syntax are worlds apart from Huck's. His long, dense, convoluted sentences do not manifest the repetition or serial verb construction that characterize Huck's speech, and Sut's sentences contain much more subordination. Sut uses no redundancy of subjects and does not use adjectives in place of adverbs.

Sut Lovingood's character and stance toward life are as far from Huck's as the language in which he describes them:

> Every critter what hes ever seed me, ef he has sence enuff to hide from a cummin kalamity, ur run from a muskit, jis' knows five great facks in my case es well es they knows the road to their moufs. *Fustly*, that I hain't got nara a soul, nuffin but a whiskey proof gizzard, sorter like the wus half ove a ole par ove saddil bags. *Seconly*, that I'se too durn'd a fool to cum even onder millertary lor. *Thudly*, that I hes the longes' par ove laigs ever hung to eny cackus. . . . *Foufly*, that I kin chamber more cork-screw kill-devil wisky, an' stay on aind, than enything 'sceptin' only a broad bottum'd chun.[120]

Whereas Jimmy and Huck had a clear aversion to cruelty, Sut was, in Edmund Wilson's words, "always malevolent and always excessively sordid." "His impulse," Wilson maintains, "is avowedly sadistic."[121]

> An' yere's anuther human nater: ef enything happens to sum feller, I don't keer ef he's yure bes' frien, an' I don't keer how sorry yu is fur him, thars a streak ove satisfackshun 'bout like a sowin thread a-runnin all thru yer sorrer. Yu may be shamed ove hit, but durn me ef hit ain't thar. . . .[122]

When Sut sees a "littil long laiged lamb . . . dancin' staggerinly onder hits mam a-huntin fur the tit, ontu hits knees," his first impulse—indeed, he asserts it as a universal impulse—is

> to seize that ar tail an' fling the little ankshus son ove a mutton over the fence amung the blackberry briars, not tu hurt hit, but jis' tu disapint hit.[123]

Sut's sadism isn't limited to "littil long laiged lambs." Affronted by innocence, he also welcomes the thought of kicking a calf fifteen feet in the air when it's trying to suck at its mother's breast, and would relish the chance to wallop a nursing human baby, too, "tu show hit what's atwixt hit an' the grave."[124]

In "Simon Suggs," another Southwestern character cited as a precursor to Huck,[125] we see a similar strain of selfishness, malevolence, and sadism. Summarizing one episode in his adventures, Kenneth Lynn writes,

> Deciding that his parents are of no use to him . . . he laughs aloud at the thought that he has secretly stuffed his mother's pipe with gunpowder instead of tobacco, and that soon she will be lighting it.[126]

Simon Suggs's character is as different from Huck's as Sut Lovingood's is. Franklin J. Meine describes Suggs as "a sharp, shrewd swashbuckler," whose whole philosophy "lies snugly in his favorite aphorism—'it is good to be shifty in a new cuntry'—which means that it is right and proper that one should live as merrily and as comfortably as possible at the expense of others. . . ."[127]

Critics who place Twain in the tradition of the Southwestern humorists note that he "had the advantage of having been born later as well as innately superior to the rest of them."[128] But when it came to the crafting of Huck's voice, the gaps between Twain's art and theirs must be explained by something more than birth order or innate superiority. While Huck may have been related to Simon Suggs or Sut Lovingood or Petroleum V. Nasby on Pap's side of the family, that literary genealogy is woefully incomplete.

Something else helped make Huck who he was, helped catapult him beyond the ephemeral popularity these other characters enjoyed, to immortality. That "something else" may turn out to have been Jimmy and the memories of African-American speech he helped Twain recall.[129] Although Kenneth Lynn and others may see enough of a family resemblance to call a character like Sut Lovingood "a prototypical Huck Finn," the resemblances between Huck and Jimmy—on the level of both language and character—are infinitely stronger.[130]

2

Oh by and by, by and by

Although there is good reason to believe that Huck's voice was inspired in good part by Jimmy's voice, the question of the extent to which Huck's speech—or Jimmy's, for that matter—would have been considered at the time, or would be recognized now, as characteristically "black" remains unanswered.[1]

For obvious reasons, the question has never even been asked before: Huck's speech was not interpreted as "black" by readers in Twain's day or our own because both Huck as a character and Twain's stated model for him were white. Yet the question, "How 'black' is Huck's speech?" is an intriguing one.

During the 1870s and 1880s publications like *Appleton's Journal of Literature, Science and Art* and *Anglia* published articles about what made African-American speech (then called "Negro Patois" or "Negro English") distinctive.[2] A forty-seven-page article entitled "Negro English" published by an American dialect scholar named James Harrison in *Anglia* in 1884 is particularly relevant. Harrison's study focused on "the area lying between the Atlantic Ocean on the East, the Mississippi River on the West, the Gulf of Mexico on the South, and the 39th parallel [the Mason-Dixon line] on the North."[3] "This area," Harrison writes,

> now contains between 6,000,000 and 7,000,000 negroes, who speak, in large measure, the English to which attention is drawn in this paper.[4]

His purpose was to provide "an outline of Negro language-usage," with the caveat that his study is "far from exhaustive or immaculate."[5]

Harrison emphasized that his "life-long residence in the Southern States of North America" gave him confidence "that what is here given is at least approximately correct."[6] In a later publication, he repeated that the experience on which he based the article was acquired through his "lifelong residence in the South in many different states."[7] His interest, it should be noted, was at least partially antiquarian: he assumed that within several generations "the American public school system" would sufficiently penetrate "the wilds of the Negro South to render what is here recorded obsolete."[8]

In racist terms common to much nineteenth- and early twentieth-century writing on dialect geography, Harrison deplored the influence of black speakers on white speakers in the South:

> It must be confessed, to the shame of the white population of the South, that they perpetuate many of these pronunciations in common with their Negro dependents.[9]

Despite his acknowledgment that black and white speech patterns in the South often converged, however, Harrison endeavored to separate out and record grammatical and lexical constructions that are characteristically "negro." As it turns out, he was considerably more accurate in some aspects of this enterprise than linguists writing in our own time.[10]

Harrison based the article on both personal observation and his analysis of black dialect as rendered by writers including "J. C. Harris, J. A. Macon, Sherwood Bonner, and others,"[11] all "born Southerners, who had thrown into literary form their reminiscences of the negro."[12] It is highly unlikely that Harrison was familiar with any black dialect writing by Twain when he wrote this article.[13]

Interestingly, despite the fact that Harrison's "sample" is taken from south of the Mason-Dixon line, and Jimmy came from the Midwest, Jimmy manifests six of the seven qualities Harrison identifies as most characteristic of "Negro speech," as well as innumerable specific minor elements (a phenomenon not surprising given migration patterns during this period, and the Southern "negro speech" to which Jimmy would probably have been exposed).[14] But the larger question is to what extent does *Huck's* speech manifest qualities Harrison and others at the time would have considered "black?"

Although a number of Harrison's observations on matters of pronunciation and syntax in "Negro English" apply to Huck's speech, it is the material included under his heading, "Specimen Negroisms" that is particularly noteworthy.[15] These expressions, Harrison writes, "have so interwoven themselves with [the Negro's] daily speech as to have become an unconscious and essential part of it."[16] Many of them, as it turns out, are "essential" to Huck's speech, too. Huck's characteristic connecting phrase, "By and by," for example, appears on Harrison's list, albeit with a changed spelling:

Bimeby = after a while[17]

Other characteristic expressions of Huck's speech that Harrison labels "Specimen Negroisms" include the use of:

"Powerful" and "monstrous" to mean "very" (in Harrison, "pow'ful" and "monst'ous");

"Lonesome" to mean "depressed";

"I lay" to mean "I wager";

"To tell on" to mean "to disclose something against";

"Warn't no use" to mean "there is no use in" (in Harrison, "'tain't no use");

"Study" to mean "to meditate";

"Sqush" to mean "to crush";

"To let on" to mean "to pretend";

"I reckon" to mean "I suppose, think, or fancy" (in Harrison, "I reckin");

"Considerable" and "tolerable" as adverbs to mean "very" or "pretty" (in Harrison, "considerbul" and "tolerbul");

"Disremember" to mean "forget" (in Harrison, "dis'member").[18]

But by far the most striking examples are those that parallel Huck's famous penultimate lines:

. . . *if I'd a knowed* what a trouble it was to make a book I wouldn't a tackled it and ain't agoing to no more. But I reckon I got to *light out for* the Territory. . . .[19]

Harrison lists both of these italicized expressions as "Specimen Negroisms":

Ef I'd a knowed = if I had known.
To *light out fer* = to run for.[20]

It is also worth noting that some of the general characterizations of "negro speech" that Harrison and others record—such as its use of slang and figurative expressions, its lucidity and directness—strongly resemble qualities critics have identified as being at the heart of Huck's language, as well. Recall, for example, Richard Bridgman's comment that the effect of many of Huck's words, "dialect, nonce, slang—is that of poetry. . . ."[21] Harrison writes that much of "the Negro's . . . talk" deals in

> picture words, like the poet; the slang which is an ingrained part of his being as deep-dyed as his skin is, with him, not mere word-distortion; it is his verbal breath of life caught from his surroundings and wrought up by him into the wonderful figure-speech specimens of which will be given later under Negroisms. . . .[22]

(Zora Neale Hurston refers to the same qualities in her essay "Characteristics of Negro Expression," where she too cites "picture" words as central to African-American speech. Also similar to Harrison's "wonderful figure-speech specimens" is Hurston's discussion of "the will to adorn," by which she means, in part, the abundant use of "metaphor and simile."[23])

Or recall those qualities Lionel Trilling emphasized when he lauded the language with which Huck transformed American literature:

> Forget the misspellings and the faults of grammar, and the prose will be seen to move with the greatest simplicity, directness, lucidity, and grace.[24]

These same qualities were cited as characteristic of "English, as used by the negro" in an 1870 article in *Appleton's Journal* on "Negro Patois and Its Humor":

> There is no language more lucid. Emotions flow in a crystal stream through its simple forms. Meaning is never obscure. Force is never wanting.[25]

If Huck's speech manifests a number of expressions and qualities that dialect scholars from the 1870s and 1880s would have identified as African-American, how would it measure up along dimensions that concern linguists today? How "black" is Huck's speech? Contemporary scholarship on "Black English" suggests some interesting answers to this question—answers that must necessarily remain on the level of conjecture, but that are intriguing nonetheless.

Discussions by linguists about the role of tense marking in "Black English," for example, illuminate characteristics not only of contemporary "Black English," but of Huck's speech patterns as well. J. L. Dillard observes,

> . . . tense, although an obligatory category in Standard English, can be omitted in Black English sentences. The sequence
>
> . . . he go yesterday . . .
>
> is perfectly grammatical, provided the surrounding clauses or sentences give the needed time cues. Action in the past may thus be represented by the base form of the verb . . .

> The boy carried the dog dish to the house and put some dog food in
> it and put some water in and bring it out and called his dog . . . (A
> Washington, D.C. informant)

In high-quality collections of speeches by American Blacks, like those of the
outstanding folklorist B. A. Botkin, we find

> When the day begin to crack, the whole plantation break out with all
> kinds of noise, and you could tell what was going on by the kind of
> noise you hear. (*Lay My Burden Down*, 60)

Any facile assumption about "historical present" is broken by the occurrence of forms like . . . *carried* and *called* . . . . The verb forms *bring, begin,
break, going,* and *hear* are consistent with occurrence in the past, insofar as
the grammar of Black English is concerned. Such occurrence is *non-redundantly* marked in the language. Whereas in Standard English every verb in a
sequence (in a sentence or in a related series of sentences) must be marked as
either present or past, in Black English only one of the verbs need so be
marked—although more than one may be marked.[26]

Huck characteristically shifts tense within a single paragraph or
sentence, as do Jimmy and Jim. This is not a habit shared, for the most
part, with other nonblack characters in the novel, but it is central to
the establishment of Huck's particular voice.[27] In the following quotations, the non-redundantly marked verbs are italicized for clarity:[28]

1. I never waited for to look further, but uncocked my gun and went
   sneaking back on my tip-toes as fast as ever I could. Every now and then
   I stopped a second, amongst the thick leaves, and listened; but my breath
   come so hard I couldn't hear nothing else.
2. A little ripply, cool breeze begun to blow, and that was as good as saying the night was about done. I *give* her a turn with the paddle and
   brung her nose to shore; then I got my gun and slipped out and into the
   edge of the woods. I set down there on a log and looked out through the
   leaves. I *see* the moon go off *watch* and the darkness begin to blanket
   the river.
3. Well, the second night a fog begun to come on, and we made for a tow-
   head to tie to, for it wouldn't do to try to run in fog; . . . I passed the line
   around one of them right on the edge of the cut bank, but there was a
   stiff current, and the raft *come* booming down so lively she tore it out by
   the roots and away she went.
4. I didn't answer up prompt. I tried to, but the words wouldn't come. I
   tried, for a second or two, to brace up and out with it, but I warn't man
   enough—hadn't the spunk of a rabbit. I *see* I was weakening; so I just
   give up trying, and up and *says*—
       "He's white."[29]

Both Jimmy and Jim mark verb tenses with similar non-redundancy.
Jimmy says, for example,

> De ole man, he tuck de bottle and shuck it, and shuck it—he seed it was
> blue . . . drat if it wa'n't blue vittles, sho' nuff, when de doctor *come*.

And Jim says,

> Well, all de niggers went in, but dey didn' have much. I wuz de on'y one dat had much. So I stuck out for mo' dan fo' dollars, en I said 'f I didn' git it I'd start a bank mysef. Well o'course dat nigger *want'* to keep me out er de business, bekase he *say* dey warn't business 'nough for two banks, so he *say* I could put in my five dollars en he pay me thirty-five at de en' er de year.[30]

Dillard maintains that the use of tense as an optional category in "Black English" is likely to be the product of a grammatical system that differs on this point from Standard English and that may have its origins in the grammars of various African languages.[31] He observes that non-redundant tense marking in "Black English" probably developed in the last quarter of the eighteenth century and continues to be found today.[32]

Several linguists have connected these tense marking traits to specific African languages.[33] Molefi Kete Asante, for example, traces tense marking patterns in African-American speech "to the Yoruba, whose speakers do not distinguish between the past and present indefinite forms of a verb. When it is necessary to make a distinction between past and present, the Yoruba use an adverb of time."[34] "I see it," in Black English "may mean 'I see it' or 'I saw it,' depending on the speaker's context."[35] A range of African and New World languages, including many Niger-Congo languages, Jamaican Creole, and Gullah, evidently "exhibit a similar lack of inflection to show time. Past, present, and sometimes future time are indicated by context rather than verb inflection."[36]

Another feature that linguists usually cite in their discussions of "Black English" is the deletion of the copula.[37] (For example, Jimmy's comment, "I ben mos' halfway to Dockery," would be "I've been" in Standard English. Similarly, the Standard English version of Jim's comment, "I ben rich wunst,"[38] would be "I've been.") While Huck usually does not delete copulas, it is striking that one of Huck's best-known lines, the one with which his narrative ends—"*I been there before*"—uses the zero copula construction.

A second aspect of this famous line, Huck's use of the word "been," may be characteristic of "Black English" as well. Robert Fasold has noted in *Tense Marking in Black English*, "a few features [of 'Black English'] such as . . . the remote time construction with *been*, are extremely rare or nonexistent in other dialects of American English, at least in the urban North."[39] Fasold notes that his research on "Black English" in Washington, D.C. confirms findings of William Labov in New York City and Walt Wolfram in Detroit.[40]

Of course, these studies in the late twentieth century do not necessarily explain anything about the speech Twain heard and wrote a hundred years earlier. It is interesting, however, that some of the most distinctive dimensions of "Black English" speech patterns linguists study today duplicate habits of speech and turns of phrase that Twain imprinted indelibly on our national consciousness as characteristic of the voice of Huck.

Perhaps the syntactical feature of "Black English" most characteristic of Huck's speech is what linguists call the use of "serial verbs," or the tendency to describe every detail of an action or event from start to finish with its own special verb, a trait that has been traced to a number of African languages. Mervyn C. Alleyne notes, for example, that "a very typical aspect of the syntax of the verb in Kwa languages is the existence of what have been called 'serial verbs.'"[41] African linguist Ayọ Bamgboṣe cites as an example of this phenomenon the Yoruba speaker who would say something to the effect of "'He took book come,' meaning, 'he brought a book.'"[42] One finds serial verb constructions in other branches of the Niger-Congo language subfamily as well. Bamgboṣe notes that a speaker of Vagala (in the Gur language group) would say, "'He took knife cut meat,' meaning, 'he cut the meat with a knife.'"[43] Alleyne finds that the same "syntactic structure also exists in Afro-American, and the rules which account for it are basically the same in Afro-American as in Kwa languages."[44]

Like Alleyne, Asante finds serial verb construction a leading characteristic of "Black English"; he also shares Alleyne's opinion that this syntactic structure may be "evidence of the same function semantically as the serial constructions of many West African languages."[45] He asks us to consider the command recorded in the Federal Writers Project's "Slave Narratives—Alabama," "Turn loose and drap down from dar," meaning, "Come down from there." The "Black English" speaker

> finds it necessary to tell the person to first turn the tree branch loose and then drop down from it. Again, note the tendency to segment the action and, more important, the fact that this segmentation appears on the surface, in the form of two verbs. For the English speaker it is sufficient to focus on the main action, falling or dropping from the tree.[46]

Huck Finn, too, characteristically describes "every detail of an action by using a special verb":

> When I got half way, first one hound and then another *got up* and *went for me*, and of course I *stopped*, and *faced them*, and *kept still*. . . . I was a kind of hub of a wheel, as you may say—spokes made out of dogs—circle of fifteen of them packed together around me, with their necks and noses

stretched up towards me, *a-barking* and *howling*; and more *a-coming*; you could see them *sailing over fences* and around corners, from everywheres.[47]

Huck's tendency to break each action into its component parts rather than unite several actions into one umbrella term may have the same roots as speech patterns documented by scholars of "Black English."

"Negro dialects in the United States," Dillard tells us, ". . . are all related historically to Gullah."[48] Students of Gullah, "the most conservative form of 'Black English' spoken in the United States today,"[49] have pinpointed, in addition to the elements noted above, a number of other grammatical features that have their roots in African systems of grammar; some of these elements are characteristic of Huck's speech (and Jimmy's) as well. Building on the pathbreaking work of Lorenzo Turner, Ivan Van Sertima wrote, for example,

> Gullah has no passive voice. Black English verbs are always active. . . . Gullah uses what may be called the double negative or multiple negative, that is, negation is expressed not once as in Standard English, but twice or several times at various parts of the sentence. . . . Gullah frequently duplicates words also in conversation and, particularly in narrative, words and phrases are often repeated. . . . The subject or object is stated in Gullah, then repeated by the use of a personal pronoun, then a statement is made about the subject. . . .[50]

The use of repetition, active verbs, double negatives, and redundancy of subject ("Tom he"), as noted in Chapter 1, are often cited as characteristic features of Huck's speech.[51]

Several of the syntactical elements discussed here resemble those singled out by Richard Bridgman as characteristic of American "colloquial style" in general. When describing a phenomenon much like the serial verbs found in so many African languages, for example, Bridgman writes,

> The compound sentence characteristic of colloquial prose is basically a list— a list of actions. The vernacular speaker offers those actions in an unsubordinated series, just as he does physical objects. He seems to display only the crudest awareness of how the actions are related, not because of stupidity, but because he literally recounts the events in the order in which they occurred. This focuses attention upon the single unit of action as it is caught and isolated between commas and conjunctions.[52]

Does Bridgman's assertion that these qualities are characteristic of what he calls American "colloquial style" in general lessen the probability that they have African-American roots? I think not, for what Bridgman is referring to is a *literary* phenomenon—one that Mark Twain helped shape in major ways:

One can observe the increased technical proficiency with which the compound sentence is managed beginning with the irregular extravagance of an 1843 dialect story, then moving to the fluent simplicity of *Huckleberry Finn* in the 1880s, and finally to the deliberately angular rhythm of a Hemingway sentence written in the 1930s.[53]

Mark Twain's writing, then, shaped our very definitions of "colloquial style" in American literature. The influence that African-American speech patterns had on Southern speech in general (a subject I will explore in Chapter 9) and the ways in which a black child helped inspire the distinctive voice of Huck Finn make it plausible to explore the possible African-American roots of a style that we have come to view as quintessentially American.

Part Two

JERRY

3

I do believe without a doubt,
  Let my people go;
That a Christian has the right to shout,
  Let my people go.

When Twain introduces Huck Finn to the world in *Tom Sawyer*, he tells us that Huck was "cordially hated and dreaded by all the mothers of the town" and that, therefore, all their children "delighted in his forbidden society." Tom Sawyer, like the others, "was under strict orders not to play with him. So he played with him every time he got a chance."[1] And early in the novel, when his teacher asks him to explain why he was late for school, Tom confesses that he had stopped to talk to Huckleberry Finn; the result is a serious beating: "The master's arm performed until it was tired and the stock of switches notably diminished."[2]

Some twenty-five years later, in a piece that was not published until after his death, Twain once again described in precisely the same language a childhood "friend whose society was very dear to me because I was forbidden by my mother to partake of it." Twain went on to tell how his mother beat him seriously when she caught him listening to this person talk—but no matter: young Sam Clemens returned daily, beating or not. Tom Blankenship? Not at all, although Twain would later describe him in similar terms, as well. The subject of Twain's comments in 1901[3] is a slave named "Jerry," a master of the African-American art of "signifying" who helped introduce Clemens, at age fifteen, to the power of satire as a tool of social criticism.

In his pathbreaking 1988 book, *The Signifying Monkey: A Theory of African-American Literary Criticism*, Henry Louis Gates, Jr., places the idea of "signifyin(g)" within a double-voiced tradition in which texts "talk to other texts," defining the term as "repetition and revision, or repetition with a signal difference."[4] "Signifyin(g)," for Gates, "epitomizes all of the rhetorical play in the black vernacular," particularly its penchant for satire and indirection.[5]

Mark Twain was fortunate enough to be exposed to brilliant and memorable "signifying" on a daily basis during his adolescence, and he was smart enough to appreciate it for what it was: one of the most impressive rhetorical performances he had ever heard. The scene I am about to relate took place one year before Twain wrote his first extant published sketch. Although the essay in which Twain recreates this scene, "Corn-Pone Opinions," is quoted often enough, what is usually cited is Twain's opinion on the subject of conformity, the topic of the latter part of the essay. Embedded in the beginning of the essay, however, we find an early, direct tribute to the power of African-American "signifying." Twain writes,

> Fifty years ago, when I was a boy of fifteen and helping to inhabit a Missourian village on the banks of the Mississipi, I had a friend whose society was very dear to me because I was forbidden by my mother to partake of it. He was a gay and impudent and satirical and delightful young black man—a slave—who daily preached sermons from the top of his master's woodpile, with me for the sole audience. He imitated the pulpit style of the several clergymen of the village, and did it well, and with fine passion and energy. To me he was a wonder. I believed he was the greatest orator in the United States and would some day be heard from. But it did not happen; in the distribution of rewards he was overlooked. It is the way, in this world.
>
> He interrupted his preaching, now and then, to saw a stick of wood; but the sawing was a pretense—he did it with his mouth; exactly imitating the sound the bucksaw makes in shrieking its way through the wood. But it served its purpose; it kept his master from coming out to see how the work was getting along. I listened to the sermons from the open window of a lumber room at the back of the house. One of his texts was this:
>
> "You tell me whar a man gits his corn-pone, en I'll tell you what his 'pinions is."
>
> I can never forget it. It was deeply impressed upon me. By my mother. Not upon my memory, but elsewhere. She had slipped in upon me while I was absorbed and not watching. The black philosopher's idea was that man is not independent, and cannot afford views which might interfere with his bread and butter. If he would prosper, he must

train with the majority; in matters of large moment, like politics and religion, he must think and feel with the bulk of his neighbors, or suffer damage in his social standing and in his business prosperities. He must restrict himself to corn-pone opinions—at least on the surface. . . .⁶

The image of this "gay and impudent and *satirical* . . . young black man" preaching daily sermons from the top of the woodpile with Twain as his sole audience—and Twain's being punished by his mother for listening—is full of telling reverberations. As Jerry "signifies" upon the sermons of the local preachers, he also "signifies" upon his own text at the same time. For he is making the case for the irresistible pull of conformity as he himself is performing a nonconformist rhetorical tour-de-force from the top of the woodpile—for an audience of one. But *what* an audience of one that was! The transgressive nature of Jerry's art is clear from the fact that Twain's mother forbade him to listen to the heretical orations, a restriction Twain claims that young Sam violated daily with glee.⁷

The audacious doubleness of Jerry's verbal brilliance thrilled Twain, as did its intertextuality and its attention to the gaps between "surface" and deeper meaning. Twain claims that he had the good sense to know he was in the presence of a real master—even if that master was a slave. The manuscript of "Corn-Pone Opinions" in the Mark Twain Papers reveals that Twain initially wrote that he believed Jerry was "the greatest *man* in the United States."* In the version that was printed posthumously in *Europe and Elsewhere*, however, Jerry became simply "the greatest orator." Jerry's impact on Twain must have indeed been momentous for Twain to remember him, fifty years later, as someone who had impressed him as the "greatest man" in the country. One can imagine Twain having listened to Jerry much as he had listened to Jimmy: "as one who receives a revelation." The revelation in this case was of the power of satire—satire in an African-American vein, the indirect, double-voiced variety of satire known as "signifying."

One must, of course, allow for what Louis Budd has called Twain's "incorrigible yarning,"⁸ and acknowledge that the scene may not have taken place precisely as Twain describes it. In Twain's version, Jerry does no work at all, and his master never figures that out. The real Jerry obviously must have cut some wood at some point, or his master would probably have grown suspicious. Twain undoubtedly allowed his imagination some play in shaping his memories of Jerry. However, this does not diminish the likelihood that Jerry or someone very much like him really existed, and that scenes generally like the one Twain describes actually took place.

Corn-Pone Opinions.

=

Fifty years ago, when I was a boy of fifteen & helping to inhabit a Missourian village on the banks of the Mississippi, I had a friend whose society was very dear to me because I was forbidden by my mother to partake of it. He was a gay & impudent & satirical & delightful young black man — a slave — who daily preached sermons from the top of his master's woodpile, with me for sole audience. He imitated the pulpit style of the several clergymen of the village, & did it well, & with fine passion & energy. To me he was a wonder. I believed he was the greatest orator in the United States, & would some day

"*I believed he was the greatest ~~man~~ orator in the United States.*" * Manuscript pages of "Corn-Pone Opinions." (Courtesy, the Mark Twain Papers, The Bancroft Library)

he heard from. But it did not happen;
in the distribution of rewards he
was overlooked. It is the way, in this
world.

He interrupted his preaching, now
& then, to saw a stick of wood; but
the sawing was a pretence — he did
it with his mouth; exactly imitating
the sound the buck-saw makes in
shrieking its way through the wood.
But it served its purpose: it kept his
master from coming out to see how
the work was getting along. I listened
to the sermons from the open window
of a lumber-room at the back of our
house. One of his texts was this:

"You tell me whar a man gits his
corn-pone, en I'll tell you what his
opinions is."

I can never forget it. It was deeply
impressed upon me. By my mother.
Not upon my memory, but elsewhere.

Manuscript pages of "Corn-Pone Opinions." (continued)

One might wonder why Twain mentions Jerry so many years after the fact. One possibility is that Twain was never fully conscious of what it was he learned from Jerry. Jerry may have been memorable, but not unique: Twain may have been exposed frequently to slaves who "signified" and played "trickster" roles. These rhetorical stances were a pervasive part of the world in which he grew up. Jerry may have just been better at it than most.[9]

What was the content and style of Jerry's "impudent and satirical" sermons? We can never know precisely what he said and how he said it. But the African-American folk tradition of "signifying" satire, which has been widely documented in slave culture, and the African-American trickster tradition intimately connected with it can provide some clues to help us understand the nature of the performances to which Twain responded so enthusiastically. Twain would borrow from these African-American folk traditions in *Huckleberry Finn* and throughout his career as an artist.

Twain tells us that Jerry "imitated the pulpit style of the several clergymen of the village"—clearly an example of what Gates refers to as "repetition with a signal difference." What was the content of those sermons that he satirized? We can glean some sense of what those clergymen had been saying (and not saying) when we read Twain's description of them in his *Autobiography*. Twain's mother, he notes, had never heard slavery

> assailed in any pulpit but had heard it defended and sanctified in a thousand; her ears were familiar with the Bible texts that approved it but if there were any that disapproved it they had not been quoted by her pastors; as far as her experience went, the wise and the good and the holy were unanimous in their conviction that slavery was right, righteous, sacred, the peculiar pet of the Deity and a condition which the slave himself ought to be daily and nightly thankful for.[10]

This perspective is echoed by descriptions of the role of the clergy in antebellum nonfiction and fiction by black writers. In his 1847 narrative, for example, former slave William Wells Brown recalled hearing a Missouri auctioneer brag that a woman he was trying to sell "has got religion!" The fact increased her value, Brown wrote, because

> the religious teaching consists in teaching the slave that he must never strike a white man; that God made him for a slave; and that, when whipped, he must not find fault,—for the Bible says, "He that knoweth his master's will and doeth it not, shall be beaten with many stripes!" And slave-holders find such religion very profitable to them.[11]

William Van Deburg observes that

> In black-authored plays and novels, theology often reinforced slave-
> holders' prerogative and southern social practices. Christian ministers
> used their catechisms to teach subservience to planters' wishes. . . .[12]

The ploy was by no means original with nineteenth-century
Southern slaveholders. In 1706, Cotton Mather in "The Negro Christianized" had developed theological principles to reassure those who
were apprehensive about the compatibility of Christianity and slavery.[13] Indeed, several years earlier, in 1693, in the revised version of
the Ten Commandments that Mather wrote for slaves to memorize,

> submissiveness to and respect for the master were substituted for the
> similar deference which the owners gave to God. The Fifth Command-
> ment ("Honor thy Father and Mother, . . .") was twisted to mean for
> the slave "I must show all due respect unto everyone and if I have a
> master or mistress, I must be very dutiful unto them." For the slave the
> Tenth Commandment ("Thou Shalt not Covet, . . .") was interpeted as
> "I must be patient and content with such a condition as God has
> ordered for me."[14]

"Mather's precepts," as Lorenzo Johnston Greene notes, "set a precedent for using the religious indoctrination of the slaves as a subtle
device for slave control and throughout the eighteenth century other
ministers carried on the tradition."[15]

By the 1830s, as Eugene Genovese has observed, Southern whites
"took the political orthodoxy of their ministers increasingly for
granted and came to regard them as supporters of the plantation
order."[16] Genovese documents the case of one minister (probably not
atypical) who "dutifully served his turn on the hated and feared slave
patrols."[17] The cozy arrangement was not lost on the slaves. As Genovese tells us, Nancy Williams of Virginia, for example, noted that

> "Ole white preachers used to talk wid dey tongues widdout sayin'
> nothin' but Jesus told us slaves to talk wid our hearts." . . . The
> favorite text of the white preachers, as the Reverend C. C. Jones
> proudly acknowledged, was Paul's "Servants, obey in all things your
> masters. . . ."[18]

The slaves' response to such teachings comes across clearly in
William Wells Brown's 1853 novel *Clotel*. After being subjected to a
catechism in the spirit of Cotton Mather's, several slaves have the following conversation:

> "Didn't you like de sermon?" asked Uncle Simon. "No" answered
> four or five voices. . . .
> "I think de people dat made de Bible was great fools," said Ned.
> "Why?" asked Uncle Simon.
> "'Cause dey made such a great big book and put nuttin' in it, but
> servants obey yer masters."

"Oh," replied Uncle Simon, "thars more in de Bible den dat, only Snyder never reads any other part to us; I use to hear it read in Maryland, and thar was more den what Snyder lets us hear."[19]

The clergymen that Jerry heard, then, presumably promoted as a general principle the idea that slavery is in everyone's best interest. Jerry, however, advances the general idea that self-interest is always more powerful than principle, no matter what the words may seem to say on the surface. (In an unpublished fragment probably written around 1907, Twain echoed the lesson Jerry had taught him. He wrote, "He would be a fool & called a fool, who should claim that when the master makes laws that are to govern both himself & his slave, he will take as good care of the slave's interest as his own. (Haw-haw!)."[20]*

In other words, Jerry's "signifying" intimates that while the clergymen may say that slavery is just, right, and justified by the Bible, the slave must decode that message and understand that it is all of those things only if one is a slaveholder.[21] For the slave, slavery is unjust, wrong, and hurtful, and the Bible may be invoked as supporting liberation, as it often was, in coded form, in spirituals.[22] The clergymen may say slavery is good for everyone, but in reality it is good only for them and the slaveholding whites who provide their livelihood, or their "corn-pone." What Jerry may have preached, in short, is the idea that reading beyond the surface meaning of the words is essential to survival.

The subject of Jerry's sermon turns out to be the essence of "signifying." As Claudia Mitchell-Kernan observes in her key article on the subject,

> The Black concept of *signifying* incorporates essentially a folk notion that dictionary entries for words are not always sufficient for interpreting meanings or messages, or that meaning goes beyond such interpretations.[23]

In "signifying," Mitchell-Kernan writes, "the apparent significance of the message differs from its real significance."[24] Jerry's sermon certainly preaches the message that whoever accepts at face value the surface meaning of the words will be misled.[25]

The gap between what words say on the surface and what they really mean is central to Jerry's sermon and to African-American "signifying."[26] In Twain's writing, as well, the pitfalls of accepting the literal meaning of a text became a common theme. Twain pointed out the gaps, for example, between stock prospectuses and the realities they purported to describe; between guide books to the Holy Land

and the actual scene one encountered there; between Sunday-school books and genuine moral behavior.[27] Indeed, Twain devoted a major portion of his writing to the project of helping his reader learn to avoid the sin of literalness.[28] Training his readers to read between the lines became an important goal; and packing as much as he could between his own lines became a central part of his method.[29]

As Gates notes, "in the literature of Signifyin(g) . . . linguists stress indirection as the most salient feature of this rhetorical strategy."[30] Folklorist Alan Dundes believes that it is quite likely that "the origins of 'signifying' lie in African rhetoric,"[31] and research by Gates and others supports this hypothesis.[32] "Subtlety and wry indirection are the requirements of African verbal wit," William D. Pierson notes, "and the demonstration of verbal skill more than circumspection demanded a satire by allusion."[33] In the New World, these African rhetorical traditions of indirection stood the slaves in good stead. Here caution and circumspection were necessary for survival: in an environment where slaveholders exercised total, absolute power, the ironic doubleness of "signifying" speech and song became the source of the impunity with which slaves could voice the unspeakable. On the surface, nothing subversive may have been said. Below the surface, however, the speaker sketched a highly subversive critique of the strong by the weak. For "signifying" speech can generate two meanings: one appears neutral and unobjectionable; the other may embody potentially dangerous information and ideas.

This was precisely what W. E. B. DuBois tried to explain to the readers of the *Mark Twain Quarterly* in the Fall–Winter issue of 1943 in an essay titled "The Humor of Negroes." Central to Negro humor, DuBois noted, was "the dry mockery of the pretensions of white folk. . . . Many is the time that a truculent white man has been wholly disarmed before the apparently innocent and really sophisticated joke of the Negro, whom he meant to berate."[34]

As Michael Cooke notes,

> The one form of Afro-American expression that most white people would have commonly encountered is known as "signifying." And one of the home traits of signifying was that it did not confess itself, but kept an innocuous air; it was a way of using words that mean one acceptable thing to resonate with or *signify* another of a dangerous or insubordinate or forbidden character.[35]

One need look no further than *Huckleberry Finn* itself for proof that Twain not only understood the nature of African-American "signifying," but appreciated the genius of it—particularly in the service of moral ends. In Chapter 28, Huck, who has convinced the Grangerford household that his name is "George," relates the following exchange between himself and the young black man who has been assigned to him as his personal servant.

> I went off down to the river, studying over this thing, and pretty soon I noticed that my nigger was following along behind. When we was out of sight of the house, he looked back and around a second, and then comes a-running, and says:
>
> "Mars Jawge, if you'll come down into de swamp, I'll show you a whole stack o' water-moccasins."
>
> Thinks I, that's mighty curious; he said that yesterday. He oughter know a body don't love water-moccasins enough to go around hunting for them. What is he up to anyway? So I says—
>
> "All right, trot ahead."
>
> I followed a half a mile, then he struck out over the swamp and waded ankle deep as much as another half mile. We come to a little flat piece of land which was dry and very thick with trees and bushes and vines, and he says—
>
> "You shove right in dah, jist a few steps, mars Jawge, dah's whah dey is. I's seed 'm befo', I don't k'yer to see 'em no mo.'"
>
> Then he slopped right along and went away, and pretty soon the trees hid him. I poked into the place a-ways, and come to a little open patch as big as a bedroom, all hung around with vines, and found a man laying there asleep—and by jings it was my old Jim!
>
> I waked him up, and I reckoned it was going to be a grand surprise to him to see me again, but it warn't. He nearly cried, he was so glad, but he warn't surprised. Said he swum along behind me, that night, and heard me yell every time, but dasn't answer, because he didn't want nobody to pick *him* up, and take him into slavery again. . . .
>
> "Dey's mighty good to me, dese niggers is, en whatever I wants 'm to do fur me, I doan' have to ast 'm twice, honey. Dat Jack's a good nigger, en pooty smart."
>
> "Yes, he is. He ain't ever told me you was here; told me to come, and he'd show me a lot of water-moccasins. If anything happens, *he* ain't mixed up in it. He can say he never seen us together, and it'll be the truth."[36]

The "signifying" speech with which Jack apprises Huck of Jim's whereabouts manifests six of the eight characteristics linguist Geneva Smitherman associates with "signification" in *Talkin' and Testifyin'*.[37] When Jack tells Huck he is taking him to see water moccasins, he uses irony, indirection, and circumlocution. His speech is "metaphorical-imagistic (but images rooted in the everyday, real world)," is "directed at [a] person or persons usually present in the situational context," and includes the "introduction of the semantically or logically unexpected."[38] Jack's use of the incongruous word "stack" to describe the snakes demonstrates what Smitherman calls "rhythmic fluency and sound," since "stack o'" will be echoed by "mocca." Jack demonstrates "the trickster's ability to talk with great innuendo," a quality Roger Abrahams identifies closely with "signifying" in *Deep Down in the Jungle*.[39] Jack may also be signifying on the society's conventions of slave speech behavior. His suggestion that he take Huck to an unusually large assemblage of water moccasins is fully in keeping with the repertoire of things a slave assigned to a young man might be expected to say: told to serve Huck's needs, he is pointing out to him the local sights, trying to keep him entertained. To some extent, then, Jack is engaged in what Gates calls "repetition with a signal difference," as he "signifies" on the discourse he is allowed as a slave by using it to help him hide a fugitive.[40]

For "signifying" to work, as Gates notes, citing Mitchell-Kernan, the speaker and his audience must realize that

> "signifying is occurring and that the dictionary-syntactical meaning of the utterance is to be ignored." In addition, a silent second text, as it were, which corresponds rightly to what Mitchell-Kernan is calling "shared knowledge," must be brought to bear upon the manifest content of the speech act and "employed in the reinterpretation of the utterance."[41]

Huck acquires the "shared knowledge" to understand that Jack has been "signifying" when he realizes he has been led not to a bunch of snakes, but to Jim. As he has Huck theorize about the effectiveness of Jack's rhetorical strategy, Twain also shares with his reader a working definition of "signifying" itself, which, as Gates describes it, "presupposes an 'encoded' intention to say one thing but to mean quite another."[42] Jack's coded language is different from an ordinary lie, in that on a figurative level he is being truthful and precise: he promised, after all, to take Huck to a place crawling with danger. And that's exactly what he did.

Like Jack, Twain preserves the option of denying all subversive intentions in *Huckleberry Finn*. "Persons attempting to find a motive in this narrative will be prosecuted," he tells us in the "Notice" that appears at the beginning of *Huckleberry Finn*, "persons attempting to find a moral in it will be banished."[43] Indeed, many readers took him at his word, and read *Huckleberry Finn* as a "boy's book," a companion volume to its predecessor, *Tom Sawyer*. But such a limited reading denies the corrosive satire of white society (and of the many "texts" that undergird its position of alleged racial superiority) that is at the book's core.[44]

As Pierson observes, "Africanists have long recognized the cultural significance of satire in African societies,"[45] and have noted that

Africans seemed especially to enjoy lampooning Europeans with whom they had dealings. Through the satire of derisive songs African societies discouraged unpleasant and dangerous face-to-face confrontations. [46]

Satirical speech and song allowed one to avoid direct insults and their cost, while still expressing opprobrium when it was deserved. It was a relatively "safe" means of protest and critique that nonetheless hit its mark, playing a key role in shaping social norms and individual behavior.[47] Indeed, as Theodore Van Dam notes, "Songs of Derision . . . sometimes were so powerful that an intended victim paid the local troubadors *not* to sing them." In the New World, Van Dam observes, "Songs of Derision" were sung by slaves to cast "satirical aspersions upon their owners."[48]

Commentators in the New World noted slaves' use of satire to voice encoded criticisms of their owners as early as the eighteenth century. Nicholas Cresswell, writing between 1774 and 1777, observed in his journal,

> In [the blacks'] songs they generally relate the usage they have received from their Masters or Mistresses in a very satirical stile [*sic*] and manner.[49]

Bryan Edwards noted in 1801 that blacks in the New World improvised ballads that directed "ridicule and derision" at their "owners or employers," and in 1843 James Phillippo described songs improvised by blacks that typically satirized white people.[50] Observers in French-speaking parts of the New World made similar comments about the satirical inclinations of African Americans they encountered: the blacks, said Father Jean Baptiste Labat, "are satirical to excess," and apply themselves particularly to mocking "the defects of people, and above all of the whites."[51]

Just as "whites at all levels of the social spectrum were the targets of black humor,"[52] so, too, no white character in *Huckleberry Finn* is immune from Twain's satiric barbs. Whether it is "Pap Finn" railing against a "guv'ment" that lets a black college professor have a vote equal to his own, or whether it is Aunt Sally saying, when she hears that "only a nigger" was killed in the steamboat accident, "Well, it's lucky because sometimes people do get hurt," Twain is specific and merciless in his exposure of the vicious underpinnings of their world view. The "text" on which Twain is signifying is the subtext of these characters' remarks: it is the familiar assumption that their kind alone are superior beings with special claims to empathy and privilege as embodiments of "civilization." Twain's acidic treatment of bigoted white folks in *Huckleberry Finn* may well reflect some of his early exposure to African-American satirical social critique, to the practice Lawrence Levine calls "laughing at the man."

Did Jerry help Twain understand the potential of satire in "exposing the absurdity of the American racial system"?[53] What might have prompted Twain to call Jerry "the greatest man in the United States"? It is likely that this appraisal was prompted by Jerry's ability to harness the power of satire to his own ends, an ability Twain himself would hone throughout his long career.

Jerry's behavior may have also helped Twain understand the special power of that particular strain of wit and satire embodied in the African-American tradition of the "trickster," a tradition in which Jerry was clearly operating. When Jerry made the sawing sound with his mouth to trick his master into thinking he was working, he demonstrated a particularly creative brand of what Kenneth Stampp has called the "ingenious subterfuge" by which slaves often tried to avoid an exhausting schedule of work.[54] He was also behaving as a "trickster," a figure intimately linked with "signifying" in both African and African-American folklore.[55]

In traditional trickster tales from both Africa and the United States, a weak figure outwits a stronger and more powerful one with cleverness and guile.[56] Popular among those at the bottom of the social structure in rigidly hierarchical African societies, "African trickster tales often 'illustrate the traditional right of the individual to contest irrational authority.'"[57] The implications of the smaller, weaker, more cunning figure outwitting the larger, stronger, more dull-witted one remained the same when these tales took root in the United States. It was a source of hope for those at the bottom.

As Levine notes,

> The white master could believe that the rabbit stories his slaves told were mere figments of a childish imagination, that they were primarily humorous anecdotes depicting the "roaring comedy of animal life." Blacks knew better. The trickster's exploits, which overturned the neat hierarchy of the world in which he was forced to live, became their exploits; the justice he achieved, their justice; the strategies he employed, their strategies. From his adventures they obtained relief; from his triumphs they learned hope.[58]

Twain's introducing Huck and Jerry in virtually identical language suggests that Jerry hovered someplace in Twain's mind when he was creating Huck. Is Huck, like Jerry, a trickster figure, a master of "signifying" who rhetorically outwits his stronger, more powerful adversaries? A number of occasions can, in fact, be identified when

Huck behaves in just such a manner to save himself and Jim from detection and betrayal.[59]

In the African-American trickster tale, Levine writes, "the strong attempt to trap the weak but are tricked by them instead."[60] The "strong" in *Huckleberry Finn* may be, like Mrs. Judith Loftus, deceptively congenial but dangerous nonetheless (her husband is out hunting for Jim with a band of slave-catchers). Huck, with nothing to his name but his wits, turns her efforts to expose him as a fraud into a joke on her: convinced she has found him out, she persists in believing he's a "runaway 'prentice."

Huck plays the trickster on another occasion, when he gets rid of two slave-hunters by pretending that he eagerly wishes them to board his raft. They become suspicious of his entreaties and decide that his relative really has smallpox.[61] Huck reluctantly assents to this, implying that he has been found out, and justifies his "desperation" so well that the two slave-hunters float two twenty-dollar gold pieces to him on a board to assuage their guilt at refusing to help.

Traditional African-American trickster tales, as one commmentator has noted, encapsulate "the kernel of an entire philosophy of black survival."[62] The "white man is unethical [and] the black man is victim; [and] the black man must deal with such unethical behavior as he is able. . . . Thus to be black in America and survive necessitates being a trickster."[63] From the moment Huck throws in his lot with Jim's—when he shouts "They're after us!"—Huck is required to play the trickster if he and Jim are to survive.[64]

Huck's performance in this trickster role is brilliantly intuitive. For example, he instinctively pays lip service to popular racist stereotypes at those moments when he is undermining them most severely. Trying to locate Jim to rescue him from his captors, Huck invents a narrative that is believed as readily as it is because it confirms popular racial prejudices:

> I run across a boy walking, and asked him if he'd seen a strange nigger, dressed so and so, and he says:
>
> "Yes."
>
> "Whereabouts?" says I.
>
> "Down to Silas Phelps's place, two mile below here. He's a runaway nigger, and they've got him. Was you looking for him?"
>
> "You bet I ain't! I run across him in the woods about an hour or two ago, and he said if I hollered he'd cut my livers out—and told me to lay down and stay where I was; and I done it. Been there ever since; afeard to come out."[65]

Huck is betting that the boy accepts the racist stereotype of the black "savage"—dangerous, violent, in need of the beneficent influence of white slaveholders to keep his malevolence in check. By affirming, in this tricksterlike manner, his adherence to what he assumes to be the basic contours of his informant's world view, Huck avoids arousing suspicion. *He's* not looking for any runaway slave, *he's* not plotting to set him free, no sir: he's doing all he can to *avoid* the degenerate brute.

Huck remains unthreatening and is consequently positioned to pick up the maximum possible information that could help him free Jim. His performance is analogous to that of Jerry, who, in a similarly unthreatening manner, manages to confirm his master's assumption that he is, indeed, doing just what he is expected to be doing—working—when in fact, he is engaged in a highly subversive activity: teaching a perceptive white boy about "signifying."[66]

4

When Israel was in Egypt's land:
Let my people go,
Oppressed so hard they could not stand,
Let my people go.

Twain was clearly cognizant of the double message that his art embodied. In an autobiographical dictation on 31 July 1906, Twain observed, "Humor must not <u>professedly</u> teach and it must not professedly preach, but it must do both if it would live forever. By forever, I mean thirty years. . . . I have always preached. That is the reason that I have lasted thirty years."* (For unknown reasons, either Albert Bigelow Paine or the printer deleted the underlining of the word "professedly" when the autobiography was published after Twain's death, thereby reducing the author's emphasis on "doubleness" that the original wording carried.[1])

We can read Twain's "Notice"—no motive, no moral, no plot contained here—as his effort to deny any "professed" or overt "preaching" in *Huckleberry Finn.* The novel's affinities with the genre of the "boy book," and the fact that it is set in long-ago antebellum times lend further support to Twain's surface denial that the book is anything more than an amusing, innocuous adventure story of a raft trip on the Mississippi. Twain retains the same kind of plausible "deniability" that the slave Jack did when he told Huck to come see the "water moccasins": nothing subversive going on here, Jack (and Twain) could have insisted, if pressed.

We find an analogous option of deniability that both the preacher and the poet himself affirm in Paul Laurence Dunbar's 1890s poem,

"An Ante-Bellum Sermon." The sermon is about the liberation of an oppressed people—a potent subject both in antebellum times and in the 1890s. Twice, however, the preacher insists that he's simply telling a tale from the Bible:

> But fu' feah some one mistakes me,
>   I will pause right hyeah to say,
> Dat I'm still a-preachin' ancient,
>   I ain't talkin' 'bout to-day. . . .

And later,

> But I think it would be bettah,
>   Ef I pause agin to say,
> Dat I'm talkin' 'bout ouah freedom
>   In a Bibleistic way.[2]

If Dunbar's preacher, preaching in antebellum times, talked about freedom in a "Bibleistic way," Twain, writing in the 1870s and 1880s, talked about freedom and American race relations in an "antebellum way," maintaining the option of denying that he was making any comment at all on the present. Yet *Huckleberry Finn* is increasingly coming to be understood as having a great deal to say about race relations in the period in which Twain wrote it.[3]

A closer look at two key points in the book—Twain's decision to smash the raft that was to carry Huck and Jim to freedom, and his decision to end the book with an elaborate burlesque farce—reveals the possibility that Twain may, in fact, have had in mind a story other than the one he was ostensibly telling. Twain may have been "signifying," like Jerry, like Jack, like Dunbar's preacher, and like Dunbar himself, pointing up in subtle, covert ways the gaps between the unthreatening surface meaning of his text—a boys' adventure story—and a more subversive hidden meaning: a critique of race relations in the post-Reconstruction South.

Clearly, it cannot be proved beyond a shadow of a doubt that Twain intentionally wove these implications into his text. Nonetheless, a good case can be made for their presence. As Toni Morrison recently observed, Twain's conscious intentions should not play a decisive role in our understanding of the implications of his work. We still have much to learn, Morrison noted, about the process by which artists transmute dimensions of their social and political environment into art.[4]

In July 1876, Twain began what he probably believed at first was a sequel to *Tom Sawyer*, another nostalgic boys' book. But the narrative was soon hijacked by a black man and a white boy on a quest for freedom. Shortly thereafter, Twain temporarily scuttled that quest by having Huck and Jim miss Cairo in the fog. Then Twain abandoned it—not casually or passively, but violently: he "smashed all to flinders" the raft that was to carry Huck and Jim to freedom.[5]

It is significant, I believe, that Twain both began and abandoned this book during the summer of 1876. One hundred years after the signing of the Declaration of Independence, that summer marked the greatest formal celebration of liberty in the nation's history. But historians would eventually remember that period not for its celebration of freedom, but for its impending denial of it.[6] Twain stopped work on *Huckleberry Finn* that summer just at the point where Buck Grangerford was about to try—and fail—to explain the rationale behind the bloody, pointless feud.[7] Like the charade of chivalry that prevented the fictional Grangerford family from seeing the barbarity of their way of life, the rhetoric of freedom that dominated the national discourse that summer tended to obscure the fact that the freedom of African Americans was about to be dealt a near-fatal blow.

The promise of genuine freedom and participation in the polity seemed within sight for African Americans during Reconstruction, as blacks shared political power in every former Confederate state, occupied certain high offices, and were guaranteed—on paper at least—equal protection under the law and full enjoyment of public facilities, through the laws and Constitutional Amendments.[8]

But racist opposition to blacks' actually exercising the rights of citizenship had been building for some time. The tactics of such terrorist groups as the Knights of the White Camelia, the White Brotherhood, the Rifle Clubs of South Carolina, and the Ku Klux Klan included intimidation, force, bribery at the polls, arson, and murder. Twain, an avid reader of the press, was clearly aware of these trends. In 1872, for example, *Harper's Weekly*, a magazine we know Twain read, carried a terrifying drawing of a Klansman paying a nighttime "visit" to a rural black family.[9] In 1873 a stack of telegraphic headings Twain clipped from daily newspapers included one that bore the headline "A Court House Fired, and Negroes Therein Shot While Escaping" and another titled "Ku Klux Murders."[10] In 1874, *Harper's Weekly* printed a stark and brutal illustration captioned, "A Company of Whites Lay in Ambush for a Party of Negroes Returning from Church, Killed Ten, and Wounded Thirteen."[11] Also in 1874, *Harper's Weekly* ran a wood engraving by Thomas Nast featuring a forlorn black couple and their child on a coat-of-arms propped up on one side by a member of the "White

League," and on the other by a hooded Klansman; emblazoned on the shield (under a skull and crossbones) were the words "Worse Than Slavery," a graphic image of the grim plight of African Americans in the post-Reconstruction South.[12]

These tensions climaxed during the summer of 1876. That summer brought bombastic orations that were reported widely in the national press. (Some were collected in a pamphlet Twain owned entitled *National Centennial Commemoration. Proceedings on the One Hundredth Anniversary of the Introduction and Adoption of the "Resolutions Respecting Independency." Held in Philadelphia on the Evening of June 7, 1876.* Twain himself was formally invited to attend the Centennial celebrations, and to contribute an essay to a "Centennial Collection."[13]) The same summer also brought some of

"Worse Than Slavery." Thomas Nast cartoon from Harper's Weekly *in 1874, depicting the condition of African Americans in the South.*

"A Company of Whites Lay in Ambush for a Party of Negroes Return-ing from Church, Killed Ten, and Wounded Thirteen." Illustration for Eugene Lawrence's report on recent atrocities in Harper's Weekly *in 1874.*

the worst racial violence the country had ever seen. A host of particu-larly brutal racial clashes in July—such as the Hamburg and Ellenton massacres in South Carolina—was reported fully in the New York papers that Twain read, alongside columns quoting Centennial speeches about the excellent health of liberty in America.

The election of 1876 led to the end of Reconstruction. "Do you mean to make good to us the promises in your Constitution?" Fred-erick Douglass asked a national gathering of Republicans in the sum-mer of 1876.[14] But by this time, as Eric Foner has noted, "most Republican leaders had concluded that the Northern public would no longer support federal intervention in Southern affairs."[15] The Com-promise of 1877 and the "withdrawal" of Federal troops from the

South that it entailed marked a key change in national policy. The Chicago *Tribune* proclaimed, "The long controversy over the black man seems to have reached a finality," while the *Nation* asserted that "the negro will disappear from the field of national politics. Henceforth, the nation, as a nation, will have nothing more to do with him."[16]

The intimidation that white supremacists earlier had to carry out at night could now be accomplished in broad daylight. The official government policy was now to look the other way as African Americans' civil rights were flagrantly violated and as thousands of African Americans were effectively re-enslaved through such means as sharecropping, lynchings, and the convict-lease system. Under the convict-lease system, for example, thousands of free black men were picked up throughout the South on "vagrancy" charges, or, if poor, on charges of "intent to steal." Once convicted they were leased out as cheap labor for extended periods of time. As Victor Doyno has noted, the convict-lease system, which "involved the captivity, imprisonment, or re-enslavement of legally freed Black men" used

> the vocabulary of the Phelps episode, including such terms as "prisoner," "chains," "shackles," "guards," and "escape." . . . Tom Sawyer's participation in Jim's captivity may represent figuratively the injustice done to countless Black freedmen under the convict-lease system.[17]

As Doyno points out, it would have been virtually impossible for Twain to have been unaware of the convict-lease system and its implications for black men in the South. Articles on the subject ran prominently in the early 1880s in two magazines Twain always read, the *Atlantic* and the *Century*.[18]

The freedom of African Americans in the post-Reconstruction era was sharply curtailed not only by sharecropping, lynchings, and the convict-lease system, but also by direct action of the Federal government, when, in the Civil Rights Cases of 1883, the Supreme Court declared the Civil Rights Act of 1875 illegal. A minister writing in the *Southwestern Christian Advocate* concluded that white Southerners were more determined than ever "to keep blacks enslaved."[19] As Reconstruction collapsed, the hypothetical fear Frederick Douglass had expressed in 1862 actually came to pass: black people had been emancipated from the relation of "slavery to individuals, only to become slaves of the community at large."[20]

Our contemporary sense of just how far off freedom was in that summer of 1876 may help explain why Twain decided to abandon the journey to freedom in the novel. The confirmation of these fears during the next eight years may well have induced him to end his novel with an unsatisfying farce that reflected the travesty that "freedom" had become for African Americans in the post-Reconstruction era, both in the South and in the North.[21] What Bernard DeVoto called the "chilling descent" of the novel's ending mirrors the equally chilling descent embodied in that chapter of history. As DuBois put it in his book *Black Reconstruction*, "The slave went free; stood a brief moment in the sun; then moved back again toward slavery."[22]

Twain himself may have embraced Jerry's trickster strategy to call into question the very possibility of writing a slavery-to-freedom narrative in the 1870s and 1880s, a time when the nation was effectively re-enslaving its black citizens by law and by force. *Huckleberry Finn* presents itself as a simple boys' book as slyly as the traditional trickster tale presents itself as a simple animal story. Just beneath the surface, however, it dramatizes, as perhaps only a work of art can, both the dream and the denial of the dream, both the spectacular boldness of the promise of liberty and justice for all, and the nation's spectacular failure to make that promise a reality.[23]

Louis J. Budd suggested in 1962 that *Huckleberry Finn* may have been a comment not only on the 1830s and 1840s but also on the 1880s, and scholars have subsequently built an increasingly solid case for the idea that the last portion of the novel may be read as a commentary on American race relations in the post-Reconstruction era.[24] In 1965, Tony Tanner observed that "Tom's treatment of Jim can easily be seen as a clumsily emerging comment on the South's treatment of the Negro."[25] Neil Schmitz expanded on this theme in 1971. Richard and Rita Gollin explored it in 1979, followed by Laurence B. Holland in 1982, Stephen Mailloux in 1985, and Harold Beaver in 1987.

Charles Nilon, in his 1984 essay, "The Ending of *Huckleberry Finn*: 'Freeing the Free Negro,'" provided an overview of scholars' growing critical support for this perspective, citing, in addition to some of the work mentioned, writing by Philip S. Foner, Justin Kaplan, Roger Salomon, Kenneth Lynn, and Arthur G. Pettit.[26] Lawrence Berkove's discussions of Twain's treatment of the free man of color should be added to this list, along with Sherwood Cumming's analysis of the allegorical implications of the evasion, and Victor Doyno's examination of the novel in the context of the convict-lease system.[27] Also relevant is Toni Morrison's discussion of why "the fatal ending [of *Huckleberry Finn*] becomes the elaborate deferment of a necessary and necessarily unfree Africanist character's escape," an interpretation that argues that we understand the novel's ending in the context of "the parasitical nature of white freedom."[28]

Other critics have offered distinctive readings of particular dimensions of the last ten chapters. For example, Twain's decision to have Tom reject Huck's simple plan for freeing Jim in favor of one that "could be strung out to as much as eighty year" struck L. Moffitt Cecil as a possible allusion to the eighty years it took our country to free the slaves—the time that lapsed from the 1783 peace treaty with England to the Emancipation Proclamation in 1863.[29] Harold Beaver has flagged the potential significance of the fact that Twain finished *Huckleberry Finn* in 1883, the very year that the Supreme Court declared the Civil Rights Act unconstitutional.[30] Scholars are increasingly coming to understand the evasion as a satire on the way the United States botched the enterprise of freeing its slaves.[31]

The sermons Twain heard Jerry preach in 1850 may have helped make Twain aware of the gaps between the literal or surface meaning of a text and the larger, implicit meanings that might lie behind it. The role Jerry and other slaves may have played in shaping Twain's awareness of satire as a tool of social criticism must remain, of course, on the level of conjecture. Interestingly, however, we have no evidence of any other specific figure impressing Twain with the potential "doubleness" of a text *before* his encounter with Jerry in 1850, nor do we have any reference by Twain to any earlier exposure to satire. Later, Twain would be exposed to satire from a variety of sources. But his early exposure to the centuries-old African and African-American tradition of using satire to criticize the pretensions and foibles of white folks proved to be particularly fruitful. Once introduced, through Jerry, and probably other slaves as well, to African-American forms of satiric discourse, Mark Twain incorporated this rhetorical mode into his own artistic repertoire. His target was often the same as theirs: racism.

As Mikhail Bakhtin observed,

> Generally speaking, to understand a genre's way of perceiving and representing the world, "a writer need not know all the links and all the branchings of that tradition. A genre possesses its own organic logic, which can to a certain extent be understood and creatively assimilated on the basis of a few generic models, even fragments."[32]

Great writers, Bakhtin claims, were able to "imagine the potential uses, both past and possible, to which" the resources of traditions to which they had been exposed "could be put." In addition, they were able to "plant more potentials for unexpected development in the future."[33] By making a particularly African-American "way of perceiving and representing the world" a central component of his own art, and, consequently, of the mainstream American literary tradition, Twain helped make clear the literary potential of that mode of expression to writers who came after him, even if they hadn't a clue as to where it originally came from.[34] The prevailing wisdom, Toni Morrison writes,

> holds that traditional, canonical American literature is free of, uninformed, and unshaped by the four-hundred-year-old presence of, first Africans and then African-Americans in the United States. It assumes that this presence—which shaped the body politic, the Constitution, and the entire history of the culture—has had no significant place or consequence in the origin and development of that culture's literature. Moreover, such knowledge assumes that the characteristics of our national literature emanate from a particular "Americanness" that is separate from and unaccountable to this presence.[35]

The truth, as Morrison's comments imply, is more complicated and more interesting. Even the word "vernacular," after all, as Barbara Johnson has observed, "comes from the Latin 'verna,' which means 'a slave born in his master's home'. . . . And the 'master's home' could not be what it is without all it has stolen from the slave."[36]

Ever since Hemingway and Faulkner paid homage to him, Twain's centrality as a major force in our culture has been secure. But if we fail to include that "signifying" black philosopher in Twain's literary genealogy, and if we fail to recognize in Twain's prose the "inventive, disruptive, masked and unmasking language" that, in Toni Morrison's view, helps make a work "Black,"[37] we will have a distorted, false, and incomplete picture of the development of American literature. We cannot understand fully that key strain of American literary history that runs from Twain to Hemingway and Ellison and innumerable white and black writers in the twentieth century without taking into account the African-American roots of Twain's double-voiced, ironic art.

Part
Three

JIM

5

*O, nobody knows a who I am, a who I am,
a who I am*

In *Huckleberry Finn* and throughout his life and work, Mark Twain interrogated his culture's categories and conventions of what it meant to be "black" or "white." This is not to say that he did so consistently or consciously, or that he invariably succeeded in transcending those categories and conventions. On the contrary, it could be argued that, in a number of key ways, he left them in place. Rather, Twain wove back and forth between challenge and affirmation, rejection and assent, as regards his culture's norms of "blackness" and "whiteness." The issues explored in this book suggest the merits of re-examining some of the assumptions that have informed discussions of Twain's response to the racial discourse of his time.

In this context, the verdict offered by Guy Cardwell in 1991 is unwarranted and reductive. He writes,

> It becomes obvious that the attitudes toward race that Clemens held during his maturity were unremarkable and essentially unambiguous. . . . He and most other humane writers of the period assumed the existence of a natural racial hierarchy, accepted as a premise the biological inferiority of Negroes.[1]

Despite Cardwell's contention, little about Twain's attitudes toward race is either "obvious" or "unambiguous," and the extent to which he "assumed the existence of a natural racial hierarchy," implicitly reaffirming it in his art, is by no means clear.

Cardwell states, quite rightly, that "until he was thirty-two years old, Clemens was by almost any standards blatantly racist,"[2] and notes that a dramatic change took place in the late 1860s, after which time "his writings were free of anything like frank racism."

> By our current standards, however, evidence that he retained racist sentiments is overwhelming. His later racist attitudes may be seen in part as the residue of boyhood biases; but in part they belonged to his time. They were very much those of his genteel friends and of his rich relatives by marriage.[3]

One need not quarrel, for the most part, with the idea that Twain may never have outgrown what Louis Budd once called a "substratum of condescending paternalism."[4] What Cardwell ignores, however, is the extent to which Twain was open to, and appreciative of, dimensions of his culture—the culture of his childhood as well as of his adulthood—that his "genteel friends" might have missed. (Cardwell also inaccurately maligns "rich relatives by marriage" such as Jervis Langdon, Twain's father-in-law, who by any standards seems to have been markedly progressive for his times.[5])

We can accept the idea that Twain shared, with peers of his race and class, simple assumptions about "the existence of a natural racial hierarchy" only if we blind ourselves to those instances in which Twain subverted and radically deconstructed the racial categories of his day. Clearly Twain's ability to take a black child named Jimmy, a black teenager named Jerry, and a white child named Tom Blankenship (with a smidgeon of his brother Bence thrown in, and perhaps some of his sidekick, "Black John," as well) and transmute them into a white child named Huck Finn—who would transform the shape of American literature—involved a measure of racial alchemy unparalleled in American letters.

Of interest here is not so much the question "Was Twain a racist?," which may be answered "yes" or "no" depending on how the term is defined, but rather how Twain intermittently played havoc with his culture's categories of "blackness" and "whiteness" in fresh and surprising ways.

In 1958, Ralph Ellison observed,

> Writing at a time when the blackfaced minstrel was still popular, and shortly after a war which left even the abolitionists weary of those problems associated with the Negro, Twain fitted Jim into the outlines of the minstrel tradition, and it was from behind this stereotype mask that we see Jim's dignity and human capacity—and Twain's complexity—emerge.[6]

In recent years, some critics have suggested that Jim suffocated behind that mask, that the demeaning stereotype of the gullible, superstitious, laughable, ridiculous minstrel-show darky prevented Jim's "dignity and human capacity" from showing through.[7] For example, Fredrick Woodard and Donnarae MacCann maintain that "The problematical elements of Jim's character are too thoroughly embedded in the convention of blackface minstrelsy for Twain to have made a literary gesture that carries far beyond the conventions of his own time."[8] At a centennial symposium on the novel in 1984 a professor of Afro-American studies charged that the novel consisted of "white men blacking up to entertain other whites at the expense of black people's humanity."[9]

To the extent that these arguments focus on Jim's captivity at the Phelps plantation, their impact is muted by the reading offered here in Chapter 4, in which we can see Twain using Jim's debasement to comment on the treatment of blacks in the post-Reconstruction South. The points these critics raise in connection with the first two-thirds of the book, however, still need to be addressed. The most eloquent and insightful response to these arguments is David L. Smith's 1984 essay, "Huck, Jim, and American Racial Discourse." Noting the importance of reading Twain's book against the context of the racial discourse to which it responds, Smith asserts that "Twain adopts a strategy of subversion in his attack on race" by focusing "on a number of commonplaces associated with 'the Negro' and then systematically dramatiz[ing] their inadequacy."[10] The result, Smith states, is a book almost "without peer among major Euro-American novels for its explicitly antiracist stance."[11]

On the question of folk beliefs, Smith acknowledges that Jim often "closely resembles the entire tradition of comic darkies." But, he adds, "in some instances apparent similarities conceal fundamental differences."

> The issue is: does Twain merely reiterate cliches, or does he use these conventional patterns to make an unconventional point? A close examination will show that, in virtually every instance, Twain uses Jim's superstition to make points that undermine rather than validate the dominant racial discourse.[12]

In Chapter 2, Tom, with Huck in tow, plays a prank on Jim by stealing his hat while he is sleeping and hanging it from a tree branch. Twain writes,

> Afterwards Jim said the witches bewitched him and put him in a trance, and rode him all over the State, and then set him under the trees again and hung his hat on a limb to show who done it. And next time Jim

told it he said they rode him down to New Orleans; and after that, every time he told it he spread it more and more, till by and by he said they rode him all over the world, and tired him most to death, and his back was all over saddle-boils. Jim was monstrous proud about it, and he got so he wouldn't hardly notice the other niggers. Niggers would come miles to hear Jim tell about it, and he was more looked up to than any nigger in that country. . . . Jim was most ruined, for a servant, because he got so stuck up on account of having seen the devil and been rode by witches.[13]

Smith notes that this episode

has often been interpreted as an example of risible Negro gullibility and ignorance as exemplified by blackface minstrelsy. . . . [T]he information that Jim becomes, through his own story telling, unsuited for life as a slave introduces unexpected complications. . . . Regardless of whether we credit Jim with forethought in this matter, it is undeniable that he turns Tom's attempt to humiliate him into a major personal triumph. . . . It is also obvious that he does so by exercising remarkable skills as a rhetorician.[14]

Smith comes up with an analogous reading of several other episodes in the novel, including that involving the "hair ball." Here, as elsewhere in the book, "Twain shows Jim self-consciously subverting the prescribed definition of 'the Negro,' even as he performs within the limitations of that role."[15]

Woodard and MacCann specifically rebut Smith's claims, insisting that Jim remains "forever frozen within the convention of the minstrel darky."

Even as one examines the minstrel-like scenes for evidence that Jim may be acting the role of the trickster . . . , the lingering effect of minstrelsy provides the frame of reference through which judgment of character is made.[16]

Episodes like Jim's being ridden by witches, Woodard and MacCann argue,

can be interpreted as successful con jobs on Jim's part only if we isolate these scenes from the many additional superstitious episodes in which no hustle can be inferred. For example, Jim thinks Huck is a ghost when he encounters him on Jackson's Island. . . . Jim speaks to the ghost in a typical addle-brained manner: "I awluz liked dead people, en done all I could for 'em."[17]

Woodard and MacCann's argument has some merit. Twain's fondness for minstrel shows is well-documented, and it is fair to assume that some minstrel material worked its way into the novel.[18] But to assume that all of this material necessarily comes from minstrel routines (and is, therefore, *a priori* demeaning to blacks) is to deny that Twain had access to other sources from which it might have come just as well: African-American oral traditions.

If we posit African-American folk traditions as the frame of reference rather than white minstrelsy, Jim's utterances reveal an alternative set of meanings. This positioning is conjectural, since we do not know Twain's actual sources; however, we do know his familiarity with African-American tales—orally received—and his documented interest in folklore traditions. Folklorists have collected numerous African-American folktales of being "ridden by witches" (often considered to be of white European, as opposed to African, origin).[19] But there are some important differences between the kinds of tales most often collected and the story Jim tells in the novel. The tale of being "ridden by witches" recorded by Richard Dorson in *American Negro Folktales*, the series of tales collected by Patricia K. Rickels in "Some Accounts of Witch Riding," and nearly all of the witch-riding tales cited by Langston Hughes and Arna Bontemps in *The Book of Negro Folklore*, for example, involve a *stationary* activity. These are the familiar contours of the "Negro witch-riding tale" Rickels, Hughes, Bontemps, and Dorson collected: the witch jumps on the sleeping victim, "straddles him," and "rides" him wildly in his bed (in a manner Rickels finds possibly suggestive of European traditions of a female spirit who "descended on sleeping persons for the purpose of having sexual intercourse with them"[20]). The witch often chokes off her victim's breath, and when he tries to cry for help, no sound comes out. Only relatively rarely does the witch "ride" the person out of his bed (in one tale, she gets as far as the window of his room). Jim, by way of contrast, was taken "all over the State, . . . down to New Orleans; and . . . all over the world."

There is another tradition, I would suggest, into which the story Jim tells may fit more clearly. Jim's "superstitiousness" and "gullibility" about having been taken on a late-night ride by a supernatural being take on a different meaning in the context of material that folklorist Gladys-Marie Fry collected in her highly acclaimed book, *Night Riders in Black Folk History*, which was based on volumes of slave testimony collected in the 1870s and 1930s, as well as interviews in the 1960s with people descended from slaves.

"According to Black oral tradition," Fry notes, to frighten their slaves into submission and "to discourage night travel," masters would circulate rumors of terrifying supernatural beings who roamed the plantation at night.[21] To provide "a few critically minded slaves" the evidence they "required . . . of the kind of 'scary things' that were supposed to come out at night," the masters "often resorted to masquerading as ghosts" themselves.[22] In the stories the slaves told about these supernatural "night rides," from antebellum times through the early twentieth century,

> the pattern of the chase remained the same: a Black saw something unnatural which chased him to the point of exhaustion. . . .[23]

Jim, we recall, was "tired most to death."

The fraudulent supernatural being, Fry writes, was the "first in a gradually developed system of night-riding creatures, the fear of which was fostered by whites for the purpose of slave control."[24] She traces a direct line from these early efforts to intimidate the slaves to the terrifying night rides of the Ku Klux Klan.

In these stories, the teller of the tale is never caught. His story achieves its "comic effect through use of exaggeration of detail. . . . Only at the end of the breathless narration does the listener realize that he has been 'took' with a description of an escape that reaches Herculean proportions under impossible circumstances."[25] According to Fry, these legends served "the cultural function of preserving the heroic exploits of a suppressed people. The theme in evidence is that the Black, though manipulated, overpowered, and mistreated, emerges to some extent as a culture hero."[26] The cultural expressions of slave life (including dances, songs, folktales, and legends like the ones Fry collected) served, as John Blassingame has observed, to bolster the slave's sense of confidence, autonomy, hope and self-esteem.[27]

The similarities between the tales Fry collected and the one Jim tells suggest the possibility that Jim may have been operating out of this tradition. If he was, it would support Smith's assertions about Jim's calculated use of rhetorical performance to gain attention and respect. Since these stories, as Fry observes, were incredibly widespread, it is hard to imagine that someone who spent as much time with slaves as Twain did would not have heard of them.

Fry's fascinating book suggests that any simple equation of African-American "superstition" with gullibility and ignorance needs to be re-evaluated in the context of how superstition was used by whites as a means of maintaining power over the slaves. Tom is the agent of the prank that sends Jim on his "ride," just as Tom is the agent responsible for Jim's ornate captivity in the final section of the book. If Tom in the last portion of the novel is implicitly implicated (through Twain's satirical social criticism) in the travesty that white America made of black freedom in the post-Reconstruction South, then perhaps Tom's prank in Chapter 2 is meant to be suggestive of the "supernatural" pranks perpetrated on blacks before and after the war by the white establishment in an effort to maintain white control.

Woodard and MacCann's reference to Jim's "addle-brained"

comment "I awluz liked dead people, en done all I could for 'em" also bears a closer look. Woodard and MacCann feel that this remark clearly comes out of the minstrel darky tradition, and their conjecture, from a contemporary perspective, makes sense. But if we change our frame of reference once again from minstrelsy to African-American folk traditions, might Jim's line seem less "addle-brained"?

Jim's assertion that he always did all he could for dead people turns out to be consistent with nineteenth-century African and African-American religious traditions. As Sterling Stuckey has put it, "Being on good terms with the ancestral spirits was an overarching conceptual concern for Africans everywhere in slavery."[28] Robert Farris Thompson has documented modern survivals of this phenomenon in cemeteries in both Africa and the New World.[29] The majority of slaves in the United States were of Kongo-Angola ancestry[30] and, as Thompson has observed, "nowhere is Kongo-Angola influence in the New World more pronounced, more profound, than in black traditional cemeteries throughout the South of the United States."[31] In these cemeteries a range of carefully selected objects and offerings decorate the graves—"gestures to the dead," including lamps "to light the way to glory," "a toy metallic airplane . . . meant to help the spirit 'get to heaven fast,'" and bright gleaming tinfoil that respectfully recalls "the flash of the departed spirit."[32] (When I accompanied Robert Thompson to an African-American cemetery in Austin, Texas, in 1992, one grave that we photographed—not, incidentally, a recent one—was newly decorated with a tiny Christmas tree upon which were hung a number of neatly wrapped miniature gifts.)

Langston Hughes and Arna Bontemps cite this phenomenon as well:

> The Ewe-speaking peoples of the west coast of Africa all make offerings of food and drink—particularly libations of palm wine and banana beer upon the graves of the ancestor. It is to be noted that in America the spirit is always given a pint of good whisky.[33]

As Stuckey has commented, slaves acknowledged "a continuous interplay between the living and the dead—a reciprocity of spirit enhanced through an observance of a whole range of African burial practices."[34]

Jim comes from a tradition in which one *does* do things for dead people, and if one hasn't treated the dead properly, they come back as ghosts to complain about it.[35] That whites may have found this behavior "comical" speaks more to the limits imposed by their own ethnocentrism than to anything inherently "addled" about the tradition itself. The point is that Jim may have made this comment in the novel not because Twain heard a minstrel-show darky say it, but because African-American speakers in his past had spoken of such things in his hearing.[36]

Ironically, then, some dimensions of Jim's character that Woodard and MacCann interpreted as clearly products of the whites-in-blackface minstrel show may turn out to have their roots in his African-American and African past. In other words, instances of behavior that struck them as most artificially "white" projections may turn out to have pedigrees that are certifiably "black."

By the same token, there are also supposedly "black" elements in Twain's creation of Jim that prove, on closer look, to be demonstrably "white." Daniel Hoffman claims that most of the folk beliefs to which Jim gives credence turn out to have roots that are white European rather than African-American.[37] A more recent example is the error Guy Cardwell makes in his description of Twain's composition process for one of Jim's key scenes in the novel, the one in which he discovers, after having slapped his daughter for inattention, that "sk'yarlet-fever" had made her "plumb deef en dumb."[38] After observing that Twain had jotted down vignettes about deafness and children in his notebooks for a number of years, Cardwell writes,

> Scarlet fever was prominently in Clemens's mind during that summer of 1882, for his daughter Jean had it. In January 1884 the disease was on his mind again. Howells's son, John, was ill of it; and Clemens wrote to Howells warning that John should not be let out of bed too soon. Presumably Clemens believed that because of inadvisable activity following a case of the fever, one of the children of his coachman, a Negro named Patrick McAleer, became deaf. As the editors of the Twain-Howells letters suggest, this odd combination of aides-memoire and events from life lies behind Jim's "Oh, de po' little thing! De Lord God Almighty fogive po ole Jim, kaze he never gwyne to fogive hisseff as long's he live!"[39]

In Cardwell's view, then, the fact that Twain's "coachman, a Negro named Patrick McAleer," had a child who became deaf from scarlet fever helped prompt Twain to create the memorable scene he crafted for Jim. Cardwell cites this chain of events to delineate "something of the method of composition and of the serendipitous whimsicality of authorial process" that went into the book. He errs, however, when he says that Patrick McAleer was black: McAleer was a white Irishman in Twain's employ since his Buffalo days. Nowhere do any of the sources Cardwell cites refer to McAleer as black. His "blackness" is simply an inference Cardwell makes—incorrectly, as it turns out.[40] The implication is that a key scene of Jim's in the novel has its roots (at least in part) in real events that happened to a black person Twain knew. Twain's imagination, however, was impishly color blind. The evidence indicates that the sources for Jim's famous "deaf and dumb" soliloquy were white.

This is not to imply that on other occasions Twain did not draw elements of Jim's character from real black people he had known. As Arthur G. Pettit has pointed out, the altruism Jim shows when he "saves Tom Sawyer from blood poisoning by insisting that Huck go for a doctor after Tom is shot in the 'evasion,'" resembles, on some level, the altruism shown by John Lewis, a servant at Quarry Farm who risked his life in 1877 to stop a runaway horse that was pulling Twain's sister-in-law, her child, and the child's nurse toward a cliff that meant certain death for all of them.[41] As Herbert A. Wisbey, Jr., has noted, "Twain never forgot" the incident, and the "superhuman strength" Lewis had shown. "Although the event was not publicized at the time the whole city eventually came to know the act of heroism."[42]

To create Jim, Twain combined aspects of Patrick McAleer, a

Mark Twain and John Lewis, a servant at Quarry Farm whose altruism, strength, and courage Twain admired deeply, and who may have served as one of the models for Jim in Huckleberry Finn. (Courtesy, the Mark Twain Papers, The Bancroft Library)

white man who was, in Twain's view, the epitome of a "gentleman," with aspects of John Lewis, a black man who was for Twain a model of supererogatory altruism.[43] Twain's readiness to draw on white sources as well as black for key dramatic monologues of Jim's is consistent with his subversion of racial categories throughout the novel. As David Smith observes,

> Jim demonstrates that race provides no useful index of character. While that point may seem obvious to contemporary readers, it is a point rarely made by nineteenth-century Euro-American novelists. . . .[44]

Twain's final subversion of racial categories comes when Jim surrenders himself to help Tom get medical attention at the novel's end. David Smith writes,

> Huck declares that Jim is "white inside" (chap. 40). He apparently intends this as a compliment, but Tom is fortunate that Jim does not behave like most whites in the novel. . . . Twain also contrasts Jim's self-sacrificing compassion with the cruel and mean-spirited behavior of his captors, emphasizing that white skin does not justify claims of superior virtue.[45]

Smith concludes,

> Twain rejects entirely the mystification of race and demonstrates that Jim is in most ways a better man than the men who regard him as their inferior.[46]

Smith's argument is convincing. It remains troubling, however, that although Twain may have subverted racial stereotypes in the novel, he made no effort to prevent his text from being presented to the public in ways that emphasized its connection to familiar minstrel-show traditions, and indeed, often participated in this process himself. For example, although he complained to illustrator Edward W. Kemble that the first pictures of Huck were not "good-looking" enough, Twain raised no objection to Kemble's drawings of Jim, who (particularly in the early illustrations) looked much like all of Kemble's characteristic "comically represented Negroes."[47]

When portions of the novel were excerpted in newspapers would not a piece about "Jim's Investments" taken out of context suggest a minstrel routine more than anything else? ("Jim's Investments" ran in the "Passing Pleasantry" column in the *Cleveland Leader*, 11 January 1885, identified as reprinted from *The Century*. It also ran in the *Boston Budget* on 4 January 1885.)[48] More significantly, some of the passages from the book with which Twain most liked to entertain audiences during readings from the 1880s through the 1890s were passages that strike readers today as most redolent of the minstrel show: "King Sollermun" and "Jim's Bank."[49]

One might argue that the closing sentences of each piece took it beyond the realm of minstrelsy into a subtle or not-so-subtle critique of race slavery. Jim's comment, "I owns mysef" evokes sober pathos, not ridicule; and by the end of "King Sollermun," as David Smith has noted, Jim's argument appears more convincing than Huck's, making Huck's comment that you "can't learn a nigger to argue" sound clearly like his own "sour grapes."[30] The reader—and audience—is more likely to challenge Huck on this pronouncement than to agree with him. We do not have the evidence to prove, however, that Twain's white lecture audiences got these points; it is quite possible they responded to the pieces precisely as minstrel routines. On this point, it is interesting to note, however, that in his readings Twain sometimes preceded "Jim's Bank" with "A True Story" and "Call this a govment," setting it in a context shaped by Aunt Rachel's powerful sincerity and Pap's self-parodic racism.[51] Twain does not seem to have been particularly concerned about the links that might have been forming in the public's mind between minstrel traditions and aspects of his work.[52] What are we to make of the fact that Twain's readings were in demand among black audiences as well as white?[53]

In a 1991 interview, Ralph Ellison emphasized the complexity of understanding the role of traditions of minstrelsy in the novel.

> *Ellison:* [Jim's] a mature adult, but he's part of the minstrel tradition. So it becomes very ambiguous. But again, Mark Twain makes certain moral points through Jim, and he does that as an adult, and as one who is quite responsible within the limitations of his freedom.
>
> *Fishkin:* How would you answer those who say that he's so much a part of the minstrel tradition that his humanity doesn't shine through it as much as we would want it to?
>
> *Ellison:* Well, I would say that that's partially true. But one also has to look at the teller of the tale, and realize that you are getting a black man, an adult, seen through the condescending eyes— partially—of a young white boy.
>
> *Fishkin:* So you're saying that those critics are making the same old mistake of confusing the narrator with the author—
>
> *Ellison:* Yes.
>
> *Fishkin:* —that they're saying that Twain saw him that way rather than Huck.
>
> *Ellison:* Yes. That happens over and over again. They assume that the writer didn't see through it, but I'm pretty sure Twain saw through it.[54]

Thomas Weaver and Merline A. Williams also explore this gap between Huck's and Twain's perceptions of Jim. They believe that Twain—but not Huck—grants Jim

> a full humanity by investing his character with the same qualities Twain saw in all human beings . . . [including] an active impulse to chicanery

which parallels the artful subterfuge of Huck Finn, Tom Sawyer, or any of the other notorious tricksters and confidence men appearing throughout Twain's fiction. . . . Conditioned by a cultural paradigm that disallows blacks a fully human status, Huck is incapable of seeing Jim as a confidence man. Twain's view, however, is not so limited.[55]

While Twain may hold a larger view of Jim's basic humanity than Huck does—a point that Ellison, Weaver, and Williams all affirm—the question of Twain's attitude toward minstrel shows remains difficult and complex. From the 1880s through the end of his life, Twain rejected minstrel-show stereotypes as unrelated in any way to real black people that he knew. He recognized as legitimate the intellectual or artistic aspirations of black Yale law student Warner McGuinn, of black Lincoln University undergraduate A. W. Jones, and of black Hartford painter Charles Ethan Porter who wanted to go to Paris to study art. Twain provided financial aid to these individuals in all of these endeavors.[56] Yet he retained a lifelong affection for the minstrel shows he recalled from his Missouri childhood.

What was it that Twain saw and heard at minstrel shows? How did his attraction to minstrelsy jibe with his ability to discard in real life the stereotypes minstrel shows projected? Elbert R. Bowen's chapter on "Negro Minstrels" in *Theatrical Entertainments in Rural Missouri Before the Civil War* suggests some of the contours of the shows that Twain recalled so fondly, but sidesteps the question of their effect on the audience's attitudes toward race. Eric Lott's illuminating book, *Love and Theft: Blackface Minstrelsy and the American Working Class* (which builds on Robert C. Toll's useful earlier study), provides us with a framework for answering some of these questions.[57]

In our interview, Ellison suggested that, along with much that was inaccurate, of course, a large amount of fairly accurate African-American vernacular speech may have made its way into the general culture via the minstrel show:

> I think that you never quite know where the vernacular is moving because you can pick it up in so many ways. And that, incidentally, is a certain positive thing that was active in the minstrel show. Demeaning in many ways it certainly was, but in order to present the comic black, very often these fellows had to go and listen, they had to open their ears to speech even if their purpose was to make it comic.[58]

William J. Mahar's research on the relationships between minstrel-show dialect and Black English confirms Ellison's intuitions.[59]

The implication of Ellison's comment is that one need not challenge the general truth of Richard Dorson's charge that minstrel shows were, in large measure, "a travesty on, rather than a simu-

Warner T. McGuinn, Baltimore attorney whose expenses at Yale Law School were paid for by Mark Twain. (Courtesy, the *Baltimore Afro-American*)

Connecticut painter Charles Ethan Porter (second from right), whose apprenticeship in Paris was funded by Twain, at a birthday dinner thrown for him by his art students. (Courtesy, Ethel L. Robert)

lacrum" of African-American folklore,[60] to suggest that some authentic and genuine folk traditions may nonetheless have made their way in.[61] Dena Epstein, in her classic article on the folk banjo, observes,

> Although initially [the minstrel theater] may have included folk material, it increasingly exaggerated its characterization, evolving a grotesque

caricature that could not fail being offensive to friends of the Negro. As with the literary stereotype, rejecting the minstrels as realistic portraits of plantation Negroes seemed to require rejecting every element in their performance as well, including banjo playing.[62]

In this context, as Epstein shows, numerous writers distorted evidence to the contrary to "prove" that "the banjo was unknown to the plantation Negro."[63] Epstein's monumental assemblage of seventeenth-, eighteenth-, and nineteenth-century documents from Africa and the Americas builds an overwhelming case for the idea that the banjo was an instrument of African origin that was, in fact, extremely popular among blacks during slavery. The minstrels, despite all their offensive attitudes toward the folk culture they exploited, turned out to be right on this one.

J. L. Dillard has noted that "sensitive observers of Negro life in the United States have always been aware of the gap between the minstrel show and black reality."[64] Mark Twain himself was one such "sensitive observer." In 1873, in fact, in his publicity blurb for the Fisk Jubilee Singers, Twain expressed his skepticism about the accuracy of minstrel performances. "The so-called 'negro minstrels' simply mis-represent the thing," Twain had written. "I do not think they ever saw a plantation or heard a slave sing."[65] (Elsewhere, however, Twain expressed the delight he took in these performances, authentic or not as they may have been.)

As Dillard has observed,

> The most sensitive have made the distinction [between the minstrel show and Black reality] without making the sweeping assertion that there was nothing in Negro folk humor to furnish a model for such inferior imitations. Careful studies have shown that there was indeed a great deal.[66]

Like the minstrel show itself, Jim was an eclectic amalgam of authentic black voices, and white caricatures of them.

Although it may have included some dimensions of "Black reality," however, the minstrel show remained an inherently racist enterprise. The fact that white minstrels may have gathered African-American material for their shows did not prevent them from transforming that material into productions that demeaned blacks in the nineteenth century, and whose legacy continues to plague African Americans to this day. Twain shared with many of his peers, including some of those most outspoken on issues of racial injustice,[67] a largely uncritical response to this most American of institutions.

6

Dark midnight was my cry, dark midnight was my cry

I would be remiss, in a book subtitled "Mark Twain and African-American Voices," if I failed to devote some attention to the speech with which Twain endows Jim, the main black character in his opus.[1] If a Frenchman's a man, Jim complains in his famous argument with Huck, "Well, den! Dad blame it, why doan he talk like a man?"[2] Does Jim "talk like a man?" The question is more significant than it may seem.

While there is not space here to present a fully detailed history of the presence of African-American dialect in American fiction, a cursory overview is necessary to set Twain's achievement in perspective.[3] How did Twain's efforts to represent African-American speech compare with those of novelists who preceded him?[4] Some of the earliest efforts by white novelists to render the speech of African Americans entirely ignored the question of accuracy. As Tremaine McDowell observed,

> in *The Power of Sympathy* (1789), the first novel written and published in America, the sentimental hero made a tour of the South; there he met a female negro servant; for her he solved the problem of slavery. The anonymous author [William Hill Brown] was so faithful to the decorum of sensibility that no indelicate touches of realism are introduced in describing this comely negress; and it is even more significant that the novelist forced the slave, although a laborer in the fields of South Carolina, to speak impeccable English.[5]

A similar strategy was adopted by Richard Hildreth in his 1836 abolitionist novel *Archy Moore,* in which the eponymous slave is given lines like, "Mine are no silken sorrows nor sentimental sufferings, but . . . [the] . . . stern reality of actual woe."[6]

McDowell assigns "the distinction of introducing negro dialect into native fiction" to Hugh Henry Brackenridge. In Brackenridge's satirical novel *Modern Chivalry* (1792), a slave named "Cuff" who discovers a petrified moccasin is inducted into the American Philosophical Society. Cuff, in what McDowell considers the "earliest attempt at recording negro dialect in an American novel," speaks like this:

> Massa shentiman; I be cash crab in de Wye river: found ting in de mud; tone, big a man's foot: holes like to he; fetch Massa: Massa say, it be de Indian Moccasin. . . . O! fat de call it; all tone. He say, you be a filasafa, Cuff: I say, O no, Massa, you be de filasafa. Wel; two tre monts afta, Massa call me, and say, You be a filasafa, Cuff, fo' sartan: Getta ready, and go dis city, and make grate peech for shentima filasafa.[7]

McDowell, Dillard, and Mahar all believe that Cuff's diction reveals some keen powers of observation on Brackenridge's part.[8] Holton, on the other hand, views Brackenridge's "exaggeration of pronunciation features" as "a form of phonological caricature" that renders the character's speech "almost grotesque."

Other early efforts by white novelists to render the speech of African-American characters include those of James Fenimore Cooper in *The Spy* (1821). Cooper's "Caesar," a faithful old servant, speaks like this:

> "I been to see—Massa Harper on the knee—pray to God—no gemman who pray to God tell of good son, come to see old fader—Skinner do that—no Christian!"
>
> "I don't t'ink he look a bit like me," said Caesar, . . . "He worse than ebber now," cried the discontented African. "A t'ink colored man like a sheep! I nebber see sich a lip, Harvey; he most big as a sausage!"
>
> "Best nebber tempt a Satan," said Caesar, . . .[9]

Cooper's efforts to render the speech of African-American characters won mild praise from Sterling Brown who noted that "though crudely recorded, his dialect rises above the usually impossible Negro speech in early novels."[10] McDowell credits Cooper with using for the first time several techniques that would become staples of American dialect writing, including "the apostrophe to indicate omission of a letter."[11]

Nonetheless, McDowell's verdict is that "Cooper was wise in avoiding extensive excursions into the field of negro dialect, for his efforts in that direction are uneven and inconsistent and they reveal constant uncertainty and vacillation."[12] Twain, always impatient with Cooper's attempts to render any form of speech, undoubtedly would have agreed with him.

Hector, a slave in William Gilmore Simms's *The Yemassee* (1835), who rejects freedom in favor of continuing loyal service to his master, speaks like this:

> I d--n to h--ll, Maussa ef I guine be free! I can't loss you company. . . . 'tis onpossible, Maussa, and dere's no use for talk 'bout it. De ting ain't right; and enty I know wha' kind of ting freedom is wid black man? Ha! You make Hector free, he turn wuss more nor poor buckrah—he tief out de shop—he git drunk and lie in de ditch—den, if sick comes, he roll, he toss in de wet grass of de stable. You come in de morning, Hector dead.[13]

As Arthur Huff Fauset commented, "any writing that can be taken as an *apologia* for a social system, or the idealization of the plantation regime" may be inherently suspect as a source of accurate information about folk speech.[14] It may be difficult to separate the unreality of Hector's speech from the unreality of his salute to the Plantation Tradition stereotype of the slave who, along with his master, longs for the good old days.[15]

"In almost all the accounts of the progress of the American language," David Simpson observes in *The Politics of American English, 1776–1850*, "the place of the Black tradition can only be inferred from its absence or parodic inclusion."[16] The diction of the character Jupiter in Edgar Allan Poe's "The Gold-Bug" (1843), for example, "is contextualized as at best a source of humor, at worst of condescension or parody."[17] This condescension was not lost on Toni Morrison, who was moved to observe that it could never have occurred to Poe that

> I, for example, might read "The Gold-Bug" and watch his efforts to render my grandfather's speech to something as close to braying as possible, in an effort so intense you can see the perspiration—and the stupidity—when Jupiter says, "I knows," and Mr. Poe spells the verb "nose."[18]

White authors, as Jean Fagan Yellin has noted, typically used a black character as a source of "humor and local color," insisting on "his grotesqueness, his hilarity, and his love of servitude."[19] An author's decision to have a black character speak in dialect often signalled the limits to the human qualities the novelist was willing to assign him.[20] The "tortured syntax and strained malapropisms that Stowe intends to be amusing" in Sam's speech in *Uncle Tom's Cabin*, for example,[21] like the jarring cacography that characterizes Jupiter's speech in "The

Gold-Bug," call attention to the black character's essential "other-ness." As Poe himself once put it,

> [Some believe that Negroes] are, like ourselves, the sons of Adam and must, therefore, have like passions and wants and feelings and tempers in all respects. This we deny. . . .[22]

Some early efforts by African-American writers to translate black dialect into print may be found in novels by William Wells Brown and Martin Delany. In Brown's *Clotel, or the President's Daughter* (1853), for example, the following exchange takes place between a passing farmer and two slaves who are engaged in a "ride and tie" ruse to make their way to Canada:

> two slaves were seen passing; one was on horseback, the other was walking before him with his arms tightly bound, on a long rope leading from the man on foot to the one on horseback.
> "Oh, ho, that's a runaway rascal, I suppose," said a farmer, who met them on the road.
> "Yes, sir, he bin runaway, and I got him fast. Marser will tan his jacket for him nicely when he gets him."
> "You are a trustworthy fellow, I imagine," continued the farmer.
> "Oh, yes, sir; marser puts a heap of confidence in this nigger."[23]

Martin Delany, in *Blake, or The Huts of America* (1861–62), describes an old man falling to his knees and praying:

> "O Laud! dow has promis' in dine own wud, to be a fadah to de fadaless, an' husban to de widah! O Laud, let dy wud run an' be glo-rify! Sof'en de haud haut ob de presseh, an' let my po' chile cum back!"[24]

The black dialect written by Brown and Delany does not force read-ers to crash through distracting barriers of cacography and eye dialect, staples of the racist portraits of blacks in the writing of Southwestern newspaper humorists.[25] It never allows the phonetic reproduction of the speaker's pronunciation to interfere with the nat-ural easy flow of his voice. By and large, however, African-American writers did not include large amounts of dialect in their poetry or fic-tion until Charles W. Chesnutt's stories in the 1880s and Paul Lau-rence Dunbar's poems in the 1890s.

In 1874, when Mark Twain published "A True Story, Repeated Word for Word as I Heard It" in the *Atlantic Monthly*, Joel Chan-dler Harris was still two years away from publishing his first "Uncle Remus" stories in the *Atlanta Constitution*. (Twain proba-bly read them in the late 1870s, when they ran in Northern news-papers.)[26] Two novelists whose sympathy for African Americans would be well-known by the mid-1880s, Albion Tourgee and

George Washington Cable, were several years away from publishing their first fiction. (Tourgee's *A Fool's Errand* and Cable's *Old Creole Days* both appeared in 1879.) Charles W. Chesnutt's first short story would not be published until 1885.[27] There is no evidence that Twain was familiar with the fiction of William Wells Brown or Martin Delany.

Twain himself had no idea that "A True Story" was anything noteworthy or worthwhile. On the contrary, he simply enclosed it with a "Fable for Old Boys & Girls" and assumed that it was the "Fable" that would pique Howells's interest:

> I enclose also a "True Story" which has no humor in it. You can pay as lightly as you choose for that, if you want it, for it is rather out of my line. I have not altered the old colored woman's story except to begin it at the beginning, instead of the middle, as she did—& ~~worked~~ traveled both ways.[28]

Twain added that he "*told* this yarn" to some friends, "& they liked it. So I thought I'd *write* it."[29]

This last comment of Twain's is crucial. For a key gift Twain gave to American literature would be a standard for translating spoken speech into print without robbing it of its energy and power. Twain was totally unprepared for Howells's response. "I've kept the True Story," Howells wrote, "which I think extremely good and touching with the best and reallest kind of black talk in it."[30] Nine days later, Howells wrote, "this little story delights me more and more: I wish you had about forty of 'em!"[31]

Three days after that Twain described to Howells the process by which he transferred "Aunt Rachel's" talk to the written page:

> I amend this dialect stuff by talking & talking & *talking* it till it sounds right—& I had difficulty with this negro talk because a negro sometimes (rarely) says "goin'" & sometimes "gwyne", & they make just such discrepancies in other words—& when you come to reproduce them on paper they look as if the variation resulted from the writer's carelessness. But I want to work at the proofs & get the dialect as nearly right as possible.[32]

Twain's manuscript of "A True Story" reveals his careful efforts to hone his prose until it captured what he put forward as "Aunt Rachel's" exact words.

Aunt Rachel tells her story with moving power and directness. Although an educated, white narrator ("Misto C—") introduces her, the reigning presence in the story is the black vernacular speaker herself. After the narrator's introductory remarks—which function principally to signal the myopic limitations of his world view—Aunt

"*Dey put chains on us. . . . *" *Manuscript pages of "A True Story."* (Mark Twain Collection [#6314], Clifton Waller Barrett Library, Manuscripts Division, Special Collections Department, University of Virginia Library)

Rachel's voice performs solo, uninterrupted, in a dramatic monologue that may well have been a "first" for American literature:[33]

> Dey put chains on us an' put us on a stan' as high as dis po'ch—twenty foot high—an' all de people stood aroun', crowds an' crowds. An' dey'd come up dah an' look at us all roun', an' squeeze our arm, an' make us git up an' walk, an' den say, "Dis one too ole," or "Dis one lame," or "Dis one don't 'mount to much." An' dey sole my ole man, an' took him away, an' dey begin to sell my chil'en an' take *dem* away, an' I begin to cry; an' de man say, "Shet up yo' damn blubberin'," an' hit me on de mouf wid his han'. An' when de las' one was gone but my little Henry, I grab' him clost up to my breas' so, an' I ris up an' says, "You sha'n't take him away," I says; "I'll kill de man dat teches him!" I says. But my little Henry whisper an' say, "I gwyne to run away, an' den I work an' buy yo' freedom." Oh, bless de chile, he always so good! But dey got him—dey got him, de men did; but I took and tear de clo'es mos' off of 'em an' beat 'em over de head wid my chain; an' *dey* give it to *me*, too, but I didn't mine dat.[34]

The story confounded members of the press, who described it, in notices about the issue of the *Atlantic Monthly* in which it appeared, as "a humorous sketch by Mark Twain"—something it clearly was not.[35] In his review of Twain's *Sketches New and Old*, in which "A True Story" was reprinted the following year, Howells expressed his puzzlement over the press's confusion:

> Evidently the critical mind feared a lurking joke. Not above two or three notices out of hundreds recognized "A True Story" for what it was—namely, a study of character as true as life itself, strong, tender, and most movingly pathetic in its perfect fidelity to the tragic fact. We beg the reader to turn to it again in this book. We can assure him that he has a great surprise and a strong emotion in store for him. The rugged truth of the sketch leaves all other stories of slave life infinitely far behind, and reveals a gift in the author for the simple, dramatic report of reality which we have seen equalled in no other American writer.[36]

The dialect spoken by Aunt Rachel/Mary Ann Cord is compelling, but not distracting. In 1906 Twain recalled Mary Ann Cord's "vigorous eloquence," and observed that "she had the best gift of strong & simple speech that I have known in any woman except my mother."[37]* In an 1895 journal Twain wrote that the story

> is a ~~pitiful~~ shameful tale of wrong & hardship, but I do not tell it for that. I tell it because I think it a ~~remarkable~~ curiously strong piece of literary work to come unpremeditated from lips untrained in the literary art. . . .[38]*

Whether the words on the page were Mary Ann Cord's exact words, as Twain claimed, or whether they were shaped by Twain's own ear and imagination, Twain allows the sheer force of her character and the concrete truth of her pain to shine through her colloquial speech with clarity and radiance. But apparently neither the nation's press nor, perhaps, Twain himself was ready quite yet to come to terms with the significance of that accomplishment.

There was an enormous gulf between Twain's achievement here and the work of the man who would become known, within a few years, as the acknowledged "master" of black dialect, Joel Chandler Harris. In 1876, two years after "A True Story" appeared in the *Atlantic Monthly*, the first "Uncle Remus" stories began to be published in the *Atlanta Constitution*. "Uncle Remus," in these early sketches, spoke like this:

> . . . Gimme a two-dollar bill, an' I'm in favor uv free guv'ment and red licker right erlong; but w'en I'm a hankerin' arter a dram I kinder disremember w'ich is w'ich an' who is who, an' dar's de d'sease what I got now.[39]

In his introduction to *Uncle Remus: His Songs and Sayings* (1880), Harris noted that Uncle Remus "has nothing but pleasant memories of the discipline of slavery."[40] But Aunt Rachel's soul-wrenching pain had come from a real emotional terrain worlds removed from Uncle Remus's worry-free plantation tales.

The language in which Aunt Rachel expressed that pain found its way directly into the language in which Jim expressed his in *Huckleberry Finn*.[41] Both run directly counter to the prevailing wisdom of the day as enshrined in the popular reference source, *The American Cyclopaedia* (1875 edition), published by D. Appleton and Company (which Twain, on other points, at least, consulted often): "Negroes . . . are comparatively insensible to pain."[42] (Or, as Thomas Jefferson had put it, "Their griefs are transient."[43]) Aunt Rachel's pain at separation from her child is palpably real—as real as the pain Roxy feels in *Pudd'nhead Wilson* at the thought that her child could be sold away from her, sold down the river.[44] (Both mothers' pain prefigures that of Sethe in Toni Morrison's *Beloved*; Sethe decides, as Roxy does at one point, that death is preferable to the fate she imagines for her child under slavery.)

Consider, for example, the story Jim tells about his daughter in Chapter 23 of the novel. Huck sets the stage for Jim's tale, much as "Misto C—" introduced Aunt Rachel in "A True Story," but with a difference. While "Misto C—" had been blind to Aunt Rachel's pain, Huck is fully cognizant of Jim's:

> When I waked up, just at daybreak, [Jim] was setting there with his head down betwixt his knees, moaning and mourning to himself. I didn't take notice, nor let on. I knowed what it was about. He was thinking about his wife and his children, away up yonder. . . . and I do believe he cared just as much for his people as white folks does for theirn. It don't seem natural, but I reckon it's so. He was always moaning and mourning, that way, nights, when he judged I was asleep, and saying "Po' little 'Lizbeth! po' little Johnny! it mighty hard; I spec' I ain't ever gwyne to see you no mo', no mo'! He was a mighty good nigger, Jim was.[45]

Huck's frame for Jim's story cues the reader into the emotional plane that Jim's tale will inhabit. While some earlier exchanges between Huck and Jim might have drawn on the tropes and wordplays of the minstrel show, Huck here signals to the reader that something sad and serious—not comic—will be voiced in Jim's rough, uneducated black speech:

> . . . I somehow got to talking to him about his wife and young ones; and by and by he says: "What makes me feel so bad dis time, 'uz bekase I hear sumpn over yonder on de bank like a whack, er a slam, while ago, en it mine me er de time I treat my little 'Lizabeth so ornery. She warn't on'y 'bout fo' year ole, en she tuck de sk'yarlet fever, en had

a powerful rough spell; but she got well, en one day she was a-stannin' aroun', en I says to her, I says:

"'Shet de do'.'

"She never done it; jis' stood dah, kiner smilin' up at me. It make me mad; en I says agin, mighty loud, I says:

"'Doan you hear me?—shet de do'!'

"She jis' stood de same way, kiner smilin' up. I was a-bilin'! I says:

"'I lay I *make* you mine!'

"En wid dat I fetch' her a slap side de head dat sont her a-sprawlin'. Den I went into de yuther room, en 'uz gone 'bout ten minutes; en when I come back, dah was dat do' a-stannin' open *yit*, en dat chile stannin' mos' right in it, a-lookin' down and mournin', en de tears runnin' down. My, but I *wuz* mad. I was agwyne for de chile, but jis' den—it was a do' dat open' innerds—jis' den, 'long come de wind en slam it to, behine de chile, ker-*blam*!—en my lan', de chile never move'! My breff mos' hop outer me; en I feel so—so—I doan know *how* I feel. I crope out, all a-tremblin', en crope aroun' en open de do' easy en slow, en poke my head in behine de chile, sof' en still, en all uv a sudden I says *pow*! jis' as loud as I could yell. *She never budge!* O, Huck, I bust out a'cryin', en grab her up in my arms en say, 'O de po' little thing! de Lord God Amighty fogive po' ole Jim, kaze he never gwine to fogive hisseff as long's he live!' O, she was plumb deef en dumb, Huck, plumb deef en dumb—en I'd been a treat'n her so!"[46]

In his notes for the novel, Twain had told himself, "Let Jim say putty for 'pretty' and nuvver for 'never.'"[47] However, as Doyno observes,

> while revising this emotionally powerful scene, Twain twice wrote "never," and one of the changes is the highly unusual modification of dialect form to standard language. Moreover, in another unusual action, Twain wrote in the left margin, in pencil, "This expression shall not be changed."[48]

Twain's willingness to break his own "rules" of dialect on this occasion shows that his foremost concern was letting nothing intervene between the reader and the emotions Jim was expressing.

Jim's speech represented Twain's "pains-taking" efforts to accurately record, to the best of his ability, "Missouri Negro Dialect." But unlike virtually all other white writers of African-American dialect before him (and many who came after him), Twain refused to allow the dialect to break the flow of the speaker's words. His use of eye dialect (like "wuz") is minimal. His primary concern is communicating Jim's very human pain.

David Sewell contends that Jim's speech "is, in fact, romanticized folk speech."[49] Others have taken positions to the contrary. Sterling Brown wrote that "Jim is the best example in nineteenth century fiction of the average Negro slave. . . . [He] is completely believable";

breff mos' hop outer me; en
I feel so — so — I doan know
how I feel. I 'crope out,
all a-tremblin', en crope
aroun' en open de do' easy
en slow, en poke my head in
behine de chile, sof' en still,
en all of a sudden I says
pow! jis' as loud as I could
yell. She never move'! O, Huck, I burst out
a-cryin', en grab her up in
my arms en say, 'O de po'
little thing! de Lord God Amighty
fogive po' ole Jim, kaze
he never gwyne to fogive hisseff as long as he live!' O, she
was plumb deef en dumb, Huck, plumb
deef en dumb — en I'd ben a treat'n her so!"

"She never move!" Manuscript page of Huckleberry Finn. (Previously
unpublished material from this page is copyrighted by the Mark Twain Foundation, c/o
Chamberlain, Willi, Ouchterloney, & Watson, 15 Maiden Lane, New York, NY 10038)

Sylvia Holton observed that "Mark Twain's representation of Jim's dialect is certainly extremely well done."[50] And writing in *Negro Digest* in 1965, Martin Pedigo maintained that

> Twain's Negroes . . . spoke out—realistically, of course—to each other and to the Huck Finns who represented the wisdom of youth that [had not] been taught to hate yet.
>
> Their simple pleas for the basic comforts and dignity ring out as did Martin Luther King's plea for his "dream."[51]

Perhaps some overstatement may be attributed to both sides. The evidence suggests that Twain was striving, to the best of his ability, for accuracy as well as readability.

The "Explanatory" note that precedes Chapter 1 of the novel attests to the primary importance of this goal for Twain:

> In this book a number of dialects are used, to wit: the Missouri negro dialect; the extremest form of the backwoods South-Western dialect; the ordinary "Pike-County" dialect; and four modified varieties of this last. The shadings have not been done in a hap-hazard fashion, or by guess-work; but pains-takingly, and with these several forms of speech.
>
> I make this explanation for the reason that without it many readers would suppose that all these characters were trying to talk alike and not succeeding.
>
> THE AUTHOR.

Several scholars have explored the question of whether Twain did, in fact, use seven distinct dialects in the novel, or whether the "Explanatory" might itself have been a joke.[52] But whatever position one stakes out on the "number of dialects" question, Twain clearly was fascinated by the variety and distinctiveness of American vernacular speech.

"Privately, in notebooks and letters," as Arthur G. Pettit has shown,

> [Twain] was constantly practicing his skill with black vernacularisms—playing with alternative spellings and pronunciations, honing the sound and the nuance to the highest possible pitch of perfection. His notebooks of the eighties and nineties are filled with dialect scribblings. . . .[53]

Moreover, in 1882 Twain wrote his publisher, James R. Osgood, a letter detailing the length of a manuscript he was about to send and the kinds of editorial judgments he was willing to accept. The letter would be unremarkable were it not for the fact that Twain decided to write it entirely in black dialect:

> Dear Osgood—
> I's gwine to sen' you de stuff jis' as she stan', now; an' you an' Misto Howls kin weed out enuff o'dem 93,000 words fer to crowd de book

down to *one* book; or you kin shove in enuff er dat ole Contrib-Club truck fer to swell her up en bust her in two an' make *two* books outen her.

Dey ain't no use to buil' no index, ner plan out no 'rangement er de stuff ontwel you is decided what you gwyne to do.

I don't want none er dat rot what is in de small onvolups to go in, 'cepp'n jis' what Misto Howls *say* shel go in.

I don' see how I come to git sich a goddam sight er truck on han', nohow.

Yourn truly S L Clemens

P.S. I wrotened to Cholly Webster 'bout dem goddam plates en copyrights.[54]

Twain was obviously having fun and playfully showing off. But the letter also demonstrates his belief that the black vernacular speech he was experimenting with was as capable as any other of communicating (fairly precisely) important information. Twain may even have suspected that black vernacular speech could be a salutary corrective to some of the obfuscating abstractions and incongruities of Standard English. Indeed, in *Huckleberry Finn*, Jim's conversation often centers on issues of language and meaning, decentering and exposing the hollow conventions that pass themselves off as meaningful and authoritative in the dominant discourse of the culture.[55] In an aborted novel that Twain worked on in the late 1890s, for example, Twain had Jim cross-examine Tom about whether the term "Civil War" was not inherently oxymoronic, an impossibility.[56]

Twain continued to experiment with black vernacular speech in the 1890s. Indeed, "The Snow-Shovelers," an unpublished piece probably written around 1892, consists almost entirely of a conversation carried on in dialect between two black speakers.[57] Twain greatly admired Joel Chandler Harris's dialect writing, but Twain's own dialect writing is infinitely easier to comprehend. As Kenneth Eble has observed, the difference between "the rendering of vernacular speech in the dialogue of Mark Twain and that of any of his contemporaries" is that

> Mark Twain's dialect is readable as almost all other attempts to reproduce a dialect accurately were not. When dialect was used for humorous effect, as it often was, its unreadability was compounded.
>
> Consider, for example, the familiar Joel Chandler Harris tale, "Tar-Baby Story": "'Youer stuck up, dat's w'at you is,' says Brer Rabbit, sezee, 'en I'm gwineter kyore you, dat's w'at I'm a gwineter do,' sezee. . . . "[58]

Whereas Eble believes Twain may be "better than" Joel Chandler Harris at reproducing in print a black dialect that is clear and readable, James A. Miller has suggested that Twain may also be "better at" black dialect than Paul Laurence Dunbar.[59]

Perhaps the writer who comes closest to Twain on this front is Charles Waddell Chesnutt. For example, in "The Goophered Grape-vine," which appeared in the *Atlantic Monthly* in 1887, Chesnutt wrote,

> Atter dat de niggers let de scuppernon's 'lone, en Mars Dugal' did n' hab no 'casion ter fine no mo' fault; en de season wuz mos' gone, w'en a strange gemman stop at de plantation one night ter see Mars Dugal' on some business; en his coachman, seein' de scuppernon's growin' so nice en sweet, slip 'roun' behine de smoke-house, en et all de scupper-non's he could hole. . . .[60]

Chesnutt's black dialect is about as easy to read as Twain's. Clearly, both Chesnutt and Twain appreciated the rhythm and power of black vernacular speech in special ways.[61] Their ears and their eyes allowed them to transfer that speech onto the page in ways that preserved its natural flow. Both Twain's Jim and Chesnutt's Uncle Julius manage to speak in dialect without renouncing their claim to being human and without weakening their claim on the reader's attention. Both authors had a special talent for creating characters who, while true to their vernacular roots, also managed to "speak like a man" in a way that creates, attributes, and commands human dignity.

Twain's efforts to focus the reader's attention on Jim's humanity were not lost on Booker T. Washington. In a 1910 memorial tribute to Twain in the *North American Review*, Washington hazarded a rare foray into literary criticism. Twain's "interest in the negro race" is "perhaps expressed best," Washington wrote, in *Huckleberry Finn*. "I do not believe any one can read this story closely,

> . . . without becoming aware of the deep sympathy of the author in "Jim." In fact, before one gets through with the book, one cannot fail to observe that in some way or other the author, without making com-ment and without going out of his way, has somehow succeeded in making his readers feel a genuine respect for "Jim," in spite of the igno-rance he displays.[62]

Twain's sympathy for "the commonest man and woman," and his willingness to break all the rules of proper English to express that sympathy, Washington felt, were central to his success as an author:

> In a word, he succeeded in literature as few men of any age have suc-ceeded, because he stuck close to nature and to the common people, and in doing so he disregarded in large degree many of the ordinary rules of rhetoric which often serve merely to cramp and make writers unnatural and uninteresting.[63]

Mark Twain onstage with Booker T. Washington at Carnegie Hall at a Tuskegee fundraiser of which Twain was co-chair, 1906. (Courtesy, the Mark Twain Papers, The Bancroft Library)

Washington, who began his tribute by noting his long friendship with Twain and his several visits to him at his home, in Hartford and New York, went on to observe,

> . . . I think I have never known him to be so stirred up on any one question as he was on that of the cruel treatment of the natives in the Congo Free State. In his letter to Leopold, the late King of the Belgians, in his own inimitable way he did a service in calling to the attention of the world the cruelties practised upon the black natives of the Congo that had far-reaching results. I saw him several times in connection with his efforts to bring about reforms in the Congo Free State, and he never seemed to tire of talking on the subject and planning for better conditions.[64]

Twain's work on behalf of "the black natives of the Congo" and his efforts to make "his readers feel a genuine respect for 'Jim'" were of a piece for Washington; they both implicitly "exhibited his sympathy and interest in the masses of the negro people."[65]

Despite Washington's encomiums, however, a troubling fact remains: reading *Huckleberry Finn* in an American secondary-school classroom can be an enormously painful experience for a black student. Twain's sympathy for Jim may have been genuine, but Jim's voice retains enough of minstrelsy in it to be demeaning and depressing. Black students reading the book may well identify—as Ralph Ellison and his brother did—with Huck, instead of Jim. Given our awareness now of the extent to which *Huck's* voice was black, black students who find themselves identifying with Huck may feel somewhat less ambivalence. After all, they are not identifying "against" their race: rather, they are choosing which of two black voices in the book they find more appealing. Nonetheless, Jim, the major figure in the book who sounds black, looks black, and is black, is still there, and must be dealt with.

One cannot get around the fact that Jim's voice is, ultimately, a diminished voice, a voice cramped within boundaries as confining as his prison-shack on the Phelps Plantation. It is not a voice with which any student, black or white, whose self-esteem is intact would choose to identify for very long. Yet it is often the only black voice on the syllabus.

This state of affairs must not prevail. Jim must not be the only African-American voice from the nineteenth century that is heard in the classroom. Twain's novel must not be the only book that raises issues of American race relations. The only way to counter the demeaning experience of encountering Jim's voice is by adding others, by exposing students to the eloquence of Frederick Douglass and W. E. B. DuBois, to the "signifying" wit of Charles W. Chesnutt and Paul Laurence Dunbar, to folktales and folk sermons, to the rhetorical power of Sojourner Truth, to the lucid anger of Ida B. Wells. These voices have long deserved a place in our classrooms in their own right. But our new awareness of the role of African-American voices in shaping mainstream American literary traditions gives us a new argument against those who challenge the legitimacy of their presence.

Slave narratives, for example, inspired Twain throughout his career.[66] During much of his adult life he was surrounded by family and friends (such as Jervis Langdon and Harriet Beecher Stowe) who shared this interest. The presence of slave narratives in Twain's library, references to them in his letters and conversations, and echoes, in his fiction, of some of their characteristic incidents or strategies[67] suggest a rich familiarity and strong interest on Twain's part; slave narratives may even be the source of some of Jim's lines in *Huckleberry Finn*.[68]

Questions of cultural exchange are always complex. The distinction between, on the one hand, appreciating a culture other than one's own, allowing dimensions of that culture to infuse one's art, and, on the other, appropriating aspects of that culture as one's own, is always problematic. A model that simply assumes that powerful, dominant cultures always appropriate powerless, minority cultures is too reductive. Individual artists may be alienated from the dominant culture even if economically and socially they would seem to be a part of it; by the same token, minority artists may identify with the mainstream culture more strongly than they identify with the culture of their own community. The nature of creating art, by definition, involves simultaneously appreciating and appropriating multiple aspects of the cultures that surround one.[69] As David Bradley has noted, the notion that one particular group "owns" a particular cultural form is an assumption necessary for the concept of "appropriation" to make sense; ideas of ownership along these lines (which Bradley suggests may be rooted in Eurocentric concepts of private property) are at odds with alternative models that may prove more compelling.[70] The work of scholars in a wide range of fields, from literary theory to history, art history, music history, and cultural anthropology, suggests that cultural exchange takes place within parameters that are less predictable than those that shape a society's economic and political structures.[71]

Mark Twain's use of black voices in *Huckleberry Finn* may have been an act of appreciation, rather than appropriation. It is an act of appropriation, however, to delegate to that novel the entire burden of representing African-American voices from the nineteenth century, or of engaging students in questions about black-white relations in America. Our classrooms must be as open to and appreciative of African-American voices as was Mark Twain's imagination.

Part
Four

BREAK DANCING IN THE
DRAWING ROOM

7

Did you ever see the like before?

Mark Twain was no stranger to what Ralph Ellison has called "the interrelatedness of blackness and whiteness."[1] In the "Raftsmen's Chapter," which was written for *Huckleberry Finn*, removed at the suggestion of Twain's publisher, and restored in the California edition of the novel published in 1985, one of the raftsmen, all of whom are *white*,

> patted juba, and the rest turned themselves loose on a regular old-fashioned keel-boat break-down.[2]

"Patting juba" was a well-known African dance popular among the slaves. The name of the dance comes from Bantu, in which "juba," or "diuba," means to pat or beat time.[3] As Solomun Northup described it in his 1853 slave narrative, the dance involved "striking the hands on the knees, then striking the hands together, then striking the right shoulder with one hand, the left with the other—all the while keeping time with the feet, and singing."[4] A turn-of-the-century observer noted that the standard position for "patting juba" "was usually a half-stoop or forward bend,"[5] the standard position for a wide range of African dances to this day.[6]

The African and African-American roots of the "break-down" that the other raftsman danced are also well-documented. "Break-downs," the dance from which our contemporary "break dancing" developed,[7] had been observed among slaves as early as 1700.[8]

Charles Dickens, in his *American Notes*, described a break-down dancer he had seen in 1842:

> Single shuffle, double shuffle, cut and crosscut: snapping his fingers, rolling his eyes, turning in his knees, presenting the back of his legs in front, spinning about on his toes and heels . . . dancing with two left legs, two right legs, two wooden legs, two wire legs, two spring legs— all sorts of legs and no legs.[9]

Dickens's reference to the break-down dancer's dancing with "no legs" is echoed by James Haskins's 1990 description of some typical break-dancing routines: "Lofting (diving into the air and landing on the hands with the body still in the air and the legs high), the Bridge (a backward handstand), and the Backspin (spinning on the floor, with the back as a fulcrum)."[10]

In Hartford in 1874, on the snowy evening when Twain found it hard to "come back" from the trance he had sung himself into singing "Swing Low, Sweet Chariot," "Go Down, Moses," and "Golden Slippers," his guests, the Aldriches and the Howellses, soon "saw another aspect of their extraordinary host."[11] Justin Kaplan writes that after singing the spirituals, Twain "wanted to go for a walk. They had run out of ale, and though he could call on the servants to run errands for him," he decided to go himself.

> . . . He tried the whiskey at the saloon where he bought the ale. He came back excited, hilarious, distinctly overheated. . . . And, in a crowning act of confident alienation from his guests, he twisted his body into the likeness of a crippled uncle or a Negro at a hoe-down and danced strange dances for them. Howells always remembered that evening, the joy and disoriented surprise of the guests, Livy's first reaction of dismay and "her low, despairing cry of, 'Oh, Youth!'"[12]

Could Twain have been dancing a "break-down" himself that memorable evening in 1874?

Mrs. Thomas Bailey Aldrich, one of the visitors who witnessed his "strange dances," described his performance like this:

> . . . the wet low shoes had been exchanged for a pair of white cowskin slippers, with the hair outside, and clothed in them, with most sober and smileless face, he twisted his angular body into all the strange contortions known to the dancing darkies of the South.[13]

Twain's choice of soft cowskin slippers instead of shoes, and his "strange contortions" would not have seemed strange to dance historians Marshall and Jean Stearns, who would probably have associated them with those elements they label as the first two "key characteristics of African dance."

> First, because it is danced on the naked earth with bare feet, African dance tends to modify or eliminate such European styles as the Jig and the Clog in which the sound of shoe on wooden floor is of primary importance. . . . Second, African dance is frequently performed from a crouch, knees flexed and body bent at the waist.[14]

Whites in the South customarily had extensive exposure to black dances. As James Haskins has observed,

> From the very beginning, the dances of the slaves interested and intrigued their white masters, and before long slave dances were being used as a form of entertainment for whites. When the master had a party, he would summon the most talented dancers from the slave quarters and have them dance for his guests. At other times, he might take his guests to the slave quarters on a Saturday night to watch the slaves dancing for themselves. . . . Sometimes, whites danced right along with the slaves. Isaac Jefferson, a slave at Thomas Jefferson's plantation at Monticello, reported that Thomas' brother, Randolph Jefferson, "used to come out among black people, play the fiddle, and dance half the night."[15]

Like Randolph Jefferson, and like the white raftsmen in *Huckleberry Finn*, Twain apparently relaxed by dancing African-American dances. Some of those present when he did responded with "joy" as well as shock.[16] Others found their sense of propriety offended. Dancing "break-downs" in the servants' quarters was one thing; but doing it in the drawing room was quite another. Break dancing in the drawing room can serve as a nice metaphor for Twain's behavior as an artist in *Huckleberry Finn*.

In November of 1874, "Sociable Jimmy" ran in the *New York Times* and "A True Story" was published in the *Atlantic Monthly*. In that one month, Twain thereby got two feisty, earthy, vernacular-speaking African-American figures into some of the finest drawing rooms in America.[17] Several months before, Twain had committed to paper in the manuscript of *Tom Sawyer* his earliest sketch of an innocent, ignorant, vernacular-speaking white boy named Huckleberry Finn. But all of these figures remained contained within a narrative "frame" in which the author, a Standard-English-speaking narrator, bracketed their tale. Such a "frame," as Kenneth Lynn notes, was "the structural trademark of Southwestern humor."[18] Augustus Baldwin Longstreet and his successors

> found that the frame was a convenient way of keeping their first-person narrators outside and above the comic action, thereby drawing a *cordon sanitaire*, so to speak, between the morally irreproachable Gentleman and the tainted life he described. . . . [The] literary mask of the Southwestern humorists was that of a cool and collected personality whose own emotions were thoroughly in hand.

Mark Twain's elegant drawing room in his home in Hartford. (Courtesy, the Mark Twain Memorial, Hartford)

By containing their satires within a frame, the humorists also assured their conservative readers of something they had to believe in before they could find such humor amusing, namely, that the Gentleman was in complete control of the situation he described, as he was of himself. . . . Finally, the frame device was a way of driving home, explicitly and directly, the social values of the author. . . . To convert the entire community to the temperate values of Whiggery was the ultimate purpose of Southwestern humor, and the frame was the place where those values were most overtly insisted on.[19]

Jimmy, Aunt Rachel, and Huck as he appears in *Tom Sawyer* are formally "introduced" to the reader by the educated narrator who, in reassuringly conventional prose, frames their informal, lower-class, colloquial speech.[20] Ushered into polite society as the rather eccentric guests of Mr. Mark Twain, these characters' first appearances in the best drawing rooms drew relatively little notice.

Everything changed when Huck made *his* debut as an "author."[21] He entered the drawing room uninvited and unannounced and started talking immediately—coarse talk, irreverent talk, *black* talk. Imagine this unrefined young man behaving the way Jimmy did in "Sociable Jimmy":

> He sat down in a big arm-chair, hung both his legs over one of the arms, and looked comfortable and conversational.[22]

Imagine that he doesn't stop talking until several hundred pages later!

In this context, the objections of the Concord Public Library to Twain's book when it first appeared take on a special edge. The *Boston Transcript* reported,

> The Concord (Mass.) Public Library committee has decided to exclude Mark Twain's latest book from the library. One member of the committee says that, while he does not wish to call it immoral, he thinks it contains but little humor, and that of a very coarse type. He regards it as the veriest trash. The librarian and the other members of the committee entertain similar views, characterizing it as rough, coarse and inelegant.[23]

The same member of the committee who regarded the book as "the veriest trash" was quoted as expounding on his objections as follows:

> It deals with a series of adventures of a very low grade of morality; it is couched in the language of a rough, ignorant dialect, and all through its pages there is a systematic use of bad grammar and an employment of rough, coarse, inelegant expressions. It is also very irreverent. To sum up, the book is flippant and irreverent in its style. It deals with a series of experiences that are certainly not elevating. The whole book is of a class that is much more profitable for the slums than it is for respectable people. . . .[24]

The *Boston Globe* seemed to understand that Twain's departure from conventional, high-flown "literary" language in the book had a great deal to do with the library's contempt. Citing the library's position that the book was "too 'coarse' for a place among the classic tomes that educate and edify the people," a *Globe* reporter quipped,

> When *Mark* writes another book he should think of the Concord School of Philosophy and put a little more whenceness of the hereafter among his nowness of the here.[25]

The journalist understood the significance of Twain's linguistic challenge to genteel literary norms. As Peter Messent has put it, "Twain, in writing *Huckleberry Finn*, opposed and thus deprivileged this official voice," "completely shattering," in the process, "the accepted boundaries of literary language" in America.[26]

The *Boston Evening Traveller* weighed in with a front-page editorial in support of the Concord Library's decision, asserting that the portions of the book that "have disfigured the *Century* magazine, are enough to tell any reader how offensive the whole thing must be."

The Library Committee did well to banish the book, the *Traveller* contended, on the

> ground that it is trashy and vicious. It is time that this influential pseudonym should cease to carry into homes and libraries unworthy productions. . . . The trouble with Mr. Clemens is that he has no reliable sense of propriety.[27]

The man is break dancing in the drawing room! Can't a stop be put to it?

Kenneth Lynn marks 1876 as the year "Mark Twain began to pit himself in imaginative opposition to the respectable community whose mores he had so eagerly adopted at the beginning of the '70s and whose approval he had so anxiously cultivated."[28] For Lynn, the defining event of this new stance vis-à-vis propriety and respectability is the subversive story Twain wrote and read to the Monday Evening Club that year, "Facts Concerning the Recent Carnival of Crime in Connecticut," in which the main character quite literally kills his conscience.

Lynn contends that starting that year, and "in his major works of fiction that came after 'Carnival,'" both Twain and his heroes (to varying degrees) endeavored to disrupt and elude "the coercions of social conventions."[29] Lynn's idea that in 1876 Twain decided (as an artist) to break with the "respectable community" whose values had defined him since shortly before his marriage is consistent with all that the phrase "break dancing in the drawing room" is meant to suggest. For 1876, after all, is also the year Twain took the daring step of making Huck an author.

Innumerable other writers since at least the 1830s had made vernacular speakers, white and black, the focal points of their fiction. But Twain's novel was different. What was so offensive about *Huckleberry Finn*, and what helped destine it to outdistance all of the productions of his peers and precursors in the immortality sweepstakes, were one and the same thing: by making Huck the "author" of his own book, Twain validated the *authority* of vernacular culture more boldly than any book that had gone before.[30]

By empowering Huck to tell his own story in his own words, Twain staked out a vast new territory of American experience as the stuff from which one could fashion "art."[31] In the process, the "black" dimension of Huck's voice made its mark on our culture as well. It prepared the way for generations of white Americans to appreciate, at least to some degree, the artistic productions of African-American writers. It also helped some African-American writers gain the confidence to shape their own traditions and experience into art.[32]

Why was Twain himself so silent on the role of African-American voices—like Jimmy's and Jerry's—in shaping his art? It is possible, of course, that he was unaware of the roots of his inspiration.[33] Jimmy's voice and Jerry's satire may have become so incorporated into Mark Twain's own artistic persona that he forgot that they were not always there. Such blurring of lines of origin is understandable. But, by the same token, it would be naive to assume that even if Twain had known exactly how indebted he was to figures like Jimmy and Jerry in his art, he would have acknowledged the fact forthrightly.

During the period in which Twain was attempting to build a reputation, achieve respectability, and earn a place for himself among the ranks of America's men of letters, claiming Jimmy or Jerry as a literary ancestor would have been akin to admitting to bastardy. It is true that Joel Chandler Harris readily acknowledged that "Uncle Remus" was a "'human syndicate' of three or four black men he had known."[34] But then Harris characterized himself as "An Accidental Author," as one who

> [knew] nothing of what is termed literary art. I have had no opportunity to nourish any serious literary ambition, and the possibility is that if such an opportunity had presented itself I would have refused to take advantage of it.[35]

Harris was prone to refer to himself as a "compiler" of tales, as distinguished from a "literary" man. At one point he even considered getting a "literary" man to "put more 'art' into his next volume" of Uncle Remus stories.[36] By way of contrast, Mark Twain (who was known to call himself a "Literary Person")[37] was so obsessed with protecting the rights of authors—of "literary men," as opposed to mere compilers—that he devoted much effort to building support for an international copyright law.[38] Although some of Harris's modesty may have been a consciously crafted part of his public persona, and although Twain only began to take himself seriously as a "literary man" relatively late in life, the fact remains that Twain never characterized himself as a mere "compiler."[39]

By the 1880s, when *Huckleberry Finn* appeared, no African-American fiction writer had yet achieved the kind of literary stature to which Twain aspired.[40] As Henry Louis Gates, Jr., has noted, early fiction by African-American writers received only very scant reviews in this country, primarily in anti-slavery newspapers.[41] The reading public had yet to be persuaded that the folk materials of African-

American life could be transmuted into a great American novel.[42] Harris's self-effacing denial of his own status as a "literary man" affirmed a paradigm that relegated folk culture to the folklorist; it was still not the stuff out of which one created "literature."

The articles dealing with African-American speech that appeared in the 1880s, the period when the *Journal of American Folklore* and the American Folklore Society came into being, failed to challenge the white supremacist ideology that ruled the day. None of the folklorists and dialect geographers had even a rudimentary acquaintance with African languages.[43] (Research informed by such knowledge would not surface until well into the twentieth century. Lorenzo D. Turner's pioneering work in 1939 was a key turning point in this field.)[44] German immigrants could make grammatical errors when speaking English and be treated with respectful indulgence; after all, their mother tongue had its own grammatical rules—indeed, it had produced some of the world's greatest literature—and they simply had not yet mastered the art of code-switching. Grammatical mistakes made by African Americans, however, were attributed to sheer denseness and stupidity by scholars who failed to recognize in their speech the "linguistic vestiges at the grammatical level" of African languages.[45] In the face of a widespread belief in race as the physical determinant of a large range of human capacities, such regularly produced grammatical deviations from Standard English as "the absence of inflectional affixes for . . . tense," and "the absence of the copula in some constructions and the use of 'be' as the habitual aspect"— were collected and presented as demonstrations of inferior mental capacity.[46]

If Twain had thought of the subject at all he might have suspected that acknowledging the African-American roots of his language and his art would not help his reputation in an era when the language of African-Americans was constantly held up to ridicule. A comment on an unlined sheet of note paper in Twain's papers suggests his keen awareness of the gap between what one said and what one really believed. "Everybody's Private Motto: It's Better to be Popular than Right."* And in a passage cancelled from "Corn-Pone Opinions," excised when this piece was published posthumously, Twain wrote, "I suppose that in more cases than we should like to admit, we have two sets of opinions: one private, the other public; one secret & sincere, the other corn-pone, & more or less tainted."* Twain may well have believed that he based Huck Finn on Tom Blankenship. Then again, that may have been simply a plausible public stance designed to avoid jeopardizing his popularity by telling the truth, assuming that he had an inkling of what the truth was. Twain may have suspected that admitting he had based his hero on a ragged, ill-mannered white child would be bad enough, that acknowledging Huck's decidedly mixed racial ancestry would saddle the child with even more trouble than either Huck or his author was ready for.

As the early reviews demonstrate, Huck's unrefined language, skepticism toward religion, and pragmatic, improvisational set of morals brought censure from many quarters. Even without his acknowledgment of a black child as a major source, Twain found the novel a source of discomfort and embarrassment. Justin Kaplan has observed,

> The spokesmen for the genteel tradition, who had taken Mark Twain to their bosoms for *The Prince and the Pauper*, a piece of literary playacting which they praised for its finish and refinement and delicacy, turned their backs on the book which sprang from his deepest personal and creative imperatives. Betrayed, rejected, and seriously confused in goal and standard, Mark Twain henceforth looked back on *Huckleberry Finn* with mingled pain, pride, and puzzlement, as on a favorite child who had brought disgrace on his father and whom the father would at times reluctantly acknowledge as his favorite and at other times reject in favor of the chaste and unexceptionable Maid of Orleans. His own conflict was mirrored within his family. Livy was fond of "dear old Huck," but was never at all comfortable with the book. Susy, whose disapproval he dreaded, disapproved of Huck, because she wanted her father not to be a humorist, naturalist, or teller of dreadful ghost stories but a writer of high seriousness, moral uplift, and thrice-purified English.[47]

It was one thing to admit to borrowing stories from Mary Ann Cord ("A True Story"), or from Uncle Dan'l ("The Golden Arm").[48] All sorts of respectable writers did that. But admitting that one's central creative strategies also emanated from the servants' quarters? That may have been too bold an idea even for Mark Twain.

It may have been too bold for the critics as well. As they turned over every proverbial stone in Twain's biography and opus for more than a century, critics managed to ignore Jimmy, Jerry, and African-American oral traditions almost completely. Why? The problem may have been the paradigm with which they approached African-American voices to begin with. Jimmy's talk and Jerry's "signifying," for example, were classified as "not art." (After all, how could utterances so coarse, illiterate, and ephemeral be "art"? And how could people of Jimmy's or Jerry's race, class, and circumstances be considered capable of producing "art"?[49]) They were not deemed important and therefore did not receive the attention devoted to other sources of Twain's work that critics did probe—such as the literary comedy of *Carpet-Bag* editor B. P. Shillaber or the novels of Charles Dickens.[50] The fact that much of Twain's humor reads not at all like that of his white contemporaries failed to give critics pause. The paradigm still went unchallenged: Twain was just "better at it," rather than qualitatively different.

Discussing African-American verbal creativity in a different context, Roger Abrahams comments on the difficulties people who "have invested their creative energies and imaginations heavily in books" may have in understanding the essentially "oral-aural world view" preserved in certain parts of the African-American community.

> Many ethnocentric judgements about blacks stem from the white man's inability to understand or appreciate the creative aspects of living in an oral atmosphere. He neither understands nor remembers the ways in which an effective talker-performer may strongly influence our attitudes. He does not value words effectively used in speaking events enough to confer high social status on the effective speaker.

This limitation often makes it hard for people rooted in a literate world view to appreciate the creativity involved in "good talking capable of totally enlisting the attention and support of an audience."[51] Mark Twain was an avid reader and a painstaking writer, but he aspired all his life to be "an effective talker-performer" as well, "capable of totally enlisting the attention and support of an audience." "Good talking" excited him. He sought it out, rejoiced in its presence, and recorded it for future reference. His greatest novel, *Huckleberry Finn*, was inspired, in large part, by the "creative aspects" of the "oral atmosphere" in which speakers like Jimmy and Jerry lived.

8

You may be a white man, white as the drifting snow

Writings left unpublished at his death, and which, for the most part, remain unpublished to this day, suggest that during the years that followed the publication of *Huckleberry Finn* Twain sporadically continued to question his culture's rigid racial divisions and hierarchies. Those were not auspicious times, however, to voice such challenges.

In the early 1890s, Dr. Eugene Rollin Corson, an erudite Savannah physician, claimed to have "proven," with the help of elaborate data and statistics, his assertion that African Americans "lacked the intelligence to care for themselves properly." Denied the benevolent control of slaveholders, they "quickly reverted to savagery" and were "destined to disappear, a victim of 'the struggle for existence against a superior race.'"[1]

In an enormously influential book entitled *Race Traits and Tendencies of the American Negro*, published in 1896, a German-born insurance statistician named Frederick L. Hoffman declared that racial characteristics "lie at the root of all social difficulties and problems." "Inferior organisms and constitutional weaknesses," Hoffman believed, were among "the most pronounced race characteristics of the American negro." Religion and education were useless, "because such external influences did not affect basic hereditary characteristics."[2] In this book, which bulges with footnotes and statistical tables,

Hoffman charges "the American negro" with, among other things, "an immense amount of immorality, *which is a race trait*."[3]

In 1900, the Chief Statistician of the United States Census Bureau, Walter F. Willcox, pronounced that blacks would eventually "succumb to the effects of the 'disease, vice, and profound discouragement' that generally accompanied the feeble efforts of a 'lower people' to compete with their racial superiors." A chorus of scholars and nonprofessional pundits confirmed the conclusion reached by Professor William Smith of Tulane University in his 1905 book, *The Color Line*, "The doom that awaits the Negro has been prepared in like measure for all inferior races."[4]

It is fashionable, among some contemporary critics, to claim that Twain generally affirmed this deafening din of racial determinism. The charge is based, most often, upon critics' interpretation of Twain's intentions when he created the character Tom Driscoll in *Pudd'nhead Wilson*, his most important work of fiction of his later period.[5] Tom, though raised to think he was white, is 1/32 part black, the son of a slave. He is also a thoroughly despicable human being— weak-willed, cowardly, brutally cruel, and dishonest. Michael Rogin argues that Twain makes Tom's

> 'one drop of Negro blood' (the Swedish title of the novel) into the sign of an explanation for his guilt. That is not just what Roxana, Tom's mother, says; it is what the novel says.[6]

Carmen Subryan reaches the same conclusion: "Twain seemed to be stressing that the one drop of Black blood in [Tom's] veins" was responsible for his failure as a human being.[7] Numerous other scholars have shared this interpretation.[8]

A passage Twain originally wrote in the manuscript but cut from the novel before he published the final version, however, suggests that, at least when he was writing the book, he was experimenting with a different, and more complex, line of reasoning. Tom ponders his fate, having just realized that he can be sold like a piece of property because of his 1/32 part black blood:

> In his broodings in the solitudes, he searched himself for the reasons of certain things, & in toil & pain he worked out the answers:
> Why was he a coward? It was the "nigger" in him. The nigger *blood?* Yes, the nigger blood degraded from original courage to cowardice by decades & generations of insult & outrage inflicted in circumstances which forbade reprisals, & made mute & meek endurance ~~acceptance~~ the only refuge & defence.
> Whence came that in him which was high, & whence that which was base? That which was high came from either blood, & was the monopoly of neither color; but that which was base was the white blood in

him debased by the brutalizing effects of a ~~long-descended~~ long-drawn heredity of slave-owning, with the habit of abuse which the possession of irresponsible power always creates & perpetuates, by a law of human nature. So he argued.'*

In this passage, Twain actually went further than any of his white peers did in their fiction—including George Washington Cable—in his rejection of a hierarchy of color.[10]

Did Twain take seriously the idea that "what was high came from either blood and was the monopoly of neither color," that human beings had different degrees of virtue and talent, but that race was simply irrelevant? If so, such a notion ran directly counter to his culture's dominant ideology of racial inferiority. Even more subversive is the implication that black could be superior to white. This idea did more than challenge the hierarchy of racial traits to which Americans at the time—often black as well as white—so readily assented. It turned it completely upside-down. Several comments in Twain's unpublished writings from the 1890s and the turn of the century suggest that Twain seriously entertained both of these ideas.

An unpublished sketch of Twain's probably dating from the 1890s entitled "The Quarrel in the Strong-Box," for example, parodies the racial discourse of his day in a fantasy in which different denominations of money represent the culture's hierarchy of color.

> Upon a certain occasion a quarrel arose among the money in the banker's strong-box, upon matters of right & privilege. It began ~~with the~~ between a Nickel & a Copper. In conversation the Nickel chanced to make a disparaging remark about the Copper, whereupon the latter spoke up with heat & said—
>
> "I will have you to know that I am as good as you are."
>
> "Since when?" retorted the Nickel, with scorn.
>
> "Since the Declaration of Independence said 'all money is created free & equal.' What do you say to that?"
>
> "I say it is nothing but a form of speech & isn't true. You know quite well that in society I am more welcome than you are; that more deference is paid to me than to you, & that no one would grant you are equal in rank to me. . . ."[11]*

The nickel is put in his place by "an emaciated half dollar," who is put in *his* place by "a Ten-Dollar Gold-Piece," who is dismissed "with asperity" by "a Hundred Dollar Bill," who is pushed to the side by "a Thousand Dollar Bond," whereupon a general free-for-all ensues, frightens away a burglar, and brings the police. The judge resolves the dispute with a disquisition on the nature of equality that makes clear the idea that while there may be differences that create inequality—differences of "strength, health, stature, weight, comeliness, complexion, intellect, & so on"—denomination (read "race") is completely irrelevant. The "Copper" and the "Thousand Dollar Bond" (in the 1890s, at least) all earn "five per cent."[12]*

The meaninglessness of race as a category is a theme Twain addressed once again in the unpublished "Family Sketch" he wrote in 1906. During the financial panic of 1893, Twain was back in New York after two years in Europe and was pleasantly surprised by a visit from George Griffin, his former butler from Hartford. "George called at the hotel, faultlessly dressed, as was his wont, & we walked up town together. . . ."

> He had been . . . serving as a waiter a couple of years, at the Union League Club & acting as banker for the other waiters, forty in number, of his own race. . . . Also, he was lending to white men outside. . . . The times were desperate, failure & ruin were everywhere, woe sat upon every countenance. I had seen nothing like it before, I have seen nothing like it since. But George's ark floated serenely upon the troubled waters. . . . he was a prosperous & happy person & about the only one thus conditioned I met in New York.[13]*

Twain provided more detail about George's financial dealings in a letter he wrote to Livy that night. Evidently members of the Club, "gentlemen who were wealthy till the panic struck them," now found they had "to borrow of George on their watches & diamonds to pay their Club dues & escape expulsion."[14]* Twain's own severe financial problems during these years probably contributed to his admiration of George's skills at making and managing money.

Twain decided on the spur of the moment to visit the offices of the *Century Magazine* and *St. Nicholas Magazine* with George. Years later, Twain recorded his memories of that afternoon:

> On our way uptown that day in New York I turned in at the Century building, & made George go up with me. The array of clerks in the great counting-room glanced up with curiosity—*a "white man" & a negro walking together was a new spectacle to them.* The glances embarrassed George, but not me, for the companionship was proper: in *some ways he was my equal, in some others my superior*; & besides, deep down in my interior I knew that the difference between any two of those poor transient things called human beings that have ever crawled about this world & then hid their little vanities in the compassionate shelter of the grave was but microscopic, trivial, a mere difference between worms.[15]*

Twain's decision to put quotation marks around the words "white man" is interesting. Does it reflect the irony inherent in our often wildly inaccurate color-labeling of racial and social categories? Or might it imply his desire to distance himself from the privileges a "white" skin entailed? Might it suggest that he considered it foolish to take the term as indicating anything at all about a person? Does it reflect a thought that "race" may be more a social construction than a biological determinant?

And what of the idea of black "superiority"? In the case at hand, Twain suspected, probably correctly, that George Griffin's talent for making and holding onto money was better than his own. The superhuman strength and extraordinary altruism demonstrated by John Lewis when he had stopped a runaway horse to save the lives of Twain's sister-in-law, her child, and the child's nurse remained in Twain's mind for years. If in 1850 Twain considered Jerry to be "the greatest man in the United States,"* clearly he thought of him as superior to himself, a mere child with no sense of what the future might bring. Some of the most powerful, eloquent, and moving speakers Twain had ever met—such as Mary Ann Cord, Frederick Douglass, and "Uncle Dan'l"—were black. Twain appreciated their superior gifts from the vantage point of a writer who struggled all his life to have an effect on his audience equal to the effect these speakers had on him. Twain could, and did, entertain this notion seriously, on the basis of personal experience.

The language of that suppressed passage from *Pudd'nhead Wilson*, however, also suggests the intriguing possibility that Twain may have been exposed to some of these ideas by black speakers during his childhood. Twain's comment that "what was base" in Tom Driscoll's character stemmed from "the white blood in him debased by the brutalizing effects of a long-drawn heredity of slave-owning" curiously echoes comments that were commonly expressed in the slave quarters, and were recorded in slave narratives. Thomas L. Webber writes,

> Each generation of slaveholding families was thought to become more and more debased. According to [James C.] Pennington, "this decline in slaveholding families is a subject of observation and daily remark among slaves. . . . As far back as I can recollect, indeed, it was a remark among slaves, that every generation of slaveholders are more and more inferior."[16]

"Black superiority," Webber notes, was one of the "broad themes which gave shape and meaning to the way [slaves] understood their world and acted in it."[17]

Twain's writing on the subject of race remains complex and ambiguous, but these unpublished comments absolutely contradict the simplistic contention that he assumed "the existence of a natural racial hierarchy" and accepted "as a premise the biological inferiority of Negroes."[18] That is not to say, however, that he eliminated all paternalistic condescension from his behavior, nor to imply that he systematically expunged all expressions that reflected these popular prejudices from his conversation and correspondence. The assumption of "a natural racial hierarchy," for example, informs the joke Twain made in a letter to William Dean Howells in 1872 after reading Howells's favorable review of *Roughing It*. "I am as uplifted and reassured" by the review, Twain wrote, "as a mother who has given birth to a white baby when she was awfully afraid it was going to be a mulatto."[19]

The premise that presumably gives the joke its edge is that the mother's fears may be justified. In other words, she knows that she has already broken the taboo against miscegenation as well as that against female promiscuity. What anxieties might be reflected in Twain's telling of that joke? Married to Olivia Langdon for two years, after an arduous course of proving his "respectability" to her family, Twain was still preoccupied with securing his place in the literary world of the East. If we put Twain, who has just given birth to a book, in the place of the white mother with whom he identifies in the joke, his fear, literally, is that his book will turn out to be noticeably part-black. What he meant, of course, was that he feared his book might turn out to be coarse or unrefined—insufficiently "respectable." What he said, however, was "mulatto."

The idea of a "natural racial hierarchy," the implicit subtext of Twain's "mulatto" joke, remained firmly in place in American popular thought throughout Twain's lifetime. In 1910, the year of Twain's death, for example, the Chicago *Broad-Ax* ran the following news item:

Negro Blood Divorce Cause

Hidden Negro blood in the wife's veins is sufficient ground for annulment of her marriage to a white husband, according to a decision of the courts of this state, handed down today.

Wm. Horton, a wealthy plumber, who received an interlocutory decree of annulment today in the State Supreme Court, charged that his wife, Edith May Williams, although really a mulatto, had represented herself to him before marriage as of Spanish descent.[20]

While popular thought reiterated the familiar prejudices, however, Twain himself changed his view on this subject. By the 1890s Twain could not have told that "mulatto" joke: the notion of mixing races now struck him as a rather salutary idea. Black Africans, he wrote, in *Following the Equator*, "should have been crossed with the Whites. It would have improved the Whites and done the Natives no harm."[21] It is impossible to know whether Twain was ever even partially aware of the extent to which black voices had crossed with white ones to produce *Huckleberry Finn*.

More than eighty years after Twain's death we are just beginning to reconstruct his imaginative melding of black and white voices, traditions and sensibilities in this novel. A critic who died when Twain was still a boy, however, was certain that such a blending would have to take place if a genuinely American literature were to come into being. In 1846 Margaret Fuller wrote, "it does not follow because many books are written by persons born in America that there exists an American literature."[22] One day—but not in her lifetime, Fuller predicted—American literature would come into its own. But, she sagely wrote, *"that day will not rise till the fusion of races among us is more complete."*[23] In this novel by the man William Faulkner called "the first truly American writer,"[24] Fuller's prophecy, uncanny in its prescience, came true.

9

The more come in with a free good will,
Make the band seem sweeter still.

In his pathbreaking 1970 essay, "What America Would Be Like Without Blacks," Ralph Ellison wrote,

> If we can resist for a moment the temptation to view everything having to do with Negro Americans in terms of their racially imposed status, we become aware of the fact that for all the harsh reality of the social and economic injustices visited upon them, these injustices have failed to keep Negroes clear of the cultural mainstream; Negro Americans are in fact one of its major tributaries.[1]

One important dimension of the "cultural mainstream" that African Americans have shaped, Ellison noted, is the language. "The American nation," he wrote,

> is in a sense the product of the American language, a colloquial speech . . . that began by merging the sounds of many tongues, brought together in the struggle of diverse regions. And whether it is admitted or not, much of the sound of that language is derived from the timbre of the African voice and the listening habits of the African ear.[2]

Ellison called *"the black man a co-creator of the language that Mark Twain raised to the level of literary eloquence. . . ."*[3] My research and interpretations clearly support this assertion.

"The spoken idiom of Negro Americans," Ellison declared,

> its flexibility, its musicality, its rhythms, freewheeling diction, and metaphors, as projected in Negro American folklore, were absorbed by

the creators of our great nineteenth-century literature even when the majority of blacks were still enslaved. Mark Twain celebrated it in the prose of *Huckleberry Finn*; without the presence of blacks, the book could not have been written. No Huck and Jim, no American novel as we know it.[4]

As the foregoing chapters make clear, Ellison's intuitions were stunningly correct—in general terms, and in particular terms as well. Rather than reflecting a consensus of twentieth-century scholarly opinion, however, Ellison's insights stick out like a car headed the wrong way down a one-way street.

The role of "the spoken idiom of Negro Americans" in shaping the language of Southerners was doggedly denied by scholars throughout most of this century. Their comments echoed the dismissive tone Thomas Jefferson had used when describing African-American speech. "Never yet could I find a black had uttered a thought above the level of plain narration," Jefferson wrote; he found the imagination of African-Americans to be "dull, tasteless and anomalous."[5]

In a 1924 article entitled "The English of the Negro" in the *American Mercury*, George Krapp wrote that "it is reasonably safe to say that not a single detail of Negro pronunciation or Negro syntax can be proved to have other than English origins."[6] And in 1928 H. P. Johnson announced that ". . . Negroes have made only one contribution to the language of the English speaking world. They have given it the word, buckra, which means white man."[7]

As J. L. Dillard, a leading authority on the subject, observed in 1972,

> Without evidence, but loyal to a commitment to the British origins theory, dialect geographers have assumed that the Negro got his dialect from the Southern white—that the influence has been almost exclusively unidirectional.[8]

According to Dillard, scholars often "disallowed" evidence to the contrary. They preferred to believe in theories that

> will not allow for the spread of Negro dialect features to the white Southern population, except in very restricted areas adjacent to Gullah territory. Orthodox works like Cleanth Brooks's *The Relation of the Alabama-Georgia Dialect to the Provincial Dialects of Great Britain* (1935) have been specifically aimed at dispelling the heretical notion of Negro influence on white speech which was propounded in L. W. Payne's article "A Word List from East Alabama." . . .[9]

Payne had written, in the 1905 article Dillard cites,

> The ordinary southerner would scoff at the idea that it is the negro dialect of his section that has largely molded its own speech. For my

own part, after a somewhat careful study of East Alabama dialect, I am convinced that the speech of the white people, the dialect I have spoken all my life and the one I have tried to record here, is more largely colored by the language of the Negroes than by any other single influence.[10]

Although Brooks's position generally found favor among twentieth-century scholars,[11] many casual eighteenth- and nineteenth-century observers often made comments similar to Payne's. In 1746, for example, a visitor to the United States observed in the *London Magazine* that the American planters gave their children too much freedom "to prowl amongst the young Negroes, which insensibly causes them to imbibe their Manners and broken Speech."[12] Fanny Kemble, in *A Journal of Residence on a Georgia Plantation in 1838–39*, observed, ". . . The children of the owners, brought up among [the slaves] acquire their Negro mode of talking."[13] And in 1864, Thomas L. Nichols noted in *Forty Years of American Life* that

> Southern speech is clipped, softened, and broadened by the Negro admixture. The child learns its language from its Negro nurse, servants, and playmates, and this not unpleasant patois is never quite eradicated.[14]

John Bennett recalled in 1909 that among the Charleston aristocracy of his day, "It is true that, up to the age of four, approximately, the children of the best families, even in town, are apt to speak an almost unmodified *Gullah*, caught from brown playmates and country bred nurses. . . ."[15]

While some twentieth-century scholars like Brooks resisted the idea, innumerable observers throughout the nineteenth century felt that "the ever-present Negro had more influence on the speech of the Southern white than the far-away East Anglian—or the occasional Scotsman or Irishman."[16]

This perception turns out to be largely correct. W. J. Cash, C. Vann Woodward, and Melville Herskovits concur with Dillard on this point.

As W. J. Cash noted,

> . . . in this society in which the infant son of the planter was commonly suckled by a black mammy, in which gray old men were the most loved story-tellers . . . in this society in which by far the greater number of white boys of whatever degree were more or less shaped by such companionship, and in which nearly the whole body of whites, young and old, had constantly before their eyes the example, had constantly in their ears the accent of the Negro, the relationship between the two groups was, by the second generation at least, nothing less than organic. Negro entered into white man as profoundly as white man entered into Negro.[17]

C. Vann Woodward noted the "lamentations of the [nineteenth-century] planters that *their children talked like Negroes*, sang Negro songs, preferred Negro music at their dances, and danced like Negroes."[18]

And Melville Herskovits averred that

> [I]t is not only phonetically that Southern speech has been influenced by the Negro. It is trite to point out how "musical" is Southern speech. Cadenced more than any other American dialect, it may almost be said to have melodic line, and it is not insignificant in this connection that a basic aspect of West African speech is the presence of what linguists call "significant tone" [meaning] that to pronounce a word—a phonetic combination—in different tonal registers gives it different meaning.[19]

For much of the twentieth century, however, this perspective was rarely voiced, or, when it was voiced, it was attacked vociferously. A 1935 essay entitled "Southern Speech" by William Cabell Greet is a case in point. Greet opined that while in America's "songs and dances [the negro] has added zest,"

> He has in the main used language to so little purpose that there I cannot find he has contributed anything at all.[20]

As late as the 1960s folklorists and ethnographers still found resistance to the idea that "the terms *OK*, *wow*, *uh-huh* and *unh-unh*" were African-American contributions to the American language.[21]

"Prior to the Emancipation," as Ernest F. Dunn observes,

> most well-to-do [white people in the South] tolerated the Black speech patterns in their children only up to a certain age. The formal educational experience was designed, in part, to extricate out of the child the linguistic and behavioral patterns he or she had acquired under the tutelage of her "mammy" and the "plantation playmates."[22]

After the war, Southern whites of all classes came to view "the influence of black speech patterns" as "a stigma with which [they] did not wish to be marked."[23] Part of the tenacity with which Southern whites clung to segregation might be linked, in Dunn's opinion, to these linguistic legacies: "The process of white education could not succeed in the presence of Blacks since part of the purpose of that education was to put aside Black influence."[24] Thus while educators struggled to suppress linguistic habits white children had acquired naturally living in an environment shaped by black as well as white speech patterns, numerous scholars labored tenaciously to deny any evidence of black influence on Southern white speech.[25]

If linguists were so resistant to recognizing the influence of African-American speech patterns on both Southern speech and American speech in general, it is not surprising that their colleagues in literature were content to ignore the influence of African-American traditions on mainstream texts. It may be one thing to acknowledge the black sources of the dialect spoken by black characters in a novel, or a white novelist's use of black folktales and folk beliefs. But it is quite another to explore the ways in which African-American vernacular traditions may have shaped mainstream American literature at its core.

Ellison is virtually alone in making this claim. As he put it in 1969, "I recognize no American culture which is not the partial creation of black people. I recognize no American style in literature, in dance, in music, even in assemblyline processes, which does not bear the mark of the American Negro."[26] Art historian Robert Farris Thompson voiced a variation on this theme in a lecture on "The Kongo Atlantic Tradition" in 1992: "To be white in America is to be very black. If you don't know how black you are, you don't know how American you are." Or, as C. Vann Woodward put it in 1969, "so far as their culture is concerned, all Americans are part Negro."[27]

In "Going to the Territory," Ellison elaborated on the process by which "America" became "American."

> American culture is of a whole, for that which is essentially "American" in it springs from the synthesis of our diverse elements of cultural style. . . . [I]n the days when our leaders still looked to England and the Continent for their standards of taste, the vernacular stream of our culture was creating itself out of whatever elements it found useful, including the Americanized culture of the slaves. . . . Ironically, it was the vernacular which gave expression to that very newness of spirit and outlook of which the leaders of the nation liked to boast.[28]

Ellison makes a strong case for why the vernacular is so central to our definitions of who and what we are:

> . . . on the level of culture no one group has managed to create the definitive American style. Hence the importance of the vernacular in the ongoing task of naming, defining and creating a consciousness of who and what we have come to be.[29]

Mark Twain, according to Ellison, played a key role in making the vernacular as important as it is to our sense of how we think of ourselves as a nation. Twain

> . . . transformed elements of regional vernacular speech into a medium of uniquely American literary expression and thus taught us how to capture that which is essentially American in our folkways and manners. For indeed the vernacular process is a way of establishing and discovering our national identity.[30]

It is easy to assemble a diverse litany of attestations to Twain's centrality as the quintessentially "American" artist. H. L. Mencken, for example, called Twain "the true father of our national literature, the first genuinely American artist of the blood royal."[31] Louis Budd noted that the story *Reader's Digest* ran during the *Huckleberry Finn* centennial

> quoted Charles Kuralt as speaking for the "feelings of millions of the book's admirers" when he declared on TV: "If I had to say as much about America as I possibly could in only two words, I would say these two words: 'Huck Finn.'"[32]

Budd reports that ". . . a supposedly scientific poll showed that 96% of college faculty now put *Huckleberry Finn* at the very head of the reading list for entering freshmen," and a feature article in the *Washington Post* in January 1986 deemed *Huckleberry Finn* "the greatest work of art by an American, the Sistine Chapel of our civilization."[33]

Budd finds these attitudes in earlier periods as well. He cites William Lyon Phelps's declaration in the 1920s that *Huckleberry Finn* "is not only the great American novel. It is America." In 1940 Clifton Fadiman dubbed Twain "'our Chaucer, our Homer, our Dante, our Virgil' because *Huckleberry Finn* 'is the nearest thing we have to a national epic. Just as the Declaration of Independence . . . contains in embryo our whole future history as a nation, so the language of *Huckleberry Finn* (another declaration of independence) expresses our popular character, our humor, our slant.'"[34] As David Sloane has noted, "with over 150 editions in print, selling over a quarter of a million copies a year, if American sales are added to the panoply of foreign translations in German, French, Russian and other major world languages, *Huckleberry Finn* is one of the most steadily experienced projections of America and the American spirit."[35] By 1976, 696 foreign editions of the novel had been published.[36]

In the thousands of books and articles written on *Huckleberry Finn*, however, the role of African-American oral traditions in shaping Twain's achievement gets virtually no attention.[37] Ellison was certain about that influence despite the fact that he adduced no specifics to support his theory. In a 1976 interview in *Pulp*, for example, Ellison claimed that "the American vernacular culture out of which what we identify as American writing arose was very much influenced by the oral lore, the oral literature of the Afro-American. This appears in Mark Twain."[38] Ellison's conviction on this point dates back to his high school days, when it occurred to him that

> what some of my "teachers" were calling "white literature" was not really *white* at all. . . . Part of the music of the language, part of the folklore which informed our conscious American literature came

through the interaction of the slave and the white man, and particularly
so in the South.[39]

Much as the observations of lay commentators on black and white
speech patterns in the nineteenth century resemble theories that are at
the cutting edge of dialect study today, Ellison's intuitive understanding of the dynamics of Twain's culture and of our own resonates with
insights that frame perfectly the ideas explored in this book.

"Materially, psychologically, and culturally," Ellison wrote, "part of
the nation's heritage is Negro American, and whatever it becomes
will be shaped in part by the Negro's presence. . . ."[40] As he put it
elsewhere, "American culture is part Afro-American culture, and
that's especially true in music, in literature, in dance. . . ."[41] These
statements are neither radical nor extravagant; yet Ellison knew that
they would meet with strong resistance.

> . . . by ignoring such matters as the sharing of bloodlines and cultural
> traditions by groups of widely differing ethnic origins, and by overlook-
> ing the blending and metamorphosis of cultural forms which is so char-
> acteristic of our society we misconceive our cultural identity. It is as
> though we dread to acknowledge the complex, pluralistic nature of our
> society, and as a result we find ourselves stumbling upon our true
> national identity under circumstances in which we least expect to do so.[42]

I had not yet stumbled upon either Jimmy or Jerry when I interviewed Ralph Ellison in July 1991.[43] But months later, as I listened to
the tape of our two-hour conversation and read the notes I had taken
on Ellison's work in preparation for the interview, I realized that Ellison had played an important role in preparing and shaping my
awareness of the role of African-American voices in Twain's art.

Ellison told me he first encountered Mark Twain when he was
around eight years old and promptly nicknamed his brother Herbert,
"Huck." He returned to *Huckleberry Finn* when he started to write.
"When I began to think consciously about writing naturally I went
back to it." What was it that spoke to him in Twain's work as a
writer? Were there things that it taught him that he valued when he
began writing himself?

Ellison responded,

> Well, for one thing, Mark Twain, as against so many other writers,
> knew more about the country. He knew something of its geographical
> and cultural variety. And being from the section of the country from
> which he came, he knew something about my own people. The other
> thing to say here is that as a newspaperman and as a writer he was
> interested (at least certainly aware of, maybe not at first consciously—

but he became so) in the vernacular language, which was so very important in conveying the essence of people, the spoken speech. He didn't always do it so well, but he was a pioneer.

Did Twain make Ellison aware of some of the possibilities of vernacular speech?

Oh yes. His attempts to render the speech of Southern negroes—it was very important to see the efforts, and to see what he grasped in the personalities behind the speech.

At what point did Ellison begin to understand that Twain was doing more than just writing a boys' book? At what age did he understand that it was a book that he could learn from as someone who aspired to using satire himself? Ellison says it must have been in his twenties, when he "read a lot, and after I got into Hemingway I went back to Twain." In Hemingway (who said all "modern American literature comes from . . . *Huckleberry Finn*"), Ellison was struck by

the use of vernacular speech, the rhythms, the ability to use understatement, which again, I have a connection with through my own folk tradition: so much is said, implied, in negro folk songs, negro folklore, and so on.

Ellison was aware of Twain's presence as well in the work of William Faulkner, who also acknowledged a strong debt to Twain.

. . . And of course, when I began to read Faulkner—I didn't really begin to read Faulkner until the forties, but I read it before he was rediscovered—there, reading a Southern writer who had lived very closely with Southern negroes, and who was closer to Slavery through his own family and so on, and through the manners which still obtained, again, I went back to Twain to make comparisons and to try t› trace influences.

Ellison believes the vernacular is as shaped by African-American voices today as it was in Twain's day. "Today's slang is always influenced by what comes from the Afro-American background. Just as the music is influenced by jazz, by the blues—you wouldn't have an American music without it." No one would attempt to write a segregated history of American music, but the history of American literature has, for the most part, been a segregated enterprise: white writers come from white literary ancestors, black writers from black ones. It is time to acknowledge the very mixed literary bloodlines on both sides. Ellison found Twain's "free-wheeling appropriation of the vernacular, his transforming it into an agency of literature," exhilarating and inspiring. His influence on Ellison's own work—both direct and indirect—and on the work of other African-American writers, was profound. As Ellison put it in our interview, *"he made it possible for many of us to find our own voices."*

The implications of this statement are provocative and intriguing. In what ways—conscious and unconscious, direct and indirect— might Twain have empowered black writers? Charles W. Chesnutt kept a bust of Twain in his library.[44] Ralph Ellison has a photo of Twain over his desk.[45] Other twentieth-century African-American writers, such as Langston Hughes, David Bradley, and Richard Wright, have paid eloquent homage to Twain. What did they learn from him?

In our interview, Ellison credited Twain with having been a "pioneer" in opening up new possibilities for the literary use of African-American vernacular. Ellison also appreciated Twain's use of comedy to "allow us to deal with the unspeakable," as he put it. In Ellison's view, the unspeakable that Twain addressed was "the moral situation of the United States and the contrast between our ideals and our activities," the ways in which the realities of American race relations always so sharply rebuked our national ideals, a subject that has remained central to twentieth-century African-American fiction.

Did he return to Twain at all when he was writing *Invisible Man*? "Not consciously," Ellison responded,

> but what reading does for a writer . . . [is] that you build up a bank within your unconscious. You might not even realize at the time you're putting stuff down that you're being influenced. . . .

His language is curiously reminiscent of Twain's, on a similar subject.

Did Twain shape Ellison's writing in *Invisible Man*? Some of Trueblood's lyrical descriptions have always struck me as evoking Huck's language and angle of vision. Trueblood says, for example,

> . . . I'd be awake lookin' at the lights comin' up from the water and listenin' to the sounds of the boats movin' along. . . . I'd be layin' there and it would be quiet and I could hear it comin' from way, way off. Like when you quail huntin' and it's getting dark, and you can hear the boss bird whistlin' tryin' to get the covey together again, and he's coming toward you slow and whistlin' soft 'cause he knows you somewhere around with your gun.[46]

Was Huck lurking in the background? Ellison said he "couldn't deny it." Twain's influence on him, he suggested, may have been unconscious, but it was there.[47]

Could some of the things Ellison learned from Twain be things Twain himself learned from the rhetorical performances of African-Americans? Ellison responded, *"I think it comes full circle."*

Richard Wright, too, saw in Twain's work some potent echoes

Novelist Charles W. Chesnutt (center) celebrating Mark Twain's seventieth birthday dinner in 1905 at Delmonico's restaurant in New York.
(Courtesy, the Mark Twain Papers, The Bancroft Library)

of his own childhood that he found "strangely familiar." David Bradley asked a stunned audience in Hartford in 1985 whether, even though Sam Clemens was white, Mark Twain might have been black? He then proceeded to make a case for Twain as a key figure in the development of African-American fiction.[48] Given Ellison's own debt to Twain, it is possible that some African-American writers in the twentieth century may have been influenced by Twain as mediated *through* Ellison;[49] others may have encountered him on their own.

Almost as little attention has been paid to Twain's influence on African-American voices as to the influence of African-American voices on Twain. One notable exception to this general pattern of neglect, however, is Arnold Rampersad's important 1984 essay, "*Adventures of Huckleberry Finn* and Afro-American Literature."[50] Rampersad cites some key ways in which Twain's novel "differs from the bulk of black American fiction." These include (1) Twain's use of a first-person narrator (the autobiographical voice being largely absent from African-American fiction until very recent times); (2) Twain's use of dialect (dialect did not play a central role in black fiction until the 1930s); (3) Twain's decision to entrust his story to a child (something "the black writer has been reluctant until recently" to attempt); (4) the book's status as a work "of adult fiction readily accessible to young readers" (virtually unheard of in black fiction); (5) Twain's use of humor to explore the subject of race (a generally taboo combination in black fiction—with notable exceptions, like that of Charles Chesnutt); (6) Twain's "'twinning' of white and dark-skinned characters to suggest an ideal American hero who combines the best qualities of the white and some darker race in a merger of complementary abilities and values" (an approach to characterization rejected by black fiction writers); and (7) Twain's focus on "the great question of Nature and its relationship to humanity," which Rampersad takes "to be at the heart of Mark Twain's depiction of the river" in the novel (a theme that has been largely unimportant in African-American fiction).[51]

However, Rampersad observes, the differences between *Huckleberry Finn* and African-American fiction narrow in the twentieth century. In 1943 Langston Hughes

> began building perhaps the best achievement in the fictional use of dialect by a black author when he created in the *Chicago Defender* his extremely popular character Jesse B. Semple, or "Simple." . . . The books that resulted between 1950 and 1965 (*Simple Speaks His Mind, Simple Takes a Wife, Simple Stakes a Claim, Simple's U.S.A.,* and *The Best of Simple*) were all very well received by critics, who persisted in pointing out, to the Missouri-born Hughes's great satisfaction, the similarities between his work and that of Mark Twain.[52]

"I'd not thought of it before myself," was Hughes's response when the resemblance was pointed out to him, "but am glad if there's something of the same quality there, naturally."[53] Rampersad cites as "examples in recent black fiction of the combining of autobiography and dialect in Twain's manner," Alice Childress's *A Hero Ain't Nothin' but a Sandwich* (1973), "whose thirteen-year-old narrator is Huck's age and even of his temperament" and Al Young's *Sitting Pretty* (1976), "whose hero has more than once been compared with Huck by reviewers." Rampersad also believes that in Alice Walker's best-seller *The Color Purple*, the "heroine, Celie, whether or not Walker herself would like the notion, is definitely a black country cousin of Huck Finn."[54]

Twain's awareness of what Rampersad calls "the subversive power of comedy" on the subject of race is echoed not only in Ellison's *Invisible Man*, but in "some of the writing of Chester Himes and . . . the most innovative recent black fiction—that of Ishmael Reed in particular, as in *Mumbo Jumbo* (1972), and of William Melvin Kelley, as in *dem* (1967)."[55]

And his depiction of "a moral dilemma, or moral inversion, as being at the heart of Southern, and by inference American society," prefigures the existential alienation of protagonists like Richard Wright's Bigger Thomas (*Native Son*) or Cross Damon (*The Outsider*), James Baldwin's Richard and Rufus (*Go Tell It on the Mountain* and *Another Country*), and Ellison's "wildly disoriented hero in *Invisible Man*." Rampersad concludes,

> In his stress on folk culture, on dialect, and on American humor, Mark Twain anticipated Dunbar, Hughes (who lauded Twain in an introduction to *Pudd'nhead Wilson*), Hurston, Fisher, Thurman, Ellison, Gaines, Childress, Reed, and Alice Walker; in his depiction of alienation in an American context, prominently including race, Twain anticipates other aspects of most of these writers' work and also that of Richard Wright, Chester Himes, Ann Petry, James Baldwin, and Toni Morrison.[56]

To Rampersad's list of the areas of influence one might add Twain's recognition of the intimate connection between oral culture and literature. In 1984, Toni Morrison noted that she tries to incorporate into her fiction "one of the major characteristics of Black art,"

> the ability to be both print and oral literature: to combine those two aspects so that the stories can be read in silence, of course, but one should be able to hear them as well. . . . To make the story appear oral, meandering, effortless, spoken . . . is what's important.[57]

When black and white writers looked for literary models in their efforts to translate oral culture into print, Mark Twain was available as a potential guide. He served that function for Ralph Ellison, David Bradley, Ernest Hemingway, William Faulkner, Sherwood Anderson, and many others—including Morrison herself, who acknowledges that she probably returned to Twain and reread him when she began honing her own skills as a writer.[58] Although such writers as Ellison and Morrison were able to hear on their own the black voices that had shaped America's past and present, Twain provided a model for some of the ways in which they could translate those voices into print. Twain helped his fellow writers learn, in very practical ways, how to write books that "talked."[59]

If Twain sometimes showed prescience about the kinds of issues and aesthetic strategies that would preoccupy black writers in the twentieth century, black writers sometimes expressed extraordinary insight into the difficulties of being Mark Twain. Perhaps the most perceptive one-sentence summary of Twain's struggle as a man and as a writer comes from Richard Wright: "Twain hid his conflict in satire and wept in private over the brutalities and the injustices of his civilization."[60]

Potential parallels, prefigurings, echoes, influences, and other links between Mark Twain and African-American writers deserve more attention than they have received. A number of unpublished fragments left by Twain, for example, curiously prefigure work by Frances E. W. Harper, Pauline Hopkins, James Weldon Johnson, Nella Larsen, W. E. B. DuBois, and Amiri Baraka. The possibility that Twain and these writers may have been responding to some of the same dimensions of our culture in similar ways is intriguing.[61]

And although Arnold Rampersad is undoubtedly right that there is no counterpart in black fiction to "the presence of the river" in *Huckleberry Finn* (with all its moral and symbolic implications), I cannot help wondering whether fellow Missourian Langston Hughes, who found "a first reading of *Adventures of Huckleberry Finn* so thrilling that he remained a lifelong admirer of Mark Twain"[62] might not have had Twain's river somewhere in the back of his mind when he wrote, "I've known rivers . . . ."[63]

Charles T. Davis noted in 1973 that "a double history" informs "every black work."

> We have, of course, the tradition of American letters, that continuity in form and ideas that contributed much, say, to the shape of Chesnutt's art, as it did to that of his contemporaries, Howells, Cable, Aldrich. But beyond this there is the hidden tradition, the rich and changing store of folk forms and folk materials, the advantages of a dialectical tongue, with a separate music of its own, and the background of rituals, learned responses, and wisdom that grew from a community given an amount of homogeneity through isolation and oppression.[64]

Could many "white works," as well, also be said to have "a double history," one intimately shaped, whether or not their creators were consciously aware of the fact, by black "folk materials and folk traditions"?[65]

With some notable exceptions, scholars of American literature have been curiously reticent about addressing, in all their rich concreteness, the mixed literary bloodlines of American fiction.[66] As Werner Sollors put it, "Do we have to believe in a filiation from Mark Twain to Ernest Hemingway, but not to Ralph Ellison (who is supposedly descended from James Weldon Johnson and Richard

Wright)?"[67] Sollors insists that we need to probe "the pervasiveness of cultural syncretism in America" if we are to get beyond reductive descent-based readings of our culture.[68]

His point resonates with an observation made by Charles Johnson in *Being and Race*:

> Our lives, as blacks and whites, we come to realize, are a tissue of cross-cultural influences. One can say as much about this book, written by a black American . . . on paper invented by the Chinese and printed with ink evolved out of India and from type developed by Germans using Roman symbols modified from the Greeks, who got their letter concepts from the Phoenicians, who had adapted them partly from Egyptian hieroglyphs.[69]

As Ellison put it in 1976,

> you can learn from [other groups]; you can make their contributions your own by the simple act of respect and showing a willingness to understand the human implications of [their traditions].[70]

Maxine Hong Kingston is surprised when readers in China insist on a direct line between her book *The Woman Warrior* and the Chinese classic *Dream of the Red Chamber*, for, when she is asked to name her literary ancestors, the ones that first come to mind are Walt Whitman and William Carlos Williams.[71] David Bradley's models were Herman Melville, Robert Penn Warren, and Robert Heinlein.[72] Tillie Olsen claims W. E. B. DuBois as a key literary forebear.[73]

I would not want my research in this book to be interpreted as suggesting that black writers in the twentieth century were attracted to Twain simply because his work was so shaped by African-American influences. Black writers like Ellison and Wright and Bradley may well have been attracted to Twain for other reasons entirely, reasons having to do with art and genius, with well-crafted sentences, and with his ability to evoke brilliantly recognizably human traits.[74] White writers—like Faulkner, for example—may have been attracted to Twain not despite the influence of African-American voices on his art but because of them.[75]

America's long history of racism has made addressing "cultural syncretism" across racial lines particularly problematical. But as these barriers gradually give way, we can begin to see a vision of our culture that is infinitely richer and more complex than any we had before. Stephen Foster's "Camp-Town Races," a song recognized throughout the world as "uniquely American"[76] turns out to be a tune sung by Yoruba mothers to their children.[77] Harriet Beecher Stowe's *Uncle Tom's Cabin* influenced slave narratives and fiction by African Americans.[78] African motifs, organizational principles, and aesthetic values may have shaped the American patchwork quilt.[79] Tones of the Jewish "shofar" may have made their way into Louis Armstrong's trumpet riffs.[80] Walt Whitman empowered June Jordan to make poetry out of her experience as a woman of color.[81] The cultural conversation turns out to be jazzy and improvisational, unpredictable and serendipitous, dynamic and tricky.

Toni Morrison's landmark essay in the *Michigan Quarterly Review*, "Unspeakable Things Unspoken: The Afro-American Presence in American Literature," and her important book *Playing in the Dark: Whiteness and the Literary Imagination*, as well as books on race and literature currently being written by a number of outstanding scholars, substantiate and amplify Henry Louis Gates, Jr.'s trenchant insight that segregation "is as difficult to maintain in the literary realm as it is in the civic one."[82]

Although the mixing of races and the mixing of cultures has been going on from the start, our country's legal system and our society's cultural narratives long accepted the fiction that it was possible to draw sharp lines of demarcation between the races. The fiction of "racial purity"—the notion that it was, in fact, possible to divide the society into "white" and "black"—justified the elaborate system of segregation statutes created in the 1890s and not dismantled until the middle of the twentieth century.

We may no longer segregate trains, schools, water fountains, waiting rooms, bibles for witnesses in courtrooms, parks, residences, textbooks, telephone booths, ticket windows, ambulances, hospitals, orphanages, prisons, morgues, and cemeteries. But segregation is alive and well among literary historians, who persist in affirming that white writers come from white literary ancestors, and black writers from black ones.[83]

The laws against miscegenation have been struck from the books. But unwritten laws prevent critics from acknowledging how fully black and white voices and traditions have mingled to create what we know as "American" culture. "The Negro looks at the white man," Ralph Ellison wrote, "and finds it difficult to believe that the 'grays'— a Negro term for white people—can be so absurdly self-deluded over the true interrelatedness of blackness and whiteness."[84] In this book I have attempted to deconstruct some of those delusions.

Toni Morrison observed, in 1992,

> There seems to be a more or less tacit agreement among literary scholars that, because American literature has been clearly the preserve of white male views, genius, and power, those views, genius, and power are without relationship to and removed from the overwhelming pres-

ence of black people in the United States. . . . The contemplation of this black presence is central to any understanding of our national literature and should not be permitted to hover at the margins of the literary imagination.[85]

David Bradley put it more bluntly. "American criticism today," he wrote in 1989, "remains both segregationist and racist."[86]

When the segregation statutes were eliminated in the middle of the twentieth century, much of American society had to alter its habits of travelling, residing, eating, learning, playing, and burying its dead. Acknowledging and understanding what Bradley has called "an integrated American Literature"[87] might well entail equally disruptive changes in familiar practice in the classroom, in the training of teachers, in institutions, and in scholarship.

A shift in paradigm is in order. Understanding African-American traditions is essential if one wants to understand *mainstream* American literary history. And understanding mainstream literary history is important if one wants to understand African-American writing in the twentieth century. We can no longer deny the mixed literary bloodlines on both sides.

Acknowledging the African-American roots of Twain's art in *Huckleberry Finn* does not make the novel any easier to teach; on the contrary, it may raise more questions than it answers. What correlation is there between listening carefully and appreciatively to African-American voices and recognizing the full humanity of the speakers to whom those voices belong? What connection is there between seeing beyond "race" to qualities that are at root simply "human," and actively challenging the racist social and political mechanisms that prevent large numbers of people in one's society from fulfilling their human potential? Can satire play a catalytic role in shaping people's awareness of the dynamics of racism, or do satire's inherent ambiguities invite too much evasion and denial?

Some of Twain's contemporaries—George Washington Cable comes immediately to mind—launched full frontal attacks against racism in the 1880s. Twain did not. Twain's attacks were more subtle, less risky, less courageous. They are also more lasting. Cable's polemics, *The Silent South* and "The Freedman's Case in Equity," for all their forceful directness, are forgotten, except among a handful of scholars. *Huckleberry Finn*, on the other hand, remains one of the most widely read and taught works by an American writer. Has it lasted despite or because of its capacity to be simultaneously all things to all people? Do its complexities contain the power of its social critique or unleash that power?

These questions remain to disturb and provoke us.[88] The research presented in this book suggests that *Huckleberry Finn* may be more subversive, ultimately, than we might have suspected. For Twain's imaginative blending of black voices with white ones (whether conscious or unconscious) effectively deconstructs "race" as a meaningful category. "Race," for Mark Twain, far from being the "ultimate trope of difference,"[89] was often simply irrelevant. The problem of racism, on the other hand, was for Twain, and continues to be for us, undeniably real.

How will Americans respond to the news that the voice of Huck Finn, the beloved national symbol and cultural icon, was part black? Will they react with the astonishment that the citizens of Dawson's Landing showed in *Pudd'nhead Wilson* when they learned that the pretentious blue-blood, Tom Driscoll, was really a mulatto? Will the forces of reaction demote Huck from his place of honor in the culture and relegate him to a lesser role in the national consciousness—the equivalent of selling him down the river, the fate that awaited Tom Driscoll? Or will Huck become an emblem of a society that is now, and has always been, as multiracial and multicultural as the sources of the novel that we have embraced as most expressive of who we really are?

Coda

Early in *Huckleberry Finn*, Huck complains about the food at the Widow Douglas's:

> When you got to the table you couldn't go right to eating, but you had to wait for the widow to tuck down her head and grumble a little over the victuals, though there warn't really anything the matter with them. That is, nothing only everything was cooked by itself. In a barrel of odds and ends it is different; things get mixed up, and the juice kind of swaps around, and the things go better.[1]

Twain's imagination was closer to Huck's barrel than to the Widow Douglas's separate pots. As he "mixed up" black voices with white ones, the flavors "swapped around" deliciously. America's taste in literature would never be the same.

Notes

Introduction

1. Ralph Ellison, "Change the Joke and Slip the Yoke," 55.

2. See, for example, Robert Alter, *Rogue's Progress: Study in the Picaresque Novel*; Alexander Blackburn, *The Myth of the Picaro*; Hugh A. Harter, "Mark Twain y la tradicion picaresca"; John B. Hughes, "*Lazarillo de Tormes y Huckleberry Finn*"; Kenneth S. Lynn, *Mark Twain and Southwestern Humor*; James M. Cox, *Mark Twain: The Fate of Humor*; Walter Blair, *Mark Twain and "Huck Finn"*; Henry Nash Smith, *Mark Twain: The Development of a Writer*; Pascal Covici, Jr., *Mark Twain's Humor*; David E. E. Sloane, *Mark Twain as a Literary Comedian*; M. Thomas Inge, ed., *The Frontier Humorists*; Leo Marx, "The Vernacular Tradition in American Literature;" Shelley Fisher Fishkin, *From Fact to Fiction: Journalism and Imaginative Writing in America*; Edgar Marquess Branch, *The Literary Apprenticeship of Mark Twain* and "Mark Twain: Newspaper Reading and the Writer's Creativity"; and Alan Gribben, "'I Did Wish Tom Sawyer Was There': Boy-Book Elements in *Tom Sawyer* and *Huckleberry Finn*."

3. Twain said, "'Huckleberry Finn' was Tom Blankenship" (*Autobiography*, 73). See also notes on Tom and Bence Blankenship in Dahlia Armon and Walter Blair, "Biographical Directory," 302–3.

4. The notable exceptions to this rule are William Andrews ("Mark Twain and James W. C. Pennington: Huckleberry Finn's Smallpox Lie"), David Bradley ("The First 'Nigger' Novel"), Ralph Ellison ("What America Would Be Like Without Blacks"), Lucinda MacKethan ("*Huck Finn* and the Slave Narratives"), and Arnold Rampersad ("*Adventures of Huckleberry Finn* and Afro-American Literature").

For critical discussions of the speech of Twain's African-American characters, see Lee A. Pederson, "Negro Speech in *The Adventures of Huckleberry Finn*"; James Nathan Tidwell, "Mark Twain's Representation of Negro Speech"; Sally Boland, "The Seven Dialects in *Huckleberry Finn*"; Curt Morris Rulon, "The Dialects in Huckleberry Finn"; and David Carkeet, "The Dialects in *Huckleberry Finn*." The best-known consideration of African-American folk beliefs in Twain's work is Daniel G. Hoffman, "Black Magic—and White—in *Huckleberry Finn*."

Critics have also approached *Huckleberry Finn* in terms of the roles played by Twain's black characters, and Twain's racial attitudes. See Ralph Ellison, "Change the Joke and Slip the Yoke" and "Twentieth-Century Fiction and the Black Mask of Humanity"; Arthur G. Pettit, *Mark Twain and the South*; Philip Foner, *Mark Twain: Social Critic*; Louis J. Budd, *Mark Twain: Social Philosopher*; Louis Rubin, Jr., "Southern Local Color and the Black Man;" Catherine

Juanita Starke, *Black Portraiture in American Fiction*; Thomas Weaver and Mer-
line A. Williams, "Mark Twain's Jim: Identity as an Index to Cultural Atti-
tudes"; Sterling A. Brown, *The Negro in American Fiction*; Sterling Stuckey,
"True Huck"; Forrest Robinson, "The Characterization of Jim in *Huckleberry
Finn*"; Sloane, *"Adventures of Huckleberry Finn": American Comic Vision*;
Sherwood Cummings, "Mark Twain's Moveable Farm and the Evasion"; Rayford
W. Logan, *The Negro in American Life and Thought: The Nadir, 1877–1901*;
Leslie A. Fiedler, "Come Back to the Raft Ag'in, Huck Honey"; Guy Cardwell,
The Man Who Was Mark Twain; and Shelley Fisher Fishkin, "Racial Attitudes"
(in *The Mark Twain Encyclopedia*). For additional references, see "For Further
Reading" by Thomas A. Tenney, in *Satire or Evasion?*

By far the most important publications on Twain's racial attitudes and on
the portrayal of black characters in his work are the 1984 special issue of the
Mark Twain Journal, "Black Writers on *Adventures of Huckleberry Finn* One
Hundred Years Later," guest edited by Thadious M. Davis, and the book into
which these and other essays were collected, *Satire or Evasion? Black Perspectives on "Huckleberry Finn,"* edited by James S. Leonard, Thomas A. Tenney,
and Thadious M. Davis. Some of the key essays on this subject included in this
volume are: Rhett S. Jones, "Nigger and Knowledge: White Double-Consciousness in *Adventures of Huckleberry Finn*"; David Smith, "Huck, Jim, and American Racial Discourse"; Bernard W. Bell, "Twain's 'Nigger' Jim: The Tragic Face
behind the Minstrel Mask"; Fredrick Woodard and Donnarae MacCann, "Minstrel Shackles and Nineteenth-Century 'Liberality' in *Huckleberry Finn*"; Charles
H. Nichols, "'A True Book—With Some Stretchers': *Huck Finn* Today"; and
Betty H. Jones, "Huck and Jim: A Reconsideration." See also Thadious Davis's
"Foreword" to the special issue of the *Mark Twain Journal*. Only rarely have
critics recognized in print some of the larger connections between Mark Twain's
work and African-American culture. See Arnold Rampersad, "Adventures of
Huckleberry Finn and Afro-American Literature," and Stewart Rodnon, "*The
Adventures of Huckleberry Finn* and Invisible Man: Thematic and Structural
Comparisons."

5. Richard Wright, "Memories of My Grandmother," quoted in Michel
Fabre, *Richard Wright: Books & Writers*, 161; Langston Hughes, "Introduc-
tion" to Mark Twain, *Pudd'nhead Wilson*, vii–xiii; Ralph Ellison, interview with
the author, 16 July 1991; David Bradley, "The First 'Nigger' Novel," speech to
Annual Meeting of the Mark Twain Memorial and the New England American
Studies Association, Hartford, Connecticut, May 1985.

6. Ellison, "What America Would Be Like Without Blacks," 109. Italics
added.

7. Twain's linguistic virtuosity is apparent from such pieces as "Italian
Without a Master," "Italian with Grammar," "The Awful German Language,"
"Concerning the American Language," "Introduction to 'The New Guide of the
Conversation in Portuguese and English,'" "'The Jumping Frog' in English. Then
in French. Then Clawed Back into a Civilized Language Once More by Patient,
Unremunerated Toil."

The most recent and sophisticated discussion of Twain's sensitivity to and
interest in diverse linguistic systems is David Sewell's stimulating book, *Mark
Twain's Languages*. Sewell argues that "Mark Twain's understanding of language, as evidenced primarily in his fiction, transcended its origin in public-
school grammar instruction and moved toward an intuition of principles just

beginning to appear in his day and fully enunciated only in our own" (Sewell, 1–2). In addition to being adept at evoking a wide range of languages and dialects, Twain demonstrated a "facile, natural control" over what psycholinguist George F. Mahl refers to as "one of the extralinguistic dimensions of speech, the 'roughness' or 'influency' or 'normal disturbances' in word-progression" (Mahl, "Everyday Speech Disturbances in *Tom Sawyer*," 295–96; Mahl, "Everyday Disturbances of Speech," 213).

In "Mark Twain and the Oral Economy: Digression in the Age of Print," David Barrow suggests that "over the course of his career" Twain was "opposed to the notion that the spoken can be translated satisfactorily into print" (10). Although he may have suspected that ultimate success in this matter was beyond his reach, Twain nonetheless labored mightily in the effort.

8. Ralph W. Ellison in Fishkin interview, 16 July 1991.

9. Richard Bridgman describes the phenomenon in this way:

> If one accepts provisionally the existence of a change in American prose style, then the next pertinent question is, when did it begin? Recently the date 1884 has been advanced from several quarters, most succinctly by Ernest Hemingway: "All modern American literature comes from one book by Mark Twain called *Huckleberry Finn.* . . ." As early as 1913 H. L. Mencken was championing Mark Twain: "I believe that he was the true father of our national literature, the first genuinely American artist of the blood royal." Later William Faulkner agreed, saying: "In my opinion, Mark Twain was the first truly American writer, and all of us since are his heirs, we are descended from him."
>
> This critical admiration has not extended to Mark Twain's work as a whole nor to his literary theories (such as they were), nor to his practical criticisms. One book alone has drawn the praise. Whatever the merits of Mark Twain's other writing, and whatever the weaknesses of *Huckleberry Finn*, everyone—literary hacks, artists, and critics—agrees that the style of this book has had a major effect on the development of American prose. (Bridgman, *Colloquial Style in America*, 5–6)

10. It is not within the scope of this book to explore the ways in which African-American voices shaped other works by Twain besides *Huckleberry Finn*, but clearly such investigations have the potential to be rich and fruitful. For example, Twain's responses to slave narratives in a range of contexts warrant further examination in this light. Werner Sollors has explored some connections between slave narratives and *A Connecticut Yankee in King Arthur's Court* (Sollors, "Ethnicity"). Lawrence Howe has noted the analogies to slave narrative themes in *Life on the Mississippi* (Howe, "Transcending the Limits of Experience: Mark Twain's *Life on the Mississippi*").

11. Twain preceded this comment with the following description of the Jubilee Singers' visit:

> The other night we had a detachment of the Jubilee Singers—6 I had known in London 24 years ago. Three of the 6 were born in slavery, the others were children of slaves. How charming they were—in spirit, manner, language, pronunciation, enunciation, grammar, phrasing, matter, carriage, clothes—in every detail that goes to make the real lady and gentleman, and welcome guest. We went down to the village hotel and bought our tickets and entered the beer-hall, where a crowd of German and Swiss men and women sat grouped at round tables with their beer mugs in front of them—self-contained and unimpressionable looking people, an indifferent and unposted and disheartened audience—and up at the far end of the room sat the Jubilees in a row. The Singers got up and stood—the

talking and glass jingling went on. Then rose and swelled out above those common earthly sounds one of those rich chords the secret of whose make only the Jubilees possess, and a spell fell upon that house. It was fine to see the faces light up with the pleased wonder and surprise of it. No one was indifferent any more; and when the singers finished, the camp was theirs. It was a triumph. It reminded me of Launcelot riding in Sir Kay's armor and astonishing complacent Knights who thought they had struck a soft thing. The Jubilees sang a lot of pieces. Arduous and painstaking cultivation has not diminished or artificialized their music, but on the contrary—to my surprise—has mightily reinforced its eloquence and beauty. (SLC to Joe Twitchell, 22 August 1897, in *Mark Twain's Letters*, ed. Albert Bigelow Paine, 2:645–46)

Twain's awareness of his countrymen's failure to appreciate the value of the spirituals is echoed by Alain Locke, who noted in 1925 in "The Negro Spirituals," that "only recently have they come to be recognized as artistically precious things. It still requires vision and courage to proclaim their ultimate value and possibilities" (199–200).

12. Gustavus D. Pike, *The Singing Campaign for Ten Thousand Pounds; or, The Jubilee Singers in Great Britain*, 14; Anon., "Coming Events," *Fun* (London), 172. The text of Twain's publicity letter for the Jubilee Singers reads as follows:

Gentlemen: The Jubilee Singers are to appear in London, and I am requested to say in their behalf what I know of them—and I most cheerfully do it. I heard them sing once, and I would walk seven miles to hear them sing again. You will recognize that this is strong language for me to use, when you remember that I never was fond of pedestrianism, and got tired of walking that Sunday afternoon, in twenty minutes, after making up my mind to see for myself and at my own leisure how much ground his grace the Duke of Bedford's property covered.

I think these gentlemen and ladies make eloquent music—and what is as much to the point, they reproduce the true melody of the plantations, and are the only persons I ever heard accomplish this on the public platform. The so-called "negro minstrels" simply mis-represent the thing; I do not think they ever saw a plantation or heard a slave sing.

I was reared in the South, and my father owned slaves, and I do not know when anything has so moved me as did the plaintive melodies of the Jubilee Singers. It was the first time for twenty-five or thirty years that I had heard such songs, or heard them sung in the genuine old way—and it is a way, I think, that white people cannot imitate—and never can, for that matter, for one must have been a slave himself in order to feel what that life was and so convey the pathos of it in the music. Do not fail to hear the Jubilee Singers. I am very well satisfied that you will not regret it. Yours faithfully, Saml. L. Clemens. Mark Twain. (SLC to Tom Hood and George Routledge and Sons, 10 March 1873, Hartford, reprinted in Pike, 14–15)

13. Katy Leary, quoted in Mary Lawton, *A Lifetime with Mark Twain: The Memories of Katy Leary, for Thirty Years His Faithful and Devoted Servant*, 212–13.

14. Justin Kaplan, *Mr. Clemens and Mark Twain*, 174.

15. Kaplan, *Mr. Clemens and Mark Twain*, 172, 174.

16. William Dean Howells, *My Mark Twain*, 99.

17. As a number of critics have noted, there are important links between speaking and singing voices in African-American culture. Henry Louis Gates, Jr.,

for example, explains the decision to include a cassette tape with the *Norton Anthology of Afro-American Literature* as follows:

> Because of the strong oral and vernacular base of so very much of our literature, we included a cassette tape along with our anthology. . . . This means that each period section includes both the printed and spoken text of oral and musical selections of black vernacular culture: sermons, blues, spirituals, rhythm and blues, poets reading their own "dialect" poems, speeches—whatever! Imagine an anthology that includes Bessie Smith and Billie Holiday singing the blues, Langston Hughes reading "[I've] Known Rivers," Sterling Brown reading "Ma Rainey," James Weldon Johnson, "The Creation". . . . We will change fundamentally not only the way our literature is taught, but the way in which any literary tradition is even conceived. . . . In our anthology we wanted to incorporate performance and the black and human voice. (Gates, Jr., "The Master's Pieces: On Canon Formation and Afro-American Tradition," 30)

As Gates notes elsewhere, "the nature of black music is the nature of black speech, and vice versa" (Gates, Jr., "Dis and Dat: Dialect and the Descent," 176).

18. *Mark Twain's Autobiography*, ed. Albert Bigelow Paine, 1:112–13. Twain often told a story he had heard at that hearth, "The Golden Arm," when he gave lectures and readings. As his cousin Tabitha Quarles recalled, every night at the Quarles farm, where Twain spent his summer, the children would gather "around the fire place and [hear] the darkies tell their ghost stories. Sam just repeated those tales Uncle Dan'l and Uncle Ned told and folks said he was smart" (Anon., "Mark Twain's Cousin," 2). Twain's older brother Orion thought Twain may have confused Uncle Dan'l with Ned, one of the Clemenses' own slaves from Hannibal (*Mark Twain's Letters*, ed. Paine, 2:403 n.1). Tabitha Quarles's comment suggests that both men were important storytellers in Twain's youth.

19. SLC to Olivia L. Langdon, 15 and 16 December 1869, *Letters, vol. 3: 1869*, ed. Victor Fischer and Michael B. Frank, 426.

20. Photocopy of manuscript of Mark Twain, "A Family Sketch," 59, 61. Mark Twain Papers. Original in Mark Twain Collection, James S. Copley Library, La Jolla, Ca. Quoted with permission.

21. Typescript of Mark Twain's notebook 35, May–Oct. 1895, 8. Mark Twain Papers. Quoted with permission. Emphasis added.

22. The night Mary Ann Cord told her story on the porch steps at Quarry Farm made a deep impression on Olivia Clemens, as well, who referred to it in a letter to her husband which was acquired in March 1992 from the Chester Davis estate by the Mark Twain Memorial, Hartford, Connecticut. I am grateful to Marianne Curling, Curator of the Mark Twain Memorial, for making the text of this letter available to me. Twain's full comment, with crossouts, in the 1895 journal, reads as follows: "but this is <direct> clear, compact & <vivid> coherent—yes, & vivid also, & perfectly simple & unconscious." (Typescript of Mark Twain's notebook 35, May–Oct. 1895, 8. Mark Twain Papers. Quoted with permission.)

Mark Twain was exposed to African-American voices during his years as a steamboat pilot and journalist, as well as during his childhood. In *Life on the Mississippi*, for example, Twain recalled that "Negro firemen, deck-hands, and barbers" who worked on such "stately craft as the Alec Scott or the Grand Turk" were "distinguished personages in their grade of life, and they were well aware of that fact, too" (124). And as a journalist in San Francisco, Twain was friends with Phillip A. Bell, outspoken editor of the African-American newspaper, the

San Francisco *Elevator* (Twain, *Early Tales and Sketches*, ed. Edgar Marquess Branch and Robert Hirst, 2:247). (Bell's newspaper was committed to advocating "the largest political and civil liberty to all American citizens, irrespective of creed or color" (Phillip Bell, "Prospectus," 1). Upon his election to the post of Assistant Sergeant-at-Arms to the State of California in 1879, Bell was described by the *Alta California* as "a political, literary and social instructor of his race" (Anon., "Assistant," 1).

23. Ernest Hemingway, *Green Hills of Africa*, 22.

24. William Faulkner, quoted in Robert A. Jelliffe, ed., *Faulkner at Nagano*, 88.

25. Toni Morrison, "Unspeakable Things Unspoken: The Afro-American Presence in American Literature," 19.

26. Sometime in 1892, Mark Twain found himself flummoxed about what to do with his current writing project. Then suddenly it became clear to him: the book he was writing "was not one story, but two stories tangled together." He wrote, "I pulled one of the stories out by the roots, and left the other one—a kind of literary Caesarean operation" (*Those Extraordinary Twins*, 119). Two books—*Pudd'nhead Wilson* and *Those Extraordinary Twins*—were the result.

Was Huck Black? Mark Twain and African-American Voices is also the result of "a kind of literary Caesarean operation." For several years I had been working on a book called *The Stories He Couldn't Tell: Mark Twain and Race* (forthcoming from Oxford), which explores Twain's attitudes toward race in the context of the racial discourse of his time. But in the spring of 1992, arguments that were forming in my mind about the genesis of *Huckleberry Finn* and about Mark Twain's response to African-American voices began to push themselves forward with unrelenting urgency. These ideas would wake me up at three in the morning. They would barge unannounced into my consciousness—at breakfast, in the library, in class. Despite my efforts to keep them "in perspective" (after all, my book was about Twain's entire career as a writer, and not just about *Huckleberry Finn*) they wouldn't subside. I began to write an essay on the subject, hoping to appease whatever force in my subconscious was responsible for those pesky three A.M. wake-up calls. It didn't work. The essay was soon well over a hundred pages long. Late one night a phrase came into my head uninvited, and refused to leave: "two stories in one" (*Those Extraordinary Twins*, 119). I decided that any solution good enough for Mark Twain was good enough for me.

The book with which I began, *The Stories He Couldn't Tell: Mark Twain and Race*, will address more ambitiously the cultural conversation that shaped Twain's writing on race and that his writing, in turn, helped shape. It will examine the controversies surrounding Twain's use of the word "nigger," and will chart the social history of efforts to ban *Huckleberry Finn* from secondary school classrooms in the 1950s and 1980s as "racist." It will explore Twain's attitudes toward various racial and ethnic "others" including African-Americans, Native Americans, Jews, and the Chinese. That study will have, I hope, time and space to examine the ways in which the ambiguities and ambivalences in Twain's work throughout his life reflect tensions inherent in his culture, and in our own, as well. By way of contrast, *Was Huck Black? Mark Twain and African-American Voices* explores in only very preliminary ways a context for understanding the attitudes toward race embodied in Twain's responses to African-American voices. However, because my argument here is so focused, specific, and coherent, I felt it could stand alone.

Chapter 1

1. Mark Twain shared W. E. B. DuBois's intense and passionate appreciation of the beauty and eloquence of African-American spirituals. In recognition of the power this music had to move and inspire Twain, I reprise DuBois's practice of printing, "before each chapter . . . a bar of the Sorrow Songs" (DuBois, *Souls of Black Folk*, 359). Both DuBois and Twain considered these songs "the most beautiful expression of human experience born this side of the seas" (*Souls*, 536–37). The bars of music and fragments of lyrics with which I begin each chapter come from songs Twain was likely to have heard the Fisk Jubilee Singers perform; they are taken from Anon., *Jubilee Songs: Complete. As Sung by the Jubilee Singers, of Fisk University* (1872) and Frederick J. Work, ed., *New Jubilee Songs, As Sung by the Fisk Jubilee Singers of Fisk University* (1902). They are, in order of appearance, Chapter 1: "Been a Listening" (Anon., *Jubilee*, 25); Chapter 2: "By and By" (Work, 45); Chapter 3: "Go down, Moses" (Anon., *Jubilee*, 22–23); Chapter 4: "Go down, Moses" (Anon., *Jubilee*, 22–23); Chapter 5: "O, Nobody Knows Who I Am" (Work, 39); Chapter 6: "Give Me Jesus" (Anon., *Jubilee*, 19); Chapter 7: "I Know the Lord's Laid His Hands On Me" (Work, 7); Chapter 8: "My Good Lord's Done Been Here" (Work, 11); Chapter 9: "I'm A-Going to Join the Band" (Work, 12). As John Lovell, Jr.'s "The Social Implications of the Negro Spiritual" makes clear, the spirituals expressed in coded language the slaves' deepest aspirations for freedom. "The spiritual," Lovell writes, "was a language well understood in all its burning import by the slave initiate, but harmless and graceful to an unthinking outsider" (462). As Frederick Douglass noted, "every tone was a testimony against slavery, and a prayer to God for deliverance from chains" (*Narrative*, 58). See also Sylvia Holton, *Down Home and Uptown: The Representation of Black Speech in American Fiction*, 48–49, and Gates, Jr., "Dis and Dat: Dialect and the Descent," 174–76.

2. Lionel Trilling, "The Greatness of *Huckleberry Finn*," 91–92.

3. Trilling, "The Greatness of *Huckleberry Finn*," 90–91. Philip Fisher, who calls "the novel told in the uniquely honest and vital voice of Huck Finn" the "most important first-person narrative in American literature," adds, "In Huck Twain invented a richer autobiographical voice than the comparatively weak first-person voices of Dickens" (Fisher, "Mark Twain," 636).

4. Louis J. Budd, "Introduction," *New Essays on "Huckleberry Finn*," 15.

5. Albert Stone, *The Innocent Eye: Childhood in Mark Twain's Imagination*, 151–52.

6. Twain also drew on an experience that had occurred to Tom's brother Bence, who had helped a runaway slave hiding on a nearby island with deliveries of food.

7. *Mark Twain's Autobiography*, ed. Paine, 2:174–75.

8. Tony Tanner, for example, observed in 1965 in *Reign of Wonder* that "Huck remains a voice. . . ." (181); and Keith Opdahl noted in 1990 in "'The Rest Is Just Cheating,'" "Huck comes to life for us not as a physical being, since his appearance is barely described in the book (we know only that he dresses in 'rags' and fidgets at the dinner table) but as a voice . . ." (277).

9. "Sociable Jimmy" ran on page 7 of the *New York Times*, 29 November 1874, over Mark Twain's by-line. All my quotations from the piece are taken from the original publication. Twain had begun to write *Tom Sawyer* the preceding summer. See Appendix for the full text of "Sociable Jimmy."

10. On pp. 31–32 I describe in more detail the obscurity of this sketch among Twain scholars. The only critical attention the sketch has received is an eleven-line note Paul Fatout appended to the sketch when he reprinted it in *Mark Twain Speaks for Himself* (92) and a brief, dismissive reference in Arthur G. Pettit's *Mark Twain and the South* (198 n.14).

11. A letter Twain wrote to Livy on 10–11 January 1872 in which he refers to the previously sent sketch suggests that he was lecturing in the Midwest when he wrote the letter enclosing the sketch, possibly near Terre Haute, Indiana (there is a reference to "Tarry Hote" in the letter). Twain's first letter and original copy of the sketch have disappeared. The second letter indicates that Livy showed or sent a copy of the sketch to Charles Dudley Warner (SLC to OLC, 10–11 January 1872, Mark Twain Papers). Another letter lends further support to the idea that Twain met Jimmy in late December 1871 or early January 1872 (SLC to OLC, 9 January 1872, Mark Twain Papers). (See p. 35.) The working copy of Twain's lecture calendar for 1871 (being prepared as part of *Letters, vol. 4:1870–1871*), which Victor Fischer of the Mark Twain Papers was good enough to share with me, allows us to narrow down the towns in which Twain met Jimmy to the following: in Illinois: Sandwich, Aurora, Princeton, Champaign, Tuscola, Danville, Matoon, and Paris; in Indiana: Logansport and Richmond; in Ohio: Wooster and Salem. (This list rules out the large cities Twain lectured in during this period, since "Sociable Jimmy" is clearly set in a less populous setting.) Victor Fischer believes the reference to Terre Haute in Twain's extant letter about "Sociable Jimmy" would make Paris, Illinois, a town thirty miles from Terre Haute, the most likely setting for the encounter (personal communication).

Another potential signpost is Jimmy's comment, "I ben mos' halfway to Dockery" and Twain's interjection, "[thirty miles]." Karla Holloway has suggested to me that "Dockery" may actually be "Decatur," a town whose "halfway" distance from Paris, Illinois, is some forty miles (not that far off from Twain's estimated thirty). Holloway notes, "Phonetically, 'Dockery' only replaces the vowel sounds and maintains the syllabic as well as the major consonant patterns. In linguistic change, even intentional change as Twain might have done, vowel shift (especially the front to back (and reverse) as happens if Decatur becomes Dockery) is still the most flexible" (personal communication). Holloway's insight lends further credence to the speculation that the encounter took place in Paris, Illinois. The name of the family for which Jimmy worked was "Aithens" (Twain changed it to "Nubbles" in the published sketch); evidence of an Aithens family in Paris, Illinois, in 1871 or 1872 may yet be found.

12. Mark Twain, "Sociable Jimmy." Emphasis added.

13. SLC to Olivia Langdon Clemens, 10–11 January 1872, Mark Twain Papers. Quoted with permission. Emphasis added. I am grateful to Victor Fischer and Louis J. Budd for having brought this letter to my attention.

14. A child's perspective surfaces briefly in his presentation of the letter he allegedly received from his niece Annie in "An Open Letter to the American People" (1866). Twain also experimented with a child narrator in his unpublished fragment, "Boy's Manuscript" (1868). See note 58.

15. Mark Twain, *Adventures of Huckleberry Finn*, Walter Blair and Victor Fischer, eds. [lvii]. Unless otherwise indicated, all citations refer to this edition. The "Explanatory" is quoted in full on page 103.

16. *Huckleberry Finn*, Chapter 39, cited in Bridgman, *The Colloquial Style in America*, 124–25. Capitals added by Bridgman.

17. Twain, "Sociable Jimmy." Capitals added.

18. Twain, *Huckleberry Finn*, 5. Capitals added.

19. Twain, "Sociable Jimmy." Capitals added.

20. Bridgman, *The Colloquial Style in America*, 117–118. Emphasis added.

21. Bridgman, *The Colloquial Style in America*, 118.

22. Emphasis added. Interestingly, although Bridgman cites these examples of Twain's (and Huck's) investing words with "new meaning," the *Oxford English Dictionary* documents several of these usages—in particular, "smouches," "clayey," "soothering," and "haggling"—as having been employed before 1884 in precisely the same manner as Twain uses them (*OED* 15:815; 3:291; 16:4; 6:1014). This does not mean that the usage is the most common, however, and Bridgman's general point may still hold. "Skreeky," "alassing," and "sqush," on the other hand, seem to be genuinely original. "Skreeky" and "alassing" are in neither the *OED* nor the *Dictionary of American Slang*, and the entry for "sqush" in the *OED*, which notes that the word is "U.S. colloq. and dial. rare," cites Twain's use of the word in *Huckleberry Finn* as the first known usage (*OED* 16:427). Jimmy's use of the verb "sloshes" turns out to be a creative amalgam of the three definitions listed for "slosh" as an intransitive verb. The closest is the second definition: "U.S. To move aimlessly; to hang or loaf about." The first example provided, dating from 1854, refers to the expression "sloshing around" as a "Louisiana negro" usage. But when Jimmy has the "sloshing" taking place in saloons, he is creatively blending the idea of aimless loafing with the two definitions associated with splashing liquids and flowing streams (*OED* 15:735). Jimmy's use of the word "buster" resembles the first OED definitions, which are "*slang* (chiefly U.S.)" (*OED* 2:699). However, both *The Dictionary of American Slang* (80) and the *OED*'s earliest citations of the word (1850 and 1860) involve references to persons rather than things, suggesting that Jimmy's use of the word to refer to a clock may be somewhat fresh, if not wholly original. Perhaps Jimmy's most creative innovation in usage among the words on this list is "scoops": "When dey ketches a cat bummin' aroun' heah, dey jis' *scoops* him—'deed dey do" (italics Twain's). The usual usage of the verb requires the word "up" or some equivalent (*OED* 15:669). Could Jimmy (unwittingly) or Twain (quite wittingly) be punning on or playing with the phrase "to scoop the kitty," a gambling expression meaning "to win all the money that is staked" (*OED* 14:669)?

23. Bridgman, *The Colloquial Style in America*, 123–24. Capitals added by Bridgman.

24. Twain, "Sociable Jimmy." Capitals added.

25. Janet Holmgren McKay, "'An Art So High': Style in *Adventures of Huckleberry Finn*," 63. "During the thunderstorm, Huck glimpses 'tree-tops *a-plunging about away* off yonder.' At the circus, the bareback riders go '*a-weaving around* the ring'" (McKay, 65, quoting from *Huckleberry Finn*, Chapter 22; emphasis added). Another example of Huck's double use of the "a-" prefix is "he set there *a-mumbling* and *a-growling*" (*Huckleberry Finn*, 24, emphasis added). As Twain characterizes his voice, Jimmy, too, employs the alliterative double "a-" in "You don't never see Kit *a-rairin* an' *a-chargin*'" ("Sociable Jimmy," emphasis added).

26. Bridgman, *The Colloquial Style in America*, 124.

27. Bridgman, *The Colloquial Style in America*, 122.

28. McKay, "'An Art So High': Style in *Adventures of Huckleberry Finn*," 67.

29. McKay, "'An Art So High,'" 64.

30. McKay, "'An Art So High,'" 66.

31. Nonstandard verb forms: Huck says, "I *seen* somebody's tracks" (19). Jimmy, in a related vein, says, "I *seed* it, when dey pulled it outen de cow" or, "I *seed* a cat in dare." Double negatives: Huck says, "I *hain't got no* money" (25); Jimmy says, "We *ain't got no* cats" or "*dey ain't got no* bell like dat in Ragtown." Redundancy of subject: Huck says, "*Tom he* showed him how unregular it would be" (309). This feature characterizes virtually all of Jimmy's constructions as well: "*Bill he* don't like 'em," "*De res' o' de people dey* had a good time," "*Bill he's* real good," "*De ole man he* gits drunk, too," "*Bob, he* don't git drunk much," "*Bob he's* next to Bill," "*Sal she's* married," "*Hoss Nubbles, he's* de las.*" Emphasis added.

32. McKay, "'An Art So High,'" 70.

33. McKay, "'An Art So High,'" 66.

34. This particular use of the word "powerful" was noted by Thomas L. Nichols in 1864 as characteristic of Southern speech in general. "The Southerner," Nichols wrote, "is apt to be 'powerful lazy' and 'powerful slow'" (Thomas L. Nichols, *Forty Years of American Life*, Vol. I, 387). In *Huckleberry Finn*, however, the only character besides Huck who uses the word "powerful" in this way is Jim (who uses it twice, as compared with Huck's sixteen times). Villy Sorensen's "*Huckleberry Finn* Concordance" in the Mark Twain Papers reveals that Huck uses the word "powerful" sixteen times in the novel, on the following pages and lines: 27.13; 45.17; 81.30; 92.3; 147.34; 149.10; 155.1; 192.7; 200.3; 204.37; 232.22; 235.2; 254.4; 264.22; 336.28; 345.1). In every case, the word is used as a synonym for "very" or "extremely." (Jim uses "powerful" on page 53, line 23 and on page 176, line 10.) I am grateful to Sterling Stuckey for having pointed out to me that Elma Stuckey, an accomplished poet and a granddaughter of slaves, uses the word "powerful" in the same manner in her poem "Defense": "De fence they keep on talking 'bout/Must gonna be powerful strong./ Done taken all them soldier boys,/ Must gonna be powerful long" (Elma Stuckey, *Collected Poems*, 163).

35. Twain, *Huckleberry Finn*, 336, 27, 45, 147, 155, 93, 31, 40, 34, 69. Demonstrative of how characteristic the word "considerable" is in Huck's lexicon is the fact that he uses it no fewer than twenty-eight times in the book, as Sorensen's "Concordance" shows. (Huck uses it on the following pages and lines: 2.17; 4.12; 14.5; 31.30; 36; 34.26; 40.16; 52.13; 60.34; 68.24; 69.9; 93.26; 104.10; 137.14; 164.11; 166.1,28; 172.28; 18.131; 183.35; 187.25; 204.8; 239.6; 271.34; 284.25; 288.37; 314.3; 319.14.) Curt Rulon notes that "uninflected intensifiers" including "*considable, considerble, tolable, tolerble, pow'ful, powful* occur pervasively without -ly in all the dialects spoken in the book (Rulon, "Dialect Areas," 220). This fact does not lessen the significance of these terms as characteristic of Huck's speech, however, since *all* speech in the book is ostensibly filtered through Huck and passed on to us in *his* version of it. Other similarities in Jimmy's and Huck's lexicons include both boys' use of the words "pison" and "truck" to refer to "poison" and "things" (or "substances"). Jimmy says, "Ain't it dish-yer blue vittles dat's pison?—ain't dat it?—truck what you pisons cats wid?" Huck says, "If I had a yaller dog that didn't know more

than a person's conscience does, I would pison him" (290), and ". . . we turned over the truck the gang had stole off the wreck" (93).

36. Twain, *Huckleberry Finn*, 299.

37. Twain, *Huckleberry Finn*, 330. If Twain is inconsistent in his spelling of this word in "Sociable Jimmy" (Jimmy says both "scacely" and "scasely"), Twain will remain inconsistent in *Huckleberry Finn*, where, on one page, Huck says both "there warn't no real *scarcity* of snakes," and "there warn't no room in bed for him, *skasely*" (emphasis added), 330.

38. Twain, *Huckleberry Finn*, 90. Emily Budick has noted that Toni Morrison uses the word "disremember" in a somewhat similar manner in *Beloved* (274) (Budick, personal communication).

39. McKay, "'An Art So High,'" 70–71.

40. Victor A. Doyno, *Writing "Huck Finn": Mark Twain's Creative Process*, 43.

41. Doyno, *Writing "Huck Finn,"* 43.

42. Twain's use of nonstandard spelling, or "eye-dialect," to render vernacular speech, for example, places Jimmy closer to Huck than to Jim. Words that are phonologically identical are transcribed by one set of rules for Jimmy and Huck, and by another set of rules for Jim. Jimmy and Huck say "was," while Jim more frequently says "wuz." Jim's speech is generally characterized by more "eye-dialect" than either Jimmy's or Huck's. As Victor Fischer has observed, Twain's distinctions on this front were often refinements he added to the manuscript as he revised (personal communication). On page 111, line 19, for example, the manuscript originally had Jim saying "was," and Twain changed it, in the first American edition of the book, to "'uz." (Victor Fischer, "*Huckleberry Finn*: Mark Twain's Usage," n.p.). Twain eventually changed "was" to "wuz" on four occasions, and "was" to "'uz" on three occasions (Jim sometimes says "was," as well, but extremely rarely) (Blair and Fischer, "Textual Introduction," 510). Jimmy and Huck say "reckoned" and Jim says "reck'n'd."

There are some strong resemblances between Jimmy and Huck on the grammatical level, as well. David Carkeet's linguistic analysis in "The Dialects in *Huckleberry Finn*" provides the most elaborate effort to differentiate among the various patterns of speech in the novel. Taking Huck's dialect as the norm, Carkeet isolates those elements of Jim's dialect, for example, that differ from Huck's. Although "grammatically, Huck's and Jim's dialects are very similar," he notes, "Jim's dialect additionally shows the *done*-perfect construction (*she done broke loose*), deletion of the copula, and an *s* suffix on second-person present-tense verbs" (317). Jimmy uses a *done*-perfect construction only once; otherwise, his speech, like Huck's, characteristically manifests none of these features (Huck's one memorable deletion of the copula in the final line of the book will be discussed in Chapter 2).

Whereas Jimmy's speech may be closer to Huck's than to Jim's grammatically, there are strong resemblances between Jimmy and Jim on the phonological level.

> Phonologically Jim shows widespread loss of *r* (*do* door, *heah* here, *thoo* through), palatalization (i.e., the insertion of a palatal glide—the initial sound of yes—in certain environments: *k'yer* care, *dish-yer* this here, *(a) gwyne* as the present participle of *go*, and substitution of voiceless *th* with *f* (*mouf* mouth) of voiced *th* with *d* (*dese* these) and of the negative prefix *un-* with *on-* (*oneasy*). (Carkeet, "Dialects," 317)

Huck's speech, unlike Jimmy's and Jim's, has none of these features. But even from a phonological standpoint, I would argue, several elements make Jimmy's dialect closer to Huck's than to Jim's. Jimmy and Huck say "considerable" while Jim says "considable." Jimmy and Huck usually preserve the final *t* in contractions even when the next word begins with a consonant, but Jim usually drops it. As James Nathan Tidwell observed, for example (based on his analysis not of the manuscript or first edition, but, as Blair and Fischer note, on the "heavily styled Harper's 'Mississippi Edition'"), "Jim tends to drop the final *t* of a contraction when the next word begins with a consonant (as in 'ain' dat'), but to retain the *t* when the next word begins with a vowel or is emphatic . . ." (Tidwell, "Mark Twain's Representation of Negro Speech," 175; Blair and Fischer, "Textual Introduction," 508). Jimmy, by way of contrast, usually *keeps* the final *t* in contractions followed by consonants: "we ain't got no cats heah," "I wouldn't like to count all dem people," "Dey ain't got no bell," "De bell . . . don't make no soun', scasely," "I don't think." (The one exception to this rule in Jimmy's speech is "I don' never git drunk.") Jimmy and Huck say "an'" or "and"—in fact, Jimmy says "and" nine times, while Jim almost always says "en'."

43. An occasional quality that Bridgman and McKay isolate as characteristic of Huck's speech, and that I have shown to be characteristic of Jimmy's speech, may also be found in other vernacular speakers Twain created. On 18 December 1869, for example, Twain published the story of Dick Baker's cat in the *Buffalo Express* (he would include the story in *Roughing It* in 1872). It was a revised and expanded version of an earlier sketch, which he had probably written in California (Twain, "Explanatory Notes," *Roughing It*, 600). The original sketch, "Remarkable Sagacity of a Cat," was written in standard English, but Twain's 1869 revision told the story in a vernacular voice (Dick Baker's), and included some of the qualities that Twain would later find or make central to Jimmy's speech and Huck's, including irregular verb forms, double negatives, "and" as a connector, and repetition (*Roughing It*, 390–91). Although these qualities are present on occasion in Baker's speech, they are not as essential to it as they will be to Jimmy's and Huck's speech. Twain's recognition in 1869 that the original "Cat" sketch held more interest and was more dramatic when told in the vernacular may be viewed as a step toward his recognition of the power of vernacular voices. Double negatives, "and" as a connector, and the use of "considerable" as an adjective are also found in Simon Wheeler's speech in "Jim Smiley and His Jumping Frog" (1865), and repetition appears in the speech of Coon in "An Unbiased Criticism" (1865). For all their vitality, however, the voices of Dick Baker, Simon Wheeler, and Ben Coon are not Huck's the way Jimmy's voice is Huck's. The striking correspondences between Jimmy's and Huck's basic syntax, diction, and cadences, as well as between the two boys' defining character traits, confirm the importance Jimmy played in revealing to Twain the narrative potential of that distinctive brand of vernacular speech.

44. Twain, *Huckleberry Finn*, 193–94. Drawing humor from a narrator who is oblivious to the implications of his own comments was, of course, a stock feature of literary humor and folklore, as well.

45. Walter Blair, *Mark Twain and "Huck Finn,"* 75.

46. Peter Messent notes that

When Bakhtin speaks of the "radical character" of a naive narrator who completely fails to understand the usual ways of looking at the world, he could have had Huck Finn in mind. Bakhtin uses the word *estrangement* (his closeness to Russian Formalist conceptions of "defamiliarization" is obvious here) to suggest what happens when a fixed way of looking at and speaking about the world meets a narrator who is uncomprehendingly naive; who "by his very uncomprehending presence . . . makes strange the world of social conventionality." (Messent, "The Clash of Language: Bakhtin and *Huckleberry Finn*," 217)

47. Twain, *Huckleberry Finn*, 65.

48. Sloane, *Mark Twain as a Literary Comedian*, 132.

49. Twain, *Huckleberry Finn*, 153.

50. Twain, *Huckleberry Finn*, 135, 89, 166, 90.

51. Jimmy tells us, "Pa used to git drunk, but dat was befo' I was big—but he's done quit. He don' git drunk no mo' now. Jis' takes one nip in de mawnin', now cuz his stomach riles up, he sleeps so soun'. Jis' one nip—over to de s'loon—every mawnin'." With similar nonchalance, Huck notes that the judge who tried to reform Pap "reckoned a body could reform the ole man with a shot-gun, maybe, but he didn't know no other way" (28).

52. Jimmy enthusiastically admires the clock on the local church: "Dat clock ain't just a striker, like dese common clocks. It's a *bell*—jist a reglar *bell*—and it's a buster." Huck is just as impressed by the clock he encounters on the Grangerford mantelpiece: "It was beautiful to hear that clock tick; and sometimes when one of these peddlers had been along and scoured her up and got her in good shape, she would start in and strike a hundred and fifty before she got tuckered out. They wouldn't took any money for her" (136). Both Jimmy and Huck on occasion set themselves up as judges of refinement, unaware of the irony that their taking this role inevitably entails. Thus Jimmy passes judgment on the manners of the women in his house, and Huck on the wall markings left by some rough characters. Jimmy pronounces, "All dem brothers an' sisters o' his'n ain't no 'count—all ceptin' dat little teeny one dat fetched in dat milk. Dat's Kit, Sah. She ain't only nine year ole. But she's de mos' lady-like one in de whole bilin'." And Huck tells us, "There was heaps of old greasy cards scattered over the floor, and old whisky bottles, and a couple of masks made out of black cloth; and all over the walls was the ignorantest kind of words and pictures, made with charcoal" (61). The incongruity of a speaker who uses the word "ignorantest" while passing judgment on whether or not something is "ignorant" is lost on Huck. Similarly, Jimmy sees nothing amiss about putting himself forth as an authority on female refinement.

53. Twain, *Huckleberry Finn*, 137, 140.

54. Twain, *Huckleberry Finn*, 157.

55. Twain, *Tom Sawyer*, 74. Also on Huck's tongue shortly after he enters *Tom Sawyer* is the nickname "Hoss" (he refers to "Hoss Williams" on page 76; later in the book the Judge calls this person "Horse Williams.") "Hoss" is the nickname Jimmy expatiates on at some length in "Sociable Jimmy." Huck in *Tom Sawyer* shares some characteristic sentence constructions with Jimmy, as well. Huck, for example, says, "A body *can't be too partic'lar* how they talk about *these-yer* dead people" (*Tom Sawyer*, 93, emphasis added); Jimmy says, "People *can't be too particlar* 'bout sich things," and frequently says, "*dish-yer*," as well (emphasis added). Huck (in *Tom Sawyer*, 177–78) and Jimmy (in "Sociable Jimmy") both use the word "gal," while Tom makes it clear to Huck that (at least when referring to Becky Thatcher) he prefers the word "girl."

56. Twain, *Huckleberry Finn*, 198.

57. Twain, quoted in Walter Blair and Hamlin Hill, *America's Humor*, 322.

58. In a sketch written in 1868, which remained unpublished until Bernard DeVoto included it in *Mark Twain at Work* in 1942, Twain had experimented with telling a story from a boy's point of view. Twain presented the sketch as the diary of a boy named Billy Rogers. The sketch is, in some ways, a preparation for *Tom Sawyer*, and Billy is a precursor of Tom. The diary is dominated by Billy's admiration for "a heroine named Amy who inflicts on the hero the same agonies and ecstasies that Becky Thatcher was to inflict on Tom" (DeVoto, *Mark Twain at Work*, 6). But, as DeVoto comments, "It is Tom Sawyer untouched by greatness, and Tom Sawyer . . . without Huck Finn. It is crude and trivial, false in sentiment, clumsily farcical, an experiment in burlesque with all its standards mixed" (DeVoto, *Mark Twain at Work*, 7). The "Boy's Manuscript" is reprinted in Dahlia Armon and Walter Blair, eds., *Huck Finn and Tom Sawyer Among the Indians and Other Unfinished Stories*, 1–19. Armon and Blair assign 1868 as its date of composition ("Explanatory Notes," 265–66).

Although "Sociable Jimmy" is Twain's first published piece dominated by the perspective of a child narrator, he had shown an interest as early as 1866 in children's tendency to be oblivious to the import of what they reveal. In a letter Twain presents as being from his eight-year-old niece "Annie," for example, Twain had the child sociably prattle on about a range of news items, including the fact that "Sissy McElroy's mother has got another little baby. She has them all the time. It has got little blue eyes, like Mr. Swimey that boards there, and looks just like him" (Twain, "An Open Letter to the American People," 1). I am grateful to Victor Fischer for bringing this piece to my attention. For more on Twain's interest in the speech patterns of real children, including his own, see Doyno, *Writing "Huck Finn,"* 41–42, 131–32.

59. Twain, quoted in Blair and Hill, *America's Humor*, 327.

60. Doyno, *Writing "Huck Finn,"* 40.

61. Anon., "Mark Twain Tells the Secrets of Novelists," *New York American*, 26 May 1907, in Neider, ed., *Life as I Find It*, 388. Emphasis added.

62. Mark Twain, "The Art of Composition," 227.

63. Blair, *Mark Twain and "Huck Finn,"* 59. In addition to being the year *Tom Sawyer* appeared, 1876 was, of course, the year Twain began writing *Huckleberry Finn*. During that year, Blair tells us, Twain showed particular interest in a chapter on plagiarism in Henry H. Breen's *Modern English Literature: Its Blemishes and Defects*.

> On page 218 Breen scornfully quotes a statement of Alexander Dumas, whom he calls, rather sweepingly, "the most audacious plagiarist of any time or country." Says Dumas: "The man of genius does not steal; he conquers, he annexes to his empire. He makes laws for it, peoples it with subjects, and extends his golden scepter over it. And where is the man who, in surveying his beautiful kingdom, shall dare to assert that this or that piece of land is no part of his property?" Though Breen calls this a barefaced plea for literary thievery, Clemens agrees with Dumas in a marginal comment: "A good deal of truth in it. Shakespeare took other people's quartz and extracted the gold from it—it was a nearly valueless commodity before." (Blair, *Mark Twain and Huck Finn*, 59–60)

In other marginal comments Twain voiced his conviction that, as Blair put it, "an author might make materials his own by adapting them to the fictional world he was creating" (60).

64. SLC to Helen Keller, St. Patrick's Day 1903, *Mark Twain's Letters*, ed. Paine, 2:731. Twain's comments here are echoed by Bakhtin, who, as Peter Messent notes, "stresses so importantly, our language is not our own. In everyday speech 'of all words uttered . . . no less than half belong to someone else'. . . . We constantly use the speech of another. Prior discourse . . . invades our language at every turn" (Bakhtin, *Problems of Dostoevsky's Poetics*, 339, quoted in Messent, "The Clash of Language," 223).

65. Huck's voice, of course, will be more complex than Jimmy's, and much of that complexity will stem from the fact that two languages are, in effect, warring within him. Messent writes that one is "the words the dominant culture has given him to use concerning the slave," the "language of the authorities which has helped form him," and the other is "that language which has emerged during and out of the conversation with Jim on the raft—that of equality and friendship, one rooted in pragmatic experience of doing and acting." Although the "latter language, celebrating 'an affirmation of a friendship among equals' wins out (in terms of the way Huck will act) in the contest of both language and values . . . and leads to Huck's famous decision to tear up the letter and 'go to hell,'" by the same token, "Huck cannot overthrow the monoglossic discourse which has formed (part of) him. He is caught within its terms, its judgments, even as he decides to act in a way which counters its commands" (Messent, "The Clash of Language," 233). Messent feels that Huck "increasingly finds . . . his language too weak to oppose those dominant voices which take over the raft, take over his and Jim's lives. That element of his voice which has emerged—hesitantly and sporadically—to find positive expression within the context of that community of two on the raft, is muted to greater and greater extent" (235). Although "Huck has the final word in the novel," Messent feels that "the implications of those last words are, in Bakhtinian terms, bleak" (238).

66. Sidney Andrews, *The South Since the War: As Shown by Fourteen Weeks of Travel and Observation in Georgia and the Carolinas* [1866], 229. See Walt Wolfram, "The Relationship of White Southern Speech to Vernacular Black English." Also, David Carkeet notes that in Twain's time and in the present century as well, "the speech of lower-class rural whites in the South shares a great deal with the speech of blacks" (Carkeet, "The Dialects in *Huckleberry Finn*," 332). These parallels often led dialect geographers to assume that African-American speech was identical with the speech of Southern whites, a premise most linguists today reject. As George Townsend Dorrill notes in a 1986 review article updating Raven McDavid, Jr., and Virginia McDavid's 1951 article, "The Relationship of the Speech of American Negroes to the Speech of Whites," Ralph W. Fasold "states that many of the features claimed to be unique to blacks are shared with whites in the South, but that there is still a residue of features unique to the English of blacks" (Dorrill, *Black and White Speech in the Southern United States: Evidence from the Linguistic Atlas of the Middle and South Atlantic States*, 16). (These include, incidentally, two features that will be discussed in Chapter 2: remote-aspect *been* and copula absence). J. L. Dillard notes,

> Dialect geographers, in keeping with their preconception (almost, at times, an obsession) that the dialects of American English must be basically regional in distribution, continued to assert that Black dialects were—or, at least, had been in earlier times—identical with those of Southern whites. Since any specifically Black forms must represent "archaisms," the pidgin-creole tradition was felt to be unnecessary as an explanation of Black dialects in the United States. But the

dialect geographers further asserted that these differences were solely a matter of a few relics, hardly enough to constitute a true dialect difference. The historical records did not, of course, bear them out. Neither did the evidence of listener perception tests . . . ." (J. L. Dillard, "General Introduction: Perspectives on Black English," 13)

For a fuller discussion of the controversies surrounding this issue, see Holton, *Down Home and Uptown,* 24–41; John Baugh, *Black Street Speech: Its History, Structure and Survival,* 15–19; George Townsend Dorrill, *Black and White Speech in the Southern United States,* 1–17; and Ila Wales Brasch and Walter Milton Brasch, *A Comprehensive Annotated Bibliography of Black English,* ix.

67. Mark Twain, "Villagers of 1840–3," 96.

68. A photocopy of the page from "Morris Anderson Scrapbook" is in the Mark Twain Papers at the Bancroft Library at Berkeley.

69. Victor Doyno observed to me that the phrase "naturally leading spirits" suggests figures whose leadership qualities come from "nature," as opposed to the social world, with all its hierarchy and fixity (personal communication).

70. In Jay Martin's provocative and controversial psychoanalytic essay, "The Genie in the Bottle: *Huckleberry Finn* in Mark Twain's Life" (an essay that focuses on Twain's "persistent feelings of loss, guilt, despair, and insignificance and . . . his momentary masked disclosure and transcendence of these feelings in" the novel), the following intriguing sentence appears: "To oppose his father, then, was to identify with the black—to imagine that Uncle Dan'l or Uncle Ned and Jennie were his real parents and that, like Tom and Valet in *The Tragedy of Pudd'nhead Wilson,* he too was divided; his selves were interchangeable, but *his real self was a black child disguised as a white man*" (Martin, 60, emphasis added; summary of essay from Sattelmeyer and Crowley, eds., *One Hundred Years of "Huckleberry Finn,"* 14). Twain's personal identification with the experience of black slaves is also apparent from the metaphor he uses in *Life on the Mississippi* to describe how it felt to escape unscathed from Brown, an abusive riverboat pilot to whom Twain, as a young apprentice, had been lent by his "master," Horace Bixby: "I know how an emancipated slave feels; for I was an emancipated slave myself" (160).

71. SLC to Olivia Langdon Clemens, 10–11 January 1872, in Mark Twain Papers. Quoted with permission.

72. Mark Twain, *Sketches New and Old,* 30.

73. Edgar Marquess Branch and Robert Hirst, eds., Mark Twain, *Early Tales and Sketches* II, 265.

74. Albert Bigelow Paine, *Mark Twain: A Biography* 1:217.

75. Twain's notebook entry read, "Coleman with his jumping frog—bet stranger $50—stranger had no frog, and C. got him one:—in the mean time stranger filled C.'s frog full of shot and he couldn't jump. The stranger's frog won" (Paine, *Mark Twain, A Biography* 1:273).

76. Twain, *Sketches New and Old,* 240.

77. No one has given a more illuminating and insightful reading of the scene on the porch when Mary Ann Cord told her tale than Sherwood Cummings in *Mark Twain and Science,* 126–29.

78. William Dean Howells, *Twain–Howells Letters* 1:195. In *My Mark Twain* he added, "The rugged truth of the sketch leaves all other stories of slave life infinitely behind, and reveals a gift in the author for the simple, dramatic

report of reality which we have seen equalled in no other American writer" (Howells, *My Mark Twain*, 124).

79. I am grateful to Sherwood Cummings for generously sharing his fine paper about Mary Ann Cord with me:

> Research by Elmira scholar Herbert Wisbey has endorsed the essential accuracy of the story. Twain did change Auntie Cord's first name, which was Mary Ann rather than Rachel, and he got her age wrong. She was 76 rather than 60, a mistake testifying to the vigor in which she lived until, at age 90, she died from complications resulting from falling down a well. She had, indeed, been reunited with son Henry, who had become and remained a barber in Elmira until he died there in 1927 at age 82. There is a striking corroboration from three sources concerning the commanding presence of Rachel, or Mary Ann, Cord. In the story Rachel is "of mighty frame and stature," and in her telling how as a slave for sale she was chained and put on a scaffold, Rachel, the story-teller, "towered above us, black against the stars." Twain described Mary Ann in a letter to Howells three years later as "very tall, very broad, very fine in every way" (MT–H, 195). And in photographs recently discovered by Herbert Wisbey she appears as a handsome, tall, broad-shouldered woman. . . . (Cummings, "The Commanding Presence of Rachel Cord," 2)

See also Herbert A. Wisbey, Jr., "The True Story of Auntie Cord."

80. Mark Twain, photocopy of manuscript of "A Family Sketch," 39. Mark Twain Papers. Original in Mark Twain Collection, James S. Copley Library, La Jolla, Ca. Quoted with permission.

81. Photostat of inscription reproduced in Angela Gambill, "UM Receives Rare, Signed Twain Book," 13.

82. Wisbey, "The True Story of Auntie Cord," 4.

83. Gambill, "UM Receives Rare, Signed Twain Book," 1, 13; Molly Sinclair, "Mother and Son's Amazing Reunion," 1.

84. Louis J. Budd, who plans to reprint "Sociable Jimmy" in an edition of Mark Twain's social and political writings to be published by the Mark Twain Project, tried hard, more than ten years ago, to identify the town in which Jimmy lived (Budd, personal communication).

85. Additional material, however, may yet appear. The letter Twain wrote pledging his support of Warner McGuinn, one of the first black law students at Yale, was lost for a hundred years before it resurfaced in 1985, reminding us that "lost" chapters of history may continue to reveal themselves unexpectedly. See Edwin McDowell, "From Twain, a Letter on Debt to Blacks," 1.

86. George Brownell, ["Request for Information about 'Sociable Jimmy'"], 3.

87. He stated that "the proof of Twain's authorship of the 'Sociable Jimmy' tale can be established only by the discovery of a complete copy of the magazine containing it. (Note: Despite Mr. Underhill's statement that the clipping in his scrapbook was taken from a magazine, the photostat reproduction of it presents evidence that the clipping *might* have been cut from a newspaper.)" (George Brownell, "Home," 1.)

88. Fatout, *Mark Twain Speaks for Himself*, 92. Fatout's note and another note in Pettit's *Mark Twain and the South* comprise the entirety of published critical comment that "Sociable Jimmy" has received. Fatout's note reads as follows:

> Mark Twain may have been attuning his ear to the variations of Negro dialect and attempting to get it down credibly on paper. As Arthur G. Pettit observes in *Mark Twain & the South* (1974), the notebooks of the 1880s and 1890s are full

of dialect fragments, as well as folk expressions, as if Mark Twain were testing accuracy by the sound and experimenting with spelling to make print convey the sound correctly. In *Huckleberry Finn*, he explains, there are seven varieties of dialect, black and white. Furthermore, "The shadings have not been done in a haphazard fashion, or by guesswork; but painstakingly, and with the trustworthy guidance and support of personal familiarity with these several forms of speech." Perhaps Mark Twain wrote "Sociable Jimmy" partly as an exercise in vernacular language. (Fatout, *Mark Twain Speaks for Himself*, 92)

While Fatout deserves credit for making this important article available to scholars, it should be noted that the transcription that appears in *Mark Twain Speaks for Himself* is unreliable: there are twenty-nine discrepancies between it and the original article that ran in the *New York Times* in 1874.

Pettit's reference to "a long and tedious sketch about a ten-year-old black boy named Sociable Jimmy" is brief, dismissive, and riddled with erroneous conjectures based on faulty chronology (Pettit, *Mark Twain and the South*, 198 n.14). Pettit gives the sketch slightly more attention in his unpublished dissertation, but still dismisses it as "long and tedious" and generally without significance. He complains about Jimmy's "repetitiousness," failing to see any prefiguring of that same quality in Huck's speech. He uses "Sociable Jimmy" to bolster his case for "Twain's inability, or disinclination . . . to account for deeper character traits in the black man than superlative ignorance, innocence, and gullibility," failing to recognize how positive and important these very qualities will become when transmuted into the voice and character of Huck (Arthur G. Pettit, "Merely Fluid Prejudice," 118–19).

89. Photocopy of manuscript of "A True Story." Mark Twain Papers. Original in Mark Twain Collection (#6314), Clifton Waller Barrett Library, Manuscripts Division, Special Collections Department, University of Virginia. Quoted with permission.

90. Dixon Wecter, *Sam Clemens of Hannibal*, 75; Mark Twain Papers DV 206.

91. *Mark Twain's Autobiography*, ed. Paine, 1:100. Twain followed this statement with the comment, "I say in effect, using the phrase as a modifier. We were comrades, and yet not comrades; color and condition interposed a subtle line which both parties were conscious of and which rendered complete fusion impossible" (*Autobiography* 1:100).

92. Bernard DeVoto, *Mark Twain's America*, 65.

93. The affection Twain and his cousin felt toward black childhood playmates was not unusual. Eugene Genovese notes, "Sometimes, lifelong friendships grew out of these early years. 'When I's a chile we'uns played togedder,' Betty Farrow said of her childhood with her master's three girls and four boys, 'and we'uns 'tached to each other all our lives'" (Genovese, *Roll, Jordan, Roll*, 516).

94. In July–August 1952, the *Twainian* reprinted an article containing Tabitha Quarles Greening's recollections that the editor identifies as having "appeared in print some 35 years ago and reveals valuable information concerning Mark's environment during his youth" (Anon., "Mark Twain's Cousin, His Favorite, Tabitha Quarles," *The Twainian*, 1). In the article she recalled that

The folk lore and strange African legends of "Daddy Ned" and Uncle Dan'll [sic] with the weird distorted superstitions of the slave girl, Mary, Little Sam's playmate developed the romantic nature that he inherited from his visionary father. The captivating stories that made Mark Twain famous were founded on the stories of Uncle Dan'l and Daddy Ned. Uncle Dan'l is the Nigger Jim [sic] of *Tom Sawyer*. The pages of *Huckleberrey Finn* [sic] show picture after picture of the life on the Quarles farm. . . .

We children had a mighty easy life. You see the negroes did the work and we roamed the hills gathering flowers, picking nuts, tapping the trees for sugar and at night gathered around the fire place and heard the darkies tell their ghost stories. Sam just repeated those tales Uncle Dan'l and Uncle Ned told and folks said he was smart. . . .

In a little while I will go away and if it is to a reunion with father and mother, Uncle John and Aunt Martha, Sam and Margaret, Pamela and Brother Fred, that place, wherever it may be, will be heaven. I do not think we will be altogether happy unless we have Uncle Dan'l and Jinny the slave girl who was sold down south. They are the imperishable part of our childhood days and Sam with all the honors that came to him never forgot "Puss" and his darky playmates. ["Puss" was Tabitha Quarles's nickname.] (Anon., "Mark Twain's Cousin," *The Twainian*, 1–2)

According to the 1840 census, Quarles "owned, or at least recorded" two female slaves under age ten, who would have been Twain's contemporaries (Twain being five years old in 1840); the 1850 census (when Twain was fifteen) showed Quarles owning or recording female slave children who were eight and twelve years old. (There were younger and older slaves, as well, but these were the ones who were closest to Twain in age. All of these children were probably the children of "Uncle Dan'l." Census data from Ralph Gregory, curator of the Mark Twain Memorial, Florida, Missouri, cited in Pettit, *Mark Twain & the South*, 192 n. 23). There is no record of Quarles having owned male slaves Twain's age. But this information does not rule out the possibility that there were other slave children on the farm, or on surrounding farms, with whom Twain may have played.

95. Mark Twain, *Tom Sawyer*, 46.

96. Mark Twain, in letter to unidentified person, quoted in Blair, *Mark Twain and "Huck Finn,"* 9.

97. Mark Twain, *Notebooks and Journals*, vol. 3, ed. Robert Pack Browning, Michael B. Frank, and Lin Salamo, 343.

98. [Lute Pease,] "Mark Twain Talks," Portland *Oregonian*. 11 August 1895, 10. Reprinted in Louis Budd, "A Listing of and Selection from Newspaper and Magazine Interviews with Samuel L. Clemens, 1874–1910," 51–53; and quoted in Blair and Fischer, "Explanatory Notes," *Adventures of Huckleberry Finn*, 372.

99. Fred W. Lorch, *The Trouble Begins at Eight*, 129. Citing Clara Clemens, *My Father, Mark Twain*, 50, Lorch notes, "To escape any interference with his privacy Mark Twain sometimes deliberately chose obscure hotels and occasionally employed the pseudonym 'Samuel Langhorne' while on tour" (Lorch, *The Trouble Begins at Eight*, 129).

100. Lorch, *The Trouble Begins at Eight*, 129.

101. SLC to Olivia Langdon Clemens, 9 January 1872, rpt. in *Love Letters of Mark Twain*, ed. Dixon Wecter, 172.

102. Alan Gribben, *Mark Twain's Library: A Reconstruction*, 1:xxvii.

103. For example, while the front free endpaper of Meredith White Townsend's *Asia and Europe* was torn out (perhaps something to do with jottings

that had been on it?), the front pastedown endpaper includes a note about having taken out fire insurance, and another about comments made by a palmist. Twain scribbled penciled notes about the dearth of cheap American books on the front and rear endpapers of Emile Zola's *Rome*, and his assorted arithmetical computations appear on the last page of *A Story of the Golden Age*, on the back cover of a pamphlet entitled *The Beecher Trial: A Review of the Evidence*, and elsewhere (Gribben, *Mark Twain's Library* 1:41, 56; 2:709, 787).

104. Paul Fatout, *Mark Twain on the Lecture Circuit*, 151.

105. His speaking engagements included Allentown, Wilkes-Barre, Easton, Reading, Norristown, Washington, D.C., Wilmington, Great Barrington, Milford, Brattleboro, Boston, Hartford, Worcester, Manchester, Haverhill, Portland, Lowell, Philadelphia, Brooklyn, Rondout, Bennington, Albany, Newark, Oswego, Homer, Geneva, Auburn, Warsaw, Fredonia, Erie, Jackson, Lansing, Grand Rapids, Kalamazoo, Chicago, Aurora, Sandwich, Princeton, Champaign, Tuscola, Danville, Matoon, Paris, Indianapolis, Logansport, Richmond, Dayton, Columbus, Wooster, Salem, and Steubenville (Fatout, *Mark Twain on the Lecture Circuit*, 152–70).

106. See note 11. Twain lectured in Paris, Illinois, on 30 December 1871, and remained there through at least part of the next day.

107. See note 11.

108. Jeffrey Steinbrink, *Getting to Be Mark Twain*, 190.

109. SLC to Olivia Langdon Clemens, 27 November 1871, in *Love Letters*, ed. Wecter, 166.

110. Typescript of notebook 35, May–Oct. 1895, 8. Mark Twain Papers. Quoted with permission.

111. I am very grateful to William Andrews for making this astute observation and for suggesting to me this promising line of reasoning (personal communication).

112. See, for example, Lynn, *Mark Twain and Southwestern Humor*; Sloane, *Mark Twain as a Literary Comedian*; Covici, Jr., *Mark Twain's Humor*; Walter Blair, *Native American Humor*; M. Thomas Inge, ed., *The Frontier Humorists*. Although Henry Nash Smith *(Mark Twain: The Development of a Writer)* rejects the idea that Twain was influenced by Charles Farrar Browne's Artemus Ward, David E. E. Sloane *(Mark Twain as a Literary Comedian)* makes a convincing case for a closer connection between Ward and Twain.

113. Sloane, *Mark Twain as a Literary Comedian*, 95–103; 133.

114. Lynn, *Mark Twain and Southwestern Humor*, 69.

115. Lynn, *Mark Twain and Southwestern Humor*, 81; Covici, Jr., *Mark Twain's Humor*, 13–14; Sloane, *Mark Twain as a Literary Comedian*, 134.

116. Blair, *Mark Twain and "Huck Finn,"* 62–64; Sloane, *Mark Twain as Literary Comedian*, 134.

117. Petroleum V. Nasby [Locke], "Presumptuous Freedman: 'Ef It Hadn't Bin for Their Black Faces, They Wood Have Passed for Folks'" [1866], in Locke, *The Struggles of Petroleum V. Nasby*, 75.

118. Nasby [Locke], "Ethnology at Confedrit x Roads: 'Possibly the Seat uv the Intelleck Is in the Heel,'" in Locke, *The Struggles of Petroleum V. Nasby*, 208–13; Twain, *Huckleberry Finn*, 37–39. Other characters in *Huckleberry Finn* may have been indebted to contemporary dialect writers, as well. Since Twain completed the book in the early 1880s, he may have modeled the white women's

gossip scene at the Phelps's plantation on a similar episode Joel Chandler Harris included in "At Teague Poteet's: A Sketch of the Hog Mountain Range," which appeared in *Century Magazine* in 1883. See David Carkeet, "The Source for the Arkansas Gossips in *Huckleberry Finn*," 90–92.

119. Sut Lovingood, quoted in Edmund Wilson, "Sut Lovingood," 149–50.

120. "Sut Lovingood Yarns," quoted in Franklin J. Meine, "Tall Tales of the Southwest," 22. Huck would never break down categories in this manner, as Susan Harris has observed (personal communication).

121. Wilson, "Sut Lovingood," 149, 148.

122. "Sut Lovingood," quoted in Wilson, "Sut Lovingood," 148.

123. "Sut Lovingood," quoted in Wilson, "Sut Lovingood," 148.

124. "Sut Lovingood," quoted in Wilson, "Sut Lovingood," 148–49.

125. Covici, Jr., *Mark Twain's Humor*, 40.

126. Lynn, *Mark Twain and Southwestern Humor*, 80.

127. Meine, "Tall Tales of the Southwest," 21.

128. John Donald Wade, "Southern Humor," 35.

129. It is also important to note, of course, that that "something else" involved Twain's genius for narrowing the gap between oral and written communication. Twain's dialect writing is more readable and poses fewer obstacles for the reader than any that came before him.

130. In Twain's sequels to *Huckleberry Finn* in which Huck reappears, a number of the resemblances between Huck and Jimmy still hold. In *Tom Sawyer, Detective,* for example, Huck retains in his vocabulary words he had shared with Jimmy—such as "reckon," "snake," and "powerful." And the repetition characteristic of both boys' voices is still a part of Huck's voice in *Tom Sawyer Abroad*:

> All around us was a *ring*, a perfectly round *ring*, where the sky and the water come together; yes a monstrous big *ring*, it was, and we right in the dead *centre* of it. Plum in the *centre*. We was racing along like a prairie fire, but it never made any difference, we couldn't seem to git past that *centre* no way. I couldn't see that we ever gained an inch on that *ring* (24). (Emphasis added)

Huck in *Tom Sawyer Abroad* occasionally sounds like the "old" Huck, using words like "considerable" and "lonesome," employing irregular verb forms, double negatives, and frequent "and"s as connectors, and making up effective new words ("homeful"):

> We set scrunched up together, and thought considerable, but didn't say nothing, only just a word once in a while when a body had to say something or bust, we was *so* scared and worried. The night dragged along slow and lonesome. We was pretty low down, and the moonshine made everything soft and pretty, and the farm houses looked snug and homeful, and we could hear the farm sounds, and wished we could be down there. . . . (14)

In *Tom Sawyer Abroad*, Huck manifests the same aversion to cruelty that he and Jimmy had shown earlier:

> . . . I see a bird setting on a dead limb of a high tree, singing, with his head tilted back and his mouth open, and before I thought I fired, and his song stopped and he fell straight down from the limb, all limp like a rag, and I run and picked him up, and he was dead, and his body was warm in my hand, and his head rolled about, this way and that, like his neck was broke, and there was a white skin over his eyes, and one little drop of blood on the side of his head, and laws! I

couldn't see nothing more for the tears; and I hain't ever murdered no creature
since, that warn't doing me no harm, and I ain't going to. (32)

In general, however, there is a real falling off in these works. Gratuitous eye-
dialect intrudes, as in "I was just as cam, a body couldn't be any cammer" (*Tom
Sawyer Abroad*, 19), and Huck's comments are often rather wooden. Huck's
voice is substantially diminished, and, as the titles of the volumes suggest, it is
Tom's agenda and perspective that take over despite the fact that Huck is the
ostensible narrator.

Chapter 2

1. In referring to Jimmy's or Huck's speech as "black," I mean that it manifests either (1) lexical dimensions identified by dialect scholars such as James A.
Harrison in the 1880s as characteristic of "Negro English," or (2) syntactic qualities mapped by twentieth-century linguists as characteristic of what J. L. Dillard
defines as "the language of about eighty percent of Americans of African ancestry," which "differs from other varieties of American English" (Dillard, *Black
English: Its History and Usage*, ix). Dillard notes,

> Despite the controversial and even polemical nature of much of the publication
> on the subject, it is now generally recognized that there is a language variety
> called Black English. . . . This variety is spoken by the great majority of poor
> ("disadvantaged") Black citizens of the United States, the descendants of the
> plantation field hands, although not by many middle-class Negroes, descendants
> of house servants and freedmen. Recognition of the relationship of this variety to
> the pidgin and creole varieties of West Africa and of the Caribbean . . . is also
> becoming general. This variety is, in the terms of Stewart (1968), a vernacular: it
> has a large body (perhaps 18 to 20 million of living speakers, its history is trace-
> able (see Dillard 1972), and its rules are essentially autonomous (regarded only
> by the linguistically naive as "distortions" of other varieties of English). It has
> not undergone standardization—in the familiar sociolinguistic sense of codifica-
> tion and legitimization. (Dillard, "General Introduction: Perspectives on Black
> English," 9)

Dillard observes that "American Black English is different in grammar (in syntax) from the Standard American English of the mainstream white culture," and
"can be traced to a creolized version of English based upon a pidgin spoken by
slaves" which "probably came from the West Coast of Africa" (*Black English:
Its History and Usage*, 6).

One might note that the creolist perspective Dillard advocates (along with
many other scholars including William Stewart and Mervyn C. Alleyne) is not
without its critics. Indeed, the debate between, on the one hand, linguists like
William Labov, Ralph W. Fasold, and Walt Wolfram, who share with the cre-
olists an emphasis on the distinctive qualities of Black English, and, on the other
hand, dialect geographers including Hans Kurath, Raven McDavid, and Juanita
Williamson, who emphasize regional elements of dialect variation, has been quite
heated at times. As Sylvia Holton notes, "Today the position of the [dialect geog-
raphers] is weakening" (*Down Home and Uptown*, 39). For an illuminating and
evenhanded overview of the controversy, see Holton, *Down Home and Uptown*,
24–41. See also George Townsend Dorrill, *Black and White Speech in the South-*

ern United States, 1–17; and Ila Wales Brasch and Walter Milton Brasch, *Black English and the Mass Media*, 256–82. Holton observes that "no matter which hypothesis [dialect geographers' or creolist] one finds most convincing, one can certainly be cognizant of African remnants in sentence structure . . . and in vocabulary" (30).

Dillard notes that "Black English" is "also called Negro Non-Standard English or Merican" by other scholars (*Black English: Its History and Usage*, ix); to these terms we would add "Ebonics"(Molefi Kete Asante), "Black English Vernacular" (William Labov), and "American Black English" (Walter F. Edwards), as well. While Dillard uses the term "Black English" historically, a number of scholars cited in this section use the term to refer to contemporary "urban black speech" (Ralph W. Fasold, *Tense Marking in Black English*, ix). The term "Black English" was first used in 1734 (Hennig Cohen, "A Southern Colonial Word List," cited in Dillard, "General Introduction," 10). (See also Marvin D. Lofflin, "Black American English and Syntactic Dialectology"; William A. Stewart, "The Problems of Defining Negro Dialect," "Sociolinguistic Factors in the History of American Negro Dialects," and "Continuity and Change in American Negro Dialects"; and J. L. Dillard, "The Writings of Herskovits and the Study of the Language of the Negro in the New World.")

Molefi Kete Asante notes in "African Elements in African-American English," that

> recent linguistic studies define a language variously referred to as Black English, African-American English, or, more appropriately, Ebonics. This language has systematic rules different from English as it is popularly learned and spoken. . . . Ebonics contains structural remnants of certain African languages even though the vocabulary is overwhelmingly English. (22)

Asante's analysis is based on "the languages spoken by most African linguistic groups," which "are considered to be in the Niger-Congo family" (23).

As will be clear from Chapter 3, I share Wahneema Lubiano's opinion that

> African-American vernacular is not necessarily synonymous with "Black English" or any form of Black dialect (rural or urban), although the vernacular and vernacular users often employ Black English and/or Black dialects. African-American vernacular is an attitude toward language, a language dynamic, and a technique of language use. (Lubiano, "But Compared to What?," 279)

See Ila Wales Brasch and Walter Milton Brasch, *A Comprehensive Annotated Bibliography of American Black English*, for a wide range of references on the subject.

2. See, for example, Anon., "Negro Patois and Its Humor," *Appleton's Journal of Popular Literature, Science and Art*, 161–62; and James A. Harrison, "Negro English," *Anglia*, 232–79.

3. Harrison, "Negro English," *Anglia*, 232.

4. Harrison, "Negro English," *Anglia*, 232.

5. Harrison, "Negro English," *Anglia*, 235.

6. Harrison, "Negro English," *Anglia*, 235.

7. James Harrison, "Negro-English," *Modern Language Notes*, 123.

8. Harrison, "Negro English," *Anglia*, 235.

9. Harrison, "Negro English," *Anglia*, 232.

10. Dillard, *Black English: Its History and Usage*, 61–62.

11. Harrison, "Negro English," *Anglia*, 279.

12. Harrison, "Negro-English," *Modern Language Notes*, 123.

13. It is highly unlikely that Harrison, who lived in Lexington, Virginia ("Negro English," *Anglia*, 279), would have read "Sociable Jimmy" in the *New York Times*, particularly since the piece was never reprinted, and the *Times* was much less a national newspaper then than it is today. It is possible that he had read "A True Story" in either the *Atlantic Monthly* or *Sketches New and Old*, or had read *Tom Sawyer*, in which the black dialect is minimal, but if he had he would probably have included Twain in the list of authors whose writings helped "in forming this collection" ("Negro English," *Anglia*, 279). Harrison would probably not have been able to see a copy of *Huckleberry Finn* until its American publication in 1885, a year after his first article on "Negro English" appeared. Harrison does not include any black writers among his sources.

14. These qualities are Aphaeresis (initial clipping), Prothesis (initial addition), Syncope (medial clipping), Epenthesis (medial addition), Apocope (final clipping), and Epithesis (final addition). The one quality Jimmy's speech lacks is Transposition.

15. Harrison, "Negro English, *Anglia*, 261–79. Unless otherwise indicated, all references to Harrison from here on are to his 1884 article in *Anglia* rather than his 1892 article. Both the brief letter to the editor of 1892 and the long article of 1884 bear the same title, "Negro English." But the 1892 piece includes a hyphen: "Negro-English."

16. Harrison, "Negro English," 279.

17. Harrison, "Negro English," 271.

18. Harrison, "Negro English," 263–74.

19. Twain, *Huckleberry Finn*, 362. Emphasis added. "If I'd a knowed" is a characteristic expression of Huck's. See, for example, *Huckleberry Finn*, 105.

20. Harrison, "Negro English," 271, 274. Emphasis added.

21. Bridgman, *Colloquial Style in America*, 118.

22. Harrison, "Negro English," 233. Joel Chandler Harris, around this time, also commented on the "poetic imagination" manifested in the speech of African-Americans (*Atlanta Constitution* editorial, 9 April 1880, quoted in R. Bruce Bickley, Jr., *Joel Chandler Harris*, 38).

23. Zora Neale Hurston, "Characteristics of Negro Expression," 24–25.

24. Trilling, "The Greatness of *Huckleberry Finn*," 91.

25. Anon., "Negro Patois and Its Humor," 161. Interestingly, William Labov noted similar qualities in Black English in 1972, when, as Sylvia Holton observes, he

> stated his belief that much Standard English, which at its best is direct and forthright, is too often full of empty verbiage, . . . of passive voice, of vague and abstract jargon and fillers. For Labov, however, Black English is direct and meaningful more frequently than is Standard English. In many cases its speakers have simplified Standard English diction and are often able to make their points more vividly than Standard English speakers can. (Holton, *Down Home and Uptown*, 37)

26. Dillard, *Black English: Its History and Usage*, 41–42.

27. Janet Holmgren McKay, for example, noted that Huck "often shifts tense within the same sequence" ("'An Art So High,'" 64).

28. Non-redundantly marked verbs in the cases cited here are present-tense

verbs in sentences describing actions that clearly took place in the past (and that are described in past-tense verbs earlier in the sentence).

29. Twain, *Huckleberry Finn*, 48, 48, 99, 125. See also the following examples (emphasis added):

> I peeped out through the willow branches, and there it was—a skiff, away across the water. I couldn't tell how many was in it. It kept a-coming, and when it was abreast of me I *see* there warn't but one man in it. (42)
>
> I slunk along another piece further, then listened again; and so on, and so on; if I *see* a stump, I took it for a man. (48)

30. Twain, *Huckleberry Finn*, 55–56.
31. Dillard, *Black English: Its History and Usage*, 50. Dillard notes,

> There are hints of what need to be accounted for in published observations like those of Walter Loban, "Problems in Oral English," . . . which shows that the Negro group chosen had more "difficulties" with tense than the "Low White" group, the "High White" group, or the "Random" group. . . . there is strong reason to believe that the differences in language behavior of the Negro group result from something different in their own grammatical system, not from chance "mistakes" or any randomness in their language. (*Black English: Its History and Usage*, 49–50)

32. Dillard, *Black English: Its History and Usage*, 93.
33. As Ernest F. Dunn has noted, Europeans who went to Africa

> found themselves in a diverse linguistic environment, encountering innumerable tribes and countless unrelated spoken languages, languages so unique to European experience that they had to be regarded as void of intellectual rhyme or reason.
>
> Such was the perception, but not the reality. Although the languages were many and various, there were typological and lexical features which allowed for linkages into families. Africa was not a wild Babel of mutually exclusive languages. Using rigorous, linguistic methodology, African languages can be classified and grouped into four major families: Congo-Kordofanian, Nilo-Saharan, Afroasiatic, and Khoisan. Of particular significance is the fact that the Blacks who were brought to the Americas during the slave trade era spoke almost exclusively the languages of only a subfamily within one of the families [of African languages], that is, the Niger Congo of the Congo-Kordofanian. The linguistic diversity so apparently lacking in pattern or structural framework was, in reality, a subfamily of languages woven together in a fabric of structural similarities. It was this commonality which eventually provided for the broad grammatical base on which to build the bridge of communication between African and European, and which previously provided for communication between African and African of differing language backgrounds. ("The Black–Southern White Dialect Controversy," 106)

Ivan Van Sertima observed in 1970,

> Under the surface of differences—there existed certain basic patterns, patterns which were to assert themselves like engineering building blocks and architectural blueprints when it became necessary for the slaves to build a bridge of communication between the European and African tongues. (Quoted in Dunn, 112)

As Holton put it, despite the linguistic multiplicity, "the West African languages tended to share many structural features of grammar and syntax, even though their vocabularies were quite different" (26).

34. Joseph E. Holloway, ed., *Africanisms in American Culture*, xiv.

35. Asante, "African Elements in African-American English," 24.

36. Jeutonne Brewer, "Possible Relationships between African Languages and Black English Dialect," quoted in Asante, "African Elements," 24.

37. John Victor Singler notes in "Copula Variation in Liberian Settler English and American Black English" that "in recent times no feature of American Black English (ABE) has been analyzed so extensively as its copula system" (129). For an overview of research on copula deletion in Black English, see John Baugh, "A Reexamination of the Black English Copula." See also William Labov, "Contraction, Deletion, and Inherent Variability of the English Copula"; Dillard, *Black English: Its History and Usage*, 49; Elizabeth Closs Traugott, *Pidgins, Creoles, and the Origins of Black English*, 67, 88; and Singler, "Copula Variation," 129–64.

38. Twain, *Huckleberry Finn*, 55.

39. Fasold, *Tense Marking in Black English*, 2. Emphasis added.

40. Fasold, *Tense Marking*, ix–x. Walt Wolfram, in his widely cited article, "The Relation of White Southern Speech to Vernacular Black English," suggests that "the copula absence in white Southern speech may have been assimilated from decreolizing black speech" (93).

41. Mervyn C. Alleyne, *Comparative Afro-American: An Historical Comparative Study of English-Based Afro-American Dialects of the New World*, 167.

42. Ayọ Bamgboṣe, "On Serial Verbs and Verb Status," cited in Asante, "African Elements," 26.

43. Ayọ Bamgboṣe, "On Serial Verbs and Verb Status," cited in Asante, "African Elements," 26. The Niger-Congo subfamily of languages, to which the Gur subgroup (including Vagala) and the Kwa subgroup (including Yoruba) belong, is the largest in Africa, and includes the languages originally spoken by the majority of slaves imported to America. (Kenneth Katzner, *The Languages of the World*, 6, 29, 292; Merritt Ruhlen, *A Guide to the World's Languages, Vol. I: Classification*, 305; Dietrich Westermann and M. A. Bryan, *The Languages of West Africa*, 54, 62, 76, 84, 85; Dunn, "The Black–Southern White Dialect Controversy," 106). See note 33.

44. Alleyne, *Comparative Afro-American*, 167.

45. Asante, "African Elements," 28–29. Asante, who prefers the term "Ebonics" to refer to the group of African-derived languages that includes "Black English," cites the following example:

> The Ebonics expression, "I took consideration and joined de lawd" can be paraphrased as "I accepted religion" or "I became a Christian.". . . . English usually focuses on the main verb, and it is the main verb that usually surfaces; therefore, on the surface of the English translation we get the verb "accept." The Ebonics speaker, tending to surface a larger number of words to express the same action, surfaces the verb participle "took consideration" for the act of having thought about or pondered and "joined" for the actual step in accepting that faith. The Ebonics speaker here seems to want to express each event, as does the speaker in many West African languages. (Asante, "African Elements," 27)

46. Asante, "African Elements," 28.

47. Twain, *Huckleberry Finn*, 277. Emphasis added. Leo Marx has also noted Huck's characteristic tendency to use "a series of verbs . . . strung together largely by the word 'and,'" and has commented on the impact of this technique

on writers after Twain (Marx, "The Vernacular Tradition in American Literature," 15).

48. Dillard, *Black English: Its History and Usage*, 26.

49. Frederick G. Cassidy, "Gullah," 772.

50. Ivan Van Sertima, "My Gullah Brother," 142–43. Other scholars have examined some of these elements in Black English generally. Baugh, for example, analyzes the phenomenon of "multiple negation" (*Black Street Speech*, 82–85).

51. The "repetition" that Bridgman stressed as central to Huck's voice also characterizes the speech of slaves whose recollections were collected by James Mellon in *Bullwhip Days*, lending support to the notion that some of the rhythms and cadences of Huck's and Jimmy's speech may have been characteristic of the speech of African-Americans. Mellon quotes Thomas Cole, for example, as follows: "*Corn* was *hauled off*, cotton was *hauled off*, hogs and cattle was rounded up and *hauled off*, and things begins lookin' bad. Instead of eatin' *corn* bread made outen *corn*meal, we eats *corn* bread made outen kaffir *corn* and maize" (Mellon, 63). (Emphasis added.) These repetitions greatly resemble those commonly used by both Jimmy and Huck, as we have shown. The rhythms and cadences of African-American speech have been neglected by linguists in favor of issues of phonology, syntax, and diction, and might be a potentially fruitful field for further research.

52. Bridgman, *Colloquial Style in America*, 31.

53. Bridgman, *Colloquial Style in America*, 31.

Chapter 3

1. Mark Twain, *Tom Sawyer*, 73–74.

2. Twain, *Tom Sawyer*, 78.

3. Mark Twain, "Corn-Pone Opinions," *Europe and Elsewhere*, 399–406. This essay was found in Twain's papers at his death, and its exact date of composition is unknown. I assign it the 1901 dating following Paul Baender, who made the most recent effort to date it (Baender, ed., *What Is Man?*, 544). Paine dates the essay 1900 in *Europe and Elsewhere* (399). Dixon Wecter dates it 1896 (*Sam Clemens of Hannibal*, 290 n. 16).

4. Henry Louis Gates, Jr., *Signifying Monkey*, xxiv. Gates uses the bracketed (g) to distinguish the "black term" for a specific rhetorical practice (with its connotations of indirection, double-voiced word play, etc.) from the "white term," by which he refers to the Standard-English denotation of the term "signifying" (*Signifying Monkey*, 46).

5. Gates, Jr., *Signifying Monkey*, 53.

6. Twain, "Corn-Pone Opinions," 399–400. Jerry, like Jimmy, has received almost no critical attention. The one mention we find of him is by Dixon Wecter, who, in his chapter on Twain's summers at the Quarles farm in Florida, Missouri, says simply that the slave to whom Twain referred in "Corn-Pone Opinions" may have been "quite possibly another Quarles servant" (Wecter, *Sam Clemens of Hannibal*, 99–100). This would be possible only if Wecter's dating (1896) is correct and Baender's (1901) and Paine's (1900) are not, since fifty years before the date of composition, by Baender's and Paine's timetable, would have set the encounter after Twain's family had ceased spending summers

at the Quarles farm, to which they went through 1847 or 1848. (Of course, Twain's reference to "fifty years" may have been an approximate rather than an exact figure.) Wecter cites no other evidence to support his contention that Jerry was from Florida, Missouri, rather than Hannibal. We simply have no additional information to help us identify him. The idea that Jerry was, indeed, a real person is supported by the fact that other specific slaves Twain recalls from his childhood (like "Uncle Dan'l") have also been described, by others who knew them (see Anon., "Mark Twain's Cousin"). We have no reason to believe that Jerry was an invention of Twain's; on the contrary, it is likely that he existed, and that an encounter close to the one Twain described actually happened.

7. Twain's mother's reaction suggests the possibility that Jerry may have been "signifying" about sexual matters, as well, or that she feared he might.

8. Louis J. Budd, personal communication, 16 June 1992.

9. Another possibility is that Twain acquiesced to the racist mores of his time and stifled the impulse to openly acknowledge, in print, the rhetorical talents of an African-American. (Theodore Dreiser, for example, was subjected to broad public ridicule in 1893 for praising, in print, the singing talents of an African-American soprano. See Fishkin, *From Fact to Fiction*, 103.) Even fifty years after the fact, Twain refrained from publishing his comments: "Corn-Pone Opinions" was published only posthumously.

10. Mark Twain, *Autobiography*, ed. Charles Neider, 32.

11. William Wells Brown, *Narrative*, 83–84.

12. William L. Van Deburg, *Slavery and Race*, 63. Van Deburg cites as novels in which this depiction of the role of the clergy may be found, William Wells Brown's *The Escape* and *Clotel*, and Martin R. Delany's *Blake* (Van Deburg, 183).

13. Lorenzo Johnston Greene, *The Negro in Colonial New England*, 264.

14. Mather, quoted in Greene, *The Negro in Colonial New England*, 286.

15. Greene, *The Negro in Colonial New England*, 286. I am indebted to Katherine Clay Bassard's fine 1992 Ph.D. dissertation, "Spiritual Interrogations: Conversion, Community and Authorship in the Writings of Phillis Wheatley, Ann Plato, Jarena Lee, and Rebecca Cox Jackson" for having drawn my attention to these passages from Lorenzo Johnston Greene's *The Negro in Colonial New England*, and to Cotton Mather's "The Negro Christianized: An Essay to Excite and Assist That Good Work, the Instruction of Negro Servants in Christianity" (1706).

16. Genovese, *Roll, Jordan, Roll*, 203.

17. Genovese, *Roll, Jordan, Roll*, 206.

18. Genovese, *Roll, Jordan, Roll*, 208.

19. William Wells Brown, *Clotel*, 86–87.

20. [Mark Twain], [fragment], DV Box 37, old DV 128, Mark Twain Papers. Quoted with permission.

21. Thomas L. Webber, in *Deep Like the Rivers*, notes that "perhaps the most pervasive religious theme of the [slave] quarter community centered upon the immorality of slavery and the necessity of distinguishing between the concepts of true Christianity and the falsehoods of the slaveholders' preaching" (80). Webber elaborates on this theme in Chapter 6 of his book, entitled "True Christianity Versus Slaveholding Priestcraft: The Immorality of Slavery" (80–90).

22. See Lovell, Jr.'s, "The Social Implications of the Negro Spiritual."

23. Claudia Mitchell-Kernan, "Signifying," 314.

24. Mitchell-Kernan, "Signifying," 325.

25. Interestingly, this is not the message that Twain himself emphasized in "Corn-Pone Opinions," where he used Jerry's sermons as a jumping-off point for a discourse on the nature of conformity. We must try to distinguish, however, between what impressed the boy of fifteen about Jerry's sermons, and what the man of sixty-five found worth expatiating on. We see both, of course, through the eyes of the sixty-five-year-old writer. The portion of Jerry's text that Twain quotes—"You tell me whar a man gits his corn-pone, en I'll tell you what his 'pinions is"—embraces much more than just the issue of conformity. But conformity must have been much on Twain's mind around 1900, when he was turning out piece after piece that he chose not to publish. The question of how the pressure to conform to certain political and literary standards influenced Twain's self-censorship during these years is a topic that can be mentioned only in passing here; it will be central to *The Stories He Couldn't Tell: Mark Twain and Race.*

26. As Henry Louis Gates, Jr., notes,

> Black people have always been masters of the figurative: saying one thing to mean something quite other has been basic to black survival in oppressive Western cultures. Misreading signs could be, and indeed often was, fatal. "Reading," in this sense, was not play; it was an essential aspect of the "literacy" training of a child. This sort of metaphorical literacy, the learning to decipher complex codes, is just about the blackest aspect of the black tradition. ("Criticism in the Jungle," 6)

27. Mark Twain, "A Gorgeous Swindle," 119–21; *The Innocents Abroad*, 368–70; "The Story of the Good Little Boy Who Didn't Prosper," 49–55.

Frederick Douglass also emphasizes the importance of recognizing the gap between the surface meaning of words and the truth that may lie behind them when he urges readers to discount and dismiss the fulsome praise of slavery on the part of slaves that fills books prepared by pro-slavery forces. He tells the story of the slave who worked on a large plantation, who had never set eyes on his master. The slave made the mistake of being candid with an unknown white man who stopped him on the road one day and asked how he was treated. For his honesty he was sold down the river. The story, and others like it, quickly made their way into the oral lore, Douglass remarks; accordingly it soon became impossible to find a slave in the neighborhood without praise for his master (Douglass, *Narrative*, 61–62). Ethan A. Andrews commented on this phenomenon in 1936, noting that

> When visitors in the South asked a slave whether he wished to be free, he usually replied: "No, massa, me no want to be free, have good massa, take care of me when I sick, never 'buse nigger; no, me no want to be free. (Ethan Andrews, *Slavery and the Domestic Slave Trade*, 97–99, cited in Stampp, *The Peculiar Institution*, 87)

The slaves, like the clergymen, said slavery was good because it was in their interest to say so. Those who mistook the slaves' *words* about their kind treatment for the *truth* about how they were treated, Douglass points out, were grossly misled. Also misled were those who "could speak of the singing among slaves, as evidence of their contentment and happiness. It is impossible to conceive of a greater mistake" (Douglass, *Narrative*, 58).

Interestingly, in "A True Story, Repeated Word for Word as I Heard It," Mark Twain has his stand-in, "Misto C—," make an analogous mistake. Observing a former slave's cheerfulness and readiness to laugh, he asks,

> "Aunt Rachel, how is it that you've lived sixty years and never had any trouble?"
> . . . She turned her face over her shoulder toward me, and said, without even a smile in her voice:
> "Misto C—, is you in 'arnest?" ("A True Story," 240)

After sharing a story that begins with her separation from her child on the auction block and ends with their reunion years later, Aunt Rachel "signifies" on "Misto C's" initial comment in the line that closes the story—a fine example of "repetitition with a signal difference":

> "Oh no, Misto C—, *I* hain't had no trouble. An' no *joy*!" (247)

28. For a fuller discussion of this point, see Fishkin, "Mark Twain," in *From Fact to Fiction*, 61–63, 66–68.

29. Indeed, this textual complexity affects the ways that Twain's writings continuously reward rereadings.

30. Gates, Jr., *Signifying Monkey*, 103. See also Roger Abrahams, *Positively Black*, 41.

31. Alan Dundes, *Mother Wit*, 310.

32. As Alan Dundes recommends,

> For an excellent study of the importance of indirection or allusion in an African society, see Ethel M. Albert, "'Rhetoric,' 'Logic,' and 'Poetics' in Burundi: Culture Patterning of Speech Behavior," in John J. Gumperz and Dell Hymes, "The Ethnography of Communication," *American Anthropologist*, 66, no. 6, part 2 (1964) pp. 35–54. . . . For an interesting application of signifying to poetry, see Carolyn M. Rodgers, "Black Poetry—Where It's At," *Negro Digest*, vol. 18 (September, 1969), pp. 7–16." (*Mother Wit*, 310)

33. William D. Pierson, "Puttin' Down Ole Massa: African Satire in the New World," 22.

34. W. E. B. DuBois, "The Humor of Negroes," 12. DuBois gave the following example in the ellipsis between the two sentences that are quoted: "I remember when a celebrated Texan politician was shouting a fervent oration, two undistinguished Negroes listened to him from a distance: 'Who is dat man?' said one. The other looked on, without smiling: 'I dunno, but he sutin'ly do recommen' hisself mos' high'" (DuBois, "Humor," 12).

35. Michael G. Cooke, *Afro-American Literature in the Twentieth Century: The Achievement of Intimacy*, ix.

36. Twain, *Huckleberry Finn*, 149–51.

37. These are:

1. indirection, circumlocution
2. metaphorical-imagistic (but images rooted in the everyday, real world)
3. humorous, ironic
4. rhythmic fluency and sound
5. teachy but not preachy
6. directed at person or persons usually present in the situational context
7. punning, play on words

8. introduction of the semantically or logically unexpected (Geneva Smitherman, *Talkin' and Testifyin'*, cited in Gates, Jr., *Signifying Monkey*, 94).

38. Smitherman, cited in Gates, Jr., *Signifying Monkey*, 94.

39. Roger Abrahams, *Deep Down in the Jungle*, 62–63.

40. As Gates notes, "Signification is a complex rhetorical device that has elicited various, even contradictory, definitions from linguists . . ." (*Signifying Monkey*, 88).

41. Gates, Jr., *Signifying Monkey*, 86.

42. Gates, Jr., *Signifying Monkey*, 82.

43. Twain, *Huckleberry Finn*, [lv].

44. For an analysis of Twain's satire on a range of texts in the novel, see Fishkin, "Mark Twain," in *From Fact to Fiction*, 79–84.

45. African satire was both political and social. Brodie Cruickshank reported from the Gold Coast in 1853 that satirical songs were improvised by singers who indulged in "mocking ridicule" or "biting sarcasm" as the "circumstances seemed to demand" (Cruickshank, *Eighteen Years on the Gold Coast of Guinea*, II: 265–66). As Pierson notes in "Puttin' Down Ole Massa," to this day, "throughout much of Africa," satiric songs still "lampoon the pompous and condemn those who neglect their duties, or who are cruel and overbearing" (21).

46. Pierson, "Puttin' Down Ole Massa," 20. Pierson refers readers to the following research by Africanists:

> Alan P. Merriam, "African Music," in *Continuity and Change in African Culture*, ed. William R. Bascom and Melville Herskovits (Chicago: Phoenix Books, 1963), pp. 51, 55; Alan P. Merriam, "Music and the Dance" in *The African World*, ed. Robert A. Lystad (New York: Praeger, 1965) pp. 464–66; Waterman and Bascom, "African and New World Folklore," p. 21; and Melville J. Herskovits, *The New World Negro* (Bloomington: Minerva Press, 1969), pp. 137–40. (Pierson, 31)

47. Cruickshank, *Eighteen Years on the Gold Coast of Guinea*, II: 265–66. Cruickshank writes,

> This habit of publishing praise or shame of individuals in spontaneous song, exercises no little influence upon conduct; for the African is most sensitive to public opinion, and dreads being held up to ridicule, while the incense of flattery incites him to actions which will gain for him the admiration of his countrymen. In this way these singing men and women become the organs of public opinion. The acrimony of their censure is sometimes so severe, that it leads to contentions, especially when a whole company or division of a town forms the subject of a derisive attack. If a white man were to pass these songsters while thus employed, they would quickly seize upon some peculiarity of his character, whether good or bad, and elaborate it aloud, amidst the unrestrained merriment of the bystanders." (Cruickshank, *Eighteen Years on the Gold Coast of Guinea*, II, 265–266)

48. Theodore Van Dam, "The Influence of West African Songs of Derision in the New World," 53.

49. Nicholas Cresswell, *Journal of Nicholas Cresswell, 1774–1777*, 17–19, cited in Gates, Jr., *Signifying Monkey*, 66.

50. Bryan Edwards, *The History of the British Colonies in the West Indies* 2:103; James M. Phillippo, *Jamaica: Its Past and Present State*, 75, cited in Pierson, "Puttin' Down Ole Massa," 24.

51. Jean Baptiste Labat, *Nouveau voyage aux isles de l'Amerique*, 57–58, cited in Pierson, "Puttin' Down Ole Massa," 25. "Considering the substantial scholarship examining both the resistance of American slaves to bondage and their musical contribution to American culture," Pierson writes, "it is suprising that more attention has not been paid to the satirical songs and mimicry used by black bondsmen to lampoon the shortcomings of their white masters" (20). "The first scholarly recognition of the satiric song as a category of Afro-American folksong," Pierson notes,

> came in the chapter "Satirical Songs of the Creoles," in Henry E. Krehbiel, *Afro-American Folksongs* (New York: G. Schirmir, 1914), pp. 140–53. An important modern study concerned in part with such songs is Harold Courlander, *The Drum and the Hoe* (Berkeley: Univ. of California Press, 1960), chapters 12–13; and a general summary discussion is available in Richard A. Waterman and William R. Bascom, "African and New World Negro Folklore," in *Dictionary of Folklore, Mythology and Legend*, ed. Maria Leach (New York: Funk and Wagnalls, 1949), I, 21. A relevant article is Theodore Van Dam, "The Influence of the West African Song of Derision in the New World," *African Music*, I (1954), pp. 53–56, which connects such early Afro-American songs to the American "blues" and a variety of West Indian music. (Pierson, 31)

Russell Ames's "Protest and Irony in Negro Folksong" offers a useful analysis of how slaves masked their protest in satire, and connects this phenomenon with more recent traditions of African-American folksong.

52. Lawrence W. Levine, *Black Culture and Black Consciousness*, 317.

53. Levine, *Black Culture and Black Consciousness*, 335.

54. Twain, "Corn-Pone Opinions," 104. We can get a sense of the kind of work schedule Jerry may have had to contend with from an article on slave management published in *Southern Cultivator* in 1850 in which a planter wrote that slaves "should rise early enough to be at work by the time it is light. . . . While at work they should be brisk. . . . I have no objection to their whistling or singing some lively tune, but no drawling tunes are allowed in the field, for their motions are almost certain to keep time with the music" (quoted in Stampp, *The Peculiar Institution*, 78).

55. For an extended discussion of the divine African trickster figure (of Yoruba mythology), Esu-Elegbara, and his relation to versions of the trickster that may be found in the United States, see Gates, Jr., "A Myth of Origins: Esu-Elegbara and the Signifying Monkey" in *The Signifying Monkey*, 3–43. See also Robert Farris Thompson, *Flash of the Spirit*, 18–33. John Blassingame notes that

> Animal stories are constant throughout West Africa. The trickster figures—the Nigerian Tortoise, the Ghanaian ananse or spider, and the rabbit—are ubiquitous. Congenitally weak, slow moving, or looked down upon by the stronger animals, the tortoise, spider, and rabbit are wise, patient, boastful, mischievous, roguish, guileful, cunning, and they always outwit their stronger foes and triumph over evil." (*The Slave Community*, 24)

Blassingame cites Northcote W. Thomas, *The Ibo-Speaking Peoples of Nigeria*, I, 139–40; Amaury Talbot, *Tribes of the Niger Delta*, 336–44; G. T. Basden, *Niger Ibos*, 424–36.

Trickster tales are not, of course, unique to Africa, and African-Americans may have been exposed to European (and Native American) trickster traditions.

Wherever they place themselves in the debates over African versus European-derived folktales, however, folklorists assume that Africa was the source of at least some of the tales. (For discussions of this debate, see Richard M. Dorson, *American Negro Folktales*; Alan Dundes, "African and Afro-American Tales"; Stephen S. Jones, "'The Rarest Thing in the World': Indo-European or African?"; Richard M. Dorson, "The African Connection: Comments on *African Folklore in the New World*.") While other cultures have trickster-tale traditions, the black trickster-slave who outwits his white master was a specific African-American tradition that has been widely documented. See Dorson, *American Negro Folktales*, for numerous examples of African-American trickster figures. Although one can find tricksters in other cultures (Native American, Jewish-American, etc.), Mark Twain's principal exposure to this form was through African-American traditions.

John W. Roberts observes in "The African American Animal Trickster as Hero" that

> Trickster-tale traditions, especially those in which clever animals act as human, were ubiquitous in the cultures from which Africans enslaved in the United States had come. Therefore it is not surprising that tales of trickery that were developed around the exploits of anthropomorphized animals occupied a central tradition in the oral narrative performances of the enslaved Africans. (97)

It should also be pointed out that when Jerry made the sound of sawing wood with his mouth, he was showing his skill at a tradition of making ideophones that was widespread throughout Africa (Robert Farris Thompson, personal communication). He was also engaged in the "avoidance of work," a theme that, as Houston Baker stresses, was an important subliminal component of many African-American trickster tales (Baker, *Long Black Song*, 22). See note 66.

56. Roberts, "The African American Animal Trickster as Hero," 106–9. See also Roger Abrahams, *Positively Black*, 63–69.

57. Susan Feldmann, cited in Roberts, "The African American Animal Trickster as Hero," 106.

58. Levine, *Black Culture and Black Consciousness*, 114.

59. Arnold Rampersad referred to Huck and Tom as tricksters in 1984 in his article in the *Mark Twain Journal* which was later reprinted in *Satire or Evasion?* (Rampersad, "*Huckleberry Finn* and Afro-American Literature," 222).

60. Levine, *Black Culture and Black Consciousness*, 106.

61. As William Andrews has observed, Huck's smallpox lie echoes a similar lie with which fugitive slave W. C. Pennington deceived some slave-catchers in his narrative. He also describes striking "similarities of substance, tone, and thematic purpose" in the use the authors make of this episode in the two books ("Mark Twain and James W. C. Pennington," 107). There is no proof that Twain had read Pennington's narrative, but the ex-slave was well-known in New York when Twain was there in 1853, and Twain could also have been familiar with him through the positive comments about him that appear in the conclusion of Harriet Beecher Stowe's *Uncle Tom's Cabin*, a novel Twain had definitely read. Andrews concludes this perceptive and intriguing article with the conjecture,

> Through *The Fugitive Blacksmith*, therefore, Samuel Clemens may have received not only the germ of a memorable scene for *Huckleberry Finn* but also a stimulus

to reflect back on his own boyhood, from which the heroes of his greatest work would come, led by a fugitive white youth whose unresolved ethical dilemmas and quest for an uncompromised freedom made him the spiritual brother of fugitive slave narrators like James. W. C. Pennington. (Andrews, "Mark Twain and James W. C. Pennington: Huckleberry Finn's Smallpox Lie," 111)

See also MacKethan, "Lighting Out as Design."

62. Nigel Thomas, *From Folklore to Fiction: A Study of Folk Heroes and Rituals in the Black American Novel*, 82.

63. Thomas, *From Folklore to Fiction*, 82.

64. Twain, *Huckleberry Finn*, 75. In "The Spunk of a Rabbit: An Allusion in *Huckleberry Finn*," William Scheick notes that shortly before he saves Jim from the slave-hunters, Huck tells us that he couldn't speak up because he lacked "the spunk of a rabbit." Huck then drives them away by begging them to come onto the raft to help with his father, who has smallpox. Scheick notes the resemblance between Huck's asking for the opposite of what he wants here and Brer Rabbit's begging Brer Fox not to throw him into the briar patch in *Uncle Remus, His Songs and His Sayings* (1880). Twain was a great admirer of Joel Chandler Harris, author of the Uncle Remus stories, which became a best-seller in the 1880s, and considered him "the only master" of black dialect (Twain, quoted in Kaplan, *Mr. Clemens and Mark Twain*, 245).

65. Twain, *Huckleberry Finn*, 267.

66. Jerry, of course, would not have characterized his behavior this way, although this is, in fact, what he was doing. What he probably would have said he was doing was cleverly getting out of work. Outwitting the white master by making him think you were working when you weren't is a common theme in African-American oral tradition. For example, among themselves, slaves would sing the following song:

> You may call me Raggedy Pat
> 'Cause I wear this raggedy hat,
> And you may think I'm a workin'
> But I ain't.

(George P. Rawick, ed., *The American Slave*, "Arkansas Narratives," vol. 8, part 2, 335.)

Chapter 4

1. Underlining of "professedly" appears on TS 1 Carbon, verified by SLC, and TS 2 Ribbon, prepared by typist for 31 July 1906 autobiographical dictation (Mark Twain Papers, 988). Quoted with permission.

2. Paul Laurence Dunbar, "An Ante-Bellum Sermon," 27–29.

3. Critics are increasingly taking this approach to other work by Twain, as well. For readings of *Pudd'nhead Wilson* as a commentary on the 1890s, see Eric J. Sundquist, "Mark Twain and Homer Plessy," and Shelley Fisher Fishkin, "Race and Culture at the Century's End: A Social Context for *Pudd'nhead Wilson*."

4. Toni Morrison, personal communication.

5. The recently recovered manuscript of the first half of *Huckleberry Finn* requires us to revise the standard notions of precisely where Twain left off writ-

ing in 1876. These revisions, however, do not affect the basic argument expressed here. The 1876 stint of composition was thought to have ended in Chapter 16 with the smashing of the raft. We now know that Twain ended the 1876 portion of the manuscript in the middle of the feud chapter (Chapter 18) instead. Thus, rather than ending his first period of work with the words "smashing straight through the raft," Twain ended it with the words, "tell me about it." Although a bit of momentum may have carried Twain along into some of the Grangerford-Sheperdson feud material, the fact remains that in the summer of 1876 he smashed the raft that was to carry Huck and Jim out of slave territory and into freedom, and he did not return to the manuscript until 1879. (Victor Fischer, "Discovery," and personal communication.) (As it happened, the raft would later turn out not to have been "smashed" after all—but Huck and Jim, and perhaps Twain himself, didn't know that at the point Twain abandoned the manuscript in 1876).

6. See, for example, George C. Rable, "1876: The Triumph of Reaction," in Rable, *But There Was No Peace: The Role of Violence in the Politics of Reconstruction*, 162–85.

7. Fischer, "Discovery," 3.

8. See Eric Foner, *Reconstruction: America's Unfinished Revolution, 1863–1877*, and its bibliography. See also W. E. B. DuBois, *Black Reconstruction*.

9. Drawing by Frank Bellew reproduced in Gladys-Marie Fry, *Night Riders in Black Folk History*.

10. Merle Johnson, *Bibliography*, 21.

11. Anon., [illustration], *Harper's Weekly* 18, no. 934 (21 November 1874): 958. The caption and illustration referred to an event that took place in Choctaw County, Alabama, around 1 August 1874. The article it accompanied, "A Dying Rebellion" by Eugene Lawrence, described numerous similar crimes whites had perpetrated on innocent blacks throughout the South in 1874 (Lawrence, 958).

12. Thomas Nast, [cartoon], *Harper's Weekly*, 878. Twain was a fan of Nast's cartoons in *Harper's Weekly*, where Nast was staff artist, and he was probably aware of this one. In November 1872, he had congratulated Nast for his anti-Greeley cartoons during the Grant campaign (*Mark Twain's Letters*, ed. Paine, 1:202). Others, as well—including Frederick Douglass—drew connections between the post-war treatment of blacks and slavery (see Shelley Fisher Fishkin and Carla Peterson, "'We Hold These Truths to Be Self-Evident': The Rhetoric of Frederick Douglass's Journalism," 202–4). It is interesting that Nast's coat-of-arms and the coat-of-arms Tom designs for Jim in Chapter 38 of *Huckleberry Finn* both feature emblems of abusive white power: Tom's shield includes a chain and a dog, both of which are used to recapture and re-enslave the runaway (322); Nast's depicts a lynching, a burning schoolhouse, the White League, and the K.K.K., all of which conspire to defraud the freedmen of their liberty.

13. Twain's short essay, on Declaration of Independence signer Francis Lightfoot Lee, was published under the title "Centennial Collection," in the *Pennsylvania Magazine of History and Biography* 1, no. 3 (1877). It is not clear whether Twain actually attended the Centennial celebrations in Philadelphia or whether he simply sent his manuscript (Robert Pack Browning to Thomas E. Bass, III, 20 January 1988). (The manuscript of "Francis Lightfoot Lee" is at the Historical Society of Pennsylvania.)

14. Frederick Douglass, quoted in Eric Foner, *Reconstruction*, 567.

15. Eric Foner, *Reconstruction*, 567.

16. Cited in Eric Foner, *Reconstruction*, 582. The complexities of the Compromise of 1877 and of Hayes's military policy (which involved a transfer of personnel rather than a withdrawal) are carefully delineated in Vincent P. DeSantis's essay, "Rutherford B. Hayes and the Removal of Troops and the End of Reconstruction," 417–50.

17. Doyno, *Writing "Huck Finn,"* 229. Doyno qualifies his interpretation with the *caveat*, "the quality of evidence one would desire has not yet been found, and perhaps does not exist. . . . When exploring this theory, we deal not with exclusive, conclusive proof, but with congruence and analogy" (229). Nonetheless, his measured and responsible scholarship—which includes a painstaking reading of Twain's manuscript revisions and insertions—is compelling. He makes a good case for the idea that "The convict-lease system provides an important additional historical resonance for the novel's ending" (239).

18. Doyno, *Writing "Huck Finn,"* 234.

19. E. W. S. Hammond, quoted in John David Smith, *An Old Creed for the New South*, 75, 95.

20. Frederick Douglass, "The Work of the Future," 292.

21. Although Twain left unpublished the plot outline for a novel that would have addressed directly the issue of racial discrimination in the North after the Civil War, the existence of the fragment demonstrates that he was aware of the fact that the South had no monopoly on racism in the 1880s. (See Shelley Fisher Fishkin, "False Starts, Fragments and Fumbles: Mark Twain's Unpublished Writing on Race" for a discussion of this fragment ("The man with negro blood") and its dating (I determined that Twain wrote it between 1883 and 1889).

22. DuBois, *Black Reconstruction*, 30.

23. As I have argued elsewhere, the difficulties of bringing out these ironies in the secondary-school classroom are daunting but not insurmountable. See Shelley Fisher Fishkin, "Mark Twain and the Risks of Irony," "Selected Bibliography for the Study of *Adventures of Huckleberry Finn*," and "*Huckleberry Finn* Is Not a Racist Novel." Albert V. Schwartz's "What Help for Teachers?" in *Interracial Books for Children* provides a useful overview of the failure of "teacher-training texts on literature for children and adolescents" to "even [hint] that racial issues might be a concern when teaching the novel," or to "suggest how teachers might deal with issues of race raised by the book" or by "the novel's extensive use of the word 'nigger'" (Schwartz, 6). Other worthwhile discussions of some of the challenges and difficulties of *Huckleberry Finn* in the classroom are: Peaches Henry, "The Struggle for Tolerance: Race and Censorship in *Huckleberry Finn*," Eric Solomon, "My *Huckleberry Finn*: Thirty Years in the Classroom with Huck and Jim," James M. Cox, "A Hard Book to Take," and Jocelyn Chadwick-Joshua, "Mark Twain and the Fires of Controversy: Teaching Racially-Sensitive Literature: Or, 'Say that 'N' Word and Out You Go!'"

24. Louis J. Budd explored this in *Mark Twain: Social Philosopher*, 95–106. Budd's important 1959 article "Southward Currents Under Huck Finn's Raft" also suggests some of this argument.

25. Tanner, *Reign of Wonder*, 156–57.

26. Charles H. Nilon, "The Ending of *Huckleberry Finn*: 'Freeing the Free Negro,'" 62–63.

27. Lawrence Berkove, "The Free Man of Color in The *Grandissimes* and Works by Harris and Mark Twain," and "The 'Poor Players' of *Huckleberry Finn*"; Cummings, *Mark Twain and Science*, 151–58; Doyno, *Writing "Huck Finn,"* 228–55.

28. Morrison, *Playing in the Dark*, 54–57.

29. L. Moffitt Cecil, "The Historical Ending of *Adventures of Huckleberry Finn*: How Nigger Jim [*sic*] Was Set Free," 281–82. (The derogatory phrase "Nigger Jim" appears nowhere in *Huckleberry Finn* nor anywhere else in Twain's writings. Critics have used the phrase in ways that imply that Twain used it as well; Twain did not.)

30. Harold Beaver, *Huckleberry Finn*, 38.

31. James M. Cox, in *Mark Twain: The Fate of Humor*, suggests that Twain raises readers' awareness of another aspect of the "doubleness" of the narrative to new levels:

> [T]he judgment which the last ten chapters render upon Tom is surely the judgment rendered upon the moral sentiment on which the book has ridden. If the reader sees in Tom's performance a rather shabby and safe bit of play, he is seeing no more than the exposure of the approval with which he watched Huck operate. For if Tom is rather contemptibly setting a free slave free, what after all is the reader doing, who begins the book after the fact of the Civil War? This is the "joke" of the book. . . . To see that Tom is doing at the ending what we have been doing throughout the book is essential to understanding what the book has meant to us. (175)

In a provocative and insightful reading of the novel, Forrest G. Robinson expands on this argument, noting that

> The novel continues to speak to our condition because it makes us mindful of the legacies of race-slavery in our midst; but it is a great favorite with us, an American "classic," in good part because it seems to invite the dismissal or disavowal of as much of its darkness as we cannot bear to own. *Huckleberry Finn* draws us close to a harsh center of our reality, and we follow willingly, unthreatened by more discomposure than we can comfortably manage because the narrative enables the relatively effortless reader capitulation of its lie of silent assertion. (Forrest G. Robinson, *In Bad Faith: The Dynamics of Deception in Mark Twain's America*, 214–15)

32. Gary Saul Morson and Caryl Emerson, *Mikhail Bakhtin: Creation of a Prosaics*, 296, quoting Bakhtin, *Problems of Dostoevsky's Poetics*, 106.

33. Morson and Emerson, *Mikhail Bakhtin*, 297.

34. "After understanding the genre's logic," Bakhtin felt, "a great writer can guess the uses to which it must have been put by someone or other at some time or other; and the writer can imagine how the resources of his own age or experience might better realize the genre's potential. Having understood the spirit of Menippean satire, Dostoevsky recognized how his own polyphonic method could combine with it so that both would be enriched" (Morson and Emerson, *Mikhail Bakhtin*, 296).

35. Morrison, *Playing in the Dark*, 4–5.

36. Barbara E. Johnson, "Response" [to Henry Louis Gates, Jr., "Canon-Formation and the Afro-American Tradition"], 42.

37. Morrison, "Unspeakable Things Unspoken: The Afro-American Presence in American Literature," 11.

Chapter 5

1. Guy Cardwell, *The Man Who Was Mark Twain*, 194, 200.

2. I, too, made this point in a 1985 television debate on CNN's "Freeman Reports."

3. Cardwell, *The Man Who Was Mark Twain*, 188.

4. Louis J. Budd, personal communication, 3 January 1991.

5. See, for example, Jervis Langdon, Jr.'s letter to the *New York Times*, on 7 April 1985. Langdon writes: "To the Editor: This relates to the wonderful 'From Twain, a Letter on Debt to Blacks' (page 1, March 14)." He notes that his great-grandfather, Jervis Langdon, Mark Twain's father-in-law, "felt so strongly on the issue of slavery that he left his old church, where there was indecision, and established another where there could be none, the Park Church of Elmira. . . . In addition, my great-grandfather ran a secret station on the underground railroad and helped hide countless slaves on their way north to freedom. . . ."

6. Ralph Ellison, "Change the Joke and Slip the Yoke," 215–16.

7. See Woodard and MacCann, "Minstrel Shackles and Nineteenth-Century 'Liberality' in *Huckleberry Finn*"; Fredrick Woodard and Donnarae Mac-Cann, "*Huckleberry Finn* and the Traditions of Blackface Minstrelsy"; Bernard W. Bell, "Twain's 'Nigger' Jim: The Tragic Face Behind the Minstrel Mask"; John H. Wallace, "The Case Against *Huck Finn*"; Cardwell, *The Man Who Was Mark Twain*, 183–200; Leo Marx, "Mr. Eliot, Mr. Trilling and *Huckleberry Finn*"; and Henry Nash Smith, *Mark Twain: The Development of a Writer*, 134.

8. Woodard and MacCann, "Minstrel Shackles and Nineteenth-Century 'Liberality' in *Huckleberry Finn*," 151.

9. Unnamed professor quoted in Leslie Fiedler, "*Huckleberry Finn*: The Book We Love to Hate," 6–7. For an interesting overview of critics' responses to Jim that focuses on a number of issues not discussed here, see the 1980 article by Thomas Weaver and Merline A. Williams, "Mark Twain's Jim: Identity as an Index to Cultural Attitudes."

10. David Smith, "Huck, Jim, and American Racial Discourse," 105.

11. David Smith, "Huck, Jim, and American Racial Discourse," 104. Smith prefaces this comment with a reference to Melville. His full statement is ". . . except for Melville's work, *Huckleberry Finn* is without peer among major Euro-American novels for its explicitly antiracist stance" (104).

12. David Smith, "Huck, Jim, and American Racial Discourse," 108.

13. Twain, *Huckleberry Finn*, 7–8.

14. David Smith, "Huck, Jim, and American Racial Discourse," 109–10.

15. David Smith, "Huck, Jim, and American Racial Discourse," 111.

16. Woodard and MacCann, "Minstrel Shackles and Nineteenth-Century 'Liberality' in *Huckleberry Finn*," 143.

17. Woodard and MacCann, "Minstrel Shackles and Nineteenth-Century 'Liberality' in *Huckleberry Finn*," 145.

18. Twain lamented in 1906 the death of "the real nigger show—the genuine nigger show, the extravagant nigger show—the show which to me has no peer and whose peer has not arrived, in my experience. . . . To my mind it was a thoroughly delightful thing, and a most competent laughter-compeller and I am sorry it is gone" (*Mark Twain in Eruption*, ed. Bernard DeVoto, 110, 115).

19. Richard Dorson, in *American Negro Folktales*, gives an extensive list of

references to English and American white, as well as African-American, examples of "Witch-Riding" tales (238–39). And in *American Folklore* he notes, "The luminous ghosts who alarm colored folk at dusk dark, and the shape-shifting witches who straddle them in bed, are English not African creations" (169). Patricia K. Rickels notes that many of these tales are curiously reminiscent of tales associated with the Salem witch trials ("Some Accounts of Witch Riding," 57).

20. Rickels, "Some Accounts of Witch Riding," 61.

21. "Ghost stories and supernatural disguises" were used by masters and overseers to "restrain the nocturnal ramblings of their slaves between visits of the county patrols. Fear on the part of the Blacks was the key emotion produced but it was not so much fear of unknown ghosts as it was of known whites" (Gladys-Marie Fry, *Night Riders in Black Folk History*, 79).

22. Fry, *Night Riders in Black Folk History*, 69, 71. Fry tends to refer to the supernatural beings as "ghosts," and Jim describes being ridden by "witches."* It's not clear, however, that Twain made much of a distinction between the two. In the manuscript of "A Family Sketch," for example, Twain wrote that Mary Ann Cord was in great demand among the children as a storyteller because she "had ghosts in stock, & these were a novelty to the children."* He inserted "& witches"* after the word "ghosts," suggesting that he thought of the two together, almost in one breath. Twain, "A Family Sketch," 60. Quoted with permission.

23. Fry, *Night Riders in Black Folk History*, 72.

24. Fry, *Night Riders in Black Folk History*, 73.

25. Fry, *Night Riders in Black Folk History*, 75–76.

26. Fry, *Night Riders in Black Folk History*, 9–10.

27. John W. Blassingame, *The Slave Community*, 105.

28. Sterling Stuckey, *Slave Culture*, 43.

29. See Robert Farris Thompson, *Flash of the Spirit*, and "Kongo Influences on African-American Artistic Culture."

30. Thompson, personal communication. See Joseph E. Holloway, "The Origins of African-American Culture" for a description of the origins of slaves imported to various parts of the United States.

31. Thompson, *Flash of the Spirit*, 132.

32. Thompson, *Flash of the Spirit*, 142.

33. Langston Hughes and Arna Bontemps, eds., *Book of Negro Folklore*, 191.

34. Stuckey, *Slave Culture*, 109. For an insightful commentary on this phenomenon, see David Bradley's novel *The Chaneysville Incident*, 206–15.

35. The recently recovered manuscript of the first half of *Huckleberry Finn* contains another episode (excised from the published version of the novel) involving Jim and the possibility that the dead may return as ghosts to haunt the living (Fischer, personal communication).

36. This possibility does not rule out that Twain probably would have known that this line in this context would suggest minstrelsy to his readers. Another passage that Woodard and McCann do not cite, but that others have referred to as having originated in minstrelsy, may also have roots in authentic folk traditions: Jim's comment, "Yes—en I's rich now, come to look at it. I owns mysef, en I's wuth eight hund'd dollars. But live stock's too resky, Huck;—I wisht I had de eight hund'd dollars en somebody else had de nigger" (57). The idea that Twain might have actually heard slaves expressing pride in

their dollar worth is supported by Kenneth Stampp's observation that many whites had

> heard slaves boast of the prices their masters had paid for them, or of the handsome offers their masters had rejected from would-be purchasers. A thousand-dollar slave felt superior to an eight-hundred-dollar slave. "When we recollect that the dollars are not their own," wrote an amused traveler, "we can hardly refrain from smiling at the childlike simplicity with which they express their satisfaction at the high price set on them." (Stampp, *The Peculiar Institution*, 339)

But although this traveller may have been "amused" by such talk, Mark Twain was aware of the pathos and injustice that lay behind it. A comment Twain made in 1906 underlines his awareness of the seriousness of Jim's pleasure in owning himself. "Is it conceivable," Twain asked, "that there can be a 'fair market price,' or any price whatever, estimable in gold, or diamonds, or bank notes, or government bonds, for a man's supremest possession—that one possession without which his life is totally worthless—his liberty?" (*Mark Twain in Eruption*, DeVoto, ed., 91).

37. Daniel G. Hoffman, "Black Magic—and White—in *Huckleberry Finn.*"

38. Twain, *Huckleberry Finn*, 201–2.

39. Cardwell, *The Man Who Was Mark Twain*, 202.

40. Perhaps Cardwell's inference is shaped by his recollection of Twain's oft-cited (and disturbing) comment that he kept a black butler because he couldn't bear to give orders to a white man (Cardwell, *The Man Who Was Mark Twain*, 186). Cardwell may have taken Twain at his word and assumed that all of Twain's servants were black. But here, as elsewhere, it is risky to take Twain at his word: Twain did give orders to a white man—Patrick McAleer—daily, and to white groundskeepers and gardeners Daniel Molloy and John O'Neill, as well. Other white servants included Katy Leary, the family's maid, a German nursemaid named Rosa, and innumerable others over the years. Patrick McAleer began working for Twain on Twain's wedding day in 1870, and Twain served as pallbearer at his Hartford funeral thirty-six years later. Shortly thereafter Twain eulogized McAleer before an audience of 10,000 who had come to hear Twain present an evening of "Reminiscences" at the Majestic Theater in New York. If pressed to come up with a "definition of what is a gentleman," Twain said, he would simply define the ideal gentleman as "Patrick McAleer." Paine describes Twain's remarks in a chapter of the biography titled, "The Definition of a Gentleman" (*Mark Twain: A Biography* 3: 1272–78); "Family Sketch"; personal communication, Marianne Curling, Curator, Mark Twain Memorial, Hartford.

41. Pettit, *Mark Twain and the South*, 105.

42. Herbert A. Wisbey, Jr., "John T. Lewis," 1. The headline on Lewis's obituary in the *Elmira Gazette and Free Press* in 1906 read: "John T. Lewis, Colored Hero, Dies on Way to Hospital. Mark Twain's Warm Friend and the Man Who Saved the Lives of Mrs. Charles J. Langdon and Mrs. E. E. Loomis Passes Away in Ambulance . . ." (Wisbey, Jr., "John T. Lewis," 1).

43. There are, of course, other black sources for Jim. "Uncle Dan'l," a slave on John Quarles's farm near Florida, Missouri, has often been cited. (See, for example, Cummings, *Mark Twain and Science*, 125–26.) Twain also notes in his *Autobiography* that he based Jim, in part, on "'Uncle Dan'l,' a middle-aged slave

whose head was the best one in the negro quarter, whose sympathies were wide and warm . . ." (*Mark Twain's Autobiography*, ed. Paine, 1:100).

44. David Smith, "Huck, Jim, and American Racial Discourse," 112.

45. David Smith, "Huck, Jim, and American Racial Discourse," 115.

46. David Smith, "Huck, Jim, and American Racial Discourse," 116. Jim's stunning altruism somehow defies being adequately dealt with in print. As David Barrow rightly observes, "it is telling that so many critics focus on Huck's decision to free Jim as the moral pinnacle of the novel and so few upon Jim's decision to stay with the wounded Tom, or Jim's refusal to betray Huck to his captors" ("Mark Twain and the Oral Economy," 77). Twain found that John Lewis's equally stunning altruism also defied being dealt with in print. (He described it to William Dean Howells in a letter, but noted that he would never write about it for publication (SLC to WDH, 25–27 August 1877, *Mark Twain-Howells Letters* 1:194). Barrow writes, "If we do not see that Tom's evasion is meant to thwart our conversion of Jim into just another member of the 'damned human race,' we have missed the significance of both Jim's character and of the dynamic which governs it. . . . We prefer to believe that Jim has made a choice [that of giving up his freedom to remain to nurse a wounded Tom] which is unbelievable rather than to see that he believes what we can no longer believe or what we can believe only at the expense of appearing foolish" (Barrow, "Mark Twain and the Oral Economy," 77–78). Jim's altruism, Barrow suggests (and, I would add, John Lewis's as well) is fueled by the values of an oral community in which people are experienced as concrete, present, and important, in contrast to a literate community capable of turning people into fungible abstractions. Interestingly, writers (the critics and Twain himself) rooted, by definition, in the world of texts, have generally refrained from exploring in print these nearly incomprehensible incidents of self-sacrifice.

47. Cardwell, *The Man Who Was Mark Twain*, 196.

48. The text, in both cases, from Chapter 8 of the novel, ran from "Jim knowed all kinds of signs. . . ." to "I owns mysef, en I's wuth eight hund'd dollars. But live stock's too resky, Huck;—I wisht I had de eight hund'd dollars en somebody else had de nigger." Twain changed this line in the first American edition to read as follows: "I owns mysef, en I's wuth eight hund'd dollars. I wisht I had de money, I wouldn' want no mo'." (While recognizing the comic value of exchanges such as Jim's "experience with high finance," Sterling Brown notes, "the fun is brought up sharp by Jim's 'Yes, en I's rich now. . . . want no mo'." Brown comments, on this last line, "But he did want more. He wanted to get to a free state and work and save money so he could buy his wife, and then they would both work to buy their children, or get an abolitionist to go steal them." The line helps make Jim "completely believable" for Brown. See Brown's *Negro in American Fiction*, 68.) Twain seems to have remained somewhat unsatisfied with this line. Blair and Fischer observe in the "Textual Notes" to the novel that Twain proposed several changes in this line for his lecture programs. In 1895, for example, he followed "I wouldn' want no mo'" with "Cuz niggers is mighty resky property." See Blair and Fischer, "Textual Notes," *Huckleberry Finn* (528) for a detailed description of Twain's various experiments with this line.

49. Twain [Samuel Clemens], typescript of Notebook 23, Old 18, September–April 1885, 4, 15; typescript of Notebook 34, Old 28, March–December 1895.

50. David Smith, "Huck, Jim, and American Racial Discourse," 98. Smith writes,

> . . . most of this debate is, as several critics have noted, conventional minstrel-show banter. Nevertheless, Jim demonstrates impressive reasoning abilities despite his factual ignorance. For instance, in their argument over "Poly-voo-franzy," Huck makes a category error by implying that the difference between languages is analogous to the difference between human language and cat language. Although Jim's response—that a man should talk like a man—betrays his ignorance of cultural diversity, his argument is otherwise perceptive and structurally sound. The humor in Huck's conclusion, "you can't learn a nigger to argue," arises precisely from the reader's recognition that Jim's argument is better than Huck's. ("Huck, Jim, and American Racial Discourse," 111)

51. Twain [Samuel Clemens], typescript of Notebook 35, May–October 1895, 5. The fullest discussion of Twain's public readings from the novel is Walter Blair and Victor Fischer, "Mark Twain's Revisions for Public Reading," Appendix C in the University of California Press edition of *Huckleberry Finn* (765–841).

52. Anthony J. Berret argues convincingly in *"Huckleberry Finn* and the Minstrel Show" that much of the aesthetic structure of the novel as a whole may have minstrel-show roots.

53. For example, Twain noted in a letter to Howells, "On the evening of March 10th, I am going to read to the colored folk in the African church here, (no whites admitted except such as I bring with me,) & a choir of colored folks will sing Jubilee songs. I count on a good time, & shall hope to have you folks there, & Livy" (SLC to Howells, 27 February 1881, *Mark Twain-Howells Letters*, 356). There are other references to readings for black audiences. With one exception, we do not generally know which pieces Twain included on these occasions. The notebook entry we have for one reading to a black audience does not include "Sollermun" or "Jim's Bank" (Typescript of Notebook 29 (Old 24), 3, "Colored folk, Unity Hall, May 22. [Skinned Man.] boyhood. [Mate & Gov Gardner Interviewer ("Lying) [Artemus Ward & the 'lone hand Christening.]") Among the letters written to Twain in the Mark Twain Papers, for example, one finds a warm thank-you note from the pastor of a black church in Hartford who evidently used a reading by Twain as a major fundraiser to reduce the church's debt. Twain's sympathy for black charities was apparently well-known among African Americans by the early 1880s. In 1881 Thomas A. Davis, pastor of the Zion A. M. E. Church at 112 Montgomery in a city other than Hartford (return address is illegible; possibly it is "Trenton, N.J.") seemed to feel Twain would respond positively to his request for help in funding a black home for the aged. He notes his people's reliance on "men like your self who feel for us as I have a knowledge of your large Christian heart as a philanthropist" and asks Twain to send "twenty five dollars as the gift of a great writer and friend of the colored man." The pastor adds in a postscript that "Rev. R. R. Morris, Pastor of Pearl St. Church Your City—is my Cousin" (Thos. A. Davis to SLC, 17 March 1881, in Mark Twain Papers).

The 1881 memoirs of a subscription agent for *Tom Sawyer* suggest that Twain's writing before *Huckleberry Finn* enjoyed some popularity among black readers as well as white. While the author of these memoirs (who identifies herself only as "a woman") describes a black barber's reaction to Twain's work in an exaggerated dialect designed to be humorous in and of itself, we have no reason to doubt the genuineness of the barber's enthusiasm: "[Twain's] one ob dem humiferous fellers, too, what teches de ticklin' spot ob a sobrificated man when he don't 'spect de larfs comin' on, an' it biles all ober him hot, shakin' his whole sittin' constarution right in ter de 'musin' jollifercatin' joys ob life, doin' as much good to de sighin' mortals as de revivin' meetin' preachers to de prayin' an confessin' sinners ob dat devartin' fraternity in de gospel communerations. Yes, dat 'Mark Twain's' done a heap ob good to des United States ob Americay." The barber proceeded to buy the subscription agent's most expensive, sturdy, library-bound copy of *Tom Sawyer*, explaining that he needed a copy that "can stand handlin' by de neighborin' hands" since he planned to pass it around to all his friends (Anon., *Facts, by a Woman*, 139). I am grateful to Louis J. Budd for bringing the existence of this volume to my attention, and to Ken Sanderson for sharing his copy with me.

54. Fishkin, Interview with Ralph Ellison, 16 July 1991.

55. Weaver and Williams, "Mark Twain's Jim: Identity as an Index to Cultural Attitudes," 119, 124.

56. See Edwin McDowell, "From Twain, a Letter on Debt to Blacks," *New York Times*, 14 March 1985, 1, 16. See also Thomas P. Riggio, "Charles Ethan Porter and Mark Twain."

57. Lott's book is forthcoming from Oxford University Press. See also Lott's bibliography; Robert C. Toll's *Blacking Up: The Minstrel Show in Nineteenth-Century America*; the chapter on "Negro Minstrels" in Elbert R. Bowen's *Theatrical Entertainments in Rural Missouri Before the Civil War* (37–43), and Bowen's bibliography, particularly 137–39. Also relevant to any examination of Twain's inconsistent challenges to racial stereotypes is Rhett S. Jones's fine essay, "Nigger and Knowledge: White Double-Consciousness in *Adventures of Huckleberry Finn*." Lott's study provides the best discussion to date of the complex ways in which minstrel shows "[opened] the culture of the dispossessed to view while simultaneously refusing the social legitimacy of its members, a truly American combination of acknowledgment and expropriation" (*Love and Theft: Blackface Minstrelsy and the American Working Class*, ms. p. 98).

58. Ellison in Fishkin interview, 1991.

59. William J. Mahar's intriguing article, "Black English in Early Blackface Minstrelsy" argues that

> songwriters borrowed from BEV [Black English Vernacular], especially when they were depicting black stereotypes or when creating totally fictional characters who hid behind the burnt-cork mask. A close reading of the song texts shows that a narrow interpretation emphasizing only their alleged prejudice-producing characteristics removes the topical and satirical songs from their appropriate context. (283)

The early songs, Mahar writes, "show a clear pattern of language borrowing" (284). Mahar goes on to suggest that minstrel-show patterns may be more indebted to African-American traditions of satirizing *white* people than previously recognized:

> Following patterns commonly found in European culture, where the greatest insults to cultivated behaviors came from the lowest classes—servants, peasants, itinerant tradesmen, and those generally without optimistic futures, the comedy presented by the burnt-cork entertainers was not directed at blacks, but used the blackface foil as a means of criticizing whites. The dialect songs and the comic

behavior associated with their delivery may have been based on a white predis-
position to accept the alleged inferiority of blacks, but the actual reasons why
the caricatures of white gentlemen worked rested more on whites' own insecuri-
ties than on any behavior by blacks. (284)

While not mistaking what took place on the minstrel stage as a simulacrum for
black folk culture, Mahar concludes that "The discovery of common characteristics in blackface songs and black English suggests that there was much truth to
the contention that the early minstrels borrowed from black culture" (284).
Mahar's conclusions reinforce Ellison's sense of the minstrel show as a means by
which Black English Vernacular infiltrated Standard American English:

> As a form of entertainment, the blackface comedy certainly did have a negative
> influence on race relations (though it would never have convinced anyone who
> wasn't already predisposed to accept the "reality" of the minstrel's disguise),
> but, from the evidence discussed above, the differences between the two races
> and cultures were used as a means of injecting a vital, discordant, and satirical
> language into popular comedy. (285)

60. Dorson, *American Folklore*, 172.

61. Writing by Dena Epstein, James Haskins, Robert Farris Thompson, and
Geraldine L. Wilson supports this idea. In a brief piece entitled "On Twain and
Minstrelsy," published in *Interracial Books for Children* in 1984, Geraldine L.
Wilson (while faulting Twain for perpetuating exploitative, degrading stereotypes) raised some similar points. Wilson cites examples from James Haskin's
Black Theater in America and from Robert Farris Thompson's *The Four Moments
of the Sun* that trace several key dimensions of the minstrel show (including the
semicircle of chairs and "argumentative tradition") to well-documented, distinctively African traditions. For more on this point, see Hans Nathan, *Dan Emmett
and the Rise of Early Negro Minstrelsy*.

62. Dena J. Epstein, "The Folk Banjo: A Documentary History," 348.

63. Epstein, "The Folk Banjo: A Documentary History," 350.

64. J. L. Dillard, *Lexicon of Black English*, 149.

65. SLC to Tom Hood and George Routledge and Sons, 10 March 1873,
Hartford, reprinted in Pike, *The Singing Campaign for Ten Thousand Pounds*,
14–15.

66. Dillard, *Lexicon of Black English*, 149. Robert C. Toll concurs on this
point:

> Although no other area of early minstrelsy was as strongly indebted to blacks as
> the dance, it is clear that minstrels borrowed other material as well. George
> Nichols, a blackface circus clown who was one of the pioneers of minstrelsy,
> learned some of his "original" songs, like "Clare de Kitchen," from anonymous
> blacks on the Mississippi and from two New Orleans Negro singers, Picayune
> Butler and "Old Corn Meal." . . . Although blackface performers rarely credited
> specific material to blacks because they wanted to be known as creative artists as
> well as entertainers, many early minstrels claimed that they did "field work"
> among Southern Negroes while they were traveling. . . . Since these performers
> had both the opportunities and motives to do it, and since Afro-American cul-
> ture did influence minstrelsy, these claims probably represent what at least some
> minstrels did to find new material. (Toll, *Blacking Up*, 44–45)

Toll notes that "minstrels made extensive use of nonsense humor, fantasy, and
animal fables that they almost certainly derived from Afro-American folk song
and narrative, which relied heavily on animal symbolism, used indirection and

guile to voice protests or attack adversaries, and featured victories for the weak over the strong," as contrasted with Anglo-American traditions (also eclectically employed by the minstrels), which were "direct and 'realistic,' employed overt protest, and presented direct conflicts, in which the strong always won out" (48). William J. Mahar offers numerous examples of the claim by many early black-face entertainers that "they borrowed their comic material from black steve-dores, preachers, laborers, or ex-slaves" ("Black English in Early Blackface Min-strelsy," 260). Eric Lott, building on earlier work by John Szwed, offers additional useful insights into this issue. "The minstrel show," he notes, "was on one hand a socially approved context of institutional control; on the other, it continually acknowledged and absorbed black culture even while defending white America against it" (Lott, *Love and Theft*, ms. p. 83). Music historian Eileen Southern contends that "to obtain materials for their shows, the minstrels visited plantations, then attempted to recreate plantation scenes on the stage . . ."(91–92; cited in Lott). Lott suggests that in the North, "the minstrel men vis-ited not plantations but racially integrated theaters, taverns, neighborhoods, and waterfronts—and *then* attempted to recreate plantation scenes" (ms. p. 85).

67. Lott, *Love and Theft: Blackface Minstrelsy and the American Working Class*, ms. pp. 54–55.

Chapter 6

1. Some of the earliest examinations of Jim's speech, like the three-page article James N. Tidwell published in 1942, "Mark Twain's Representation of Negro Speech," ignored important dimensions of language and its literary repre-sentation that advances in linguistics over the last fifty years have highlighted. Tidwell's conclusion that "Twain includes only two Negro language features in Jim's speech" is refuted by current standards of scholarship. Sumner Ives, in "A Theory of Literary Dialect" (1950), examines some of the problems with Tid-well's general approach to literary dialect, and his essay offers a useful corrective, although it does not focus on Twain. David Carkeet, in "The Dialects in *Huckle-berry Finn*" (1979), briefly surveys and evaluates more recent research on Twain's dialect in general, including a dissertation by Rulon (1967), and articles by Pederson (1965 and 1967) and Boland (1968). Bernard W. Bell's call for new work evaluating Twain's representations of "Missouri negro dialect" "in the contexts of [Twain's] belief in the authenticity of minstrelsy, his having been influenced by the eye dialect of southwestern humorists, his delineation of other blacks in the novel as comic servants, his own speech features, and all the distinc-tive grammatical, lexical, and phonetic features of nineteenth-century black Mis-souri speech," is well-taken, and suggests the complexity of this issue (Bernard Bell, "Twain's 'Nigger' Jim," 140). As Bell suggests, examinations in the past have often focused rather narrowly on questions of Jim's pronunciation. Ques-tions of phonology have received a disproportionate share of dialect scholars' attention to the novel. (Curt Morris Rulon acknowledges, for example, in his dis-sertation on "The Dialects in *Huckleberry Finn*," that "the major emphasis of the analysis will be on phonology" (57).

2. Twain, *Adventures of Huckleberry Finn*, 98.

3. See Sylvia Holton's chapter on "Black English in Fiction, 1790–1900" in *Down Home and Uptown*, for a broader and more detailed survey of the subject

(Holton, 55–94). See also Walter M. Brasch, *Black English and the Mass Media* (1–145), and Tremaine McDowell, "Notes on Negro Dialect in the American Novel to 1821." For a consideration of the larger question of how African Americans were represented in general in American fiction, see Sterling Brown, "The American Race Problem as Reflected in American Literature," *The Negro in American Fiction,* and "Negro Character as Seen by White Authors"; Jean Fagan Yellin, *The Intricate Knot: Black Figures in American Literature, 1776–1863;* Seymour L. Gross, "Stereotype to Archetype: The Negro in American Literary Criticism"; Milton Cantor, "The Image of the Negro in Colonial Literature"; Tremaine McDowell, "The Negro in the Southern Novel Prior to 1850"; Leslie A. Fiedler, "The Blackness of Darkness: The Negro and the Development of American Gothic"; William Stanley Braithwaite, "The Negro in American Literature"; and Arthur Huff Fauset, "American Negro Folk Literature."

4. Black English appeared in drama before it made its way into novels. For a discussion of early examples of literary Black English in such plays as John Leacock's *The Fall of British Tyranny* (Philadelphia, 1776) and Samuel Low's *The Politician Outwitted* (New York, 1789), see Mahar, "Black English in Early Blackface Minstrelsy."

5. Tremaine McDowell, "Notes," 291.

6. Richard Hildreth, *Archy Moore,* cited in Yellin, *The Intricate Knot,* 88.

7. Hugh Henry Brackenridge, *Modern Chivalry,* quoted in Tremaine McDowell, "Notes," 291–92. McDowell notes that he is quoting from an 1815 version of Brackenridge's 1792 novel. See also Walter M. Brasch's analysis of Brackenridge's black dialect in *Black English and the Mass Media,* 18–19.

8. Tremaine McDowell, "Notes," 292; Dillard, *Black English: Its History and Usage,* 129, 190–91; Mahar, "Black English in Early Blackface Minstrelsy," 268. See also Sylvia Holton's detailed analysis in *Down Home and Uptown* (60–63).

9. James Fenimore Cooper, 1831 revision of *The Spy,* quoted in Tremaine McDowell, "Notes," 294.

10. Sterling Brown, *The Negro in American Fiction,* 8.

11. Tremaine McDowell, "James Fenimore Cooper," 513. J. L. Dillard also credited Cooper with having accurately transcribed Plantation Creole (Black English).

12. McDowell, "Notes," 294. Walter Brasch similarly finds Cooper's black dialect inconsistent (*Black English and the Mass Media,* 25–28). David Sloane, however, observes the difficulty of assembling evidence to prove "constant uncertainty and vacillation" on the part of a writer, given the inconsistencies and vacillations common to real speech. Throughout the nineteenth century, from the 1830s on, he noted, jokes circulated about an Irishman newly arrived in New York "who overheard a negro talking in his dialect and wanted to go back to Ireland before he turned black, too" (personal communication).

13. William Gilmore Simms, *The Yemassee,* quoted in Starke, *Black Portraiture in American Fiction,* 36. For more on Simms's black dialect, see Brasch, *Black English and the Mass Media,* 35–41.

14. Fauset, "American Negro Folk Literature," 241.

15. Charles S. Watson notes in "Portrayals of the Black and the Idea of Progress: Simms and Douglass," that Hector's refusal of freedom in this novel resembles "a similar scene described by James Kirke Paulding, in which, how-

ever, the slave, Little Pompey, does not speak. See *Westerward Ho! A Tale* (New York, 1832; rpt. Grosse Point, Michigan, 1968), I:58" (Watson, "Portrayals of the Black," 341). Watson feels Simms "probably borrowed" from Paulding.

16. David Simpson, *The Politics of American English, 1776–1850*, 17.

17. Simpson, *The Politics of American English, 1776–1850*, 16. See also Holton, *Down Home and Uptown*, 63–66; Eric Stockton, "Poe's Use of Negro Dialect in 'The Gold-Bug,'" 193–214; and Brasch, *Black English and the Mass Media*, 32–35.

18. Morrison, "Unspeakable Things Unspoken," 13–14.

19. Yellin, *The Intricate Knot*, 16.

20. Sometimes a writer fudged the issue by allowing a black character to speak in dialect, but a dialect more acceptable as "human speech" to readers' eyes and ears than the one he actually would have spoken. Tremaine McDowell, for example, found that much of the speech of Uncle Tom and his fellow slaves in *Uncle Tom's Cabin* (1852) "might come from the lips of semi-literate European immigrants." He cited this example:

> . . . I have principles, and I sticks to 'em like forty—jest anything that I thinks is principle, I goes in to't; I wouldn't mind if dey burn me 'live, I'd walk right up to de stake, I would, and say, Here I comes to shed my last blood fur my principles, fur my country, fur der gen'l interests of s'ciety. (*Uncle Tom's Cabin*, quoted in Tremaine McDowell, "Stowe," 323–24)

McDowell notes, "A few touches of revision would make such a harangue appropriate, not to a Southern negro, but to one of the characters of Artemus Ward" ("Stowe," 324). Such speech might also be found in an African-American speaker of Northern roots, as David Sloane suggests (personal communication). Thus, Stowe's failure to make Uncle Tom sound like a Southern black might be explained, in part, by her exposure to the speech of blacks in the North.

21. Richard Yarborough, "Strategies of Characterization in *Uncle Tom's Cabin* and the Early Afro-American Novel," 47.

22. Poe, quoted in Sterling Brown, "Negro Character," 182. For a discussion of Poe's racial attitudes, see Bernard Rosenthal, "Poe, Slavery, and the *Southern Literary Messenger*: A Reexamination" (29–38) and Dana Nelson, "'Race' in *Pym* and Poe," in *The Word in Black and White* (90–92).

23. William Wells Brown, *Clotel*, 148.

24. Martin R. Delany, *Blake*, 10. Also of interest is Frances E. W. Harper's poem "Aunt Chloe's Politics" (1872), in which Aunt Chloe's dialect is suggested rather than delineated. Paul Lauter notes, "Harper is remarkably successful in suggesting the speech patterns, syntax, and vocabulary of an unschooled southern black woman without, on the whole, presenting her in dialect. . . ." The sophisticated middle ground that Harper stakes out between Standard English and Southern black dialect is designed, in Lauter's view, to help "legitimate [Aunt Chloe's] keen political commentary" in the poem (Paul Lauter, "Is Frances Ellen Watkins Harper Good Enough to Teach?," 31).

25. On rare occasions a white writer before Twain managed to have an African American speak in dialect that was relatively readable. David Sloane suggests that J. L. Trowbridge, in *Cudjo's Cave* [1863], accomplishes this feat (personal communication). The dialect spoken by Toby and Cudjo in this novel, while rather inconsistent, is, on the whole, generally easy to understand. For

Twain's familiarity with Trowbridge's work, see David Sloane, *"Adventures of Huckleberry Finn": American Comic Vision*, 19, 46–47, 147–48.

26. The work of Irwin Russell, the man whom Joel Chandler Harris credited with having brought accurate black dialect into American literature, did not begin to appear in Northern magazines until January 1876, when *Scribner's* published his earliest dialect poems. Harris praised the "fidelity" of Russell's "bold and striking plantation pictures" (Harris, quoted in G. William Nott, "Irwin Russell, First Dialect Author," 809). Not all critics, however, were as enamored as Harris was of Russell's efforts. William Stanley Braithwaite, for example, in "The Negro in American Literature," had this to say about him:

> Irwin Russell was the first to discover the happy, care-free, humorous Negro. He became a fad. It must be sharply called to attention that the tradition of the ante-bellum Negro is a post-bellum product, stranger in truth than in fiction. Contemporary realism in American fiction has not only recorded his passing, but has thrown serious doubts upon his ever having been a very genuine and representative view of Negro life and character. (31–32)

And Sterling Brown, noting Russell's insistence on "the slave's docility toward, and worship of his master," observes that "on reading Russell's few poems, one is struck by the limited gamut of characteristics allowed to Negroes" ("Negro Character," 184).

It is possible that a precedent for Twain's achievement in "A True Story" may be James Redpath's *The Roving Editor; or Talks with Slaves in the Southern States*, which was published in New York in 1859. Although we have no confirmation that Twain was familiar with this book, his "long, congenial association, both personal and professional" with Redpath (*Mark Twain's Letters* 3:199), who became booking agent for his lecture tours, as well as the admiration Twain expressed for Redpath's abolitionist activities (*Mark Twain's Letters* 3:217–18), suggest that the work may have been known to him. Redpath's book, as Walter M. Brasch observes, is distinguished not only by Redpath's admirable transcriptions of black speech, but also by his ability to draw, from his interviews with slaves, moving first-person testimonies to the cruelty inflicted by the slave system. One slave says, for example, "I had twelve [children] by my firs' wife. I got her when she was seventeen, and I lived wid her twenty-four years. *Den da sold her and all de chil'ren.* I married anoder wife, 'bout nine years since; but I had her little more dan tree years. *Da sold her too*" (slave interviewed by Redpath, 117—emphasis Redpath's, quoted in Brasch, *Black English and the Mass Media*, 45).

27. His daughter, Helen Chesnutt, noted that he sold his first piece of fiction, "Uncle Peter's House," to S. S. McClure's newspaper syndicate in 1885 and was delighted when the story appeared in the *Cleveland News and Herald* in December of that year. During the next three years, he wrote a number of stories for McClure's syndicate, and also for *Family Fiction, The Great International Weekly Story Paper*. "The Goophered Grapevine" was published in the *Atlantic Monthly* in 1887 (Helen M. Chesnutt, *Charles Waddell Chesnutt: Pioneer of the Color Line*, 39–40).

28. SLC to Howells, 2 September 1874, *Mark Twain-Howells Letters* 1:22–23.

29. SLC to Howells, 2 September 1874, *Mark Twain-Howells Letters* 1:23.

30. William Dean Howells to SLC, 8 September 1874, *Mark Twain-Howells Letters* 1:24. Walter M. Brasch concurs with Howells's verdict about the accuracy of Twain's rendition of black dialect in this piece.

> Twain shows a great consistency in his writing, and because he is able to distinguish a number of hard-to-detect speech patterns (for example, *s'ef*), it might be assumed that the preservation of the voiced labio-dental fricative [v] rather than its replacement by the voiced bilabial stop [b] (as in *over* and *of*) reflects not an error, but what Twain actually heard or honestly perceived. (Brasch, *Black English and the Mass Media*, 100)

31. Howells to SLC, 17 September 1874, *Mark Twain-Howells Letters* 1:25.

32. SLC to Howells, 20 September 1874, *Mark Twain-Howells Letters* 1:26.

33. I will always be indebted to Charles T. Davis for having drawn my attention, some sixteen years ago, to the power of this remarkable story.

I agree with William Andrews's interesting suggestion that Fleece's famous sermon to the sharks in *Moby Dick* (Melville, Chapter 64, 288–89) may "[anticipate] some of the important changes that Mark Twain brings to the depiction of dialectal speakers and black dialect as well" (William Andrews, personal communication). In a similar vein, Holton observes that Fleece's "'special speech,' far from making him the object of satire . . . actually gives Fleece a kind of moral distance, allows him to comment analogically and ethically on the conduct of the 'carnivoracious' sharks and sailors." The "'specialness' of Fleece's dialect speech," Holton notes, "establishes for him an authority that makes his sermon a window through which the reader can attain a moral perspective on the action of the book" (*Down Home and Uptown*, 68).

34. Twain, "A True Story," 204. Aunt Rachel's speech throughout "A True Story" manifests a number of the same features we have discussed in connection with the speech of Jimmy, Jim, and Huck. These include repetition: "An' we had *chil'en*—seven *chil'en*—an' we *loved* dem *chil'en* jist de same as you *loves* yo' *chil'en*. Dey was *black*, but de Lord can't make no *chil'en* so *black* but what dey mother *loves* 'em an' wouldn't give 'em up no, not for anything dat's in dis whole world" (203, emphasis added); use of the word "bymeby" (204); zero copula construction: "he always so good!" (204); non-redundancy of tense: "dey got off him, de men did; but I took and tear de clo'es mos' off of 'em an' beat 'em over de head wid my chain; an dey give it to me, too, but I didn't mine dat" (204); and so on. To his credit, Twain makes Aunt Rachel a repository not only of pain, but of other human qualities as well—the feeling of being disoriented or disconcerted, for example, or proud. The surprise at the realization that, since thirteen years had passed, she was now looking not for a small boy, but a man, is believable and real, as is the pride Aunt Rachel takes in her roots—"I's one o' de ole Blue Hen's Chickens, I is!" (203). This pride prefigures the pride that Roxy will have for her son's blue-blood genealogy in *Pudd'nhead Wilson*.

Aunt Rachel's story has some affinities with slaves' recollections of similar scenes as recorded by James Mellon in *Bullwhip Days: The Slaves Remember: An Oral History*, 287–96.

35. Howells, *My Mark Twain*, 123.

36. Howells, *My Mark Twain*, 123–24.

37. Twain [Samuel Clemens], manuscript of "A Family Sketch," 59, 61.

38. Twain [Samuel Clemens], typescript of Notebook 35, May–October 1895, 8.

39. Joel Chandler Harris, "Uncle Remus's Politics," *Atlanta Constitution*, quoted in William Bell, "The Relationship of Joel Chandler Harris and Mark Twain," 99.

40. Harris, quoted in William Bell, "Joel Chandler Harris and Mark Twain," 100.

41. Jon Powell's analysis in his essay, "Trouble and Joy from 'A True Story' to *Adventures of Huckleberry Finn*: Mark Twain and the Book of Jeremiah," echoes the argument presented here. Noting that both Aunt Rachel and Jim use the words "trouble" and "joy," Powell states, "Twain's giving Jim Aunt Rachel's epiphanic words from 'A True Story' clearly illustrates Twain's respect for Jim in a context outside *Huckleberry Finn* . . . and forces . . . a broader perspective of the novel which includes the Biblical Rachel of the Old and New Testaments . . ." (50).

42. Anon., "Negro," 216. *American Cyclopaedia: A Popular Dictionary of General Knowledge*, ed. George Ripley and Charles Anderson Dana, 16 vols. (New York: D. Appleton and Co., 1873–1876) was donated by Clemens to the Mark Twain Library in Redding, Conn. (Gribben, *Mark Twain's Library*, 1:23). Alan Gribben documents numerous statements from Twain to support the idea that he generally consulted this source for information on American history and biography (Gribben, *Mark Twain's Library*, 1:25).

43. Thomas Jefferson, *Notes on Virginia*, 194.

44. There are a number of other resemblances between Aunt Rachel and Roxy. Both are physically impressive: Twain refers to Aunt Rachel's "mighty frame and stature" ("True Story," 202) and to Roxy's "majestic form and stature" (*Pudd'nhead Wilson*, 8). Both are women of strong character, both are mothers passionately devoted to their children, and both express pride in their own or their child's aristocratic ancestry. Both use "signifying": Aunt Rachel in her revision of Misto C—'s remark that she must have seen "no trouble and no joy" in her life ("True Story," 207); Roxy in the wordplay she engages in with Jasper (*Pudd'nhead Wilson*, 7–8), perhaps one of the earliest documented versions in American fiction of a verbal style Claudia Mitchell-Kernan describes in her 1971 article on "Signifying." The exchange between Roxy and Jasper resembles the exchange between Mitchell-Kernan and one of her subjects ("Signifying,"319). Mitchell-Kernan analyzes a "'fluent and lively way of talking characterized by a high degree of personal style,' . . . laced with innuendo—signifying because it alludes to and implies things which are never made explicit" ("Signifying," 319). Like Jasper's early remark to Roxy ("I's gwine to come a-court'n' you bimeby, Roxy"), her subject's opening remark to Mitchell-Kernan ("Mama, you sho is fine") "was intended from all indications as a compliment and was accepted as such. The manner in which it was framed is rather stylized and jocularly effusive, and as such makes the speaker's remarks less bold and presumptuous and is permissive of a response which can acknowledge the compliment in a similar and jokingly impersonal fashion" ("Signifying," 319). "The most salient purpose of the compliment" (in both cases) was initiating a conversation with a woman (Mitchell-Kernan, "Signifying," 319).

Roxy's exchange with Jasper manifests the trading insults and one-upmanship ("Dat's de time I got you," Jasper says midway through the exchange) that are basic to "signifying" exchanges like "the dozens," as William Andrews has observed (personal communication); and the fact that the "friendly duel" between Jasper and Roxy "went on and on," to the enjoyment of both parties, suggests the extended, ritualistic nature of the exchange. The narrator in the book—whom we tend to view as synonymous with Twain, but who may or may not be—takes a dismissive stance toward the kind of wordplay in which Roxy and Jasper are engaged, calling it "idle and aimless jabber," and "wit . . . for wit they considered it" (*Pudd'nhead Wilson*, 8). It is not clear, however, whether or not Twain shared his narrator's view. We know, for example, that despite the fact that black dialect was ridiculed and belittled during Twain's lifetime, Twain painstakingly collected examples of it throughout his journals; this suggests that while his narrator may have expressed the "conventional wisdom" regarding such speech, Twain himself was intrigued by it, and appreciated its creative and vital energy.

45. Twain, *Huckleberry Finn*, 201.

46. Twain, *Huckleberry Finn*, 201–2. The manuscript of the final page of this passage reveals that Twain crossed out one letter and let the rest of the material stand as he originally wrote it. The only line he seems to have added is "She never move!" In the first American edition of the novel, for reasons unknown, Twain changed the line to "She never budge!"

47. Doyno, *Writing "Huck Finn,"* 122.

48. Doyno, *Writing "Huck Finn,"* 122. Doyno finds in this passage and in Twain's special concern with the word "never" a possible allusion to "King Lear's tragic situation with Cordelia and his famous line, 'Never, never, never, never, never'" (122). He feels the resonances between this speech of Jim's and King Lear's

> could be interpreted to mean that tragic emotions can occur in the life of a low-status, traditionally voiceless person such as Jim just as they can in those of higher birth. For a moment Twain has created, in this richly allusive context, a dramatization of immense, irreparable human sadness, the inconsolable grief about a sick child that can torment any parent. This suffering, limitless in depth, transcends cultural status and racial boundaries to serve as the best argument in favor of Jim's shared humanity. (122–23)

Doyno goes on to point out that only two paragraphs later we find a specific reference (in a very different context) to *King Lear*.

49. Sewell, *Mark Twain's Languages*, 95. Sewell follows his statement that Jim's speech "is, in fact, romanticized folk speech," with the observation that his speech is "purified of any forceful hostility that might, coming from a black speaker, have seemed threatening to a white readership even in the postwar North." While this latter point may be true, it does not prove that Jim's speech is inherently "romanticized" (95).

50. Sterling Brown, *The Negro in American Fiction*, 68. Brown believed that "the characterization of Jim, superstitious but shrewd, kindly, self-sacrificial, but determined to be free, not contented in slavery—all of these are vividly rendered. A single passage of dialogue and the pretensions of the plantation tradition are shredded away" (Sterling Brown, "A Century of Negro Portraiture," 341). Holton, *Down Home and Uptown*, 88. Holton adds,

> If Jim's speech were set beside "Standard English," it might well have made him the object of ridicule. But, of course, it is not so juxtaposed. For the whole

novel is in dialect, and Jim's speech, although highly individuated, cannot be judged against any standard. Huck's speech is similarly without a Standard English context. . . . The reader, deprived as he is of received linguistic standard, must—like Huck—perceive experience anew. (*Down Home and Uptown*, 88–89)

51. Martin Pedigo, "Mark Twain's Views on Race," 47.

52. Victor Fischer's records and calculations indicate that Twain used mor than seven dialects (personal communication). See also articles by Carkeet, Tic well, Pederson, and Boland. The most perceptive and useful of these publishe studies is Carkeet's "The Dialects in *Huckleberry Finn*" (1979). Among Ca keet's interesting observations is the notion that Twain made dialect choices usu ally associated with race to establish differences in class—that is, that he gav some characteristically "black" pronunciations and speech patterns to his "lov est" white characters (such as the gang of robbers on the steamboat, and th Bricksville loafers).

It is worth pointing out that there is a contradiction between the positic Twain takes in the "Explanatory" and his simultaneous insistence that the boc is told entirely by Huck. For both of these premises to hold, Huck would have 1 be a consummate dialectologist—for all the speech the reader "hears" is filtere presumably, through Huck's consciousness.

53. Pettit, *Mark Twain and the South*, 128.

54. SLC to James R. Osgood, 4 March 1882, in *Mark Twain's Letters : His Publishers*, ed. Hamlin Hill, 152–53.

55. Peter Messent observes, "Introducing a black voice into the litera mainstream, and registering its appearances and disappearances as it responds t and briefly avoids, the pressure of a dominant discourse, [Twain] further que tions any notion of a common value system, a unitary literary language. If, f Bakhtin, society consists of a plurality of voices in dialogue, then in the use of distinctive black voice," Messent notes, as well as "in the use of Huck's vernac lar, Twain points the way to the seeing of American literature as a clash voices—ethnic, class, regional, gendered—which cuts against the grain of a notion of a fixed, stable and unitary literary canon" (Messent, "The Clash Language," 240).

56. See David Barrow's illuminating discussion of this conversation (whic takes place in "Tom Sawyer's Conspiracy") in "Mark Twain and the Oral Eco omy: Digression in the Age of Print" (27–29). Barrow cites the following di logue:

Jim was a studying and studying, and pretty soon he says—

"Mars Tom, what do dat word mean—*civil*?"

"Well, it means—it means—well, anything that's good, and kind, and polite, and all that—Christian, as you may say."

"Mars Tom, doan dey fight in de wars, en kill each other?"

"Of course."

"Now den, does you call dat civil, en kind en polite, en does you call it Christian?"

"Well—you see—well, you know—don't you understand, it's only a *name*."

"Hi-yah! I was layin' for you, Mars Tom, en I got you dis time, sho! Jist a name! *Dat's* so. *Civil* war! Dey ain' no sich war. De idear!—people dat's good en kind en polite en b'long to de church a-marchin' out en slashin' en choppin' en cussin' en shootin' one another. . . ." (Mark Twain, *Hannibal, Huck and Tom*, Walter Blair, ed., 165–66, cited in Barrow, 27–28)

As Barrow notes, "Jim's impertinences are vexing to Tom precisely because he has no way of showing Jim that they *are* impertinences without revealing the arbitrariness of his own [Tom's] discourse" (27).

57. In this piece Twain shows his sensitivity to the rhythms of black vernacular speech by his careful underlining of accented terms:

> *Aleck.* . . . Ef a man want his snow shoveled by de job, let him go git somebody else; I ain't gwine rassle round rackin my bones outen jint on no job, now you hear *me*!
> *Hank.* No, *sir*! When you wants *me* to shovel snow, s'I, you'll pay me by de *hour*, s'I, en its thutty *cents*, too, s'I, en don't you fogit it! (Manuscript of "Snow-Shovelers," 3–4, Mark Twain Papers. Quoted with permission)

The snow-shovelers go on to have a heated discussion about anarchism, socialism, and work, all of which is carried on in black dialect.

58. Kenneth E. Eble, *Old Clemens and W. D. H.*, 66. Eble goes on to cite several other examples of fairly unreadable dialect writing by Twain's contemporaries, and concludes,

> What may have been a listener's delight was certainly a typesetter's and a reader's nightmare. Howells, in a far-ranging essay about dialect in *Harper's Weekly* in 1895, concluded that the general reader "has got tired of dialect" and that the "conscientious artist" should consider "how little dialect he can get on with, and how much can be done by suggestion, without actual representation." (Eble, *Old Clemens and W. D. H.*, 66–67)

59. James A. Miller made this comment during a public talk at the Mark Twain Memorial in Hartford, Connecticut, in the fall of 1989, and reaffirmed it in conversation during the summer of 1990 (personal communication).

60. Charles W. Chesnutt, "The Goophered Grapevine," 17. As William Andrews has noted,

> "The Goophered Grapevine," an unusual dialect story that displayed intimate knowledge of black folk culture in the South, was Chesnutt's first nationally recognized work of fiction. Its publication in the August 1887 issue of the *Atlantic Monthly* marked the first time that a short story by a black had appeared in that prestigious magazine. (William Andrews, "Chesnutt," 203)

61. Dillard gave Chesnutt high marks for understanding dialect variation within the black community (*Black English: Its History and Usage*, 223). See also Holton's analysis of Chesnutt's representation of dialect (*Down Home and Uptown*, 82–84).

62. Booker T. Washington, ["Tributes to Mark Twain"], 829.

63. Washington, ["Tributes to Mark Twain"], 829.

64. Washington, ["Tributes to Mark Twain"], 829.

65. Washington, ["Tributes to Mark Twain"], 829. Plot summary was not Washington's forte in this article. He gave the following garbled précis of *Huckleberry Finn*: "In this story, which contains many pictures of Southern life as it was fifty or sixty years ago, there is a poor ignorant negro boy who accompanies the heroes of the story, Huckleberry Finn and Tom Sawyer, on a long journey down the Mississippi on a raft" (Washington, ["Tributes to Mark Twain"], 828–29). Interestingly, Washington's confusion resembles that found by six graduate students at the State University of New York at Albany who interviewed 400 randomly selected adults in the 1980s (John C. Gerber, "The Continuing Adventures of *Huckleberry Finn*," 4–5).

66. See MacKethan, "Huck Finn and the Slave Narratives: Lighting Out as Design"; Andrews, "Mark Twain and James W. C. Pennington: Huckleberry Finn's Smallpox Lie"; and Sollors, "Ethnicity." See also Howe, "Transcending the Limits of Experience: Mark Twain's *Life on the Mississippi*," which notes striking resemblances between Twain's work and Frederick Douglass's narrative (425).

67. MacKethan, *"Huck Finn* and the Slave Narratives," 253.

68. Lucinda MacKethan argues this point in *"Huck Finn* and the Slave Narratives," where she writes,

> Pennington, describing his feelings when he realized that he must be near free soil, said that "my spirits were so highly elated, that I took the whole of the road to myself; I ran, hopped, skipped, jumped, clapped my hands, talked to myself." Huck tells us that Jim, seeing one last light that looks like Cairo, says, "We's safe, Huck, we's safe! Jump up and crack yo' heels, dat's de good ole Cairo at las', I jis knows it." (MacKethan, 260)

Twain's characterization of Huck, too, MacKethan claims, may have been influenced by slave narratives. For example, she offers this fascinating analysis of parallels between slave narratives by Pennington, Brown, and Douglass and Chapter 17 of the novel.

> When Huck crawls up the bank on the Kentucky side of the river, he is set upon by dogs and threatened by guns before he is taken into the Grangerford house, much in the way that Pennington was attacked when he was caught in Maryland. . . . The generosity with which the Grangerfords welcome Huck is reminiscent of Pennington's description of his arrival at a Quaker Pennsylvanian's home, where wet, cold, and hungry, he heard the magical words, "Come in and take thy breakfast, and get warm." Once the Grangerfords adopt Huck, he becomes an observer of this southern slaveholding family in much the same position as Brown was as he observed life in Dr. Young's household. And finally, when Huck tricks Buck Grangerford into helping him to remember the alias he invented when he arrived, he employs a strategy that duplicates one that Frederick Douglass devised. (MacKethan, 262)

69. Stuart Hall's comments on the complex relationship between "popular culture" and the "dominant culture" have bearing on this point:

> There is a continuous and necessarily uneven and unequal struggle, by the dominant culture, constantly to disorganise and reorganise popular culture; to enclose and confine its definitions and forms within a more inclusive range of dominant forms. There are points of resistance; there are also moments of supercession. This is the dialectic of cultural struggle. ("Notes on Deconstructing 'the Popular,'" 233)

70. David Bradley, personal communication, 26 July 1992.

71. John Szwed offers some illuminating insights on this issue:

> At once limited in the variety and forms of occupation open to them and at the same time isolated from the central resources of the society, often ghettoized or kept on the margins, the low status groups live largely on their own cultural resources. The irony of the situation is obvious: the low status group, though cut off from the sources of power and production in the larger society, is at the same time less alienated from its own cultural productions. The twist is that the elite of the society is free to draw on the lower group's cultural pool. Were there ever more massive examples of the conversion of community life and culture into

commodity than those in which black folk life has been turned into national culture in the U.S., Brazil, or Cuba? . . . As Roger Bastide has said of the spread of African and Afro-American cuisine, dance, music, art forms, religion, and speech in the Americas: "That spiritual void which the city creates at the heart of each human individual is resented, naturally, just as much by the European as by the Negro. As a result the European turns increasingly to Africa or Black America for the satisfaction of those vital needs which industrial society can no longer answer." . . . Perhaps we are the butt of our own historical joke: we now find ourselves becoming famished and desperate students of the discredited and displaced in a pastoral of ludicrous dimensions. ("Race and the Embodiment of Culture," 30–31)

Chapter 7

1. Ralph Ellison, "Change the Joke and Slip the Yoke," 55.

2. Twain, *Huckleberry Finn*, 112.

3. Beverly J. Robinson, "Africanisms and the Study of Folklore," 215.

4. Solomon Northup, *Twelve Years a Slave*, 219.

5. John Allan Wyeth, *With Sabre and Scalpel*, 59, 62, cited in Blair and Fischer, "Explanatory Notes," 395.

6. Robert Farris Thompson, personal communication.

7. Thompson, personal communication.

8. Roi Ottley and William J. Weatherby, eds., *The Negro in New York*, 25–26, cited in Blair and Fischer, "Explanatory Notes," 395.

9. Charles Dickens, *American Notes*, 36, cited in Blair and Fischer, "Explanatory Notes," 395.

10. James Haskins, *Black Dance in America*, 188.

11. Justin Kaplan, *Mr. Clemens and Mark Twain*, 174.

12. Kaplan, *Mr. Clemens and Mark Twain*, 174. The phrase "crippled uncle" comes from William Dean Howells's account of the evening: Twain came "into his drawing-room at Hartford in a pair of white cowskin slippers, with the hair out, and [did] a crippled colored uncle to the joy of all beholders. Or, I must not say all, for I remember also the dismay of Mrs. Clemens, and her low, despairing cry of, 'Oh, Youth!'" (Howells, *My Mark Twain*, 6–7).

13. Mrs. Thomas Bailey Aldrich, *Crowding Memories*, 160.

14. Marshall Stearns and Jean Stearns, *Jazz Dance: The Story of American Vernacular Dance*, 15.

15. Haskins, *Black Dance in America*, 14.

16. Howells, *My Mark Twain*, 6.

17. William Dean Howells believed that in 1874 the *Atlantic Monthly* was "the most scrupulously cultivated of our periodicals" (Howells, *My Mark Twain*, 19; Blair, *Mark Twain and "Huck Finn,"* 19).

18. Kenneth Lynn, *Mark Twain and Southwestern Humor*, 64.

19. Lynn, *Mark Twain and Southwestern Humor*, 64–65.

20. In one of these instances—"A True Story"—the narrator ("Misto C—") has the first word, but not the last. It is a hint of things to come, for two years later, when Twain began *Huckleberry Finn*, his vernacular-speaking protagonist dispensed with the "frame" altogether and told his own story in his own words.

21. The closest approximation of a "frame" in this book was the heliotype illustration of Karl Gerhardt's elegant bust of Twain that appeared opposite the frontispiece. The bust, like the traditional frame, reminded readers that the book's author (Mark Twain) and its narrator (Huck Finn) were not one and the same. For more on the heliotype, see Louis J. Budd, "'A Nobler Roman Aspect' of *Adventures of Huckleberry Finn.*" The author's "Notice" ("By Order of the Author") and "Explanatory" ("From the Author") also serve a "framing" function in the novel (Twain, *Huckleberry Finn*, xv, xvii).

22. Twain, "Sociable Jimmy," 7.

23. Anon., *"Huckleberry Finn* Barred Out," *Boston Transcript*, 17 March 1885, 6.

24. Anon., "Mark Twain's Last Book Excluded from a Public Library," *St. Louis Globe Democrat*, 17 March 1885, 1.

25. Anon., ["Members of Concord Public Library Committee Have Drawn Line on Literature"], *Boston Daily Globe*, 17 March 1885, 2.

26. Peter Messent, "The Clash of Language," 210. Messent's insightful Bakhtinian reading of the novel illuminates the ways in which "'official' voices are subject to contest, to potential overthrow, from many different directions" (214). David Sewell complicates the polarity between "official," or "genteel," and "vernacular" in important ways in *Mark Twain's Languages*, making a compelling case for the idea that there are, in fact, "two different vernaculars and two standard languages in the novel" (Sewell, 86–87). When I use the term "vernacular" throughout this chapter, I am referring primarily to the variety of the vernacular that is spoken by Huck.

27. Anon., *"Huckleberry Finn," Boston Evening Traveller*, 17 March 1885, 1.

28. Lynn, *Mark Twain and Southwestern Humor*, 204.

29. Lynn, *Mark Twain and Southwestern Humor*, 204.

30. This was far from Twain's first foray into vernacular narration. As Everett Emerson has observed,

> By the time he began *Huckleberry Finn*, Mark Twain was experienced in using vernacular narrators, such as Simon Wheeler of the Jumping Frog story, and during the years between 1876, when he began the new novel, and 1884, when he finished it, Mark Twain contrived to make use of such storytellers: Jim Baker, who tells the Blue Jay Yarn, Rob Styles and Uncle Mumford of *Life on the Mississippi*. (Emerson, *The Authentic Mark Twain*, 128)

Never before, however, had the vernacular been given as much authority.

As Henry Nash Smith pointed out, it was not just the language of vernacular speakers that Twain validated, but also "the values, the ethical and aesthetic assumptions they represent" (*Mark Twain: The Development of a Writer*, 20).

This validation of the vernacular, as Peter Messent has noted, may be seen as related to Bakhtin's notion of "carnivalization." "Life here is turned upside down as conventional barriers are removed." Bakhtin, like Twain, demonstrated a "preference for 'low' languages over 'high,' realized in literary terms in the comic overturning of official systems of life and thought by an unofficial folk culture and the energies with which it is associated (Messent, "The Clash of Language," 212). Huck's own voice, as Messent notes, cannot escape the influence of the cultural authorities it challenges (240); nonetheless, it is a vision of the potential of Huck's voice to undercut and displace those authorities that continues to attract us.

As David Barrow has observed, at the novel's close, Huck "had to decide forever 'betwixt' two sources of authority, between the power of textuality to order the world and the power of human contact to make the world worth ordering. And having made his decision, he had to flee the world of Tom Sawyer, for to stay was to become, like Jim, a slave, or like Pap, a hopeless outsider" (Barrow, "Mark Twain and the Oral Economy," 33).

31. David Sewell notes in *Mark Twain's Languages*,

> From the perspective of Standard English, Huck's speech is riddled with errors. But that perspective is impossible to maintain during a reading of *Huckleberry Finn*; since Huck is the narrator, his speech becomes normative for the duration of the novel. Read his narrative aloud, and only with difficulty can you resist modifying your speech towards your best approximation of Missouri dialect. Indeed, the only successful resistance is to close the book and retreat into silence. . . . In compelling readers to mimic Huck, Mark Twain implicitly asserts that the narrator's language is a valid literary dialect. (85–86)

32. Both of these are points on which I will expand shortly.

33. Twain may have internalized the values of his age in ways that prevented him from consciously recognizing the role African-American voices had played in his creation of this novel. Interesting in this context is Bakhtin's comment that "The author is a captive of his epoch, of his own present. Subsequent times liberate him from this captivity, and literary scholarship is called upon to assist in this liberation. The technique of liberation is called 'creative understanding'" (Bakhtin, quoted in Morson and Emerson, *Mikhail Bakhtin: Creation of a Prosaics*, 288–89). In "creative understanding," in Bakhtin's view, the interpreter or critic, "not satisfied with recreating the text's original context," also "takes advantage of his own," or brings his or her own cultural context to bear on the work (Morson and Emerson, 289). It may well be that the advances in our own time in the fields of linguistics, folklore, and African-American literature and theory had to precede our "creative understanding" of how African-American traditions shaped Twain's art.

34. Bruce R. Bickley, Jr., *Joel Chandler Harris*, 31.

35. Joel Chandler Harris, "Accidental Author," quoted in Bickley, Jr., *Joel Chandler Harris*, 47–48.

36. Bickley, Jr., *Joel Chandler Harris*, 39. Bickley remarks that there may have been more than a little false modesty at work in these disclaimers, and points out that one must take Harris's claim to be only a "compiler" with a grain of salt. Harris "often spun several-page tales from the one-paragraph summaries sent to him by his readers" (Bickley, 39).

37. Mark Twain, "My Debut as a Literary Person."

38. The best discussion of Twain's work on behalf of an International Copyright Act is Victor A. Doyno's chapter, "Literacy, Copyright and Books," in *Writing "Huck Finn,"* 174–219.

39. Louis J. Budd explains the difference in achievement between Twain and Joel Chandler Harris in terms of "1) innate genius and 2) their underlying political-social, that is, racial-cultural attitudes" (Budd, personal communication, 16 June 1992).

40. The first novel by an African-American, William Wells Brown's *Clotel; or, The President's Daughter*, was published in London in 1853. As Henry Louis Gates, Jr., notes,

> curiously enough [the first version of *Clotel*] was not published in America until 1969, perhaps because of its claim that Thomas Jefferson had kept a mistress who was a slave, Sally Hemmings, that she had borne his children, and that Jefferson had sold them. References to Jefferson's paternity disappear completely in the other American editions of *Clotel*. (Gates, Jr., "Introduction," *Three Classic African-American Novels*, x)

Frederick Douglass's only work of fiction, "The Heroic Slave," also appeared in 1853. Frank J. Webb's *The Garies and Their Friends* was published in London in 1857. The first novel by an African American published in the United States appeared in 1859, Harriet E. Wilson's *Our Nig; or, Sketches from the Life of a Free Black*. Martin R. Delany's novel *Blake* was published serially in 1859, 1861, and 1862. Charles W. Chesnutt's "The Goophered Grapevine" appeared in 1887.

41. Henry Louis Gates, Jr., "Introduction," *Our Nig*, xxx.

42. They also failed to recognize that one could make poetry out of this material. As late as 1896, William Dean Howells wrote in his preface to Paul Laurence Dunbar's *Lyrics of Lowly Life*, "These are divinations and reports of what passes in the hearts and minds of a lowly people whose poetry had hitherto been inarticulately expressed in music, but now finds, for the first time in our tongue, literary interpretation of a very artistic completeness" (Howells, "Introduction," xix).

43. Ernest F. Dunn notes that many Europeans failed to recognize "the fact that the Africans spoke actual languages" and "usually concluded that the African spoke a savage black gibberish" ("The Black-Southern White Dialect Controversy," 109). One might cite, in support of this notion, John Campbell's comment, in 1851, that "the typical woolly-haired races have never . . . framed a grammatical language" (Campbell, *Negromania: An Examination of the Falsely Assumed Equality of the Various Races of Men*, cited in John Baugh, *Black Street Speech*, 13). Dunn observes that

> Even today, White comedians, and, sad to say, even Black comedians, flippantly give forth a meaningless variety of gibberish whenever they give impersonations of African encounters. In similar situations where they are mimicking European languages, usually some care is taken to provide some phonological, morphological, and even some lexical features of the language. . . . Such "courtesy" is never afforded African languages. ("The Black-Southern White Dialect Controversy," 109)

The pidgin languages that developed to facilitate communication between Africans and Europeans, which "Europeans interpreted as 'baby talk' dialects,"

> surely reinforced the misconceived inferences by Europeans concerning the African's linguistic or cognitive capacity. Even now, it is still assumed and asserted that the background of such a language was obviously an imperfectly learned form of English or whatever language in question. This assertion, however, implies or presupposes ipso facto that perfect English was the linguistic goal of the speakers. It further presupposes that the African moved into a linguistic ambience, the parameters and perimeters of which were defined by the

European languages only. (Dunn, "The Black-Southern White Dialect Controversy," 109–10)

Lorenzo Turner offers a useful critique of the effect that ignorance of African languages had upon early investigations of Gullah in "Problems Confronting the Investigator of Gullah," 126–35.

44. Ernest F. Dunn provides an illuminating overview of this issue in "The Black-Southern White Dialect Controversy." See also Lorenzo D. Turner, *Africanisms in the Gullah Dialect.*

45. Dunn, "The Black-Southern White Dialect Controversy," 114.

The dominant society "reinvented" and perpetuated a theory of racial inferiority to account for any deviations from standard exhibited in Black speech. . . . Constantly confronted by a system that condemned their speech as inferior, infantile, and incorrect, Blacks slowly began to accept this dogma as truth. . . . (Dunn, 118–19)

For a fuller discussion of this issue, see Dunn, 116–19.

46. Dunn, "The Black-Southern White Dialect Controversy," 114, 116–19. Carter G. Woodson observed,

In the study of language in school pupils were made to scoff at the Negro dialect as some peculiar possession of the Negro which they should despise rather than directed to study the background of this language as a broken-down African tongue—in short to understand their own linguistic history. . . . To the African language as such, no attention was given except in the case of the preparation of traders, missionaries and public functionaries to exploit the natives. This number of persons thus trained, of course, constituted a small fraction hardly deserving attention. From literature the African was excluded altogether. He was not supposed to have expressed any thought worth knowing. The philosophy in the African proverbs and the rich folklore of that continent was ignored to give preference to that developed on the distant shores of the Mediterranean. (*The Mis-Education of the Negro,* 19)

Woodson made these comments in 1933. By 1976 Ernest F. Dunn was able to affirm that "Research has shown that many more African linguistic structures exist in American Black English than previously assumed" ("The Black-Southern White Dialect Controversy," 119).

47. Kaplan, *Mr. Clemens and Mark Twain,* 270. As Leslie Fiedler notes,

Even William Dean Howells, his life-long devotee, as well as his editor and censor and close friend, though he rushed into print enthusiastically in behalf of *Innocents Abroad, The Prince and the Pauper,* and *A Connecticut Yankee in King Arthur's Court,* published no review of *Huckleberry Finn.* Good and sufficient reasons may have been offered for this (he had no regular reviewing assignment at the moment; he was too deeply involved in editing the book etc. etc.); but his perhaps embarrassed silence is too much like that of most of his respectable contemporaries to be easily explained away. ("*Huckleberry Finn*: The Book We Love to Hate," 3)

The idea that "whatever Twain wrote in *Huckleberry Finn,* it wasn't 'literature'" lasted well into the twentieth century. In 1905 a children's librarian named Asa Don Dickinson argued unsuccessfully to allow the book on the shelves of the children's rooms at the Brooklyn Public Library; his fellow-librarians objected that "Huck was a deceitful boy" who "said sweat when he should have said perspiration"

(Dickinson, "Huckleberry Finn Is Fifty Years Old," 6). As late as 1920, a Professor John T. Rice insisted in *The Missouri Historical Review* that Mark Twain "lacks the refinement which would render it impossible for him to create such coarse characters as Huckleberry Finn" (quoted in Fiedler, "*Huckleberry Finn*: The Book We Love to Hate," 2).

48. Twain credits Uncle Dan'l as the source of "The Golden Arm" in his *Autobiography*:

> I can hear Uncle Dan'l telling the immortal tales which Uncle Remus Harris was to gather into his books and charm the world with, by and by; and I can feel again the creepy joy which quivered through me when the time for the ghost story of the "Golden Arm" was reached—and the sense of regret, too, which came over me, for it was always the last story of the evening and there was nothing between it and the unwelcome bed. (15)

49. A widely read book published in 1896, *Race Traits and Tendencies of the American Negro*, included the following statements:

> Nowhere in the region inhabited by [the negro] race do we perceive indications of higher powers of either work or thought. No monuments of architecture appear, no philosophies, or literatures have arisen. And in their present condition they stand mentally at a very low level. (Frederick L. Hoffman, quoting a "Mr. Morris," in Hoffman, *Race Traits and Tendencies of the American Negro*, 313)

50. Sloane, *Mark Twain as a Literary Comedian*, 59–60; Blair, *Mark Twain and "Huck Finn*," 61; DeVoto, *Mark Twain's America*, 14, 137.

51. Roger Abrahams, *Deep Down in the Jungle*, 39.

Chapter 8

1. George M. Fredrickson, *The Black Image in the White Mind*, 248.

2. Frederick L. Hoffman, cited in Fredrickson, *The Black Image in the White Mind*, 249–51.

3. Frederick L. Hoffman, *Race Traits and Tendencies of the American Negro*, 95. Emphasis added.

4. William Smith, cited in Fredrickson, *The Black Image in the White Mind*, 257. Academic "scholars" of the day produced books with titles such as *The Negro, A Menace to American Civilization* (C. Vann Woodward, *The Strange Career of Jim Crow*, 78). In 1903 Charles Chesnutt was moved to remark, "the rights of Negroes are at a lower ebb than at any time during the thirty-five years of their freedom, and the race prejudice more intense and uncompromising" (quoted in Woodward, *The Strange Career of Jim Crow*, 80–81).

As Fredrickson has noted in *The Black Image in the White Mind*,

> If the blacks were a degenerating race with no future, the problem ceased to be one of how to prepare them for citizenship or even how to make them more productive and useful members of the community. The new prognosis pointed rather to the need to segregate or quarantine a race liable to be a source of contamination and social danger to the white community. (255)

African Americans, Fredrickson notes,

> became the scapegoat for the political and economic tensions of the period. The result was legal disfranchisement, the passage of rigorous Jim Crow laws, new and more horrible forms of lynchings, and a series of one-sided race riots which took a heavy toll of defenseless blacks. (266)

Ironically, one such race riot took place in Cairo, Illinois, the place that held such talismanic power for Jim in *Huckleberry Finn* as the site where freedom could be realized.

5. Although this view is represented by the critics cited in this chapter—Michael Rogin, Carmen Subryan, and Guy Cardwell—a more complex perspective emerges in recent work by David Smith and Susan Gillman. David Smith's important paper on "Racial Discourse and Its Critics" sets Twain's racial attitudes in the 1890s and at the turn of the century in the context of his time in fresh and provocative ways. And in her fascinating book *Dark Twins*, Gillman maintains that "the tendency in the thoroughly grounded, deeply historical *Pudd'nhead Wilson* to question conventional boundaries of racial identity expands in the dream tales into challenging the borders of reality itself" (Gillman, *Dark Twins*, 95).

6. Michael Rogin, "Francis Galton and Mark Twain," 74.

7. Carmen Subryan, quoted in Anon., "Experts Split on Whether Twain, His Work, Racist," *Jet*, 15 April 1985, 39.

8. A number of the contributors to *Mark Twain's "Pudd'nhead Wilson,"* edited by Susan Gillman and Forrest G. Robinson, share this perspective.

9. Twain [Samuel Clemens], Autograph Manuscript of *Pudd'nhead Wilson*, Pierpont Morgan Library, New York, MA 241–42. Quoted with permission. It is not clear why Twain chose to omit this passage from the published version of the novel.

10. "Despite his ability and boldness in portraying black characters of impressive complexity, Cable's fiction tended to see virtue in a hierarchy of color, with the lighter race superior to the darker (Louis D. Rubin, Jr., in "Southern Local Color and the Black Man," summarized in William Roberson, *George Washington Cable*, 167).

11. Twain [Samuel Clemens], manuscript of "The Quarrel in the Strong-Box," 1–2. Mark Twain Papers. Quoted with permission.

12. Twain [Samuel Clemens], manuscript of "The Quarrel in the Strong-Box," 7. Quoted with permission.

13. Twain [Samuel Clemens], photocopy of manuscript of "A Family Sketch," 18b. Mark Twain Papers. Quoted with permission.

14. SLC to Olivia Langdon Clemens, 26 September 1893. Mark Twain Papers. Quoted with permission.

15. Twain [Samuel Clemens], photocopy of manuscript of "A Family Sketch," 24b/27. Emphasis added. Published with permission.

16. Thomas Webber, *Deep Like the Rivers, Education in the Slave Quarter Community*, 93. As William Andrews notes in "Mark Twain and James W. C. Pennington: Huckleberry Finn's Smallpox Lie," it is possible that Twain may have read Pennington's book, *The Fugitive Blacksmith; or, Events in the History of James C. Pennington, Pastor of a Presbyterian Church, New York, Formerly a Slave in the State of Maryland, United States* (1849), at some point before he

wrote *Huckleberry Finn*. Although there is no proof that Twain read the book, Andrews observes that Pennington was prominent in New York in 1853. He was also praised in the conclusion of *Uncle Tom's Cabin*. If one might ever prove that Twain had read Pennington, it would still leave open the question of whether Twain absorbed these ideas from Pennington's book or from the slaves he knew himself.

17. Webber, *Deep Like the Rivers*, xi. "'Dat dere fellow am ill as if he were one of de white pop'lation,' remarked one old black man about another showing signs of syphilitic deformities" (Webber, 92).

18. Cardwell, *The Man Who Was Mark Twain*, 200.

19. SLC to William Dean Howells, n.d. June 1872, *Mark Twain-Howells Letters* 1:10–11.

20. Anon., "Negro Blood Divorce Cause," *Broad-Ax*, 28 May 1910, 2.

21. Mark Twain, *Following the Equator*, 265.

22. Margaret Fuller, "American Literature; Its Position in the Present Time and Prospects for the Future," 122.

23. Fuller, "American Literature," 124. Emphasis added.

24. William Faulkner, quoted in Robert Jelliffe, *Faulkner at Nagano*, 88.

Chapter 9

1. Ralph Ellison, "What America Would Be Like Without Blacks," 108.

2. Ellison, "What America Would Be Like Without Blacks," 109.

3. Ellison, "What America Would Be Like Without Blacks," 109. Emphasis added.

4. Ellison, "What America Would Be Like Without Blacks," 109.

5. Thomas Jefferson, *Notes on Virginia*, 195. Houston Baker has observed,

> If blacks "entered" the English language with values and concepts antithetical to those of the white externality surrounding them, then their vocabulary is less important than the underlying codes, or semantic fields, that governed meaning. What I am suggesting is the possibility that whites—moving exclusively within the boundaries of their own semantic categories—have taken the words of the black work of verbal art at face value, or worse, at a value assigned by their own limiting attitudes and patterns of judgment. (*The Journey Back*, 157)

Clearly, Jefferson's appraisal of African-American language use was the product of his "own limiting attitudes and patterns of judgment," and of his inability to grasp the "underlying codes, or semantic fields, that governed meaning" in the speech of African Americans.

6. George Philip Krapp, "The English of the Negro," 190. Eight years after Krapp issued this judgment George Pullen Jackson argued that African-American spirituals similarly had purely Anglo-American origins. In *White Spirituals in the Southern Uplands*, Jackson claimed that African Americans borrowed "both texts and tunes" from early white "revival hymns and other religious folksongs" (Richard Dorson, *American Folklore*, 179). As Dorson notes, throughout the 1930s, '40s, and '50s, "Southern white scholars maintained white cultural supremacy against the new generation of college-educated Negroes, who found support in the Africanist anthropologists of Northwestern University led by Melville J. Herskovits" (Dorson, *American Folklore*, 178–79). "The most sweeping turn of the argument," Dorson writes,

appeared in 1953 under the imprint of the American Historical Association. *Negro Slave Songs in the United States,* by the Negro theological scholar, Miles Mark Fisher, relied on the 1867 volume of *Slave Songs* for its basic text, but bolstered its position with ample documentation from ante-bellum writings and post-bellum collections. Fisher contended that African slaves carried to the United States their cultural trait of using songs for historical records and for satirical purposes. (Dorson, *American Folklore,* 179–80)

(For a useful summary of the debate over the origins and nature of African-American spirituals, see D. K. Wilgus, "The Negro-White Spiritual," 67–80.)

7. H. P. Johnson, "Who Lost the Southern R?," 381.

8. Dillard, *Black English: Its History and Usage,* 186.

9. Dillard, *Black English: Its History and Usage,* 187. Dillard notes, "Payne, let it be pointed out, suggests several areas of influence which were not dealt with by Brooks, who limited himself to a highly unsystematic approach to pronunciation matters" (Dillard, *Black English: Its History and Usage,* 187). Dillard adds that

> The decisions that the Blacks were imitators of European immigrants and that the Europeans themselves brought "regional" varieties to the New World were made in dialectology before any appreciable part of the Black evidence was in. From these hastily formulated theories, it was deduced that investigation of Black populations would turn up no evidence contrary to the Eurocentric picture. Studies of Black language varieties were, therefore, not undertaken, except as Eurocentric or "white-washing" operations. ("General Introduction: Perspectives on Black English," 26)

See also Cleanth Brooks, "The English Language of the South." While claiming that he did not wish "to deny that the blacks influenced the language—through their intonation, through their own rhythms, through the development of striking metaphors, new word coinages and fresh idioms," Brooks reiterated a largely Anglicist position as late as 1985 in his book, *The Language of the American South* (12; 1–17).

10. L. W. Payne, "A Word List from East Alabama," 279.

11. For a useful summary of the Anglicist position, see Holton, *Down Home and Uptown,* 19–23. One of the key problems, as Lorenzo Turner noted, stemmed from the unfamiliarity of white dialect researchers with either African languages or Gullah. Given their ignorance, it is not surprising that "white American linguists refused to consider the possibility that blacks used African words in their vocabularies." The researchers would not have recognized them if they had encountered them (Asante, "African Elements in African-American English," 30).

12. *London Magazine,* 1746, quoted in A. W. Reed, "British Recognition of American Speech in the Eighteenth Century," *Dialect Notes* 6 (1933): 329, cited in John F. Szwed, "Race and the Embodiment of Culture," 26.

13. Fanny Kemble, quoted in Dillard, *Black English: Its History and Usage,* 192.

14. Thomas L. Nichols, *Forty Years of American Life,* 1:385.

15. John Bennett, "Gullah: A Negro Patois," *South Atlantic Quarterly* 7 (October 1908): 339. Cited in Stewart, "Continuity and Change in American Negro Dialects," 237–38.

16. Dillard, *Black English: Its History and Usage,* 216.

17. W. J. Cash, *The Mind of the South,* 51.

18. C. Vann Woodward, "Clio with Soul," 17. Emphasis added.

19. Melville Herskovits, "What Has Africa Given America?," 93. Emphasis added.

20. William Cabell Greet, "Southern Speech," 614. Ironically, black writers and critics coming from vastly different points on the political spectrum from Greet often expressed similar skepticism that anything of value was to be found in Southern black vernacular culture. Wahneema Lubiano notes, for example, that Zora Neale Hurston was marginalized by black writers and critics

> because of her insistence on recreating and representing black southern dialect and folklore within her work. Hurston's focus on that language and folklore flew in the face of the prevailing wisdom. By the time she published *Their Eyes Were Watching God*, James Weldon Johnson had already delimited the use of dialect; at the same time, both politically conservative and Marxist critics were condemning the use of folklore materials as opportunistic and regressive—politically incorrect. For those critics the representation of folklore was a recourse to exploitation of the most oppressed segment of the black American group. Implicit and often explicit in their condemnation was an admission that there was nothing in black southern culture worth representing and that the people of that group existed only as objects of the most abject oppression. (Lubiano, "Constructing and Reconstructing Afro-American Texts," 444)

21. Roger Abrahams and John Szwed, "Introduction," *After Africa*, 1–2.

22. Dunn, "The Black-Southern White Dialect Controversy," 117. Not until work in the 1960s and 1970s by "Black Aestheticians," including Addison Gayle, Jr., Stephen Henderson, Larry Neal, and Houston Baker, did the vernacular begin to come into its own among the critics. As Houston Baker has observed, "a Black Aesthetic generation was the first paradigmatic community to demonstrate the efficacy of the vernacular" (Baker, "Discovering America: Generational Shifts, Afro-American Literary Criticism, and the Study of Expressive Culture," 112). A "vernacular model," Baker notes, is "the analytical project that may serve as a paradigm for the future study of Afro-American literature and expressive culture" ("Discovering America," 112). Baker has continued to foreground the importance of African-American vernacular traditions (see *Blues, Ideology and Afro-American Literature: A Vernacular Theory*), as has Henry Louis Gates, Jr., whose most recent statement on this point may be found in *Loose Canons: Notes on the Culture Wars*, 83.

23. Dunn, "The Black-Southern White Dialect Controversy," 117. This idea is echoed in an anecdote related by R. MacKaye Atwood, who reports a conversation that he had with a woman from Lynchburg, Virginia, about an incident during her childhood in the 1870s or 1880s:

> She had a younger brother, perhaps ten or so, who had as his chief playmate a black boy of his own age. One day the parents of the white lad called him in for a serious talk. They knew that soon he would have to end having him as his best friend, but more to the point was his speech. It was explained that he spoke just like his black friend, and they could not be told apart. He would have to find a more suitable companion. The boy objected, asserting, "It don't matter how I talks, everybody knows who ah is." The parents remained unmoved. (R. MacKaye Atwood, personal communication)

Ernest F. Dunn observes that whites' desire to be rid of the stigma of black speech "was intensified following the so-called Emancipation."

> Scholars like Dillard (1972) rightly pointed out that the movement of the Black into a freer environment placed him in competition with the working-class White who was forced to fall back upon his "Whiteness" as his only claim to superiority. To such people the tracing of any of their language or behavior patterns to the Negro was the bitterest of insults. (Dunn, "The Black-Southern White Dialect Controversy," 116–17)

Former aristocrats whose positions were similarly reduced after the war also shunned the idea that anything in their own speech could have black roots. Their position was supported by the work of scholars like Krapp (1924) and Kurath (1928), who mounted Herculean efforts to deny any evidence of black influence on Southern white speech (Dunn, "The Black-Southern White Dialect Controversy," 117).

24. Dunn, "The Black-Southern White Dialect Controversy," 118.

25. Dunn, "The Black-Southern White Dialect Controversy," 117.

26. Ralph Ellison, quoted in James Alan McPherson, "Indivisible Man," 44.

27. Woodward, "Clio with Soul," 17.

28. Ralph Ellison, "Going to the Territory," 142.

29. Ellison, "Going to the Territory," 143.

30. Ellison, "Going to the Territory," 140.

31. H. L. Mencken, "The Burden of Humor," 69–70.

32. Louis J. Budd, "The Recomposition of *Adventures of Huckleberry Finn*," 195.

33. Budd, "The Recomposition of *Adventures of Huckleberry Finn*," 195.

34. Budd, "The Recomposition of *Adventures of Huckleberry Finn*," 200.

35. David E. E. Sloane, *"Adventures of Huckleberry Finn": American Comic Vision*, 5. See Jonathan Arac's "Nationalism, Hypercanonization, and *Huckleberry Finn*," for some interesting reflections on what Arac calls the "hypercanonicity" of this novel.

36. Robert M. Rodney, ed., *Mark Twain International: A Bibliography and Interpretation of His Worldwide Popularity*, 264. *Huckleberry Finn* has been translated into German, Dutch, French, Danish, Italian, Portuguese, Spanish, Swedish, Albanian, Bulgarian, Czech, Bohemian, Slovak, Greek, Hungarian, Polish, Rumanian, Serbian, Serbo-Croatian, Slovenian, Macedonian, Russian, Ukrainian, Lettish, Tatar, Moldavian, Georgian, Lithuanian, Azerbaidjan, Turkmen, Uzbek, Kazakh, Kirgiz, Karelo-Finnish, Farsi, Hebrew, Turkish, Arabic, Afrikaans, Singhalese, Bengali, Gujarati, Telugu, Marathi, Tamil, Malayalam, Hindi, Assamese, Indonesian, Thai, Chinese, and Japanese. See Rodney, ed., *Mark Twain International: A Bibliography and Interpretation of His Worldwide Popularity*, 45–462, for the most complete listing of foreign editions.

37. Part of this neglect may have been related to the widespread assumption, as Walter J. Ong has put it in *Orality and Literacy*, that "oral art forms were essentially unskillful and not worth serious study" (10). Interestingly, in his effort to devise an alternative for the oxymoronic term "oral literature," Ong suggests that "we might refer to all purely oral art as 'epos,' which has the same Proto-Indian European root, *wekw-*, as the Latin word *vox* and its English equivalent 'voice,' and thus is grounded firmly in the vocal, the oral. Oral performances would thus be felt as 'voicings,' which is what they are" (13–14). My emphasis in this book on voices that shaped Twain's imagination, and on the

voice of Huck Finn, stems from a similar desire to explore, in complex, nuanced ways, some of the links between oral and literate experiences.

38. Ellison, quoted in Howard Sage, "An Interview with Ralph Ellison," 12.

39. Ralph Ellison, "On Initiation Rites and Power," 47–48.

40. Ellison, "What America Would Be Like Without Blacks," 111.

41. Ellison, quoted in Sage, "An Interview with Ralph Ellison," 11.

42. Ellison, "Going to the Territory," 125.

43. In fact, I did not begin to conceptualize the argument I lay out in this book until some four months after our interview.

44. A plaster bust of Twain was given to every guest at his seventieth birthday party at Delmonico's in New York City on 5 December 1905. Chesnutt was a guest at that dinner. Chesnutt's daughter notes that "the bust of Mark Twain was put in the library [in Chesnutt's home] in a place of honor" (Helen M. Chesnutt, *Charles Waddell Chesnutt: Pioneer of the Color Line*, 214).

45. Ellison drew my attention to the picture, which was displayed on the bookshelf next to his desk, during our interview. The photo, which was a gift to Ellison from a student, showed Twain at Oxford in the gown in which he received an honorary degree.

46. Ralph Ellison, *Invisible Man*, 55. I read this passage from *Invisible Man* out loud during the interview. Ellison immediately responded by acknowledging the likelihood that he had been unconsciously influenced by Twain.

47. See also Stewart Rodnon's "*The Adventures of Huckleberry Finn* and *Invisible Man*: Thematic and Structural Comparisons," for an interesting consideration of similarities between the two novels' use of language, folklore, humor, and point-of-view.

Houston Baker's controversial discussion of Trueblood as a paradigmatic figure of the African-American artist lends added significance to the potential links between Trueblood and Huck. See Houston Baker, "To Move Without Moving: Creativity and Commerce in Ralph Ellison's Trueblood Episode," 221–48.

48. David Bradley, "The First 'Nigger' Novel."

49. I am grateful to James A. Miller for raising this interesting point (personal communication).

50. The essay first appeared in the *Mark Twain Journal* in 1984 and is included in *Satire or Evasion? Black Perspectives on "Huckleberry Finn"* (1991).

51. Rampersad, "*Adventures of Huckleberry Finn* and Afro-American Literature," 217–24.

52. Rampersad, "*Adventures of Huckleberry Finn* and Afro-American Literature," 219.

53. Langston Hughes, quoted in Arnold Rampersad, *The Life of Langston Hughes, Volume II*, 223.

54. Rampersad, "*Adventures of Huckleberry Finn* and Afro-American Literature," 218.

Richard Yarborough suggests that Albert Murray's *Train Whistle Guitar*, which is narrated in the first person from the point of view of a boy, may also have been influenced by *Huckleberry Finn* (personal communication).

55. Rampersad, "*Adventures of Huckleberry Finn* and Afro-American Literature," 222.

56. Rampersad, "*Adventures of Huckleberry Finn* and Afro-American Literature," 227.

57. Toni Morrison, quoted in Trudier Harris, *Fiction and Folklore: The Novels of Toni Morrison*, 1.

58. Toni Morrison, personal communication.

59. Interestingly, the trope of the "talking book" had a central role in African-American culture long before Twain wrote (Gates, Jr., *Signifying Monkey*, 127–216).

60. Richard Wright, quoted in Michel Fabre, *Richard Wright: Books and Writers*, 161. I am indebted to Werner Sollors for having brought his comment to my attention.

61. It is a subject I will explore in *The Stories He Couldn't Tell: Mark Twain and Race*.

62. Rampersad, *The Life of Langston Hughes, Volume I*, 19.

63. Langston Hughes, "The Negro Speaks of Rivers," 1488. Arnold Rampersad's description of the occasion when Hughes wrote this poem lends support to the idea that it was the Mississippi above all other rivers that inspired "The Negro Speaks of Rivers":

> The sun was setting as the train reached St. Louis and began the long passage from Illinois across the Mississippi and into Missouri, where Hughes had been born. The beauty of the hour and the setting—the great muddy river glinting in the sun, the banked and tinted summer clouds, the rush of the train toward the dark, all touched an adolescent sensibility tender after the gloomy day. The sense of beauty and death, of hope and despair, fused in his imagination. A phrase came to him, then a sentence. Drawing an envelope from his pocket, he began to scribble. In a few minutes Langston had finished a poem: "I've known rivers" (Rampersad, *The Life of Langston Hughes, Volume I*, 39)

Intriguing in this context, as well, is a poem Daniel Hoffman published in 1984 in the *New Yorker* entitled "Mark Twain, 1909," which reads, in part, as follows: ". . . Behind him,/ in the bookcase, only one/ title in focus, thick book:/ "THE NILE" Always rivers,/ rivers, the mind afloat on/ currents, eddies . . . Memory/ the raft that bears us onward . . ." (Hoffman, "Mark Twain, 1909," 48).

64. Charles T. Davis, "Black Literature and the Critics," 51. In a similar vein, Henry Louis Gates, Jr., has noted,

> In the case of the writer of African descent, his or her texts occupy spaces in at least two traditions: a European or American literary tradition, and one of the several but related distinct black traditions. The "heritage" of each black text written in a Western language is, then, a double heritage, two-toned, as it were. Its visual tones are white and black, and its aural tones are standard and vernacular. (Gates, Jr., "Criticism in the Jungle," 4)

65. Eric Sundquist observes

> Neither the tradition of classic American literature nor that of Afro-American literature adequately defines the problem of race; like the larger social history that they reflect, the two traditions must be read together for their interactions and conflicts, their revisions of one another. Most of all, they must be read with careful attention to the historical contexts whose pressures have in every case formed them, with or against their will, and often by placing them in a web of

reference that simple attention to the text will not uncover. (Sundquist, "Faulkner, Race and the Forms of American Fiction," 3)

66. The principal exceptions are William Andrews, David Bradley, Charles T. Davis, Henry Louis Gates, Jr., Ralph Ellison, Lucinda MacKethan, Arnold Rampersad, Werner Sollors, and Eric Sundquist.

67. Werner Sollors, "A Critique of Pure Pluralism," 257. Sollors continues,

> Can Gertrude Stein be discussed with Richard Wright or only with white women expatriate German-Jewish writers? . . . In general, is the question of influence, or who came first, more interesting than investigation of the constellation in which ideas, styles, themes and forms travel? (Sollors, "A Critique of Pure Pluralism," 257)

68. Sollors, "A Critique of Pure Pluralism," 256.
69. Charles Johnson, *Being and Race*, 43–44.
70. Ellison, quoted in Sage, "Interview with Ralph Ellison," 10.
71. Shelley Fisher Fishkin, "Interview with Kingston," 784, 790.
72. David Bradley, personal communication, 29 May 1992. Bradley bemoaned the fact that the critics "won't let me have my models" (personal communication, 29 May 1992). Presumably, he was referring to comments such as that of Charles Johnson: "Bradley has said, in his 1984 interview in *Callaloo*, that *The Chaneysville Incident*, winner of the 1982 *PEN/Faulkner Award*, is largely influenced by the writing of Robert Penn Warren, a statement that reveals more of his tendency toward self-mockery than this fascinating book, a historical novel about the historical imagination itself" (Charles Johnson, *Being and Race*, 79).
73. Tillie Olsen confirmed her debt to DuBois in December 1987, after hearing an MLA paper on "Creative Experimentation in American Nonfiction Narrative," in which I hypothesized the connection (personal communication). She reiterated the importance of this connection in a conversation on 28 December 1991. See also Shelley Fisher Fishkin, "The Borderlands of Culture: Writing by W. E. B. DuBois, James Agee, Tillie Olsen and Gloria Anzaldúa."
As Henry Louis Gates, Jr., has observed,

> [T]he most formally complex and compelling black writers—such as Jean Toomer, Sterling Brown, Langston Hughes, Zora Hurston, Richard Wright, Ralph Ellison, James Baldwin, Toni Morrison and Gwendolyn Brooks—have always blended forms of Western literature with African-American vernacular and written traditions. Then again, even a vernacular form like the spirituals took as its texts the King James version of the Old and New Testaments. . . . African-American culture, then, has been a model of multiculturalism and plurality. (Gates, Jr., *Loose Canons*, xvii)

See also Phillip M. Richards, "Phillis Wheatley and Literary Americanization."
74. *Chicago Tribune* columnist Clarence Page, for example, is a writer for whom Twain's craftsmanship (in *Huckleberry Finn*) served as a compelling example: "It was inspiring for me as a future wordsmith to see how effectively the power of words could be used to grab and persuade a reader to see a powerful point. It was inspiring enough for me to read other great American authors who were inspired by Twain. They include such great African-American authors as James Baldwin and Ralph Ellison" (Page, "Black Voice Enriches Maligned Masterpiece," 7B).

75. In 1956 William Faulkner claimed Twain as a literary grandfather. What he actually said was: "[Sherwood Anderson] was the father of my generation of American writers and the tradition which our successors will carry on. . . . Dreiser is his older brother and Mark Twain the father of them both" (Faulkner, in interview with Jean Stein, *Paris Review*, 46–47). Elsewhere he said, "In my opinion Mark Twain was the first truly American writer, and all of us since are his heirs, we descended from him" (Faulkner, quoted in Jelliffe, ed., *Faulkner at Nagano*, 88).

76. Zoe Ingalls wrote in the *Chronicle of Higher Education*,

> Stephen Foster might seem out of place at the prestigious St. Petersburg International Choir Festival, which acts as host to Europe's finest professional choirs. You'd expect Handel, perhaps, or Bach. But for William A. Wyman, director of the Nebraska Wesleyan University choir, the choice of "Camptown Races" for his group's concert is a canny assessment of what Europeans like to hear when Americans perform. "A foreign audience wants to hear the things that are uniquely American," he says. It's an assessment based on experience: During his 18-year stint as director, Mr. Wyman has led the choir on concert tours of Europe and the Orient. (Ingalls, "A Choir Festival in St. Petersburg," B6)

77. Lorenzo Turner, cited in John A. Davis, "The Influence of Africans on American Culture," 77.

78. Yarborough, "Strategies of Characterization in *Uncle Tom's Cabin* and the Early Afro-American Novel"; Robert Stepto, "Sharing the Thunder: The Literary Exchanges of Harriet Beecher Stowe, Henry Bibb, and Frederick Douglass."

79. Eli Leon, *Models in the Mind: African Prototypes in American Patchwork*.

80. Sage, "Interview with Ralph Ellison," 10.

81. June Jordan, "For the Sake of a People's Poetry: Walt Whitman and the Rest of Us." Other examples within and outside the borders of the United States abound. For instance, African-American poet Robert Hayden was heavily influenced by Stephen Benet's poem, "John Brown's Body." (Charles T. Davis, "Black Literature," 52). And an entire tradition of Czech poetry was inspired by African-American jazz (Josef Jarab, "Black Stars, Red Star, and the Blues").

82. Henry Louis Gates, Jr., "'Authenticity,' or the Lesson of Little Tree." Eric Sundquist's erudite and impressive book, *To Wake the Nations: Race in American Literature and Culture, 1830–1930*, will be published this year by Harvard University Press. Werner Sollors has been working for some time on a massive study of miscegenation in Western literature; Carla Peterson is completing a book on nineteenth-century African-American women writers; Arnold Rampersad is writing a book on race and American authors. Books by David Smith on "Racial Writing, Black and White," and by Michael North on "Race, Dialect, and the Emergence of Modernism," promise to be of great interest as well. Also useful for reframing our understanding of issues of race and American culture are Aldon Lynn Nielson's 1988 study of twentieth-century white American poets and racial discourse, and Dana Nelson's 1992 book on race in early American literature. Our understanding of "cultural syncretism" is also furthered by such works as Gloria Anzaldúa's landmark book *Borderlands/La Frontera*, with its eloquent exploration of "mestiza consciousness" and "cultural mestisaje."

American Studies Association President Cathy Davidson's comment in a recent ASA newsletter reflects the change in paradigm that is increasingly shaping the discipline:

> Multicultural representation? Gender equity? Diversity? Forget it! Just give me *good* history (whether social or literary history), a far more dangerous proposition. The investment in some kind of sanitizing, homogenizing, consensual "we" . . . may be tenable as a politician's polemic but it has weakened American Studies as a field and shut off important and fascinating areas of discussion. The Norse, probably the Chinese, and even an Italian sent by Spain to India all "discovered" a continent inhabited by various American cultures long before the Puritans made their way to these shores. Slaves and immigrants built much of the country, a country that extends far beyond New England. Roughly half of the population has always been female, not all of it was ever heterosexual, and relatively little of it (any gender, racial or immigrant group) has been rich. With a history like this, who needs affirmative action? (Cathy Davidson, "Statement")

83. The notion that white writers are the descendants of other white writers is a familiar theme, one which is central to what Henry Louis Gates, Jr., has called "'the antebellum aesthetic position,' when men were men, and men were white, when scholar-critics were white men, and when women and persons of color were voiceless, faceless servants and laborers, pouring tea and filling brandy snifters in the boardrooms of old boys' clubs" (Gates, Jr., *Loose Canons*, 17). As Paul Lauter put it in *Canons and Contexts*,

> Consider, as an example of faulty literary history, what was until the mid-1970s the usual portrait of the evolution of fiction in North America (a portrait that still shapes curricular choices). Writers such as Charles Brockden Brown, Washington Irving, and James Fenimore Cooper, it was said, were forerunners who cleared and plowed the colonial cultural wilderness so that, in the "American Renaissance," the first generation of major writers—Poe, Hawthorne, Melville—could flourish. These were succeeded by three generations of fiction writers: Twain and James, who elaborated alternative westward-looking and eastward-looking subjects and styles; realists and naturalists like Howells, Crane, and Dreiser; and finally, in the 1920s, a new, modernist renaissance exemplified by the work of Hemingway, Fitzgerald, Dos Passos, Faulkner, and a host of others. (54)

These "older accounts of American fictional history," Lauter continued, "left us asking 'where were the blacks?'" (55).

By the same token, standard accounts of African-American literary history emphasize the all-black literary genealogies of African-American writers, often to the frustration of those writers themselves. Ralph Ellison notes, for example, that the role of James Weldon Johnson (author of *Autobiography of an Ex-Colored Man*) as one of Ellison's literary forebears was much less important than critics seem willing to accept (Fishkin interview). And David Bradley complains that critics refuse to accept the idea that white writers played a key role in shaping his art (personal communication, 29 May 1992).

84. Ellison, "Change the Joke and Slip the Yoke," 55.

85. Toni Morrison, *Playing in the Dark*, 5.

86. David Bradley, "Foreword," vii. "Literary segregation," like all American segregation,

> was originally supported by perfectly legitimate nineteenth-century beliefs. . . . Indeed, one must insist that early literary segregation came about quite natu-

rally, as an expression of what was then the American reality. One can hardly condemn the New Critics for not mingling colored and white poets in the same essay in 1941 when President Roosevelt would not "mingle colored and white enlisted personnel in the same regiment" in 1944. . . . Beginning in 1948, when President Truman issued Executive Orders 9980 and 9981, ending segregation in the federal service and the armed forces, the segregation of literature began to lose the support of the social context. By 1953, when the Supreme Court struck down the separate-but-equal doctrine in *Brown v. Board of Education*, the legal basis was lost. Soon the scientific basis too was gone; in 1958 Ralph Ellison could write sarcastically, "I know of no valid demonstration that culture is transmitted through the genes." (Bradley, "Foreword," xviii)

Elsewhere Bradley has noted the impact of this segregation in American college classrooms, observing that in 1980–81, the *Bulletin* of the University of Pennsylvania advertised

> a course in "American" fiction that explicitly includes "Hawthorne, Clemens, James, Wharton, Hemingway, Fitzgerald, and Faulkner," and implicitly excludes Chesnutt, Hurston, Richard Wright and Ralph Ellison; a course in "American" poetry including "Whitman, Dickinson, Frost, Pound, Eliot, Stevens, Williams, Moore, Lowell, Roethke, and Plath," and apparently not including Dunbar, Hughes, Toomer, Gwendolyn Brooks or Sterling Brown. (David Bradley, "Black and American, 1982," 408)

An elaborate survey of forty college and university literature departments conducted by Alan Wald between 1986 and 1988 suggests that the pattern Bradley noted in the *Bulletin* of the University of Pennsylvania persists in American college classrooms. Wald found that "students across the country who enroll in courses called 'The Modern Novel' or 'Modern Poetry' will read and discuss works almost exclusively by elite white men that are interpreted through the prism of the British tradition" (Katterman, "In Search of an 'American' Literature: UM [University of Michigan] Scholar Argues that Emphasis on the British Tradition Creates Damaging Myths," 14.) "The result," Wald said, "is an approach to literature that fails to indicate, and actually distorts, the rich cultural activity that has existed and still exists in the United States" (Katterman, "In Search of an 'American' Literature," 14).

William Andrews clearly summarizes the segregated nature of one branch of critical writing in his excellent 1990 essay, "Mark Twain, William Wells Brown, and the Problem of Authority in New South Writing": "Until the late 1960s," Andrews notes,

> the history and criticism of southern literature in America proceeded from the unwritten assumption that the literature of the South was the product of white, predominantly male southerners. Black writers from the South belonged to a separate province of letters that was reconstructed into Negro American literature mainly by the literary historians and critics who taught in black colleges of the South. Owing to the enormous influence of his myth and his message on both sides of the color line, Booker T. Washington was one of the few black writers who held a secure niche in both southern and Negro literature before the onset of the civil rights movement in the late 1950s. Charles W. Chesnutt, a figure of the first importance to students of Negro literature, footnoted Joel Chandler Harris in standard accounts of southern literature. In Faulkner's shadow lurked Richard Wright, but Wright's perspective on the South was judged parochial next to Faulkner's much-vaunted universality. White southern criticism chose Faulkner more than any other single writer to explain southern race

relations to the world. Black critics accepted Richard Wright as a brave new spokesman for their side of the controversial issue. But until very recently virtually no published discourse ensued between the two literary camps. (1)

Andrews adds, in a footnote, that "A sign of a much-welcome change is Craig Werner's 'Tell Old Pharaoh: The Afro-American Response to Faulkner,' *Southern Review* 19 (Autumn 1983): 711–35" (18). For a useful overview of white critics' dismissive attitudes toward African-American writers, see Houston Baker's "Black Creativity and American Attitudes" in *The Journey Back* (144–54).

87. Bradley, "Foreword," xviii.

88. There is neither time nor space to give these important questions their due here, in part because of the complexity of Mark Twain's attitudes toward race, and in part because the jury is still out on the subject of Americans' reactions to the research at hand. I will explore these issues more fully in my next book. See Introduction, note 26.

89. Henry Louis Gates, Jr., "Introduction: Writing 'Race' and the Difference It Makes," 5. "Race," as Gates has observed,

is the ultimate trope of difference because it is so very arbitrary in its application. The biological criteria used to determine "difference" in sex simply do not hold when applied to "race." Yet we carelessly use language in such a way as to *will* this sense of *natural* difference into our formulations. To do so is to engage in a pernicious act of language, one which exacerbates the complex problem of cultural or ethnic difference, rather than to assuage or redress it. This is especially the case at a time when, once again, racism has become fashionable. ("Writing 'Race,'" 5)

Coda

1. Twain, *Huckleberry Finn*, 2.

Works Cited

Abrahams, Roger D. *Deep Down in the Jungle: Negro Narrative Folklore from the Streets of Philadelphia.* [1964]. rev. ed. Chicago: Aldine, 1970.

_____. *Positively Black.* Englewood Cliffs, N.J.: Prentice-Hall, 1970.

Abrahams, Roger D., and John Szwed. "Introduction." In *After Africa: Extracts from British Travel Accounts and Journals of the Seventeenth, Eighteenth, and Nineteenth Centuries Concerning the Slaves, Their Manners, and Customs in the British West Indies*, 1–48. New Haven: Yale University Press, 1983.

Albert, Ethel M. "'Rhetoric,' 'Logic,' and 'Poetics' in Burundi: Culture Patterning of Speech Behavior." In "The Ethnography of Communication," edited by John J. Gumperz and Dell Hymes. *American Anthropologist* 66, pt. 2 (Special issue, 1964): 35–54.

Aldrich, Mrs. Thomas Bailey. *Crowding Memories.* Boston: Houghton Mifflin Co., 1920.

Alleyne, Mervyn C. *Comparative Afro-American: An Historical Comparative Study of English-Based Afro-American Dialects of the New World.* Foreword by Ian F. Hancock. *Linguistica Extranea, Studia II.* Ann Arbor: Karoma Publishers, Inc., 1980.

Alter, Robert. *Rogue's Progress: Study in the Picaresque Novel*, 117–21. Cambridge, Mass.: Harvard University Press, 1964.

Ames, Russell. "Protest and Irony in Negro Folksong." *Science and Society* 14 (1950): 193–213. Reprinted in Dundes, Alan, ed., *Mother Wit from the Laughing Barrel*, 487–500. Jackson: University Press of Mississippi, 1990.

Andrews, Ethan A. *Slavery and the Domestic Slave Trade in the United States.* Boston: Light and Stearns, 1836.

Andrews, Sidney. *The South Since the War: As Shown by Fourteen Weeks of Travel and Observation in Georgia and the Carolinas.* Boston: Ticknor and Fields, 1866. Reprint. New York: Arno Press and the New York Times, 1969.

Andrews, William L. "Charles W. Chesnutt." In *Encyclopedia of Southern Culture*, edited by Charles Wilson Reagan and William Ferris, 202–3. Chapel Hill: University of North Carolina Press, 1989.

_____. "Mark Twain and James W. C. Pennington: Huckleberry Finn's Smallpox Lie." *Studies in American Fiction* 9 (Spring 1981): 103–12.

_____. "Mark Twain, William Wells Brown, and the Problem of Authority in New South Writing." In *Southern Literature and Literary Theory*, edited by Jefferson Humphries, 1–21. Athens: University of Georgia Press, 1990.

_____. Personal communication, 22 June 1992.

Anon. "Assistant Sergeant-at-Arms to the State of California." *Alta California*, 4 December 1879, 1.

Anon. "Coming Events." *Fun* (London), 26 April 1873, 172.

Anon. "Experts Split on Whether Twain, His Work Racist." *Jet*, 15 April 1985, 39.

Anon. *Facts, by a Woman.* Oakland, Ca.: Pacific Press Publishing House, 1881.

Anon. "*Huckleberry Finn.*" *Boston Evening Traveller*, 17 March 1885, 1.

Anon. [*Huckleberry Finn* Barred Out], *Boston Transcript*, 17 March 1885, 6. Reprinted in Champion, Laurie, ed., *The Critical Response to Mark Twain's "Huckleberry Finn,"* 13. Westport, Conn.: Greenwood Press, 1991.

Anon. *Jubilee Songs: Complete. As Sung by the Jubilee Singers, of Fisk University* (Nashville, Tenn.). Under the Auspices of the American Missionary Association. New York and Chicago: Biglow and Main, 1872.

Anon. "Mark Twain's Cousin, His Favorite, Tabitha Quarles." *The Twainian* 4 (July–August 1952): 1–2.

Anon. "Mark Twain's Last Book Excluded from a Public Library." *St. Louis Globe-Democrat*, 17 March 1885, 1.

Anon. "Mark Twain Tells the Secrets of Novelists." *New York American*, 26 May 1907. Reprinted in Neider, Charles, ed., *Mark Twain: Life as I Find It*, 388. Garden City, N.Y.: Hanover House, 1961.

Anon. ["Members of Concord Public Library Committee Have Drawn Line on Literature"]. *Boston Daily Globe*, 17 March 1885, 2.

Anon. National Centennial Commemoration. Proceedings on the One Hundredth Anniversary of the Introduction and Adoption of the Resolutions Respecting Independency. Held in Philadelphia on the Evening of June 7, 1876.

Anon. "Negro." In *American Cyclopaedia: A Popular Dictionary of General Knowledge.* Vol. 12: 215–17. New York: D. Appleton and Co., 1875.

Anon. "Negro Blood Divorce Cause." *Broad-Ax* (Chicago), 28 May 1910, 2.

Anon. "Negro Patois and Its Humor." *Appleton's Journal of Popular Literature, Science and Art* 2 (5 February 1870): 161–62.

Anon. [editor's note]. *The Twainian* 2, no. 5 (February 1943), 3.

Anzaldúa, Gloria. *Borderlands/La Frontera: The New Mestiza.* San Francisco: Spinsters/Aunt Lute, 1987.

Arac, Jonathan. "Nationalism, Hypercanonization, and *Huckleberry Finn*," in "New Americanists 2," edited by Donald Pease. *boundary 2.* 19:1 (Special issue, Spring 1992): 14–33.

Armon, Dahlia, and Walter Blair. "Biographical Directory." In *Huck Finn and Tom Sawyer Among the Indians and Other Unfinished Stories*, by Mark Twain. Foreword and Notes by Dahlia Armon and Walter Blair. The Mark Twain Library. Berkeley: University of California Press, 1989.

———, eds. *Mark Twain, Huck Finn and Tom Sawyer Among the Indians and Other Unfinished Stories.* Foreword and Notes by Dahlia Armon and Walter Blair. Berkeley: University of California Press, Mark Twain Project, 1989.

Asante, Molefi Kete. "African Elements in African-American English." In *Africanisms in American Culture*, edited by Joseph E. Holloway, 19–33. Bloomington: Indiana University Press, 1990.

Atwood, R. Mackaye. Personal communication, 17 July 1992.

Ayres, John W. "Recollections of Hannibal." Letter of 22 August 1917 to *Palmyra Spectator.* Undated clipping in Morris Anderson scrapbook, Mark Twain Museum, Hannibal, Missouri. Photocopy in Mark Twain Papers, Bancroft Library, University of California, Berkeley.

Baender, Paul, ed., and intro. *What Is Man? And Other Philosophical Writings*. The Works of Mark Twain. Berkeley: University of California Press, 1973.

Baker, Houston A., Jr. *Blues, Ideology, and Afro-American Literature: A Vernacular Theory*. Chicago: University of Chicago Press, 1984. Paperback edition, 1987.

_____. "Discovering America: Generational Shifts, Afro-American Literary Criticism, and the Study of Expressive Culture." In *Blues, Ideology and Afro-American Literature*, by Houston A. Baker, Jr., 64–112. Chicago: University of Chicago Press, 1984. Paperback edition, 1987.

_____. *The Journey Back: Issues in Black Literature and Criticism*. Chicago: University of Chicago Press, 1980.

_____. *Long Black Song: Essays in Black American Literature and Culture*. Charlottesville: University Press of Virginia, 1972.

_____. "To Move Without Moving: Creativity and Commerce in Ralph Ellison's Trueblood Episode." In *Black Literature and Literary Theory*, edited by Henry Louis Gates, Jr., 221–48. New York: Methuen, 1984.

Bakhtin, Mikhail. *Problems of Dostoevsky's Poetics* [1963 edition of Dostoevsky book]. Edited and translated by Caryl Emerson. Minneapolis: University of Minnesota Press, 1984.

Ball, Charles. *Slavery in the United States: A Narrative of the Life and Adventures of Charles Ball, a Black Man, Who Lived Forty Years in Maryland, South Carolina and Georgia, as a Slave*. New York: J. S. Taylor, 1837.

Bamgboṣe, Ayọ. "On Serial Verbs and Verbal Status." Paper presented at Tenth West African Language Congress, Ibadan, 1970.

Barrow, David. "Mark Twain and the Oral Economy: Digression in the Age of Print." Ph.D. diss. Duke University, 1991.

Basden, G. T. *Niger Ibos* [1938]. Reprint. London: Seeley, Service and Co., 1966.

Bassard, Katherine Clay. "Spiritual Interrogations: Conversion, Community, and Authorship in the Writings of Phillis Wheatley, Ann Plato, Jarena Lee, and Rebecca Cox Jackson." Ph.D. diss. Rutgers University, 1992.

Baugh, John. *Black Street Speech: Its History, Structure and Survival*. Austin: University of Texas Press, 1983.

_____. "A Reexamination of the Black English Copula." In *Verb Phrase Patterns in Black English and Creole*, edited by Walter F. Edwards and Donald Winford, 32–59. Detroit: Wayne State University Press.

Beaver, Harold. *Huckleberry Finn*. London: Allen and Unwin, 1987.

_____. "Run, Nigger, Run: *Adventures of Huckleberry Finn* as a Fugitive Slave Narrative." *Journal of American Studies* 8 (December 1974): 339–61.

Bell, Bernard W. "Twain's 'Nigger' Jim: The Tragic Face Behind the Minstrel Mask." In *Satire or Evasion? Black Perspectives on "Huckleberry Finn,"* edited by James S. Leonard, Thomas A. Tenney, and Thadious M. Davis. Durham, N.C.: Duke University Press, 1991.

Bell, P[hillip] A. "Prospectus: The Elevator, a Weekly Journal," San Francisco *Elevator*, 5 May 1865, 1.

Bell, William R. "The Relationship of Joel Chandler Harris and Mark Twain." *Atlanta Historical Journal* 30, nos. 3–4 (Fall–Winter 1986–1987): 97–112.

Bennett, John. "Gullah: A Negro Patois." *The South Atlantic Quarterly* 7 (October, 1908): 332–47.

Berkove, Lawrence I. "The Free Man of Color in *The Grandissimes* and Works by Harris and Mark Twain." *Southern Quarterly* 18:4 (Summer 1980): 60–73.

_____. "The 'Poor Players' of *Huckleberry Finn*." *Papers of the Michigan Academy of Science, Arts, and Letters* 53 (1968): 291–310.

Berret, Anthony J. "*Huckleberry Finn* and the Minstrel Show." *American Studies* 27, no. 2 (1986): 37–49.

Bickley, R. Bruce, Jr. *Joel Chandler Harris*. [1978]. Reprint. Athens: University of Georgia Press, 1987.

Blackburn, Alexander. *The Myth of the Picaro: Continuity and Transformation of the Picaresque Novel, 1554–1954*. Chapel Hill: University of North Carolina Press, 1979, 177–87.

Blair, Walter. *Mark Twain & "Huck Finn."* Berkeley: University of California Press, 1960.

_____. *Native American Humor*. San Francisco: Chandler Publishing Company, 1960.

Blair, Walter, and Victor Fischer. "Explanatory Notes." In *Adventures of Huckleberry Finn*, by Mark Twain, 371–422. The Works of Mark Twain. Berkeley: University of California Press, 1988.

_____, eds. *Mark Twain's Hannibal, Huck & Tom*. The Mark Twain Papers. Berkeley: University of California Press, 1969.

_____. "Mark Twain's Marginal Working Notes." In *Adventures of Huckleberry Finn*, by Mark Twain, 762–64. The Works of Mark Twain. Berkeley: University of California Press, 1988.

_____. "Mark Twain's Revisions for Public Reading." In *Adventures of Huckleberry Finn*, by Mark Twain, 765–841. The Works of Mark Twain. Berkeley: University of California Press, 1988.

_____. "Textual Introduction." In *Adventures of Huckleberry Finn*, by Mark Twain, 432–514. The Works of Mark Twain. Berkeley: University of California Press, 1988.

Blair, Walter, and Hamlin Hill. *America's Humor*. New York: Oxford University Press, 1978.

Blassingame, John W. *The Slave Community: Plantation Life in the Antebellum South*. New York: Oxford University Press, 1972.

Boland, Sally. "The Seven Dialects in *Huckleberry Finn*." *North Dakota Quarterly* 36 (Summer 1968): 30–40.

Bowen, Elbert R. "Negro Minstrels." In *Theatrical Entertainments in Rural Missouri Before the Civil War*. Vol. 32 of *University of Missouri Studies*. Columbia: University of Missouri Press, 1959.

Brackenridge, Hugh Henry. *Modern Chivalry: Containing the Adventures of Captain John Farrago and Teague Oregon, His Servant*, pt. 1. Philadelphia: John M. M'Culloch, 1792.

Bradley, David. "Black and American, 1982." *Esquire*, May 1982. Reprinted in Vesterman, William, ed., *Essays for the '80s*, 397–413. New York: Random House, 1987.

_____. *The Chaneysville Incident* [1981]. Reprint. New York: Harper and Row, Perennial Library Edition, 1990.

_____. "The First 'Nigger' Novel." Speech to Annual Meeting of the Mark Twain Memorial and the New England American Studies Association, Hartford, Connecticut, 1985.

_____. "Foreword." *A Different Drummer*, by William Melvin Kelley, xi–xxxii. New York: Anchor/Doubleday, 1989.

_____. Personal communication, 29 May 1992, and 26 July 1992.

Braithwaite, William Stanley. "The Negro in American Literature." In *The New Negro*, edited by Alain Locke. [1925]. New edition, with introduction by Arnold Rampersad, 29–44. New York: Atheneum, 1992.

Branch, Edgar Marquess. *The Literary Apprenticeship of Mark Twain*. Urbana: University of Illinois Press, 1950.

_____. "Mark Twain: Newspaper Reading and the Writer's Creativity." *Nineteenth-Century Fiction* 37, no. 3 (1983): 576–603.

Brasch, Ila Wales, and Walter M. Brasch. *A Comprehensive Annotated Bibliography of Black English*. Baton Rouge: Louisiana State University Press, 1974.

Brasch, Walter M. *Black English and the Mass Media*. Amherst: University of Massachusetts Press, 1981.

Brewer, Jeutonne. "Possible Relationships Between African Languages and Black English Dialect." Paper presented at the annual meeting of the Speech Communication Association, December 1970.

Bridgman, Richard. *The Colloquial Style in America*. New York: Oxford University Press, 1966.

Brooks, Cleanth, "The English Language of the South." In *A Various Language: Perspectives on American Dialects*, edited by Juanita V. Williamson and Virginia M. Burke, 136–42. New York: Holt, Rinehart and Winston, 1971.

_____. *The Language of the American South*. Mercer University Lamar Memorial Lectures, No. 28. Athens, Georgia: University of Georgia Press, 1985.

_____. *The Relationship of the Alabama-Georgia Dialect to the Provincial Dialects of Great Britain*. Baton Rouge: Louisiana State University Press, 1935.

Brown, Sterling A. "The American Race Problem as Reflected in American Literature." *Journal of Negro Education* 8, no. 3 (July 1939): 275–90.

_____. "A Century of Negro Portraiture." In *Black and White in American Culture: An Anthology from the Massachusetts Review*, edited by Jules Chametzky and Sidney Kaplan. Amherst: University of Massachusetts Press, 1969.

_____. "Negro Character as Seen by White Authors." *Journal of Negro Education* 2, no. 2 (April 1933): 179–203.

_____. *The Negro in American Fiction*. [1935] Port Washington, N.Y.: Kennikat Press, Inc., 1937.

Brown, William Wells. *Clotel; or, The President's Daughter*. [1853]. In *Three Classic African-American Novels*, edited by Henry Louis Gates, Jr., 45–223. New York: Random House, Vintage Classics, 1990.

_____. *The Escape; or, A Leap for Freedom*. [Boston: P. F. Wallcut, 1858]. Reprint. New York: Prologue Press, 1969.

_____. *Narrative of the Life and Escape of William Wells Brown*. [1847]. In *Three Classic African-American Novels*, edited by Henry Louis Gates, Jr., 5–44. New York: Random House, Vintage Classics, 1990.

Brownell, George Hiram. "The Home of the Prodigal Son." *The Twainian* 2, no. 7 (April 1943): 1.

_____. ["Request for Information about 'Sociable Jimmy'"]. *The Twainian* 2, no. 5 (February 1943): 3.

Budd, Louis J. *Critical Essays on Mark Twain, 1867–1910.* Boston: G. K. Hall, 1982.

_____. "Introduction." In *New Essays on "Adventures of Huckleberry Finn,"* edited by Louis J. Budd, 1–33. Cambridge: Cambridge University Press, 1985.

_____. "A Listing of and Selection from Newspaper and Magazine Interviews with Samuel L. Clemens, 1874–1910." *American Literary Realism* 10 (Winter, 1977): i–100.

_____. *Mark Twain: Social Philosopher.* Bloomington: Indiana University Press, 1962.

_____. "'A Nobler Roman Aspect' of *Adventures of Huckleberry Finn.*" In *One Hundred Years of "Huckleberry Finn,"* edited by Robert Sattelmeyer and J. Donald Crowley, 26–40. Columbia: University of Missouri Press, 1985.

_____. Personal communication, 3 January 1991, and 16 June 1992.

_____. "The Recomposition of *Adventures of Huckleberry Finn.*" *Missouri Review* 10 (1987): 113–29. Reprinted in Champion, Laurie, ed., *The Critical Response to Mark Twain's "Huckleberry Finn,"* 195–206. Westport, Conn.: Greenwood Press, 1991.

_____. "Southward Currents Under Huck Finn's Raft." *Mississippi Valley Historical Review* 46, no. 2 (1959): 222–37.

Budick, Emily. Personal communication, 14 July 1992.

Cable, George Washington. *Old Creole Days* [1879]. Reprint. New York: Charles Scribner's Sons, 1892.

_____. *The Silent South; Together with The Freedman's Case in Equity and The Convict Lease System.* new ed. New York: Charles Scribner's Sons, 1907.

Campbell, John. *Negromania: An Examination of the Falsely Assumed Equality of the Various Races of Men.* Philadelphia: Campbell and Power, 1851.

Cantor, Milton. "The Image of the Negro in Colonial Literature." In *Images of the Negro in American Literature,* edited by Seymour L. Gross and John W. Hardy, 29–53. Chicago: University of Chicago Press, 1966.

Cardwell, Guy. *The Man Who Was Mark Twain: Images and Ideologies.* New Haven: Yale University Press, 1991.

Carkeet, David. "The Dialects in *Huckleberry Finn.*" *American Literature* 51 (November 1979): 315–32.

_____. "The Source for the Arkansas Gossips in *Huckleberry Finn.*" *American Literary Realism* 14 (1981): 90–92.

Cash, W. F. *The Mind of the South.* New York: Alfred A. Knopf, 1941.

Cassidy, Frederic G. "Gullah." In *Encyclopedia of Southern Culture,* edited by Charles Reagan Wilson and William Ferris, 772–73. Chapel Hill: University of North Carolina Press, 1989.

Cecil, L. Moffitt. "The Historical Ending of *Huckleberry Finn:* How Nigger Jim [sic] Was Set Free." *American Literary Realism* 13 (Autumn 1980): 280–83.

Chadwick-Joshua, Jocelyn. "Mark Twain and the Fires of Controversy: Teaching Racially-Sensitive Literature: Or, 'Say That 'N' Word and Out You Go!'" In *The Critical Response to Mark Twain's "Huckleberry Finn,"* edited by Laurie Champion, 228–37. Westport, Conn.: Greenwood Press, 1991.

Champion, Laurie, ed. *The Critical Response to Mark Twain's "Huckleberry Finn."* Westport, Conn: Greenwood Press, 1991.

Cheesman, Elaine, and Earl French, eds. *Twain/Stowe Sourcebook: Curriculum Resource Materials for the Study of Mark Twain and Harriet Beecher Stowe.* Hartford: Mark Twain Memorial and Stowe-Day Foundation, 1989.

Chesnutt, Charles W. *The Conjure Woman.* 1899. Reprint. Boston: Houghton Mifflin Co., 1928.

———. "The Goophered Grapevine." *Atlantic Monthly* 60, no. 358 (August 1887): 254–60.

Chesnutt, Helen M. *Charles Waddell Chesnutt: Pioneer of the Color Line.* Chapel Hill: University of North Carolina Press, 1952.

Clemens, Clara. *My Father, Mark Twain.* New York: Harper and Brothers, 1931.

[Clemens, Samuel. See Mark Twain]

Cohen, Hennig. "A Southern Colonial Word List: Addenda to the DA." *American Speech* 27 (1952): 282–84.

Cooke, Michael G. *Afro-American Literature in the Twentieth Century: The Achievement of Intimacy.* New Haven: Yale University Press, 1984.

Courlander, Harold. *The Drum and the Hoe.* Berkeley: University of California Press, 1960.

Covici, Pascal, Jr. *Mark Twain's Humor: The Image of a World.* Dallas: Southern Methodist University Press, 1962.

Cox, James M. "A Hard Book to Take." In *One Hundred Years of "Huckleberry Finn,"* edited by Robert Sattelmeyer and J. Donald Crowley, 386–403. Columbia: University of Missouri Press, 1985.

———. *Mark Twain: The Fate of Humor.* Princeton, N.J.: Princeton University Press, 1966.

Cresswell, Nicholas. *Journal of Nicholas Cresswell, 1774–1777.* Edited by L. MacVeigh. New York: Dial Press, 1924.

Criado de Val, Manuel, ed. *La picaresca: origenes, textos y estructuras.* Madrid: Fundacion Universitaria Española, 1979.

Crowley, Daniel J. *African Folklore in the New World.* Austin: University of Texas Press, 1977.

Cruickshank, Brodie. *Eighteen Years on the Gold Coast of Guinea.* London: Hurst and Blackelt, 1853.

Cummings, Sherwood. "The Commanding Presence of Rachel Cord." Paper presented at the Annual Meeting of the Modern Language Association, Chicago, 28 December 1990.

———. *Mark Twain and Science: Adventures of a Mind.* Baton Rouge: Louisiana State University Press, 1988.

———. "Mark Twain's Moveable Farm and the Evasion." *American Literature* 63, no. 3 (September 1991): 440–58.

Curling, Marianne. Personal communication, March 1992.

Davidson, Cathy. "Statement." *American Studies Association Newsletter* 15, no. 1 (February 1992): 2.

Davis, Charles T. "Black Literature and the Critic." [1973]. In Charles T. Davis, *Black is the Color of the Cosmos: Essays on Afro-American Literature and Culture, 1942–1981,* edited by Henry Louis Gates, Jr. Foreword by A. Bartlett Giamatti, 49–62. New York: Garland, 1982.

Davis, John A. "The Influence of Africans on American Culture," *Annals of the American Academy of Political Science* 354 (July 1964): 75–83.

Davis, Thadious M., guest ed. "Black Writers on *Adventures of Huckleberry Finn* One Hundred Years Later." *Mark Twain Journal* 22, no. 2 (Fall 1984).

———. "Foreword." Thadious M. Davis, guest ed. "Black Writers on *Adventures of Huckleberry Finn* One Hundred Years Later." *Mark Twain Journal* 22, no. 2 (Fall 1984): 2–3.

Delany, Martin R. *Blake; or, The Huts of America.* [*The Weekly Anglo-African.* 26 November 1861–24 May 1862]. Reprint. Boston: Beacon Press, 1970.

DeSantis, Vincent P. "Rutherford B. Hayes and the Removal of the Troops and the End of Reconstruction." In *Region, Race, and Reconstruction: Essays in Honor of C. Vann Woodward,* edited by J. Morgan Kousser and James M. McPherson, 417–50. New York: Oxford University Press, 1982.

DeVoto, Bernard. *Mark Twain at Work.* Cambridge, Mass.: Harvard University Press, 1942.

_____, ed. *Mark Twain in Eruption.* New York: Harper and Brothers, 1940.

_____. *Mark Twain's America.* Boston: Little, Brown, 1932.

Dickens, Charles. *American Notes for General Circulation.* New York: Harper and Brothers, 1842.

Dickinson, Asa Don. "Huckleberry Finn Is Fifty Years Old—Yes; But Is He Respectable?" *Wilson Bulletin for Librarians* 10 (November 1935): 180–85.

Dillard, J. L. *Black English: Its History and Usage in the United States.* New York: Random House, 1972; Vintage edition, 1973.

_____. "General Introduction: Perspectives on Black English." In *Perspectives on Black English,* edited by J. L. Dillard, 9–32. The Hague: Mouton, 1975.

_____. *Lexicon of Black English.* New York: Seabury Press, 1977.

_____, ed. *Perspectives on Black English.* The Hague: Mouton, 1975.

_____. "The Writing of Herskovits and the Study of the Language of the Negro in the New World." In *Perspectives on Black English,* ed. J. L. Dillard, 288–95. The Hague: Mouton, 1975.

Dorrill, George Townsend. *Black and White Speech in the Southern United States: Evidence from the Linguistic Atlas of the Middle and South Atlantic States.* Bamberger Beitrage zur Englischen Sprachwissenschaft, Heraussegeben von Prof. Dr. Wolfgang Viereck, Band 19. Frankfurt am Main: Verlag Peter Lang, 1986.

Dorson, Richard M. "The African Connection: Comments on African Folklore in the New World." In *African Folklore in the New World,* edited by Daniel J. Crowley. Austin: University of Texas Press, 1977.

_____. *American Folklore.* Chicago: University of Chicago Press, 1959.

_____. *American Negro Folktales.* [1958]. Reprint. Bloomington: Indiana University Press, 1967.

Douglass, Frederick. *Narrative of the Life of Frederick Douglass, An American Slave, Written by Himself.* [1845]. Reprint. New York: Viking Penguin, 1982.

_____. "The Work of the Future." *Douglass's Monthly,* November 1862. Reprinted in Foner, Philip S., ed., *The Life and Writings of Frederick Douglass.* Vol. 3, 290–93. New York: International Publishers, 1952.

Doyno, Victor A. Personal communication, June–July 1992.

_____. *Writing "Huck Finn": Mark Twain's Creative Process.* Philadelphia: University of Pennsylvania Press, 1992.

DuBois, W. E. B. *Black Reconstruction in America: An Essay Toward a History of the Part Which Black Folk Played in the Attempt to Reconstruct Democracy in America, 1860–1880.* New York: Harcourt, Brace, 1935.

_____. "The Humor of Negroes." *Mark Twain Quarterly* (Fall–Winter, 1943):

12. [The *Mark Twain Quarterly* was renamed the *Mark Twain Journal* in 1954.]

_____. *The Souls of Black Folk.* [1903]. Reprinted in Huggins, Nathan, ed., *W.E.B. Du Bois: Writings*, 357–547. New York: Library of America, 1986.

Dunbar, Paul Lawrence. "An Ante-Bellum Sermon." In *Lyrics of Lowly Life.* [1896]. Reprint. New York: Citadel Press, 1984, 26–30.

Dundes, Alan. "African and Afro-American Tales." In *African Folklore in the New World*, edited by Daniel J. Crowley, 35–53. Austin: University of Texas Press, 1977.

_____, ed. *Mother Wit from the Laughing Barrel: Readings in the Interpretation of Afro-American Folklore.* Jackson: University Press of Mississippi, 1990.

Dunn, Ernest F. "The Black-Southern White Dialect Controversy: Who Did What to Whom?" In *Black English: A Seminar*, edited by Deborah Sears Harrison and Tom Trabasso, 105–22. Hillsdale, N.J.: Lawrence Erlbaum Associates, 1976.

Eble, Kenneth E. *Old Clemens and W. D. H.: The Story of A Remarkable Friendship.* Baton Rouge: Louisiana State University Press, 1985.

Edwards, Bryan. *The History of the British Colonies in the West Indies.* London: John Stockdale, 1801.

Edwards, Walter F., and Donald Winford, eds. *Verb Phrase Patterns in Black English and Creole.* Detroit: Wayne State University Press, 1991.

Ellison, Ralph. "Change the Joke and Slip the Yoke." *Partisan Review* 25 (Spring 1958): 212–22. Reprinted in Ellison, Ralph, *Shadow and Act*, 45–59. New York: Random House, 1953.

_____. *Going to the Territory.* New York: Random House, 1986; Vintage edition, 1987.

_____. "Going to the Territory." In *Going to the Territory*, by Ralph Ellison, 120–44. New York: Random House, 1987.

_____. Interview with Shelley Fisher Fishkin, 16 July 1991, New York City.

_____. *Invisible Man.* [1952]. New York: Vintage edition, 1989.

_____. "On Initiation Rites and Power: Ralph Ellison Speaks at West Point." *Contemporary Literature*, Spring 1974. Reprinted in *Going to the Territory*, by Ralph Ellison, 39–63. New York: Random House, 1987.

_____. *Shadow and Act.* New York: Random House, 1953.

_____. "Twentieth-Century Fiction and the Black Mask of Humanity." In *Shadow and Act*, by Ralph Ellison, 24–44. New York: Random House, 1953.

_____. "What America Would Be Like Without Blacks." *Time*, 6 April 1970. Reprinted in *Going to the Territory*, by Ralph Ellison, 104–12. New York: Random House, 1987.

Emerson, Everett. *The Authentic Mark Twain: A Literary Biography of Samuel L. Clemens.* Philadelphia: University of Pennsylvania Press, 1984.

Emery, Lynne Fauley. *Black Dance in the United States from 1619 to 1970.* New York: Books for Libraries, a Division of Arno Press, 1980.

English, Thomas H., ed. *Mark Twain to Uncle Remus: 1881–1885.* Atlanta: Emory University Sources and Reprints, series 7, no. 3, 1953.

Epstein, Dena J. "The Folk Banjo: A Documentary History." *Ethnomusicology*, September 1975, 347–71.

Fabre, Michel. *Richard Wright: Books and Writers*. Jackson: University Press of Mississippi, 1990.

Fasold, Ralph W. *Tense Marking in Black English: A Linguistic and Social Analysis*. Arlington, Va.: Center for Applied Linguistics, 1972.

Fatout, Paul. *Mark Twain on the Lecture Circuit*. Bloomington: Indiana University Press, 1960. Gloucester, Mass.: Peter Smith, 1966.

————, ed. *Mark Twain Speaks for Himself*. West Lafayette, Ind.: Purdue University Press, 1978.

Fauset, Arthur Huff, "American Negro Folk Literature." In *The New Negro*, edited by Alain Locke. [1925]. New edition, with introduction by Arnold Rampersad, 238–44. New York: Atheneum, 1992.

Feldmann, Susan. *African Myths and Tales*. New York: Dell, 1963.

Fiedler, Leslie A. "The Blackness of Darkness: The Negro and the Development of American Gothic." In *Love and Death in the American Novel*, by Leslie Fiedler, 370–414. New York: Criterion Books, 1960. Reprinted in Gross, Seymour L., and John Edward Hardy, eds., *Images of the Negro in American Literature*, 84–105. Chicago: University of Chicago Press, 1966.

————. "Come Back to the Raft Ag'in, Huck Honey," *Partisan Review* 15 (June 1948): 664–71. Reprinted in Inge, M. Thomas, ed., *Huck Finn Among the Critics*, 93–101. Frederick, Md.: University Publications of America, 1985.

————. "*Huckleberry Finn*: The Book We Love to Hate," *Proteus* (Fall 1984): 1–8.

Fischer, Victor. "Discovery of the Manuscript of *Huckleberry Finn*." Photocopied handout from presentation at the Annual Meeting of the Modern Language Association, San Francisco, 1991.

————. "*Huckleberry Finn*: Mark Twain's Usage." (Working notes for Mark Twain Project edition of *Huckleberry Finn*.)

————. Personal communication, 24 June 1992.

————. "Working Copy of Lecture Calendar." Forthcoming in *Letters, Vol. 4: 1870-1871*, by Mark Twain. Berkeley: University of California Press, Mark Twain Papers.

Fisher, Miles Mark. *Negro Slave Songs in the United States*. Ithaca, N.Y.: Cornell University Press, 1953.

Fisher, Philip. "Mark Twain." In *The Columbia Literary History of the United States*, General Editor, Emory Elliott, 627–44. New York: Columbia University Press, 1988.

Fishkin, Shelley Fisher. "The Borderlands of Culture: Writing by W. E. B. DuBois, James Agee, Tillie Olsen and Gloria Anzaldúa." In *Literary Journalism in the Twentieth Century*, edited by Norman Sims, 133–82. New York: Oxford University Press, 1990.

————. "False Starts, Fragments and Fumbles: Mark Twain's Unpublished Writing on Race." *Essays in Arts and Sciences* 20 (October 1991): 17–31.

————. "Freeman Reports." [Television Debate]. Cable News Network, 14 March 1985.

————. "*Huckleberry Finn* is Not a Racist Novel," In *Racism*, rev. ed., edited by Bruno Leone, 176–79. St. Paul, Minn.: Greenhaven Press, 1986.

————. "Interview with Maxine Hong Kingston." *American Literary History*, Winter 1991, 782–91.

————. Interview with Ralph Ellison, 16 July 1991 (unpublished).

————. "Mark Twain." In *From Fact to Fiction: Journalism and Imaginative*

Writing in America, by Shelley Fisher Fishkin, 55–84. Baltimore: Johns Hopkins University Press, 1985; New York: Oxford University Press, 1988.

———. "Mark Twain and the Risks of Irony." In *Twain/Stowe Sourcebook*, edited by Elaine Cheesman and Earl French, 49–52. Hartford: Mark Twain Memorial and Stowe-Day Foundation, 1989.

———. "Race and Culture at the Century's End: A Social Context for Pudd'nhead Wilson." *Essays in Arts and Sciences* 18 (May 1989): 1–27. Reprinted as "The Tales He Couldn't Tell: Mark Twain, Race, and Culture at the Century's End," in *Mark Twain's Humor: Critical Essays*, edited by David E. E. Sloane. Garland Studies in Humor, vol. 3, 359–88. New York: Garland, 1993.

———. "Racial Attitudes." *The Mark Twain Encyclopedia*, edited by J. R. LeMaster and James D. Wilson, 609–15. New York: Garland, 1993.

———. "Selected Bibliography for the Study of *Adventures of Huckleberry Finn*." In *Twain/Stowe Sourcebook*, edited by Elaine Cheesman and Earl French, 138–39. Hartford: Mark Twain Memorial and Stowe-Day Foundation, 1989.

Fishkin, Shelley Fisher, and Carla Peterson. "'We Hold These Truths to Be Self-Evident': The Rhetoric of Frederick Douglass's Journalism." In *Frederick Douglass: New Literary and Historical Essays*, edited by Eric Sundquist, 189–204. Cambridge: Cambridge University Press, 1990.

Foner, Eric. *Reconstruction: America's Unfinished Revolution, 1863–1877*. New York: Harper and Row, 1988.

Foner, Philip. *Mark Twain: Social Critic*. [1958]. Reprint. New York: International Publishers, 1969.

Franklin, John Hope. *From Slavery to Freedom: A History of Negro Americans*. 3d ed. New York: Alfred A. Knopf, 1967.

Fredrickson, George M. *The Black Image in the White Mind: The Debate on Afro-American Character and Destiny, 1817–1914*. Middletown, Conn.: Wesleyan University Press, 1971.

Fry, Gladys-Marie. *Night Riders in Black Folk History*. [1975]. Reprint. Athens: University of Georgia Press, 1991.

Fuller, Margaret. "American Literature; Its Position in the Present Time, and Prospects for the Future." In *Papers on Literature and Art*, part 2, by Margaret Fuller, 122–59. London: Wiley and Putnam, 1846.

[Fusscas, Helen K., ed.] *Charles Ethan Porter*. Marlborough, Conn.: Connecticut Gallery, Inc., 1987.

Gambill, Angela. "UM Receives Rare, Signed Twain Book." *The Baltimore Sun*, 27 February 1986, Maryland section, 1.

Gates, Henry Louis, Jr. "'Authenticity,' or the Lesson of Little Tree." *New York Times Book Review*, 24 November 1991, section 7, 1 (lexus).

———. "The Blackness of Blackness: A Critique of the Sign of the Signifying Monkey." In *Black Literature and Literary Theory*, edited by Henry Louis Gates, Jr., 285–321. New York: Methuen, 1984.

———. "Criticism in the Jungle," in *Black Literature and Literary Theory*, edited by Henry Louis Gates, Jr., 1–26. New York: Methuen, 1984.

———. "Dis and Dat: Dialect and Descent." In *Figures in Black: Words, Signs, and the 'Racial' Self*, by Henry Louis Gates, Jr., 167–95. New York: Oxford University Press, 1987.

_____. "Introduction." In *Our Nig; or, Sketches from the Life of a Free Black*, by Harriet E. Wilson. New York: Random House, 1983.

_____. "Introduction." In *Three Classic African-American Novels: "Clotel; or, The President's Daughter" by William Wells Brown; "Iola Leroy, or Shadows Uplifted" by Frances E. W. Harper; "The Marrow of Tradition" by Charles W. Chesnutt*, edited by Henry Louis Gates, Jr., vii–xviii. New York: Vintage Books, 1990.

_____. "Introduction: Writing 'Race' and the Difference It Makes." [1985]. In *"Race," Writing, and Difference*, edited by Henry Louis Gates, Jr., 1–20. Chicago: University of Chicago Press, 1986.

_____. *Loose Canons: Notes on the Culture Wars*. New York: Oxford University Press, 1992.

_____. "The Master's Pieces: On Canon Formation and Afro-American Tradition." In *The Bounds of Race: Perspectives on Hegemony and Resistance*, edited by Dominick LaCapra, 17–38. Ithaca, N.Y.: Cornell University Press, 1991.

_____. *The Signifying Monkey: A Theory of African-American Literary Criticism*. New York: Oxford University Press, 1988.

_____. "Talking Black: Critical Signs of the Times." In Henry Louis Gates, Jr., *Loose Canons*, 71–83. New York: Oxford University Press, 1992.

Genovese, Eugene D. *Roll, Jordan, Roll: The World the Slaves Made*. New York: Pantheon Books, 1974.

Gerber, John C. "Introduction: The Continuing Adventures of *Huckleberry Finn*." In *One Hundred Years of "Huckleberry Finn,"* edited by Robert Sattelmeyer and J. Donald Crowley, 1–12. Columbia: University of Missouri Press, 1985.

Gillman, Susan. *Dark Twins; Imposture and Identity in Mark Twain's America*. Chicago: University of Chicago Press, 1989.

Gillman, Susan, and Forrest G. Robinson, eds. *Mark Twain's "Pudd'nhead Wilson": Race, Conflict, and Culture*. Durham, N.C.: Duke University Press, 1990.

Gloster, Hugh M. *Negro Voices in American Fiction*. New York: Russell, 1965.

Gollin, Richard, and Rita Gollin. "*Huckleberry Finn* and the Time of the Evasion." *Modern Language Studies* 9 (Spring 1979): 5–15.

Greene, Lorenzo Johnston, *The Negro in Colonial New England, 1620–1776*. New York: Columbia University Press, 1942.

Greet, W. Cabell. "Southern Speech." In *Culture in the South*, edited by W. T. Couch, 594–615. Chapel Hill: University of North Carolina Press, 1935.

Gribben, Alan. "'I Did Wish Tom Sawyer Was There': Boy-Book Elements in *Tom Sawyer* and *Huckleberry Finn*." In *One Hundred Years of "Huckleberry Finn,"* edited by Robert Sattelmeyer and J. Donald Crowley, 149–70. Columbia: University of Missouri Press, 1985.

_____. *Mark Twain's Library: A Reconstruction*. 2 vols. Boston: G. K. Hall, 1980.

Gross, Seymour L. "Introduction: Stereotype to Archetype: The Negro in American Literary Criticism." In *Images of the Negro in American Literature*, edited by Seymour L. Gross and John Edward Hardy, 1–26. Chicago: University of Chicago Press, 1966.

_____. "The Negro in the Literature of Reconstruction." In *Images of the Negro in American Literature*, edited by Seymour L. Gross and John Edward Hardy, 71–83. Chicago: University of Chicago Press, 1966.

Hall, Stuart. "Notes on Deconstructing 'the Popular.'" In *People's History and Socialist Theory*, edited by Raphael Samuel, 227–40. London: Routledge and Kegan Paul, 1981.

Harris, Joel Chandler. *Uncle Remus: His Songs and His Sayings*. [1880]. Reprint. New York: D. Appleton and Co., 1881.

_____. "Uncle Remus's Politics." *Atlanta Constitution*, 28 November 1876.

Harris, Susan. Personal communication, 4 June 1992.

Harris, Trudier. *Fiction and Folklore: The Novels of Toni Morrison*. Knoxville: University of Tennessee Press, 1991.

Harrison, Deborah Sears, and Tom Trabasso, eds. *Black English: A Seminar*. Hillsdale, N.J.: Lawrence Erlbaum Associates, 1976.

Harrison, James A. "Negro English." *Anglia* 8 (1884): 232–79.

_____. "Negro-English." *Modern Language Notes* 7 (1892): 123.

Harrison, John M. *The Man Who Made Nasby, David Ross Locke*. Chapel Hill: University of North Carolina Press, 1969.

Harter, Hugh A. "Mark Twain y la tradicion picaresca." In *La Picaresca: origenes, textos y estructuras*, edited by Manuel Criade de Val, 1161–66. Madrid: Fundacion Universitaria Espanola, 1979.

Haskins, James. *Black Dance in America: A History Through Its People*. New York: HarperCollins, 1990.

_____. *Black Theater in America*. New York: Crowell, 1982.

Hemingway, Ernest. *Green Hills of Africa*. New York: Charles Scribner's Sons, 1935.

Henry, Peaches. "The Struggle for Tolerance: Race and Censorship in *Huckleberry Finn*." In *Satire or Evasion? Black Perspectives on "Huckleberry Finn,"* edited by James S. Leonard, Thomas A. Tenney, and Thadious M. Davis. Durham, N.C.: Duke University Press, 1991.

Herskovits, Melville J. *The Myth of the Negro Past*. [1941]. Reprint. Boston: Beacon Press, 1958.

_____. *The New World Negro*. [1966]. Bloomington: Minerva Press, 1969.

_____. "What Has Africa Given America?" *The New Republic* 74, no. 1083 (4 September 1935): 92–94.

Hildreth, Richard. *The Slave: or Memoirs of Archy Moore*. [1836]. Upper Saddle River, N.J.: The Gregg Press, 1968.

Hoffman, Daniel. "Mark Twain, 1909." *New Yorker*, 29 October 1984, 48.

Hoffman, Daniel G. "Black Magic—and White—in *Huckleberry Finn*." In *Form and Fable in American Fiction*, by Daniel G. Hoffman, 317–42. New York: Oxford University Press, 1961.

_____. "Jim's Magic: Black or White?" *American Literature* 32, no. 1 (March 1960): 47–54.

Hoffman, Frederick L. *Race Traits and Tendencies of the American Negro*. Publication of the American Economic Association 11, nos. 1, 2 and 3. New York: Macmillan, 1896.

Holland, Laurence B. [1979]. "A 'Raft of Trouble': Word and Deed in *Huckleberry Finn*." In *American Realism: New Essays*, edited by Eric Sundquist, 66–81. Baltimore: Johns Hopkins University Press, 1982.

Holloway, Joseph E. "Introduction." In *Africanisms in American Culture*, edited by Joseph E. Holloway, ix–xxi. Bloomington: Indiana University Press, 1990.

——. "The Origins of African-American Culture." In *Africanisms in American Culture*, edited by Joseph E. Holloway, 1–18. Bloomington: Indiana University Press, 1990.

Holloway, Karla F. C. Personal communication, 29 July 1992.

Holton, Sylvia Wallace. *Down Home and Uptown: The Representation of Black Speech in American Fiction*. Rutherford, N.J.: Fairleigh Dickinson University Press, 1984.

Howe, Lawrence. "Transcending the Limits of Experience: Mark Twain's *Life on the Mississippi*." *American Literature* 63, no. 3 (September 1991): 420–39.

Howells, William Dean. "Introduction." In *Lyrics of Lowly Life*, by Paul Laurence Dunbar. New York: Citadel Press, 1984.

——. *My Mark Twain*. New York: Harper and Brothers, 1910.

Hughes, John B. "*Lazarillo de Tormes y Huckleberry Finn*." In *La Picaresca: origenes, textos y estructuras*, edited by Manuel Criade de Val, 1167–72. Madrid: Fundacion Universitaria Española, 1979.

Hughes, Langston. *The Best of Simple*. [1961]. Reprint. New York: Hill, 1965.

——. "Introduction." In *Pudd'nhead Wilson*, by Mark Twain, vii–xiii. New York: Bantam Books, 1959.

——. "The Negro Speaks of Rivers." [1921]. In *The Heath Anthology of American Literature*. Vol. 2, edited by Paul Lauter, 1488–89. Lexington, Mass.: D. C. Heath and Co., 1990.

——. *Simple Speaks His Mind*. [1950]. Reprint. Mattituck: Aeonian, 1976.

Hughes, Langston, and Arna Bontemps, eds. *The Book of Negro Folklore*. New York: Dodd, Mead and Co., 1958.

Hurston, Zora Neale. "Characteristics of Negro Expression." In *Negro: An Anthology*, edited by Nancy Cunard. [1934]. Rev. ed., edited and abridged, with an introduction by Hugh Ford, 24–31. New York: Frederick Ungar, 1970.

Ingalls, Zoe. "A Choir Festival in St. Petersburg." *Chronicle of Higher Education* 38, no. 37 (20 May 1992): B6.

Inge, M. Thomas, ed. *The Frontier Humorists: Critical Views*. Hamden, Conn.: Archon Books, The Shoestring Press, 1975.

——, ed. *Huck Finn Among the Critics: A Centennial Selection*. Frederick, Md.: University Publications of America, 1985.

Ives, Sumner. "A Theory of Literary Dialect." *Tulane Studies in English* 2 (1950): 137–82.

Jackson, George Pullen. *White Spirituals in the Southern Uplands: The Story of the Fasola Folk, Their Songs, Singings, and "Buckwheat Notes."* Chapel Hill: University of North Carolina Press, 1933.

Jarab, Josef. "Black Stars, Red Star, and the Blues." Paper presented at the European Association for American Studies Conference, Seville, Spain, 6 April 1992. In *Defining Moments in African-American Literature and History*, edited by Werner Sollors and Maria Diedrich, forthcoming.

Jefferson, Thomas. *Notes on Virginia*. The Writings of Thomas Jefferson. definitive ed. Vol. 1. edited by Albert Ellery Bergh. Washington: Thomas Jefferson Memorial Association, 1907.

Jelliffe, Robert A., ed. *Faulkner at Nagano.* Tokyo: Kenkyusha Ltd., 1956.

Johnson, Barbara E. "Response" [to Henry Louis Gates, Jr., "Canon-Formation and the Afro-American Tradition"], in *Afro-American Literary Studies in the 1990s,* edited by Houston A. Baker, Jr., and Patricia Redmond, 39–44. Chicago: University of Chicago Press, 1989.

Johnson, Charles. *Being and Race: Black Writing Since 1970.* Bloomington: Indiana University Press, 1988.

Johnson, H. P. "Who Lost the Southern R?" *American Speech* 3, no. 4 (April 1928): 377–83.

Johnson, Merle. *A Bibliography of the Works of Mark Twain.* New York: Harper and Brothers, 1935.

Jones, Betty H. "Huck and Jim: A Reconsideration." In *Satire or Evasion?,* edited by James S. Leonard, Thomas A. Tenney, and Thadious M. Davis, 154–72. Durham, N.C.: Duke University Press, 1991.

Jones, Rhett S. "Nigger and Knowledge: White Double-Consciousness in *Adventures of Huckleberry Finn.*" In *Satire or Evasion? Black Perspectives on "Huckleberry Finn,"* edited by James S. Leonard, Thomas A. Tenney, and Thadious M. Davis, 173–94. Durham, N.C.: Duke University Press, 1991.

Jones, Steven S. "'The Rarest Thing in the World': Indo-European or African?" In *African Folklore in the New World,* edited by Daniel J. Crowley, 54–64. Austin: University of Texas Press, 1977.

Jordan, June. "For the Sake of a People's Poetry: Walt Whitman and the Rest of Us." In *Walt Whitman: The Measure of His Song,* edited by Jim Perlman, Ed Folsom, and Dam Campion, 343–52. Minneapolis: Holy Cow! Press, 1981.

Kaplan, Justin. *Mr. Clemens and Mark Twain.* New York: Simon and Schuster, 1966.

Katterman, Lee. "In Search of an 'American' Literature: UM [University of Michigan] Scholar Argues That Emphasis on the British Tradition Creates Damaging Myths." *Research News* (University of Michigan) 41, no. 1–2 (January–February 1990), 14–15.

Katzner, Kenneth. *Languages of the World.* London: Routledge, 1977; rev. ed. 1980.

Kingston, Maxine Hong. *The Woman Warrior: Memoirs of a Girlhood Among Ghosts.* New York: Alfred A. Knopf, 1976.

Krapp, George Philip. "The English of the Negro." *American Mercury* 2, no. 5 (June 1924): 190–95.

Krehbiel, Henry E. "Satirical Songs of the Creoles." In *Afro-American Folksongs,* 140–53. New York: G. Schirmir, 1914.

Labat, Jean Baptiste. *Nouveau voyage aux isles de l'Amerique.* La Haye: P. Husson, 1724.

Labov, William. "Contraction, Deletion, and Inherent Variability of the English Copula." *Language* 45: 715–62.

_____. *Language in the Inner City: Studies in the Black English Vernacular.* Philadelphia. University of Pennsylvania Press, 1972.

Langdon, Jervis, Jr. "To the Editor." *New York Times,* 7 April 1985, E16.

Lauter, Paul. *Canons and Contexts.* New York: Oxford University Press, 1991.

_____, ed. *The Heath Anthology of American Literature.* Vol. 2. Lexington, Mass.: D. C. Heath and Co., 1990.

_____. "Is Frances Ellen Watkins Harper Good Enough to Teach?" *Legacy* 5, no. 1 (Spring 1988): 27–32.

Lawrence, Eugene. "A Dying Rebellion." *Harper's Weekly,* no. 934 (21 November 1874): 958.

Lawton, Mary. *A Lifetime with Mark Twain: The Memories of Katy Leary, for Thirty Years His Faithful and Devoted Servant.* New York: Harcourt, Brace and Co., 1925.

Leon, Eli. *Models in the Mind: African Prototypes in American Patchwork* (Exhibition Catalog). Winston-Salem, N.C.: The Diggs Gallery and Winston-Salem State University, 1992.

Leonard, James S., Thomas A. Tenney, and Thadious M. Davis, *Satire or Evasion? Black Perspectives on "Huckleberry Finn."* Durham, N.C.: Duke University Press, 1991.

Levine, Lawrence W. *Black Culture and Black Consciousness: Afro-American Folk Thought From Slavery to Freedom.* New York: Oxford University Press, 1977.

Locke, Alain. "The Negro Spirituals." In *The New Negro,* edited by Alain Locke. [1925]. New edition, with introduction by Arnold Rampersad, 199–213. New York: Atheneum, 1992.

Locke, David Ross [Petroleum V. Nasby]. *The Struggles of Petroleum V. Nasby.* Original illustrations by Thomas Nast. Abridged edition, selected, edited, and with an introduction by Joseph Jones. Boston: Beacon Press, 1963.

Lofflin, Marvin D. "Black American English and Syntactic Dialectology." In *Perspectives on Black English,* edited by J. L. Dillard, 64–73. The Hague: Mouton, 1975.

Logan, Rayford W. *The Betrayal of the Negro from Rutherford B. Hayes to Woodrow Wilson* [originally published as *The Negro in American Life and Thought: The Nadir, 1877–1901*]. London: Collier-Macmillan, 1965.

Lorch, Fred W. *The Trouble Begins at Eight: Mark Twain's Lecture Tours.* Ames: Iowa State University Press, 1968.

Lott, Eric. *Love and Theft: Blackface Minstrelsy and the American Working Class.* New York: Oxford University Press, forthcoming.

Lovell, John, Jr. "The Social Implications of the Negro Spiritual." *Journal of Negro Education* 8 (1939): 634–43. Reprinted in Dundes, Alan, ed., *Mother Wit from the Laughing Barrel,* 452–64. Jackson: University Press of Mississippi, 1990.

Lubiano, Wahneema. "Constructing and Reconstructing Afro-American Texts: The Critic as Ambassador and Referee." *American Literary History* 1, no. 2 (Summer 1989): 432–47.

Lynn, Kenneth S. *Mark Twain and Southwestern Humor.* Boston: Little, Brown, 1959.

McDavid, Raven, Jr., and Virginia McDavid. "The Relationship of the Speech of American Negroes to the Speech of Whites." *American Speech* 26 (1951): 3–16.

McDowell, Edwin. "From Twain, a Letter on Debt to Blacks." *New York Times,* 14 March 1985, 1, 16.

McDowell, Tremaine. "James Fenimore Cooper as Self-Critic." *Studies in Philology* 27 (1930): 508–16.

_____. "Negro Dialect in the American Novel to 1821." *American Speech* 5, no. 4 (April 1930): 291–96.

_____. "The Negro in the Southern Novel Prior to 1850." In *Images of the*

Negro in American Literature, edited by Seymour L. Gross and John Edward Hardy, 54–70. Chicago: University of Chicago Press, 1966.

———. "Notes on Negro Dialect in the American Novel to 1821." *American Speech* 5, no. 1 (October 1929): 291–96.

———. "The Use of Negro Dialect by Harriet Beecher Stowe." *American Speech* 6, no. 5 (June 1931): 322–26.

McKay, Janet Holmgren. "'An Art So High': Style in *Adventures of Huckleberry Finn*." In *New Essays on "Huckleberry Finn,"* edited by Louis J. Budd, 61–81. Cambridge: Cambridge University Press, 1985.

MacKethan, Lucinda. "*Huck Finn* and the Slave Narratives: Lighting Out as Design." *Southern Review* 20 (1984): 247–64.

McPherson, James Alan. "Indivisible Man." In *Ralph Ellison: A Collection of Critical Essays*, edited by John Hersey, 43–57. Englewood Cliffs, N.J.: Prentice-Hall, Inc., 1974.

Mahar, William J. "Black English in Early Blackface Minstrelsy: A New Interpretation of the Sources of Minstrel Show Dialect." *American Quarterly* 37, no. 2 (1985): 260–85.

Mailloux, Stephen. "Reading *Huckleberry Finn*: The Rhetoric of Performed Ideology." In *New Essays on Adventures of "Huckleberry Finn,"* edited by Louis J. Budd. New York: Cambridge University Press, 1985.

Mahl, George F. "Everyday Disturbances of Speech." In *Language in Psychotherapy: Strategies of Discovery*, edited by Robert L. Russell, 213–69. New York: Plenum Press, 1987.

———. "Everyday Speech Disturbances in *Tom Sawyer*." In *Explorations in Nonverbal and Vocal Behavior*, by George F. Mahl, 286–309. Hillsdale, N.J.: Lawrence Erlbaum, 1987.

Martin, Jay. "The Genie in the Bottle: *Huckleberry Finn* in Mark Twain's Life." In *One Hundred Years of "Huckleberry Finn,"* edited by Robert Sattelmeyer and J. Donald Crowley, 56–81. Columbia: University of Missouri Press, 1985.

Marx, Leo. "Mr. Eliot, Mr. Trilling and *Huckleberry Finn*," *American Scholar* 22 (Autumn 1953): 423–40. Reprinted in Inge, M. Thomas, ed., *Huck Finn Among the Critics*, 113–29. Frederick, Md.: University Publications of America, 1985.

———. "The Vernacular Tradition in American Literature." In *The Pilot and the Passenger: Essays in Literature, Technology and Culture in the United States*, by Leo Marx, 3–17. New York: Oxford University Press, 1988.

Mather, Cotton. "The Negro Christianized: An Essay to Excite and Assist That Good Work, the Instruction of Negro Servants in Christianity." Boston: B. Green, [1706].

Meine, Franklin J. "Tall Tales of the Southwest." In *The Frontier Humorists: Critical Views*, edited by M. Thomas Inge, 15–31. Hamden, Conn.: Archon Books, The Shoestring Press, 1975.

Mellon, James, ed. *Bullwhip Days: The Slaves Remember: An Oral History*. New York: Avon Books, 1988.

Melville, Herman. *Moby Dick, or The White Whale*. [1851]. Reprint. New York: New American Library, 1961.

Mencken, H. L. "The Burden of Humor." *The Smart Set* (February 1913): 151–54. Reprinted in Inge, M. Thomas, ed., *Huck Finn Among the Critics*, 67–71. Frederick, Md.: University Publications of America, 1985.

Merriam, Alan P. "African Music." In *Continuity and Change in African Culture*, edited by William R. Bascom and Melville Herskovits. Chicago: Phoenix Books, 1963.

_____. "Music and the Dance." In *The African World*, edited by Robert A. Lystad. New York: Praeger, 1965.

Messent, Peter. "The Clash of Language: Bakhtin and *Huckleberry Finn*." In *New Readings of the American Novel*, 204–42. London and New York: Macmillan/St. Martins Press, 1990.

Miller, James A. "Charles Ethan Porter and the Hartford Black Community." In *Charles Ethan Porter*, [edited by Helen K. Fusscas], 88–95. Marlborough, Conn.: Connecticut Gallery, Inc., 1987.

_____. Personal communication, 10 October 1992, and July 1990.

Mitchell-Kernan, Claudia. "Signifying." In *Language Behavior in a Black Urban Community*, by Claudia Mitchell-Kernan. Monographs of the Language-Behavior Laboratory, University of California, Berkeley, no. 2 (February 1971), 87–129. Reprinted in Dundes, Alan, ed., *Mother Wit from the Laughing Barrel*, 311–28. Jackson: University Press of Mississippi, 1990.

Morrison, Toni. *Beloved*. New York: New American Library/Plume, 1988.

_____. Personal communication, 4 December 1991.

_____. *Playing in the Dark: Whiteness and the Literary Imagination*. Cambridge, Mass.: Harvard University Press, 1992.

_____. "Unspeakable Things Unspoken: The Afro-American Presence in American Literature." *Michigan Quarterly Review* 28, no. 1 (Winter 1989): 1–34.

Morson, Gary Saul, and Caryl Emerson. *Mikhail Bakhtin: Creation of a Prosaics*. Stanford, Ca.: Stanford University Press, 1990.

Murray, Albert. *Train Whistle Guitar*. [1974]. New edition, with foreword by Robert O'Meally. Northeastern Library of Black Literature, Richard Yarborough, Series Editor. Boston: Northeastern University Press, 1989.

Nast, Thomas. [cartoon, uncaptioned]. *Harper's Weekly* 18, no. 929 (24 October 1874): 878.

Nathan, Hans. *Dan Emmett and the Rise of Early Negro Minstrelsy*. Norman: University of Oklahoma Press, 1962.

Nelson, Dana D. *The Word in Black and White: Reading "Race" in American Literature 1638–1897*. New York: Oxford University Press, 1992.

Nichols, Charles H. "'A True Book—With Some Stretchers': *Huck Finn* Today." In *Satire or Evasion? Black Perspectives on "Huckleberry Finn,"* edited by James S. Leonard, Thomas A. Tenney, and Thadious M. Davis, 208–15. Durham, N.C.: Duke University Press, 1991.

Nichols, Thomas L. *Forty Years of American Life*. Vols. 1 and 2. London: John Maxwell and Company, 1864.

Nielson, Aldon Lynn. *Reading Race: White American Poets and Racial Discourse in the Twentieth Century*. Athens: University of Georgia Press, 1988.

Nilon, Charles H. "The Ending of *Huckleberry Finn*: 'Freeing the Free Negro.'" In *Satire or Evasion? Black Perspectives on "Huckleberry Finn,"* edited by James S. Leonard, Thomas A. Tenney, and Thadious M. Davis, 62–76. Durham, N.C.: Duke University Press, 1991.

Northup, Solomon. *Twelve Years a Slave*. [1853]. New edition, edited by Sue Eakin and Joseph Logsdon. Baton Rouge: Louisiana State University Press, 1968.

Nott, G. William. "Irwin Russell, First Dialect Author." *Southern Literary Messenger* 1, no. 12 (December 1939): 809–14.

Olsen, Tillie. Personal communication, 28 December 1991, and December 1987.

Ong, Walter J. *Orality and Literacy: The Technologizing of the Word*. London and New York: Methuen, 1982.

Opdahl, Keith. "'The Rest Is Just Cheating': When Feelings Go Bad in *Adventures of Huckleberry Finn*." *Texas Studies in Literature and Language* 32, no. 2 (Summer 1990): 277–93.

Ottley, Roi, and William J. Weatherby, eds. *The Negro in New York: An Informal Social History, 1626–1940*. New York: Praeger Publishers, 1969.

Page, Clarence. "Black Voice Enriches Maligned Masterpiece." (syndicated column from Chicago *Tribune*) San Jose *Mercury News*, 9 July 1992, 7B.

Paine, Albert Bigelow. *Mark Twain: A Biography*. 3 vols. New York: Harper and Brothers, 1912.

Payne, L. W. "A Word List from East Alabama." *Dialect Notes* 3 (1905): 279–328, 343–91.

Paulding, James Kirke. *Westward Ho! A Tale*. [1832]. Grosse Point, Michigan, 1968.

[Pease, Lute]. "Mark Twain Talks." Portland *Oregonian*, 11 August 1895, 10. Reprinted in Budd, Louis J., "A Listing of and Selection from Newspaper and Magazine Interviews with Samuel L. Clemens, 1874–1910." *American Literary Realism* 10 (Winter 1977): 51–53.

Pederson, Lee A. "Mark Twain's Missouri Dialects: Marion County Phonemics." *American Speech* 50, no. 4 (December 1967): 261–78.

_____. "Negro Speech in *The Adventures of Huckleberry Finn*." *Mark Twain Journal* 13 (Winter 1965–1966): 1–4.

Pedigo, Martin. "Mark Twain's Views on Race: 'The Truth Shall Make You Free.'" *Negro Digest* 14, no. 8 (June 1965): 42–48.

Pennington, James W. C. *The Fugitive Blacksmith; or, Events in the History of James W. C. Pennington*. [1850]. Reprint. New York: Negro University Press, 1971.

Pettit, Arthur G. *Mark Twain and the South*. Lexington: University of Kentucky Press, 1974.

_____. "Merely Fluid Prejudice: Mark Twain, Southerner, and the Negro." Ph.D. diss. University of California, Berkeley, 1970.

Philips, John Edward. "The African Heritage of White America." In *Africanisms in American Culture*, edited by Joseph E. Holloway, 225–39. Bloomington: Indiana University Press, 1990.

Phillippo, James M. *Jamaica: Its Past and Present State*. Philadelphia: James M. Campbell, 1843.

Pierson, William D. "Puttin' Down Ole Massa: African Satire in the New World." In *African Folklore in the New World*, edited by Daniel J. Crowley. Austin: University of Texas Press, 1977.

Pike, Gustavus D. *The Singing Campaign for Ten Thousand Pounds; or, The Jubilee Singers in Great Britain*. rev. ed. New York: American Missionary Association, 1875.

Powell, Jon. "Trouble and Joy from 'A True Story' to *Adventures of Huckleberry Finn*: Mark Twain and the Book of Jeremiah." In *Studies in American Fiction* 20, no. 2 (1992): 49–58.

Rable, George C. *But There Was No Peace: The Role of Violence in the Politics of Reconstruction.* Athens: University of Georgia Press, 1984.

Rampersad, Arnold. "*Adventures of Huckleberry Finn* and Afro-American Literature." In *Satire or Evasion?, Black Perspectives on "Huckleberry Finn,"* edited by James S. Leonard, Thomas A. Tenney, and Thadious M. Davis, 216–27. Durham, N.C.: Duke University Press, 1991.

_____. *The Life of Langston Hughes. Volume I: 1902–1941. I, Too, Sing America.* New York: Oxford University Press, 1986.

_____. *The Life of Langston Hughes. Volume II: 1941–1967. I Dream a World.* New York: Oxford University Press, 1988.

Rawick, George P., ed. *The American Slave: A Composite Autobiography.* 19 vols. Westport, Conn.: Greenwood Press, 1972–1979.

Redpath, James, *The Roving Editor; Or, Talks with Slaves in the Southern States.* New York: A. B. Burdick, 1859.

Reed, A. W. "British Recognition of American Speech in the Eighteenth Century." *Dialect Notes* 6, 1933.

Richards, Phillip M. "Phillis Wheatley and Literary Americanization." *American Quarterly* 44, no. 2 (June 1992): 163–91.

Rickels, Patricia K. "Some Accounts of Witch Riding." In *Readings in American Folklore*, edited by Jan Harold Brunvand, 53–63. New York: W. W. Norton and Co., 1979.

Riggio, Thomas P. "Charles Ethan Porter and Mark Twain." In *Charles Ethan Porter*, [edited by Helen Fusscas], 76–87. Marlborough, Conn.: Connecticut Gallery, Inc., 1987.

Ripley, George, and Charles Anderson Dana, eds. *American Cyclopaedia: A Popular Dictionary of General Knowledge.* 16 vols. New York: D. Appleton and Co, 1873–1876.

Roberson, William. *George Washington Cable: An Annotated Bibliography.* Metuchen, N.J.: Scarecrow Press, 1982.

Roberts, John W. "The African American Animal Trickster as Hero." In *Redefining American Literary History*, edited by A. LaVonne Brown Ruoff and Jerry W. Ward, 97–114. New York: Modern Language Association of America, 1990.

Robinson, Beverly J. "Africanisms and the Study of Folklore." In *Africanisms in American Culture*, edited by Joseph E. Holloway, 211–24. Bloomington: Indiana University Press, 1990.

Robinson, Forrest G. "The Characterization of Jim in *Huckleberry Finn*." *Nineteenth-Century Literature* 43, no. 3 (December 1988): 361–91. Reprinted in Champion, Laurie, ed., *The Critical Response to Mark Twain's "Huckleberry Finn"*, 207–25. Westport, Conn.: Greenwood Press, 1991.

_____. *In Bad Faith: The Dynamics of Deception in Mark Twain's America.* Cambridge, Mass.: Harvard University Press, 1986.

Rodgers, Carolyn M. "Black Poetry—Where It's At." *Negro Digest*, 18 (September 1969): 7–16.

Rodney, Robert M., ed. and comp. *Mark Twain International: A Bibliography and Interpretation of His Worldwide Popularity.* Westport, Conn.: Greenwood Press, 1982.

Rodnon, Stewart. "*The Adventures of Huckleberry Finn* and *Invisible Man*: Thematic and Structural Comparisons." *Negro American Literature Forum* 4 (July 1970): 45–51.

Rogin, Michael. "Francis Galton and Mark Twain: The Natal Autograph in *Pudd'nhead Wilson.*" In *Mark Twain's "Pudd'nhead Wilson,"* edited by Susan Gillman and Forrest G. Robinson, 73–85. Durham, N.C.: Duke University Press, 1990.

Rosenthal, Bernard. "Poe, Slavery, and the Southern Literary Messenger: A Reexamination." *Poe Studies* 7 (1974): 29–38.

Rourke, Constance. "Traditions for a Negro Literature." In *The Roots of American Culture and Other Essays* by Constance Rourke, 262–74. New York: Harcourt, Brace and Co., 1942.

Rubin, Louis, Jr. "Southern Local Color and the Black Man." *Southern Review* 6 (October 1970): 1026–30.

Ruhlen, Merritt. *A Guide to the World's Languages.* Vol. I: Classification. London: Edward Arnold, 1991.

Rulon, Curt Morris. "The Dialects in *Huckleberry Finn.*" Ph.D. diss. University of Iowa, 1967.

_____. "Geographical Delimitation of the Dialect Areas in *The Adventures of Huckleberry Finn.*" *Mark Twain Journal* 14, no. 1 (Winter 1967): 9–12. Reprinted in Williamson, Juanita V., and Virginia Burke, eds., *A Various Language,* 215–21. New York: Holt, Rinehart and Winston, 1971.

Sage, Howard. "An Interview with Ralph Ellison: Visible Man." *Pulp* 2, no. 2 (Summer 1976): 10–12.

Salomon, Roger. *Twain and the Image of History.* New Haven: Yale University Press, 1961.

Sattelmeyer, Robert, and J. Donald Crowley. "The Imagination and its Amanuensis: Huck, Twain and Clemens." In *One Hundred Years of "Huckleberry Finn,"* edited by Robert Sattelmeyer and J. Donald Crowley, 13–14. Columbia: University of Missouri Press, 1985.

_____, eds. *One Hundred Years of "Huckleberry Finn": The Boy, His Book, and American Culture.* Columbia: University of Missouri Press, 1985.

Scheick, William. "The Spunk of a Rabbit: An Allusion in *Huckleberry Finn.*" *Mark Twain Journal* 15 (Summer 1971): 14–16.

Schmitz, Neil. "The Paradox of Liberation in *Huckleberry Finn,*" *Texas Studies in Literature and Language* 13 (1971): 125–36. Reprinted in Champion, Laurie, ed., *The Critical Response to Mark Twain's "Huckleberry Finn,"* 99–107. Westport, Conn.: Greenwood Press, 1991.

_____. "Twain, *Huckleberry Finn,* and the Reconstruction." *American Studies* 12 (Spring 1971): 59–67.

Schwartz, Albert V. "What Help for Teachers?" *Interracial Books for Children Bulletin* 15, nos. 1 and 2 (1984).

Sewell, David R. *Mark Twain's Languages: Discourse, Dialogue and Linguistic Variety.* Berkeley: University of California Press, 1987.

Simms, William Gilmore. *The Yemassee.* 2 vols. New York: Harper and Brothers, 1835.

Simpson, David. *The Politics of American English, 1776–1850.* New York: Oxford University Press, 1986.

Simpson, J. A. and E. S. C. Weiner, eds. *The Oxford English Dictionary.* 2d ed. Oxford: Clarendon Press, 1989.

Sinclair, Molly. "Mother and Son's Amazing Reunion; Twain Immortalized Story of Two Slaves Who Are Ancestors of Olney Family." *Washington Post,* 27 February 1986, Maryland Weekly, Md. 1.

Singler, John Victor. "Copula Variation in Liberian Settler English and American Black English." In *Verb Phrase Patterns in Black English and Creole*, edited by Walter F. Edwards and Donald Winford, 129–64. Detroit: Wayne State University Press, 1991.

Sloane, David E. E. *"Adventures of Huckleberry Finn": American Comic Vision*. Boston: Twayne, 1988.

_____. *Mark Twain as a Literary Comedian*. Baton Rouge: Louisiana State University Press, 1979.

_____. Personal communication, 3 June 1992.

Smith, David L. "Huck, Jim, and American Racial Discourse." In *Satire or Evasion? Black Perspectives on "Huckleberry Finn,"* edited by James S. Leonard, Thomas A. Tenney, and Thadious M. Davis, 103–20. Durham, N.C.: Duke University Press, 1991.

_____. "Racial Discourse and Its Critics." Paper presented at "Fall Twain Symposium: Issues of Race and Prejudice," sponsored by the Mark Twain Memorial and Trinity College, 12 October 1991.

Smith, Henry Nash. *Mark Twain: The Development of a Writer*. Cambridge, Mass.: The Belknap Press of Harvard University Press, 1962.

Smith, John David. *An Old Creed for the New South: Proslavery Ideology and Historiography, 1865–1918*. Athens: University of Georgia Press, 1991.

Smitherman, Geneva. *Talkin' and Testifyin': The Language of Black America*. Boston: Houghton Mifflin, 1977.

Sollors, Werner. "A Critique of Pure Pluralism." In *Reconstructing American Literary History*, edited by Sacvan Bercovitch, 250–79. Cambridge, Mass.: Harvard University Press, 1986.

_____. "Ethnicity." In *Critical Terms for Literary Study*, edited by Frank Lentricchia and Thomas McLaughlin, 288–305. Chicago: University of Chicago Press, 1990.

Solomon, Eric. "My *Huckleberry Finn*: Thirty Years in the Classroom with Huck and Jim." In *One Hundred Years of "Huckleberry Finn,"* edited by Robert Sattelmeyer and J. Donald Crowley, 245–54. Columbia: University of Missouri Press, 1985.

Sorensen, Villy. "*Huckleberry Finn* Concordance." In Mark Twain Papers. Bancroft Library. University of California, Berkeley.

Southern, Eileen. *The Music of Black Americans: A History*. New York: Oxford University Press, 1983.

Stampp, Kenneth M. *The Peculiar Institution: Slavery in the Ante-Bellum South*. New York: Vintage, 1956.

Starke, Catherine Juanita. *Black Portraiture in American Fiction. Stock Characters, Archetypes, and Individuals*. New York: Basic Books, 1971.

Stearns, Marshall, and Jean Stearns. *Jazz Dance: The Story of American Vernacular Dance*. New York: Macmillan, 1968.

Stein, Jean. "The Art of Fiction XIII: William Faulkner." *The Paris Review* 12 (Spring 1956): 28–52.

Steinbrink, Jeffrey. *Getting to Be Mark Twain*. Berkeley: University of California Press, 1991.

Stepto, Robert B. "Sharing the Thunder: The Literary Exchanges of Harriet Beecher Stowe, Henry Bibb, and Frederick Douglass." In *New Essays on "Uncle Tom's Cabin,"* edited by Eric J. Sundquist, 135–54. Cambridge and New York: Cambridge University Press, 1986.

Stewart, William A. "Continuity and Change in American Negro Dialects."
Florida FL Reporter 6, no. 1 (Spring 1968): 3–4, 14–16, 18. Reprinted in
Dillard, J. L., ed., *Perspectives on Black English*, 233–47. The Hague: Mouton, 1975.

———. "Observations (1966) On the Problems of Defining Negro Dialect."
Florida FL Reporter 9, nos. 1 and 2 (Spring/Fall 1971): 47–49, 57. Reprinted
in Dillard, J. L., ed., *Perspectives on Black English*, 57–64. The Hague: Mouton, 1975.

———. "Sociolinguistic Factors in the History of American Negro Dialects."
Florida FL Reporter 5, no. 2 (Spring 1967): 11, 22, 24, 26, 30. Reprinted in
Dillard, J. L., ed., *Perspectives on Black English*, 222–32. The Hague: Mouton, 1975.

Stockton, Eric. "Poe's Use of Negro Dialect in 'The Gold Bug.'" In *A Various Language*, edited by Juanita V. Williamson and Virginia M. Burke, 193–214.
New York: Holt, Rinehart and Winston, 1971.

Stone, Albert. *The Innocent Eye: Childhood in Mark Twain's Imagination.*
1961. Reprint. Hamden, Conn.: Archon Books, 1970.

Stuckey, Elma. *The Collected Poems of Elma Stuckey.* Introduction by E. D.
Hirsch, Jr. Chicago: Precedent Publishing, 1987.

Stuckey, Sterling. *Slave Culture: Nationalist Theory and the Foundations of
Black America.* New York: Oxford University Press, 1987.

———. "True Huck." *The Nation.* 14 December 1985, 2.

Sundquist, Eric J. "Faulkner, Race, and the Forms of American Fiction." In
Faulkner and Race: Faulkner and Yoknapatawpha, 1986, edited by Doreen
Fowler and Ann J. Abadie, 1–34. Jackson, Miss.: University Press of Mississippi, 1987.

———. "Mark Twain and Homer Plessy." *Representations* 24 (Fall 1988).
Reprinted in Gillman, Susan, and Forrest G. Robinson, eds., *Mark Twain's
"Pudd'nhead Wilson,"* 46–72. Durham, N.C.: Duke University Press, 1990.

———, ed. *New Essays on "Uncle Tom's Cabin."* Cambridge and New York:
Cambridge University Press, 1986.

———. *To Wake the Nations: Race in American Literature and American Culture 1830–1930.* Cambridge, Mass.: Harvard University Press, forthcoming
1993.

———. "Uncle Remus, Uncle Julius, and the 'Noo Nigger.'" In *To Wake the
Nations: Race in American Literature and Culture, 1830–1930,* by Eric J.
Sundquist. Cambridge, Mass.: Harvard University Press, forthcoming 1993.

———. "Word Shadows, Alternating Sounds: Folklore, Dialect and Vernacular." In *To Wake the Nations: Race in American Literature and Culture,
1830–1930,* by Eric J. Sundquist. Cambridge, Mass.: Harvard University
Press, forthcoming 1993.

Szwed, John F. "Race and the Embodiment of Culture." *Ethnicity* 2, no. 1
(1975): 19–33.

Talbot, Amaury. *Tribes of the Niger Delta.* London, 1932.

Tanner, Tony. *Reign of Wonder: Naiveté and Reality in American Literature.*
Cambridge: Cambridge University Press, 1965.

Tenney, Thomas A. "An Annotated Checklist of Criticism on *Adventures of
Huckleberry Finn,* 1884–1984." In *Huck Finn Among the Critics,* edited by
M. Thomas Inge, 317–465. Frederick, Md.: University Publications of
America, 1985.

_____. "For Further Reading." In *Satire or Evasion? Black Perspectives on "Huckleberry Finn,"* edited by James S. Leonard, Thomas A. Tenney, and Thadious M. Davis, 239–69. Durham, N.C.: Duke University Press, 1977.

Thomas, H. Nigel. *From Folklore to Fiction: A Study of Folk Heroes and Rituals in the Black American Novel.* Westport, Conn.: Greenwood Press, 1988.

Thomas, Northcote W. *The Ibo-Speaking Peoples of Nigeria.* 4 vols. London: Harrison and Sons, 1913.

Thompson, Robert Farris. *Flash of the Spirit: African and Afro-American Art and Philosophy.* New York: Random House, 1983.

_____. "The Kongo Atlantic Tradition." Lecture presented at the University of Texas, Austin, 28 February 1992.

_____. "Kongo Influences on African-American Artistic Culture." In *Africanisms in American Culture,* edited by Joseph E. Holloway, 148–84. Bloomington: Indiana University Press, 1990.

_____. Personal communication, 29 February 1992.

Thompson, Robert Farris, and Joseph Cornet. *The Four Moments of the Sun: Kongo Art in Two Worlds.* Washington: National Gallery of Art, 1981.

Tidwell, James Nathan. "Mark Twain's Representation of Negro Speech." *American Speech* 17 (October 1942): 174–76.

Toll, Robert C. *Blacking Up: The Minstrel Show in Nineteenth-Century America.* New York: Oxford University Press, 1974.

Tourgee, Albion. *A Fool's Errand By One of the Fools.* [First published anonymously]. Reprint. New York: Fords, Howard and Hulbert, 1879.

Traugott, Elizabeth Closs. "Pidgins, Creoles, and the Origins of Black English." In *Black English: A Seminar,* edited by Deborah Sears Harrison and Tom Trabasso, 57–94. Hillsdale, N.J.: Lawrence Erlbaum Associates, 1976.

Trilling, Lionel. "The Greatness of *Huckleberry Finn.*" (From *The Liberal Imagination,* 1950). Reprinted in *Huck Finn Among the Critics,* edited by M. Thomas Inge, 81–92. Frederick, Md.: University Publications of America, 1985.

Trowbridge, J. T. *Cudjo's Cave.* [1863]. Reprint. Boston: Lee and Shepard, 1893.

Turner, Lorenzo D. *Africanisms in the Gullah Dialect.* Chicago: University of Chicago Press, 1949. Reprint. New York: Arno Press, 1969.

_____. "Problems Confronting the Investigator of Gullah." *Publications of the American Dialect Society,* no. 9 (1947): 74–84. Reprinted in Dundes, Alan, ed., *Mother Wit from the Laughing Barrel,* 126–35. Jackson: University Press of Mississippi, 1990.

Twain, Mark [Samuel Clemens]. *Adventures of Huckleberry Finn.* Edited by Walter Blair and Victor Fischer, with the assistance of Dahlia Armon and Harriet Elinor Smith. The Works of Mark Twain. Berkeley: University of California Press, 1988. (*Note:* All citations to *Huckleberry Finn* are to this edition.)

_____. *Adventures of Huckleberry Finn.* Edited by Walter Blair and Victor Fischer. The Mark Twain Library. Berkeley: University of California Press, 1985.

_____. *Adventures of Huckleberry Finn: A Facsimile of the Manuscript.* Introduction by Louis J. Budd. Afterword by William H. Loos. 2 vols. Detroit: Bruccoli Clark, Gale, 1983.

_____. *The Adventures of Tom Sawyer; Tom Sawyer Abroad; Tom Sawyer,*

Detective. Edited by John C. Gerber, Paul Baender, and Terry Firkins. The Works of Mark Twain. Berkeley: University of California Press, 1980.

_____. "The Art of Composition." [1890]. In *Mark Twain: Life as I Find It*, edited by Charles Neider, 226–28. Garden City, N.Y.: Hanover House, 1961.

_____. Autobiographical Dictation file. Mark Twain Papers. Bancroft Library. University of California, Berkeley.

_____. *The Autobiography of Mark Twain.* Edited by Charles Neider. New York: Harper and Row, Perennial Library, 1966. (*Note:* When the *Autobiography* is cited without a volume number, the reference is to this edition.)

_____. "The Awful German Language." [in *A Tramp Abroad*, 2]. In *The Favorite Works of Mark Twain*, Deluxe ed., 1143–56. Garden City, N.Y.: Garden City Publishing Co., Inc., 1939.

_____. "Boy's Manuscript." [1868]. "Supplement A." *The Adventures of Tom Sawyer; Tom Sawyer Abroad; Tom Sawyer, Detective.* The works of Mark Twain. Edited by John C. Gerber, Paul Baender, and Terry Firkins, 419–51. Berkeley: University of California Press, 1980.

_____. "Concerning the American Language." [in *The Stolen White Elephant*, etc.]. Reprinted in *Tom Sawyer Abroad, Tom Sawyer, Detective, and Other Stories, Etc., Etc.*, Hillcrest edition, 396–400. New York: Harper and Brothers, 1906.

_____. "Corn-Pone Opinions." [1901]. In *Europe and Elsewhere.* With an Appreciation by Brander Matthews and an Introduction by Albert Bigelow Paine, 299–406. New York: Harper and Brothers, 1923.

_____. Correspondence file (Letters to SLC). Mark Twain Papers. Bancroft Library. University of California, Berkeley.

_____. *Early Tales and Sketches.* Vol. 2 (1864–1865). Edited by Edgar Marquess Branch and Robert H. Hirst, with the assistance of Harriet Elinor Smith. The Works of Mark Twain. Berkeley: University of California Press, 1981.

_____. "The Facts Concerning the Recent Carnival of Crime in Connecticut." *Atlantic Monthly* 37 (June 1876): 641–50.

_____. "A Family Sketch," no. 1, 1906, photocopy of manuscript and typescript of manuscript in the Mark Twain Papers, Bancroft Library, University of California, Berkeley. Original in Mark Twain Collection, James S. Copley Library, La Jolla, California.

_____. *Following the Equator.* Hartford: American Publishing Company, 1897.

_____. "A Gorgeous Swindle." *Territorial Enterprise*, 30 December 1863. Reprinted in Smith, Henry Nash, ed., *Mark Twain of the Enterprise: Newspaper Articles and Other Documents, 1862–1884*, 119–21. Berkeley: University of California Press, 1969.

_____. *Huck Finn and Tom Sawyer among the Indians and Other Unfinished Stories.* Foreword and notes by Dahlia Armon and Walter Blair. Texts established by Dahlia Armon, Paul Baender, Walter Blair, William M. Gibson, and Franklin R. Rogers. The Mark Twain Library. Berkeley: University of California Press, 1989.

_____. *The Innocents Abroad.* [1869]. New York: New American Library, Signet Classic Edition, 1966.

_____. "Introduction to 'The New Guide of the Conversation in Portuguese and

English.'" In *The $30,000 Bequest*. New York: Harper and Brothers, American Artists Edition, 1917, 301–4.

_____. "Italian with Grammar." In *The $30,000 Bequest*. New York: Harper and Brothers, American Artists Edition, 1917, 243–53.

_____. "Italian without a Master." In *The $30,000 Bequest*, 229–42. New York: Harper and Brothers, American Artists Edition, 1917.

_____. "Jim's Investments." [from *Huckleberry Finn*]. *Cleveland Leader*, 11 January 1885, 11; and *Boston Budget*, 4 January 1885, 6.

_____. "The Jumping Frog in English. Then in French. Then Clawed Back into a Civilized Language Once More by Patient, Unremunerated Toil." In *Mark Twain's Sketches, New and Old*, 25–44. Hartford: American Publishing Co., 1875.

_____. *Life on the Mississippi*. New York: Penguin, 1984.

_____. *The Love Letters of Mark Twain*. Edited and with an introduction by Dixon Wecter. New York: Harper and Brothers, 1949.

_____. *Mark Twain in Eruption*. Edited by Bernard DeVoto. New York: Harper and Brothers, 1940.

_____. Mark Twain Papers. Bancroft Library. University of California, Berkeley. Under the curatorship of Robert H. Hirst.

_____. *Mark Twain's Autobiography*. 2 vols. Edited by Albert Bigelow Paine. New York: Harper and Brothers, 1924.

_____. *Mark Twain's Hannibal, Huck and Tom*. Edited by Walter Blair. The Mark Twain Project. Berkeley: University of California Press, 1969.

_____. *Mark Twain's Letters*. 2 vols. Edited by Albert Bigelow Paine. New York: Harper and Brothers, 1917.

_____. *Mark Twain's Letters, Vol. 3: 1869*. Edited by Victor Fischer and Michael B. Frank; Associate Editor, Dahlia Armon. The Mark Twain Papers, under the General Editorship of Robert H. Hirst. Berkeley: University of California Press, 1992.

_____. *Mark Twain's Letters to His Publishers, 1867–1894*. Edited by Hamlin Hill. The Mark Twain Papers. Berkeley: University of California Press, 1967.

_____. *Mark Twain's Notebooks and Journals*. Vol. 1 (1855–1873). Edited by Frederick Anderson, Michael B. Frank, and Kenneth M. Sanderson. The Mark Twain Papers. Berkeley: University of California Press, 1975.

_____. *Mark Twain's Notebooks and Journals*. Vol. 2 (1877–1883). Edited by Frederick Anderson, Lin Salamo, and Bernard L. Stein. The Mark Twain Papers. Berkeley: University of California Press, 1975.

_____. *Mark Twain's Notebooks and Journals*. Vol. 3 (1883–1891). Edited by Robert Pack Browning, Michael B. Frank, and Lin Salamo. General Editor, Frederick Anderson. The Mark Twain Papers. Berkeley: University of California Press, 1979.

_____. *Mark Twain's Sketches, New and Old*. Hartford: American Publishing Company, 1875.

_____. "My Debut as a Literary Person." In *Complete Essays of Mark Twain*, edited by Charles Neider. Garden City, N.Y.: Doubleday, 1963.

_____. Notebooks and typescripts of Notebooks. Mark Twain Papers. Bancroft Library. University of California, Berkeley.

_____. "The Notorious Jumping Frog of Calaveras County." In *Mark Twain's Sketches, New and Old*, by Mark Twain, 29–35. Hartford: American Publishing Co., 1875.

_____. "An Open Letter to the American People." New York *Weekly Review* 17 (17 February 1866): 1. (Scheduled to appear in *Early Tales & Sketches, Volume 3*, Mark Twain Project).

_____. *Pudd'nhead Wilson.* [1894]. Reprint. New York: Bantam Books, 1959.

_____. *Pudd'nhead Wilson.* Manuscript in Pierpont Morgan Library, New York City.

_____. "The Quarrel in the Strong-Box." [1890s]. Manuscript in Mark Twain Papers. Bancroft Library. University of California, Berkeley.

_____. *Roughing It.* [1872]. Edited by Franklin R. Rogers and Paul Baender. The Works of Mark Twain. Berkeley: University of California Press, 1972.

_____. SLC to Olivia Clemens, 27 November 1871. Mark Twain Papers. Bancroft Library. University of California, Berkeley.

_____. SLC to Olivia Clemens, 11–12 January 1872. Mark Twain Papers. Bancroft Library. University of California, Berkeley.

_____. "Snow-Shovelers." [c. 1892]. Manuscript in Mark Twain Papers. Bancroft Library. University of California, Berkeley.

_____. "Sociable Jimmy." *New York Times*, 29 November 1874, 7. Reprinted in *The Twainian* 2, no. 5 (February 1943), 3–5, and in Paul Fatout, *Mark Twain Speaks For Himself.* West Lafayette, Ind.: Purdue University Press, 1978, 88–92 [*Note:* reprinted versions differ from the original. All quotations from "Sociable Jimmy" refer to the original *New York Times* version of the text.]

_____. "The Story of the Good Little Boy." In *Mark Twain's Sketches, New and Old*, by Mark Twain, 56–61. Hartford: American Publishing Co., 1875.

_____. *Those Extraordinary Twins.* [1894]. Reprint. Edited by Sidney E. Berger. New York: W. W. Norton and Co., 1980.

_____. *Tom Sawyer Abroad; Tom Sawyer, Detective.* Edited by John C. Gerber and Terry Firkins. The Mark Twain Library. Berkeley: University of California Press, 1982.

_____. "A True Story, Repeated Word for Word as I Heard It." In *Mark Twain's Sketches, New and Old*, by Mark Twain, 202–7. Hartford: American Publishing Co., 1875.

_____. "A True Story." Manuscript in Clifton Waller Barrett Library, Manuscripts Division, Special Collections Department, University of Virginia. Photocopy in Mark Twain Papers. Bancroft Library. University of California, Berkeley.

_____. "Villagers of 1840–3." In *Huck Finn and Tom Sawyer Among the Indians*, by Mark Twain. Foreword and Notes by Dahlia Armon and Walter Blair. Berkeley: University of California, Mark Twain Project, 1989.

_____. *What Is Man? and Other Philosophical Writings.* Edited by Paul Baender. The Works of Mark Twain. Berkeley: University of California Press, 1973.

Twain, Mark, and William Dean Howells. *Mark Twain–Howells Letters: The Correspondence of Samuel L. Clemens and William Dean Howells, 1872–1910.* Edited by Henry Nash Smith and William Gibson, with the assistance of Frederick Anderson. 2 vols. Cambridge, Mass.: Harvard University Press, 1960.

Van Dam, Theodore. "The Influence of West African Songs of Derision in the New World." *African Music* 1 (1954): 53–56.

Van Deburg, William L. *Slavery and Race in American Popular Culture.* Madison: University of Wisconsin Press, 1984.

Van Sertima, Ivan. "My Gullah Brother and I: Exploration into a Community's Language and Myth through Its Oral Tradition." In *Black English: A Seminar*, edited by Deborah Sears Harrison and Tom Trabasso, 123–46. Hillsdale, N.J.: Lawrence Erlbaum Associates, 1976.

Wade, John Donald. "Southern Humor." In *Culture in the South*, edited by W. T. Couch [1934]. Reprinted in Inge, M. Thomas, ed., *The Frontier Humorists: Critical Views*, 32–44. Hamden, Conn.: Archon Books, The Shoestring Press, 1975.

Wallace, John. *Adventures of Huckleberry Finn Adapted.* Falls Church, Virginia: John H. Wallace and Sons, 1983.

_____. "The Case Against *Huckleberry Finn.*" In *Satire or Evasion? Black Perspectives on Huckleberry Finn,"* edited by James S. Leonard, Thomas A. Tenney, and Thadious M. Davis, 16–24. Durham, N.C.: Duke University Press, 1991.

Washington, Booker T. ["Tributes to Mark Twain"]. *North American Review* 191, no. 655 (June 1910): 828–30.

Waterman, Richard A., and William R. Bascom. "African and New World Folklore." In *Dictionary of Folklore, Mythology and Legend*, edited by Maria Leach, 18–24. New York: Funk and Wagnalls, 1949.

Watson, Charles S. "Portrayals of the Black and the Idea of Progress: Simms and Douglass." *Southern Studies* 20, no. 4 (Winter 1981): 339–50.

Weaver, Thomas, and Merline A. Williams. "Mark Twain's Jim: Identity as an Index to Cultural Attitudes." *American Literary Realism* 13 (Spring 1980): 19–29.

Webber, Thomas L. *Deep Like the Rivers: Education in the Slave Quarter Community, 1831–1865.* New York: W. W. Norton, 1978.

Wecter, Dixon. *Sam Clemens of Hannibal.* Boston: Houghton Mifflin, 1952.

Wentworth, Harold, and Stuart Berg Flexner, eds. *Dictionary of American Slang.* 2d supplemented ed. New York: Thomas Y. Crowell Company, 1975.

Werner, Craig. "'Tell Old Pharaoh': The Afro-American Response to Faulkner." *Southern Review* 19 (Autumn 1983): 711–35.

Westermann, Dietrich, and M. A. Bryan. *The Languages of West Africa.* London: Oxford University Press, 1952.

Wilgus, D. K. "The Negro-White Spiritual." In *Anglo-American Folksong Scholarship Since 1898*, 344–64. New Brunswick, 1959. Reprinted in Dundes, Alan, ed., *Mother Wit from the Laughing Barrel*, 67–80. Jackson: University Press of Mississippi, 1990.

Williamson, Joel. *A Rage for Order: Black-White Relations in the American South Since Emancipation.* New York: Oxford University Press, 1986.

Williamson, Juanita V. "Selected Features of Speech: Black and White." In *A Various Language: Perspectives on American Dialects*, edited by Juanita V. Williamson and Virginia M. Burke, 496–507. New York: Holt, Rinehart and Winston, 1971.

Wilson, Charles Reagan, and William Ferris, eds. *Encyclopedia of Southern Culture.* Chapel Hill: University of North Carolina Press, 1989.

Wilson, Edmund. "Sut Lovingood." In *The Frontier Humorists:, Critical Views*, edited by M. Thomas Inge, 146–54. Hamden, Conn.: Archon Books, The Shoestring Press, 1975.

Wilson, Geraldine L. "On Twain and Minstrelsy." *Interracial Books for Children Bulletin* 15, nos. 1 and 2 (1984).

Wisbey, Herbert A., Jr. "John T. Lewis, Mark Twain's Friend in Elmira." *Mark Twain Society Bulletin* 7, no. 1 (1984): 1–5.

———. "The True Story of Auntie Cord." *Mark Twain Society Bulletin* 3, no. 2 (1981): 1, 3–5.

Wolfram, Walt. "The Relationship of White Southern Speech to Vernacular Black English." *Language* 50 (September 1974): 498–527.

Woodard, Fredrick, and Donnarae MacCann. "*Huckleberry Finn* and the Traditions of Blackface Minstrelsy." *Interracial Books for Children Bulletin* 15, nos. 1 and 2 (1984): 4–13.

———. "Minstrel Shackles and Nineteenth-Century 'Liberality' in *Huckleberry Finn.*" In *Satire or Evasion? Black Perspectives on "Huckleberry Finn,"* edited by James S. Leonard, Thomas A. Tenney, and Thadious M. Davis, 141–53. Durham, N.C.: Duke University Press, 1991.

Woodson, Carter G. *The Mis-Education of the Negro.* 1933. Reprint. Trenton, N.J.: Africa World Press, Inc., 1990.

Woodward, C. Vann. "Clio with Soul." *Journal of American History* 1, no. 56 (June 1969): 5–20.

———. *The Strange Career of Jim Crow.* [1955]. 3d rev. ed. New York: Oxford University Press, 1974.

[Work, Frederick, J.] *New Jubilee Songs, As Sung by the Fisk Jubilee Singers of Fisk University.* Collected and Harmonized by Frederick J. Work. Nashville: Fisk University, 1902.

Wright, Richard. *Richard Wright: Books and Writers.* Edited by Michel Fabre. Jackson: University Press of Mississippi, 1990.

Wyeth, John Allan, *With Sabre and Scalpel.* New York: Harper and Brothers, 1914.

Yarborough, Richard. Personal communication, 18 July 1992.

———. "Strategies of Characterization in *Uncle Tom's Cabin* and the Early Afro-American Novel." In *New Essays on "Uncle Tom's Cabin,"* edited by Eric Sundquist, 45–84. Cambridge and New York: Cambridge University Press, 1986.

Yellin, Jean Fagan. *The Intricate Knot: Black Figures in American Literature, 1776–1863.* New York: New York University Press, 1972.

Sociable Jimmy

by Mark Twain

[I sent the following home in a private letter, some time ago, from a certain little village. It was in the days when I was a public lecturer. I did it because I wished to preserve the memory of the most artless, sociable, and exhaustless talker I ever came across. He did not tell me a single remarkable thing, or one that was worth remembering; and yet he was himself so interested in his small marvels, and they flowed so naturally and comfortably from his lips that his talk got the upper hand of my interest, too, and I listened as one who receives a revelation. I took down what he had to say, just as he said it—without altering a word or adding one.]

I had my supper in my room this evening, (as usual,) and they sent up a bright, simple, guileless little darkey boy to wait on me—ten years old—a wide-eyed, observant little chap. I said:

"What is your name, my boy?"

"Dey calls me Jimmy, Sah, but my right name's James, Sah."

I said, "Sit down there, Jimmy—I'll not want you just yet."

He sat down in a big arm-chair, hung both his legs over one of the arms, and looked comfortable and conversational. I said:

"Did you have a pleasant Christmas, Jimmy?"

"No, sah—not zackly. I was kind o' sick den. But de res' o' de people *dey* had a good time—mos' all uv 'em had a good time. Dey all got drunk. Dey all gits drunk heah, every Christmas, and carries on and has awful good times."

"So you were sick, and lost it all. But unless you were *very* sick I should think that if you had asked the doctor he might have let you get—get—a *little* drunk—and—"

"Oh, no, Sah—I don' never git drunk—it's de *white* folks—dem's de ones I means. Pa used to git drunk, but dat was befo' I was big—but he's done quit. He don' git drunk no mo' now. Jis' takes one nip in de mawnin', now, cuz his stomach riles up, he sleeps so soun'. Jis' one nip—over to de s'loon—every mawnin'. He's powerful sickly—

249

powerful—sometimes he can't hardly git aroun', he can't. He goes to de doctor every week—over to Ragtown. An' one time he tuck some stuff, you know, an' it mighty near *fetched* him. Ain't it dish-yer blue-vittles dat's pison?—ain't dat it?—truck what you pisons cats wid?"

"Yes blue vittles [vitriol] is a very convincing article with a cat."

"Well, den, dat was it. De ole man, he tuck de bottle and shuck it, and shuck it—he seed it was blue, and he didn't know but it was blue mass, which he tuck mos' always—blue mass pills—but den he 'spected maybe dish-yer truck might be some other kin' o' blue stuff, and so he sot de bottle down, and drat if it wa'n't blue vittles, sho' nuff, when de doctor come. An' de doctor he say if he'd a tuck dat blue vittles it would a highsted him, *sho'*. People can't be too particlar 'bout sich things. Yes, in*deedy!*

"We ain't got no cats heah, 'bout dis hotel. Bill he don't like 'em. He can't stan' a cat no way. Ef he was to ketch one he'd slam it outen de winder in a minute. Yes he would. Bill's down on cats. So is de gals—waiter gals. When dey ketches a cat bummin' aroun' heah, dey jis' *scoops* him—'deed dey do. Dey snake him into de cistern—dey's been cats drownded in dat water dat's in yo' pitcher. I seed a cat in dare yistiddy—all swelled up like a pudd'n. I bet you dem gals done dat. Ma says if dey was to drownd a cat for *her*, de fust one of 'em she ketched she'd jam her into de cistern 'long wid de cat. Ma wouldn't *do* dat, I don't reckon, but 'deed an' double, she *said* she would. I can't kill a chicken—well, I kin wring its neck off, cuz dat don't make 'em no sufferin scacely; but I can't take and chop dey heads off, like some people kin. It makes me feel so—so—well, I kin see dat chicken nights so's I can't sleep. Mr. Dunlap, he's de richest man in dis town. Some people says dey's fo' thousan' people in dis town—dis city. But Bill he says dey aint but 'bout thirty-three hund'd. And Bill he knows, cuz he's lived heah all his life, do' dey *do* say he won't never set de river on fire. I don't know how dey fin' out—*I* wouldn't like to count all dem people. Some folks says dis town would be considerable bigger if it wa'n't on accounts of so much lan' all roun' it dat ain't got no houses on it." [This in perfect seriousness—dense simplicity—no idea of a joke.] "I reckon you seed dat church as you come along up street. Dat's an awful big church—awful high steeple. An' it's all solid stone, excep' jes' de top part—de steeple, I means—dat's wood. It falls off when de win' blows pooty hard, an' one time it stuck in a cow's back and busted de cow all to de mischief. It's gwine to kill some body yit, dat steeple is. A man—big man, he was—bigger'n what Bill is—he tuck it up dare and fixed it again—an' he didn't look no bigger'n a boy, he was so high up. Dat steeple's awful high. If you look out de winder you kin see it." [I looked out, and was speechless with awe and admiration—which gratified Jimmy beyond expression. The wonderful steeple was some sixty or seventy feet high, and had a clock-face on it.] "You see dat arrer on top o' dat steeple? Well, Sah, dat arrer is pooty nigh as big as dis do' [door.] I seed it when dey pulled it outen de cow. It mus' be awful to stan' in dat steeple when de clock is strikin'—dey say it is. Booms and jars so's you think the world's a comin' to an end. *I* wouldn't like to be up dare when de clock's a strikin'. Dat clock ain't jest a *striker*, like dese common clocks. It's a *bell*—jist a reglar *bell*— and it's a buster. You kin hear dat bell all over dis city. You ought to hear it boom, boom, boom, when dey's a fire. My sakes! Dey ain't got no bell like dat in Ragtown. *I* ben to Ragtown, an' I ben mos' halfway to Dockery [thirty miles.] De bell in Ragtown's got so ole now she don't make no soun', scasely."

[Enter the landlord—a kindly man, verging toward fifty. My small friend, without changing position, says:]

"Bill, didn't you say dat dey was only thirty-three hund'd people in dis city?"

"Yes, about thirty-three hundred is the population now."

"Well, some folks says dey's fo' thousan'."

"Yes, I know they do; but it isn't correct."

"Bill, I don't think dis gen'lman kin eat a whole prairie-chicken, but dey *tole* me to fetch it all up."

"Yes, that's all right—he ordered it."

[Exit "Bill," leaving me comfortable; for I had been perishing to know who "Bill" was.]

"Bill he's de oldest. An' he's de bes', too. Dey's fo'teen in dis fam'ly—all boys an' gals. Bill he suppo'ts 'em all—an' he don' never complain—he's *real* good, Bill is. All dem brothers an' sisters o' his'n ain't no 'count—all ceptin' dat little teeny one dat fetched in dat milk. Dat's Kit, Sah. She ain't only nine year ole. But she's de mos' lady-like one in de whole bilin'. You don't never see Kit a-rairin' an' a-chargin' aroun' an' kickin' up her heels like de res' o' de gals in dis fam'ly does gen'ally. Dat was Nan dat you hearn a-cuttin' dem shines on de pi-anah while ago. An' sometimes ef she don't rastle dat pi-anah when she gits started! *Tab* can't hole a candle to *her*, but Tab kin *sing* like de very nation. She's de only one in dis family dat kin sing. You don't never hear a yelp outen Nan. Nan can't sing for shucks. I'd jes' lieves hear a tom-cat dat's got scalded. Dey's fo'-teen in dis fam'ly 'sides de ole man an' de ole 'ooman—all brothers an' sis- ters. But some of 'em don't live heah—do' Bill he suppo'ts 'em—lends 'em money, an' pays dey debts an' he'ps 'em along. I tell you Bill he's *real* good. Dey all gits drunk—all 'cep Bill. De ole man he gits drunk, too, same as de res' uv 'em. Bob, he don't git drunk much—jes' sloshes roun' de s'loons some, an' takes a dram sometimes. Bob he's next to Bill—'bout forty year old. Dey's all married—all de fam'ly's married—cep' some of de gals. Dare's fo'teen. It's de biggest family in dese parts, dey say. Dare's Bill—Bill Nubbles—Nubbles is de name; Bill an' Griz, an' Duke, an' Bob, an' Nan, an' Tab, an' Kit, an' Sol, an' Si, an' Phil, an' Puss, an' Jake, an' Sal—Sal she's married an' got chil'en as big as I is—an' Hoss Nubbles, he's de las'. Hoss is what dey mos' always calls him, but he's got another name dat I somehow disremember, it's so kind o' hard to git de hang of it." [Then observing that I had been taking down this extraordinary list of nicknames for adults, he said:] "But in de mawnin' I can ask Bill what's Hoss's other name, an' den I'll come up an' tell you when I fetches yo' breakfast. An' may be I done got some o' dem names mixed up, but Bill, he kin tell me. Dey's fo'teen."

By this time he was starting off with the waiter, (and a pecuniary consideration for his sociability,) and, as he went out, he paused a moment and said:

"Dad-fetch it, somehow dat other name don't come. But, anyways, you jes' read dem names over an' see if dey's fo'teen." [I read the list from the fly-leaf of Longfellow's *New-England Tragedies*.] "Dat's right, Sah. Dey's all down, I'll fetch up Hoss's other name in de mawnin', Sah. Don't you be oneasy."

[Exit, whistling "Listen to the Mockingbird."]

Note: In line 27 of this text (page 249), an obvious typographical error has been corrected: "it's" originally appeared as "i'ts."

Index